Fulfilling the Law and the Prophets

Fulfilling the Law and the Prophets

The Prophetic Vocation of Jesus in the Gospel of Matthew

Matthew Anslow

FOREWORD BY
David J. Neville

☙PICKWICK *Publications* · Eugene, Oregon

FULFILLING THE LAW AND THE PROPHETS
The Prophetic Vocation of Jesus in the Gospel of Matthew

Pickwick Publications
An Imprint of Wipf and Stock Publishers
199 W. 8th Ave., Suite 3
Eugene, OR 97401

www.wipfandstock.com

PAPERBACK ISBN: 978-1-6667-3119-4
HARDCOVER ISBN: 978-1-6667-2341-0
EBOOK ISBN: 978-1-6667-2342-7

Cataloguing-in-Publication data:

Names: Anslow, Matthew, author. | Neville, David J., foreword.

Title: Fulfilling the law and the prophets : the prophetic vocation of Jesus in the Gospel of Matthew / Matthew Anslow ; foreword by David J. Neville.

Description: Eugene, OR: Pickwick Publications, 2022 | Includes bibliographical references and index.

Identifiers: ISBN 978-1-6667-3119-4 (paperback) | ISBN 978-1-6667-2341-0 (hardcover) | ISBN 978-1-6667-2342-7 (ebook)

Subjects: LCSH: Bible. Matthew—Criticism, interpretation, etc. | Prophecy—Christianity—Biblical teaching.

Classification: BS2575.2 A575 2022 (print) | BS2575.2 (ebook)

07/15/22

Dedicated to Ashlee,
without whom this book
and my life as I know it
would be impossible.

Contents

Foreword

WERE ONE TO COMPARE Matthean studies to a gathering of specialists engaged in discussion and debate around a large seminar table, someone new to that conversation would need to have something worthwhile to say to gain a hearing. With this monograph, Matthew Anslow has earned a place at the Matthean seminar table. Thematically and methodologically, his study brings to light fresh perspectives on Matthew's Gospel.

Fulfilling the Law and the Prophets is an intrinsically important and distinctive study of a relatively neglected feature of Matthew's christology, namely, prophetic dimensions of Matthew's narrative portrait of Jesus. Indeed, the prophetic vocation of Jesus is a central christological theme for Matthew, according to Anslow, which he demonstrates by means of detailed discussion of four key passages in the Gospel. Perhaps readers may already be inclined to regard Jesus' temple disruption in Matt 21:10–17 and his tirade against scribes and Pharisees in Matthew 23 in broadly "prophetic" terms, but Anslow's argument that the beatitudes in Matt 5:3–12 compose prophetic speech and that Matthew's account of Jesus' table fellowship with tax agents and sinners (9:9–13) may be perceived as a prophetic act casts light from different angles on Matthew's complex and multi-faceted depiction of the identity and significance of Jesus. In this connection, it is perhaps worth pointing out that although Anslow's study focuses on Jesus as prophet within the Gospel according to Matthew, he does not reduce Matthew's christology to Jesus' prophetic role. By analogy with Anslow's argument that Matthew's presentation of Jesus' prophetic vocation is multi-faceted by association with a range of Israelite prophetic traditions, Matthew's depiction of Jesus as Israel's prophet *par excellence* is but one facet of a multi-faceted christological portrait.

In methodological terms, Anslow's study artfully and judiciously combines narrative-critical and socio-historical approaches. Independently, both approaches continue to be used fruitfully by Matthean scholars. In scholarly study of Matthew's Gospel, Anslow may not be the first to combine narrative and socio-historical analysis, but his careful integration of both approaches, alongside attention to intertextual resonances with a range of biblical texts and motifs, contributes to an illuminating appraisal of decisive Matthean features.

For Anslow, Matthew's prophetic christology addresses three principal issues related to his audience's concerns. Against the backdrop of social and ideological conflict with competing formative or proto-rabbinic Jewish antagonists as well as with Roman imperial pressures, Matthew's presentation of Jesus as a prophetic figure who interprets the Torah in an authoritative way served to reassure his audience of its identity as people of a renewed covenant with the God of Israel. Depicting Jesus in prophetic terms also enabled Matthew to reinforce his audience's understanding of the God of Israel as the merciful judge of the world. Together, this conception of the identity of Matthew's audience and its governing vision of God, facilitated by Matthew's prophetic portrait of Jesus, implied and perhaps even generated a corporate self-understanding of a community of disciples with a renewed imperative to fulfil Israel's vocation in the wider world. Perhaps such a vision has the compelling vibrancy to continue to inform what it means to be a disciple of Jesus in a conflicted world.

As one who learned much from Matt Anslow's research as it came to fruition, I am delighted by the publication of this book, which will make his contribution to Matthean studies more widely accessible. For anyone interested in Matthew's portrait of Jesus, I commend this study.

David J. Neville
St Mark's National Theological Centre, Charles Sturt University
August, 2021

Preface

THE SUBJECT OF PROPHECY has been of interest to me for some years now. This interest, far from being a purely intellectual curiosity, is the outworking of mainly practical and pastoral factors. Indeed, I can hardly ignore the auto-biographical influences that have contributed to the following study.

I have been fortunate enough to have amassed a broad range of experience of the Christian church. I became a follower of Jesus as a teenager in a mildly-Charismatic Evangelical church, having grown up in a nominally Catholic family. I went on to study under and spend considerable time with Pentecostals and Catholics. I eventually embraced Neo-Anabaptism while attending a Uniting Church, a Mainline denomination created by the union of the Methodist, Presbyterian, and Congregationalist churches in Australia. I completed my doctoral studies in a university whose theology departments consisted of Uniting Church and Anglican colleges, and I have lectured in Pentecostal, Baptist, and Churches of Christ institutions. At the time of writing, I attend a Baptist Church two hours west of Sydney and am employed by the Uniting Church as a theological educator. As I say, I am fortunate to have been given the opportunity to spend time with Christians from all over the ecclesial and theological map, even if I do often feel like a proverbial mongrel.

I mention all of this because each of these diverse traditions has a notion and a language of prophecy, even if those notions are in many ways divergent and, in some cases, irreconcilable. Experience with a variety of traditions has led me to appreciate their diverse approaches to prophecy. I have, however, also grown to be critical of elements of those same approaches.

In truth, I have witnessed no shortage of what I can only call abuse under the guise of prophecy and prophetic ministry. In Pentecostal and Charismatic settings, such abuses are, sadly, all too common. I am sure some of those reading these words would have heard stories of, if not directly experienced, prophetic imperatives declaring, say, the end of a person's need for vital medication, calling for an obscene financial sacrifice for the benefit of a Christian ministry, or specifying a marriage partner. I could provide many further examples. And yet, I have seen amazing instances of this Pentecostal-style of prophecy which conveyed seemingly miraculous knowledge about some otherwise unknowable situation. Still, such instances do not cancel out those deeply problematic episodes of "prophetic" activity that I have witnessed—episodes that have left people traumatized, injured, and disillusioned.

Such experiences have been a significant motivator in my desire to explore the subject of prophecy. Certainly, back when I was completing my Masters research on prophecy in Luke-Acts, I was studying in a Pentecostal institution and this context motivated my work at the time. In the end, I became unconvinced that the often exclusively individualistic and therapeutic approaches to prophecy practiced in many Pentecostal and Charismatic communities represent a faithful expression of the prophet's vocation, at least according to my understanding of Scripture.

Since then, I have also gained much experience of the distinct understanding of prophecy typically found in Mainline Protestant churches. Here, the language of the prophetic is commonly used to describe certain social and political declarations and actions. Most often such prophetic expressions are associated with the progressive side of culture and politics. Indeed, my own past work in public refugee advocacy, involving civil disobedience as it did, often earned the label "prophetic" in such communities, though I never considered it such. Again, I have witnessed the positive side of such an understanding of the prophetic. Examples come to mind of churches speaking truth to powers operating unjustly, or dramatic public acts that help reframe social and political issues around compassion and justice. But for all the beauty of such an approach to the prophetic, it can easily lead to tribalism, arrogance, and self-righteousness. I cannot say with certainty, but I suspect this is the consequence of too-easily assuming our words and actions are prophetic, thus equating them in some sense— along with the politics they represent—with God's will. In my experience, such an approach to prophecy often leads to the political more than it does to Christ, immanentizing the prophetic and detaching it from its divine source. In other words, it too easily leads to a kingdom without a King. While I am more than sympathetic to the aims of liberationist politics, I am suspicious of the reduction of prophetic language merely to describe words and actions associated with such politics.

These are no doubt simplifications of vastly complicated phenomena. Indeed, prophecy as it is practiced nowadays cannot be so neatly categorized. Still, I hope these reflections provide a window into the tensions I feel regarding the prophetic and my motivations for exploring this subject in the present study. Perhaps most crucially, it is that I think prophecy is vital to the life and mission of the church that has led me to this point.

What follows is a reworked version of my doctoral thesis, submitted through Charles Sturt University in Australia. My hope is that this study of Jesus' prophetic vocation in Matthew's Gospel will provoke important conversations about the practice of prophecy and its role in our participation in the mission of God. In this, I pray it is of some small service to the church and the kingdom.

Matthew Anslow
August, 2021

Acknowledgments

I WOULD LIKE TO express my utmost appreciation of and gratitude to my doctoral supervisor, David Neville. You have shown great care in your mentoring and oversight of my research, making many helpful comments and giving much priceless advice along the way. Further, you have continued to advise me even after the conclusion of my PhD studies, helping me to navigate to the point of publication. I am sure, given my many varied and disruptive commitments, there have been easier students to supervise. I am grateful for your never-ceasing encouragement and support.

I would also like to thank my other doctoral supervisors: Jeff Aernie, my secondary supervisor, and John Squires and Greg Jenks, both of whom served successively as my principal supervisors early in my candidature before being forced to hand over supervision for various reasons. Each of you has offered invaluable insight into the research that would become this study and I am thankful for your support and wisdom.

In addition, I can hardly overlook all those who have instructed and formed me in my theological education. I would especially like to thank Barry Chant, the late Bill Dumbrell, David Parker, Josh Dowton, Jacqueline Grey, and Shane Clifton. I have not always agreed with you all, but I have learnt much from you.

My thanks extend also to Geoff Broughton whose friendship and no-nonsense advice have been an energizing force, both for the present work and more generally in my scholarship, activism, and ministry. I wish not only for more pastor-activist-scholars like Geoff in the church, but also for more who share his vocation of mentoring younger leaders, scholars, and activists.

My church communities, past and present, also deserve my gratitude. During the process of undertaking this research, I have belonged to three church communities. When I still lived in Sydney, Kingsway Community

Church and then Hope Uniting Church were my congregations. Nowadays, my family worships as part of Blackheath Baptist Church, in the beautiful Blue Mountains, two hours west of Sydney. I am convinced that academic theological pursuits are invaluable to the life of the church, but more so that the life of one's church is indispensable to academic theological pursuits. I am who I am in part because of the church communities I have called home and the worship, fellowship, and witness we share together. To my friends, mentors, and siblings in Christ that make up these communities: thank you for your slow, quiet, and perpetual love throughout the years.

Finally, my greatest thanks go to my family, in particular my wife, Ashlee. I began this research not long before we were married and, more than a few years later, it is finally coming to fruition. Your unwavering patience, love, and support have made all the difference.

Abbreviations

ABD	Anchor Bible Dictionary
AEJT	Australian eJournal of Theology
ARNW	*Aufstieg und Niedergang der römischen Welt*
BBR	Bulletin of Biblical Research
BECNT	Baker Exegetical Commentary on the New Testament
BibInt	Biblical Interpretation
BJRL	Bulletin of the John Rylands University Library of Manchester
BR	Biblical Research
BSac	*Bibliotheca sacra*
BTB	Biblical Theology Bulletin
BZ	*Biblische Zeitschrift*
CBQ	Catholic Biblical Quarterly
CHJ	Cambridge History of Judaism
CTR	Criswell Theological Review
DSD	Dead Sea Discoveries
EuroJTh	European Journal of Theology
EvQ	Evangelical Quarterly
HTR	Harvard Theological Review
HTS	HTS Teologiese Studies/Theological Studies
HUCA	Hebrew Union College Annual
ICC	International Critical Commentary
Int	Interpretation
JBL	Journal of Biblical Literature
JBLMS	Journal of Biblical Literature Monograph Series

JETS	Journal of the Evangelical Theological Society
JJS	Journal of Jewish Studies
JSHJ	Journal for the Study of the Historical Jesus
JSJ	Journal for the Study of Judaism
JSNT	Journal for the Study of the New Testament
JSOT	Journal for the Study of the Old Testament
JSP	Journal for the Study of the Pseudepigrapha
LCL	Loeb Classical Library
LNTS	Library of New Testament Studies
NAC	New American Commentary
NICNT	New International Commentary on the New Testament
NICOT	New International Commentary on the Old Testament
NIGTC	New International Greek Testament Commentary
NovT	*Novum Testamentum*
NT	New Testament
NTG	New Testament Guides
NTL	New Testament Library
NTS	New Testament Studies
OT	Old Testament
OTP	Old Testament Pseudepigrapha
SBG	Studies in Biblical Greek
SBL	Society of Biblical Literature
SBLSP	Society of Biblical Literature Seminar Papers
SBT	Studies in Biblical Theology
SJT	Scottish Journal of Theology
SM	The Sermon on the Mount
TDNT	Theological Dictionary of the New Testament
ThTo	Theology Today
TNTC	Tyndale New Testament Commentaries
TynBul	Tyndale Bulletin
WBC	Word Biblical Commentary
WUNT	*Wissenschaftliche Untersuchungen zum Neuen Testament*
WW	Word and World
ZAW	*Zeitschrift für die alttestamentliche Wissenschaft*
ZECNT	Zondervan Exegetical Commentary of the New Testament

Apocrypha and Septuagint

Bar.	Baruch
Esd.	Esdras
Macc	Maccabees

Apostolic Fathers

Clem.	Clement
Did.	The Didache
Ign. *Eph.*	Ignatius, *To the Ephesians*
Ign. *Pol.*	Ignatius, *To Polycarp*
Ign. *Smyrn.*	Ignatius, *To the Smyrnaeans*

Dead Sea Scrolls and Nag Hammadi Codices

1QM	War Scroll
1QpHab	*Pesher Habakkuk*
1QpNah	*Pesher Nahum*
1QS	Rule of the Community
1QSa	Rule of the Congregation
4QapLam	*Pseudo-Lamentations*
4 QTestim	*Testimonia*
CD	Damascus Document
MasShirShabb	Masada Songs of the Sabbath Sacrifice
Pap. Oxyr	Oxyrhynchus papyri
Thom. Cont.	Book of Thomas the Contender

Greek and Latin Works

Aen.	*Aeneid* (Virgil)
Ann.	*Annales* (Tacitus)
Ath. pol.	Constitution of Athens (Aristotle)
Haer.	Against Heresies (Irenaeus)
Hipp.	*Hippolytus* (Euripides)
Hist. eccl.	Ecclesiastical History (Eusebius)
Prov. cons.	*De provinciis consularibus* (Cicero)
Virt. mor.	*De virtute morali* (Plutarch)

Josephus

Ag. Ap.	*Against Apion*
Ant.	*Antiquities of the Jews*
J.W.	Jewish War
Life	*Life of Josephus*

New Testament Apocrypha and Pseudepigrapha

Acts Pil.	Acts of Pilate
Gos. Thom.	Gospel of Thomas
Inf. Thom.	Infancy Gospel of Thomas
Prot. Jas.	Protevangelium of James
Ps.-Clem. Rec.	Pseudo-Clementine Recognitions

Old Testament Pseudepigrapha

Apoc. Ab.	Apocalypse of Abraham
En.	Enoch
Jos. Asen.	Joseph and Aseneth
L.A.B.	*Liber antiquitatum biblicarum* (Pseudo-Philo)
L.A.E.	Life of Adam and Eve
Lad. Jac.	Ladder of Jacob
Sib. Or.	Sibylline Oracles
T. Mos.	Testament of Moses

Philo

Good Person	That Every Good Person Is Free
Migration	On the Migration of Abraham

Rabbinic Literature

'Abot	*'Abot*
B.	Babylonian Talmud
B. Bat.	*Baba Batra*
Ber.	*Berakot*
Dem.	*Demai*
Eccl. Rab.	Ecclesiastes *Rabbah*
Git.	*Gittin*
Hag.	*Hagigah*
Ker.	*Kerithot*

Ketub.	*Ketubbot*
Lam. Rab.	Lamentations *Rabbah*
M.	*Mishnah*
Maʿaś Š.	*Maʿaser Sheni*
Mek.	*Mekilta*
Menah.	*Menahot*
Naz.	*Nazir*
Nid.	*Niddah*
Parah	*Parah*
Pesah.	*Pesahim*
Pesiq. Rab.	*Pesiqta Rabbati*
Pesiq. Rab Kah.	*Pesiqta de Rab Kahana*
Šabb.	Šabbat
Sanh.	*Sanhedrin*
Sifre Deut	Sifre to Deuteronomy
Sukkah	*Sukkah*
T.	*Tosefta*
Tg. Jer.	*Targum to Jeremiah*
Y.	Jerusalem Talmud
Yad.	*Yadayim*
Yebam.	*Yebamot*
Yoma	*Yoma*
Zebah.	*Zebahim*

Introduction

Background and Aims of this Study

MY INTEREST IN MATTHEW's Gospel as it relates to the subject of Jesus' prophetic vocation stems from a set of concerns that can be condensed into two areas. First, Matthew's Gospel makes mention of prophets and prophecy more than the other canonical Gospels.[1] Second—and despite the first reason—Matthew's Gospel is often neglected in discussions of NT prophecy, at least in comparison to other NT texts. This is also the case for the Gospels more generally, and I am somewhat concerned that studies of NT prophecy have often synthesized a uniformity of perspective in the early church by marginalizing texts that do not easily harmonize with their dominant picture of prophecy.[2] Indeed, understandings of prophets and prophecy in the NT period were probably diverse. This leads me to think that a study of Matthew's perspective is valuable as part of a larger mosaic.

Of course, Jesus as prophet is but one of many Christological lenses present in Matthew's Gospel. By employing this lens, I am in no way seeking to minimize other lenses, nor to argue that the prophetic lens is the primary

---

1. As an indication, προφήτης is used in Matthew thirty-seven times, while it appears six times in Mark, twenty-nine times in Luke and fourteen times in John. Προφητεύω appears four times in Matthew, but twice each in Mark and Luke and once in John. Προφητεία appears once in Matthew, but not at all in the other Gospels.

2. Well-known works such as Aune, *Prophecy in Early Christianity*; Hill, *New Testament Prophecy*; Witherington, *Jesus the Seer* spend the vast minority of their textual engagement focused on the Gospels, while works such as Ellis, *Prophecy and Hermeneutic in Early Christianity*; Gillespie, *First Theologians*; Grudem, *Gift of Prophecy* either do not engage with these works, or do so minimally. I do not wish to pass judgment on these works, but rather to point out the common marginalization of Gospel texts in studies of NT prophecy. It is worth noting some NT prophecy studies that have given meaningful attention to the Gospels; see Boring, *Sayings of the Risen Jesus*; Boring, *Continuing Voice of Jesus*; Forbes, *Prophecy and Inspired Speech*.

one through which to view the Matthean Jesus. I am, however, concerned to give the subject of Jesus' prophetic vocation in Matthew's Gospel the attention it warrants—attention that has generally been lacking.[3]

This study investigates the narrative theme of Jesus' prophetic vocation in selected passages of the Gospel of Matthew. It is developed through (1) an analysis of Matthew's Gospel and social world, including consideration of historical matters such as Matthew's authorship, location, genre, and purpose in order to provide a framework for reading Matthew's narrative; (2) a survey of Jewish prophecy and prophets in Syro-Palestine around the time of Jesus, as a comparison and reference point for the subsequent exegetical section; (3) an extended study of Jesus' prophetic vocation in four select texts in Matthew (5:3–12; 9:9–13; 21:10–17; 23:1–39); and (4) a conclusion of the arguments presented.

The Limitations of this Study

The confines of this study's format, as well as the potential scope of its subject matter, demands an explanation of its limitations. The first limitation is the impossibility of attending to the entirety of Matthew's Gospel. Amid the tension between breadth and depth, I have chosen to focus on four select passages. These passages have been chosen according to two criteria. First, on the basis of a typology of popular prophecy which distinguishes between *action* prophets and *oracular* prophets (explored in chapter 2); two of the select passages (Matt 9:9–13; 21:10–17) tell of Jesus acting primarily as action prophet whereas the other two passages (5:3–12; 23:1–39) have Jesus acting primarily as oracular prophet. Second, two of the passages (Matt 21:10–17; 23:1–39) are standard texts in terms of a study of Jesus' prophetic vocation, while the other two (5:3–12; 9:9–13) are less commonly associated with this subject, and thus may provide fresh insights. My hope is that this combination of predictability and novelty leads to both critical engagement with scholarship and new ground.

Beyond the obvious textual limitations are more complex methodological considerations. I will have more to say about this below, but for now it is worth noting that because I am undertaking a narrative study that seeks the literary meaning of Matthew's story I am not primarily interested in providing an "objective" account of what is going on behind the text. Rather, I must, in immersing myself in Matthew's story, reflect what I think

---

3. This is not to say the subject of Jesus as prophet in Matthew has been completely ignored. Notable examples of works addressing this subject include Allison, *New Moses*, and Turner, *Israel's Last Prophet*.

it is saying about Jesus and his prophetic vocation. In this way, the language I use may at times, given the exegetical context, seem to some overly biased, even uncritical, toward Matthew's perspective. But this is necessitated by my choice of narrative criticism, concerned as it is to take on the role of the implied audience. In doing so, I am binding myself to Matthew's commitment to the person and work of Jesus, a commitment that cannot be neatly distinguished from the meaning of his story.

Methodological Considerations

As noted, this study makes use of narrative criticism as its primary method, but complements this with socio-historical criticism. Narrative criticism has been the subject of widespread debate over recent decades, and this requires some attention, as does my choice to combine it with a historical method. In what follows, I will outline my approach to each method and also defend my decision to combine narrative criticism with socio-historical criticism. Indeed, for some narrative critics this would seem a choice that undermines narrative criticism itself.

Narrative Criticism

Narrative criticism, which treats the text as a whole unit, focuses on aspects of a story such as implied author,[4] implied reader/audience, narrator, forms of discourse, structure, plot, literary devices, setting, and characters. The aim of narrative criticism is to read the text as the implied reader,[5] the "imaginary person in whom the intention of the text is to be thought of as always reaching its fulfillment."[6] In other words, our goal is to read the text as the audience that the narrative presupposes and in whom the strategies of the narrative accomplish their purpose.

In choosing to utilize narrative criticism as the primary method for this study, I am opting for a methodology that draws contested assumptions and

---

4. Booth, *Rhetoric of Fiction*, 70–71: "As he writes, [the historical author] creates not simply an ideal, impersonal 'man in general' but an implied version of 'himself' that is different from the implied authors we meet in other men's works. . . . Whether we call this implied author an 'official scribe,' or adopt the term recently revived by Kathleen Tillotson—the author's 'second self'—it is clear that the picture the reader gets of this presence is one of the author's most important effects. However impersonal he may try to be, his reader will inevitably construct a picture of the official scribe."

5. Powell, *What Is Narrative Criticism?*, 20.

6. Kingsbury, *Matthew as Story*, 36.

generates varied approaches. The prevailing methodological paradigm in biblical studies over the last few centuries has been that of historical-critical study. In recent decades, however, the historical-critical paradigm has been questioned as the dominant method for biblical criticism. Indeed, I concur with Howell, who argues that historical critics seek to examine the narrative text not in order to understand the gospel but rather something external to it,[7] namely a hypothetical situation or text. Recognizing that biblical texts contain not only historical and theological categories, but also literary ones, I echo Howell: "The limitations of a textually disintegrative and historicist approach in the historical critical paradigm resulted in a failure by biblical critics to appreciate the narrative character of the gospel texts."[8]

Another issue arises, however, when literary critics commit an equal and opposite methodological mistake by foregoing the historical window into the text. "What is the relation between a narrative and the events it depicts?" asks David Carr in his 1986 essay entitled "Narrative and the Real World."[9] And rightly so, for although historical narratives depict events that have occurred in what most would deem reality, the methodology of narrative criticism has at times been characterized by the implicit belief that the final form of the text functions coherently apart from circumstances relating to the compositional process and the historical actuality behind the story.[10]

This raises the question: does separating a narrative from its historical inspiration—assuming it exists—provide the most comprehensive interpretive approach? Conversely, does the integration of historical concerns into a narrative/literary methodology detract from or enhance understanding of a story?

Philosopher of history, Louis Mink, speaking of historical narrative, says:

> As historical it [historical narrative] claims to represent, through its form, part of the real complexity of the past, but as narrative it is a product of imaginative construction, which cannot defend its claim to truth by any accepted procedure of argument or authentification.[11]

---

7. Howell, *Matthew's Inclusive Story*, 23.

8. Howell, *Matthew's Inclusive Story*, 24.

9. Carr, "Narrative and the Real World," 117.

10. Bowman, "Narrative Criticism," 17.

11. Mink, "Narrative Form as a Cognitive Instrument," 145.

Hence Mink's notion that, "Stories are not lived but told. Life has no beginnings, middles, or ends . . . Narrative qualities are transferred from art to life."[12] Likewise, Hayden White says:

> There has been a reluctance to consider historical narratives as what they most manifestly are: verbal fictions, the contents of which are as much invented as found and the forms of which have more in common with their counterparts in literature than they have with those in the sciences.[13]

There is no doubt that the creation of a narrative, historical or fictional, presupposes an imaginative construction and a rhetorical purpose. But, as Laughery asks, "Why should narrative construction . . . banish historical occurrence, sense and reference? Does narrative construction exclude a credible representation of the past?"[14] Why, Laughery asks, should we assume that there is no narrative structure (beginning, middle and end) to the events prior to their literary construction?[15] A. P. Norman answers in the negative:

> A good historian will interact dialogically with the historical record, recognizing the limits it places on possible construals of the past. Although the traces of the past underdetermine the stories that can be told about the past, it is simply not the case that an historian must invent and impose to achieve a concrete determination. . . . Of course historians select their facts, and obviously the stories they tell are incomplete. But by itself this does not mean that the result is distorted or false. To say so is to posit implicitly an evaluative ideal of a history that is complete and non-perspectival. But this very idea is incoherent.[16]

The implied expectations that Mink and White place on narrative in reflecting historical reality are too demanding. Indeed, a postmodern critique might argue that no genre of text, narrative or otherwise (including scientific texts), could possibly fulfil such expectations, and that if we were to accept such presuppositions then we may be forced to accept that we can never actually describe reality at all.

In my view, we ought to go beyond a mere critique of formalist literary approaches to make a counterclaim to literary formalism: narrative criticism cannot stand completely unaccompanied if it seeks to provide a meaningful

---

12. Mink, "History and Fiction as Modes of Comprehension," 557–58.

13. White, "Historical Text as a Literary Artifact," 192.

14. Laughery, "Ricoeur on History," 346.

15. Laughery, "Ricoeur on History," 346–47.

16. Norman, "Telling It Like It Was," 132.

attempt at textual interpretation. After all, words, sentences, paragraphs, episodes, and narratives do not hold a universally accessible meaning on their own; they are encoded with meaning according to their social world. Without knowledge of this social setting, a narrative's encoded cues are bypassed, making way for the "gaps" to be filled with whatever meaning the reader wills them to hold. No doubt some interpreters welcome this shift of focus toward the reader, and indeed we must take due account of the reader in our efforts of interpretation.[17] Nonetheless, if the right to the creation of meaning lies solely with the reader, necessarily influenced by their social setting as they are, then there remains no satisfactory reason to choose this or that text over another—why not invest the same meaning into another story? Indeed, when a text's meaning is allowed to become so subjective the text itself becomes effectively meaning*less*, a proverbial mirror.[18] It is not surprising, then, that "text-immanent" perspectives that set aside the social context of author and original audience have been out of favor with literary interpreters for decades now.[19]

My aim in saying all of this is not to discern how "historically accurate" Matthew's narrative may be. Strictly speaking, the object of this study is not the historical reality of Jesus' prophetic vocation, but rather Matthew's literary depiction of this vocation. Still, in describing this study's chosen method we must understand that Matthew's narrative is addressed to an historical context and that there is a relationship between the narrative and that context. To make better sense of the narrative—regardless of whether it accurately refers to an historical reality—one can utilize socio-historical research in order to determine how it held meaning in its intended recipient context. This would be the case even if Matthew were entirely fictional. Ultimately, I am not seeking to determine how Matthew's narrative supplements our understanding of the depicted reality (as with historical-critical methods[20]), but conversely how our understanding of that reality (and the understanding of the implied recipients) may affect our perception of

---

17. Bauckham, *Jesus and the Eyewitnesses*, 3: "All history . . . is an inextricable combination of fact and interpretation, the empirically observable and the intuited or constructed meaning." This applies of course to both biblical interpreters and the Gospels themselves.

18. This is not an outright rejection of reader-response approaches to texts, but just to say such an approach ought to be understood within the realm of epistemology rather than that of ontology.

19. Kermode, *Poetry, Narrative, History*, 49: "[M]ore and more people are turning away from the idea that literary works should be treated as autonomous and without significant relation to the world in which they are produced and read."

20. Kingsbury, *Matthew as Story*, 2.

Matthew's narrative. This is the primary reason for seeking understanding of the relationship between narrative and history.

This is not to say that I am denying that Matthew's narrative depicts historical reality. As we will see, part of Matthew's aim for writing is to evoke a response from his audience in light of past events—events that were within the realm of historical recollection. My estimation is that the Jesus of testimony is not as distinct from the Jesus of history as some have claimed.[21] Indeed, the only direct vision we have of the Jesus of history is through the windows of memory,[22] whether biblical or extrabiblical; it is merely a question of which memories are most trustworthy. This question of trustworthiness is of course contested, though I am inclined to agree with the "Scandinavian school,"[23] which has warned against form-criticism's inflated claims, and with Richard Bauckham's more recent articulation of the Gospels as eyewitness testimony.[24]

In the end, the historical accuracy of Matthew is not, strictly speaking, crucial to this study. What is crucial is to remember that we cannot adequately comprehend Matthew's story without an understanding of the socio-historical context of the community to whom the narrative was addressed and of the reality being depicted in the narrative. This is the nature

---

21. Vanhoozer, *First Theology*, 269: "Testimony is a speech act in which the witness's very act of stating *p* is offered as evidence 'that *p*,' it being assumed that the witness has the relevant competence or credentials to state truly 'that *p*.'" In Gospel studies, a hermeneutic of suspicion has been the dominant stance, as if the Gospel authors could be trusted only if their claims could be verified independently of them by other historical means. A central issue, though, has been the irony that scholars have needed to trust *other* sources of testimony from the same time period to "verify" the claims of the Gospels. My stance is not a form of fideism, nor baseless selectivity, but rather an acknowledgement that the biblical accounts, including Matthew, were among the earliest accounts of Jesus of Nazareth.

22. On historical reconstruction as memory, see Dunn, *Jesus Remembered*; Bauckham, *Jesus and the Eyewitnesses*, esp. 319–57; Allison, *Constructing Jesus*; Le Donne, *Historical Jesus*. Allison, in the foreword to Le Donne's study, notes the way in which subjectivity's central role in historical reconstruction casts out Cartesian certainty (xi), and that positing an antithesis between event and interpretation is a flawed concept because it is not merely memories that are distorted, but perceptions of events themselves: "all perception is—in part because it is always social—inevitably distorted and shot through with interpretation from beginning to end" (ix).

23. Davies, "Reflections on a Scandinavian Approach to 'The Gospel Tradition,'" in *The Setting of the Sermon on the Mount*, 480: "[They] have made it far more probable, and reasonably credible, over against the skepticism of much form-criticism, that in the Gospels we are within hearing of the authentic voice and within sight of the authentic activity of Jesus of Nazareth."

24. Bauckham, *Jesus and the Eyewitnesses*.

of all literature.[25] In the case of the author of Matthew, he used realistic—if not real—people, places, customs, and events to tell his story, "and the common or shared experiences of their readers enabled communication to take place."[26] The historical paradigm is essential because it provides "information for setting the parameters of valid reading of the (text)."[27] Without such we cannot truly understand the perspective of the implied audience/reader, which is the goal of narrative criticism.

Regarding the aim of narrative criticism, Bowman says that "Narrative criticism seeks to discover and disclose the narrative's own intrinsic points of emphasis, thereby facilitating its interpretation and consequently helping to discriminate among various possible interpretations."[28] While this is generally true, it must be conceded at this point that my study seeks to analyze the prophetic vocation of Jesus, and thus somewhat contrives an emphasis before the narrative has even been engaged. In this way, I am tracing one particular coherent narrative theme through four selected passages of Matthew's Gospel.

Socio-Historical Criticism

Socio-historical criticism is a broadly defined method in scholarly literature, sometimes being viewed as a synonym for social-scientific criticism.[29] According to this view, the socio-historical approach seeks to apply the allied fields of the social sciences (such as anthropology, sociology, economics, and political science)[30] to the biblical text in order to "ground all interpretation in a literal reading of the text" (*literal* referring to the historical sense).[31] Indeed, in this conception the use of socio-historical criticism aims to "expose the meaning of the texts in terms of the first-century Mediterranean . . . contexts in which they were originally produced."[32]

25. "While we may grant the basic position that literature is primarily art, it must be affirmed also that art does not exist in a vacuum. It is a creation by someone at some time in history, and it is intended to speak to other human beings about some idea or issue that has human relevance. Any work of art for that matter will always be more meaningful to knowledgeable people than to uninformed ones." Guerin et al., *Handbook of Critical Approaches*, 17.

26. Howell, *Matthew's Inclusive Story*, 28.

27. Vorster, "Historical Paradigm," 104.

28. Bowman, "Narrative Criticism," 17.

29. Such as in MacDonald, *Pauline Churches*, 19–20.

30. Anderson, "Biblical Theology and Sociological Interpretation," 294.

31. Wilson, *Sociological Approaches to the Old Testament*, 2.

32. Whitelam, "Social World of the Bible," 37. In this statement Whitelam is

Though I see value in such an approach, I conceive of socio-historical criticism as a method distinct from social-scientific criticism. The sociological approaches of the latter actively seek to apply sociological theories to the world behind the text to explain behavior and other events and actions depicted within it. Meeks has a point, even if it is overstated, when he claims that the sociological interpreter of religious texts "imposes his own belief system on his evidence, implicitly or explicitly claiming to know more about the meaning of religious behavior than did the participants."[33]

Aside from the potentially reductionist tendencies of social-scientific criticism, a reason to avoid the application of sociological frameworks is that I am not qualified to construct contemporary sociological theories. Moreover, the competing schools of sociology, anthropology, and psychology complicate matters by insisting on the question of which approach should be adopted in the first place.[34]

This is not to reject outright the use of sociological approaches; on the contrary, my own conception of socio-historical criticism will, at times, make use of such research. Following Keener, I think that current sociological and anthropological models must function heuristically, being "adjusted or discarded where they do not fit the hard data," and for this reason I will give preference to such hard data over social-scientific models derived from it.[35] I will thus be far less given to utilizing theories based solely on contemporary observations (of which I lack expertise in any case) and more interested in frameworks developed from readings of ancient texts, particularly extrabiblical sources. I emphasize extrabiblical sources not because the biblical texts are deemed unreliable, but rather because there must be some guarding against the pitfalls of circular reasoning.[36] In short, I am interested in identifying the social, cultural, political, religious, and historical interactions that are embodied within the Matthean text by means of social-historical investigation into the historical

---

speaking of anthropological approaches in particular (his quote refers to *cultural* contexts in the original), though his conclusion can apply to any of the social sciences.

33. Meeks, *First Urban Christians*, 2–3.

34. Meeks, *First Urban Christians*, 5.

35. Keener, *Gospel of Matthew*, 16.

36. This is particularly relevant for our next chapter in which we are in danger of studying Matthew's Gospel in order to discern a social background on which to build a foundation to study Matthew's Gospel. We must be cautious of such circular reasoning "in trying to extrapolate the social world of the Bible from the biblical texts themselves" (Whitelam, "Social World of the Bible," 44).

period around the first century CE. This is perhaps best labeled *social description*, as opposed to social-scientific criticism.[37]

It is important to point out a possible point of tension between socio-historical and narrative criticism, namely, how we understand the reader. Socio-historical criticism will naturally be drawn to the author's actual audience to comprehend the meaning of the text. Such understanding is not the overall aim of my research, however, but serves as a supplement for heightened narrative-critical study. Indeed, the original historical reader is not normally a concern within literary-critical biblical studies. Rather, it is the implied reader who tends to be the focus of literary-critical attention. In saying this, I see no reason why the socio-historical study of the hypothesized actual audience and the narrative-critical study of the implied audience cannot work in partnership. For this research an understanding of the actual intended reader is supplementary to the study of the way the implied reader shapes the interpretation of the story and how it depicts a particular Jewish prophet from Galilee.

Utilizing This Study

A final note before launching into the study. The first two chapters of this study, dealing first with the background and social world of Matthew and second with prophecy in first-century Syro-Palestine, are somewhat exhaustive in detail. Some readers may find these chapters unnecessary and will wish to jump straight into the exegetical aspects of the study. Though I think the detail of these initial chapters is important for establishing the foundations of the remainder of the study, I understand why some readers may be less interested in such minutiae. For them, I would suggest reading the concluding sections of chapters 1 and 2 and then heading to chapter 3. Still, I hope such detailed treatments will be interesting both as foundations for what follows and as general overviews of Matthew's Gospel and first-century prophecy.

37. Following Meeks, *First Urban Christians*, 1–7.

Chapter 1

Matthew: Background, Social Setting, Narrative

PRIOR TO DELVING INTO the select passages of Matthew that concern later chapters of this study, it is important to first attend to the background, social setting and broad narrative elements of Matthew's Gospel as a whole. To embrace the role of the implied reader we must put ourselves in their position as much as we possibly can. This is a necessarily piecemeal task, since we can never fully enter into the knowledge and experience of a person or group from a different historical context (even an implied person or group, a work of imagination such as they are). But an analysis of critical historical, social, and narrative elements will help us bridge the gap between ourselves and a plausible implied reader and thus provide a better platform for a narrative-critical interpretation of Matthew's story than if we had bypassed such considerations.

1.1 The Author

In short, we do not know who authored Matthew's Gospel—the text is anonymous. In terms of external evidence the sources most important to us are Irenaeus[1] (c. 180–90 CE) and Eusebius[2] (c. 280–340 CE; including his citing of Papias,[3] a source from the early second century CE), both of whom testify to the traditional view that the apostle Matthew was the author of the first canonical Gospel. The majority of modern commentators reject this claim and the reasons for this rejection have been explored extensively

1. Irenaeus, *Haer.* 3.1.1, 3.9.1–3, 3.11.8, 3.16.2.
2. Eusebius, *Hist. eccl.* 3.24.5–6, 3.24.13.
3. Eusebius, *Hist. eccl.* 3.39.4–5 and esp. 3.39.16.

in the commentaries.[4] Whether the apostle wrote Matthew's Gospel is not, strictly speaking, particularly important for this study. More important are the characteristics and social world of this author and indeed many of the clues are found internal to the Gospel narrative.

What does Matthew's narrative reveal about the author? What is likely, and indeed is agreed upon by most commentators, is that the author was a Jew. "The Gospel has numerous Jewish features which cannot be attributed to tradition," argue W. D. Davies and Dale Allison:

> These include the play on the Hebrew name of David in 1.2–17, OT texts seemingly translated from the Hebrew specifically for our Gospel (e.g. 2.18; 8.17; 12.18–21), concentrated focus on the synagogue (e.g. 6.1–18; 23.1–39) and affirmation of the abiding force of the Mosaic Law (5.17–20). Matthew alone moreover records Jesus' prohibitions against mission outside Israel (10.5; 15.24), disparages Gentiles as such (5.47; 6.7), and shows concern that eschatological flight not occur on the Sabbath (24.20).[5]

Some scholars have attempted to argue for a gentile identity for the author of Matthew based on a perceived gentile, and indeed anti-Jewish, bias.[6] But as Warren Carter points out, nowhere does Matthew's Gospel have Israel rejected absolutely.[7] David Garland lists several passages (Matt 6:2; 21:43; 23:6, 32–33, 35; 27:25) that suggest an anti-Jewish bias in Matthew,[8] while Michael J. Cook provides an example from Matthew 22:

> In the Markan Tribute to Caesar pericope, Mark deems Jesus' questioners guilty of "hypocrisy"; Matthew, preserving the episode, substitutes "malice" for "hypocrisy," sharpening thereby the anti-Jewish denigration.[9]

---

4. See especially Davies and Allison, *Matthew 1–7*, 7–58. Also, Witherington, *Matthew*, 3–5. Keener, *Gospel of Matthew*, 38–41 is perhaps the most open to Matthean authorship amid recent scholarship, expressing inclination but also uncertainty. So too Gundry, *Matthew*, xxii; France, *Gospel of Matthew*, 15.

5. Davies and Allison, *Matthew*, xi–xii.

6. Clark, "Gentile Bias of Matthew," 165–72; Tilborg, *Jewish Leaders in Matthew*, 171–72; Meier, *Vision of Matthew*, 17–25; Cook, "Interpreting 'Pro-Jewish' Passages in Matthew," 135–46.

7. Carter, *Matthew: Storyteller, Interpreter, Evangelist*, 18.

8. Garland, *Reading Matthew*, 2. Garland does not support the notion of gentile authorship of Matthew, he merely presents it as a perspective.

9. Cook, "Interpreting 'Pro-Jewish' Passages in Matthew," 139. Cook argues that the appeal to so-called "pro-Jewish" passages in Matthew as proof of a Jewish author are in fact unjustified since they "have been viewed out of context so that their intent is misconstrued." However, the same argument applies to "anti-Jewish" passages.

There is a critical problem with this type of argument, common as it is. With the exception of Matt 27:25 in Garland's list, each of these references provides evidence not of a general anti-Jewish bias but of a polemic against the Jerusalem politico-religious leaders. Even in 27:25, the polemic is not leveled against "Jews"—the term ὁ Ἰουδαῖος is not even used—but against a particular group of people in the narrative under the influence of the Jerusalem leaders. The failure to distinguish between "Jews" and corrupt leadership in Matthew is a misunderstanding that affects how one views Matthew's *Sitz im Leben*. At this point, I will defer further discussion of this topic since Matthean polemic against such leadership, specifically by Jesus, embodies a number of prophetic characteristics and will come under closer analysis later on. The point here is that to posit gentile authorship based on a perceived anti-Jewish bias in Matthew is at best a problematic conclusion.

An additional point derived from Papias is worthy of note. In his *Ecclesiastical History*, our only record of Papias' work, Eusebius writes: "About Matthew this was said, 'Matthew collected the oracles in the Hebrew language (διαλέκτῳ), and each interpreted them as best he could.'"[10] This passage has long been used to suggest that Matthew's Gospel as we know it in Greek is in fact a translation from an earlier Hebrew version. As early as the work of Josef Kürzinger, however, this suggestion has been challenged.[11] Kürzinger argued that διαλέκτῳ is in fact a technical term of rhetorical technique so that rather than referring to Matthew writing in the Hebrew *dialect*, Papias is referring to Matthew having written in a Hebrew rhetorical *style*. While this reading is not unquestionably convincing (Matthew Black has noted a number of issues[12]), it leaves us with four options: (1) the original author(s) wrote in Hebrew; (2) they wrote in Greek but in a Hebrew rhetorical style; (3) a hypothetical source document, written in Hebrew, was utilized by Matthew's author; or (4) Papias' testimony is to be rejected. The first three possibilities point strongly to Jewish authorship.

Without a convincing argument in favor of gentile authorship, and with several important factors pointing in the opposite direction, the majority opinion seems a more prudent estimation—the author of Matthew was in fact a Jewish follower of Jesus. Beyond this, things become even less clear. Matthew's more than competent Greek—which has been used as an argument for his gentile identity—as well as his apparent knowledge of Hebrew and Aramaic, reflects a Jew embedded in a wider Greco-Roman world in which "Jewish" and "Hellenistic" spheres cannot be neatly or clearly

---

10. Eusebius, *Ecclesiastical History*, 1:297 (3.39.15–16).

11. Kürzinger, "Das Papiaszeugnis und die Erstgestalt," 19–38.

12. Black, "Use of Rhetorical Terminology," 33–34.

delineated.[13] Indeed, in such a world, competent Greek points much less to a gentile author than does knowledge of Hebrew to a Jewish author. We could surmise from the sophistication of the author's writing that he was well educated, possibly from a scribal background;[14] given the attention focused toward scribes in Matthew, this is not improbable. Whether scribe or not, Matthew's author seems to be in dialogue with Jewish thought and debate amid his contemporaries.[15] He is also accomplished in traditional methods of Jewish interpretation of the Old Testament,[16] his exegetical skill demonstrated in his portrayal of Jesus' use of antitheses (5:22–48) and *qal wahomer* (12:9–14).[17] That Matthew's author was likely well educated and a skilled exegete does not, however, reveal a highly specific identity since such skills could be present in a figure who was anything from one formerly toward the center of the socio-religious matrix, such as a rabbi, as argued by Ernst von Dobschütz,[18] to one from a Qumran-type marginalized community, as with Krister Stendahl.[19] This situation is further complicated by the fact that these possibilities are not mutually exclusive—a "converted" Jewish rabbi could have entered a Qumran-like Matthean community. Indeed, Saul of Tarsus could fit this profile of a highly educated exegete.

Overall, we must tread lightly regarding the identification of the author of Matthew's Gospel. In this study, I will adopt a reasonably modest set of presuppositions: the author was a Jewish Christian,[20] well-educated and skilled in Jewish interpretation and exegesis, and well acquainted

---

13. Carter, *Matthew: Storyteller*, 19–21, points out that the author used words and grammatical constructions that reflect Hebrew and Aramaic influences, as well as demonstrating knowledge of the Hebrew Old Testament. Also, while it is possible that Matthew was authored by a woman, here I conform to the universal presumption that the author was male, hence the ongoing use of male pronouns.

14. Cope, *Matthew*, 10.

15. Sigal, *Halakhah of Jesus of Nazareth*, provides important examples of Matthew's Jesus offering halakhic teaching on a range of issues hotly debated throughout the first century, into the post-70 CE period and beyond to the early rabbinic period.

16. Keener, *Gospel of Matthew*, 40.

17. Segal, "Matthew's Jewish Voice," 7.

18. Dobschütz, "Matthew as Rabbi and Catechist," 32. Dobschütz's suggestion that the author was a converted Jewish rabbi is, for a number of reasons, not least its anachronism, almost certainly false. It relies on Matthew's "rabbinic style," but this judgment is made in light of much later rabbinic literature. Rabbis are discussed below in greater detail.

19. Stendahl, *School of St. Matthew*.

20. Perhaps it is more accurate to use the label "Christian Jew," although the term "Christian" is probably anachronistic in this case.

with the wider Greco-Roman world possessing a strong competency in the Greek language.

1.2 Location and the "Matthean Community"

Moving from the author to investigate the location of Matthew's Gospel is to shift from one mystery to another—scholars have suggested a variety of possible locations and there is not yet a definitive identification. It is important to note that when referring to location we are talking about destination and not provenance. In truth, they may be the same but, as Michael Bird points out, we ought not assume that because a Gospel was written *in* a community that it was written *for* that community.[21] I take for granted that the author of Matthew wrote for a particular audience and fashioned his text in relation to them. Provenance may be helpful in that it sheds light on the environmental factors that generated the text, but I consider it less important than destination. Given the sparse data for determining it, provenance is for our purposes a nonessential consideration.

Suggestions as to possible destinations for Matthew's Gospel include Jerusalem, Alexandria in Egypt, Caesarea Maritima, Pella, Tyre or Sidon, Galilee, and Syria.[22] It is Syria that is most widely supported amongst contemporary scholars, with Antioch being the most common theory therein. External evidence may lend weight to this suggestion since possible references to Matthew are found in the writings of Ignatius, bishop of Antioch, from early in the second century CE,[23] and also in the Didache,[24] a text used widely throughout Syria. In saying this, it is important to note that these texts may not actually refer to Matthew but to an earlier shared source.[25] Whatever the case, the source of this material seems to have been circulated in Syria. Internal to Matthew there is a reference at 4:24 in which, following a description of Jesus' ministry in Galilee, it is said that "his fame spread throughout all Syria." Since this reference otherwise seems out of place, it is often used as an indication of a Syrian audience.

---

21. Bird, "Bauckham's *The Gospel For All Christians* Revisited," 9.

22. Carter, *Matthew: Storyteller*, 21. Since most scholars judge that Matthew was written post-70 CE the possibility of Jerusalem is generally excluded.

23. Ign. *Smyrn.* 1:1 (cf. Matt 3:15); Ign. *Pol.* 2:2 (cf. Matt 10:16b); Ign. *Eph.* 14:2 (cf. Matt 12:33).

24. Did. 1:4–5; 8:1–3 (cf. Matt 6:9–13 in contrast to Luke 11:2–4, which has a shorter address to God).

25. Contra, for example, Carter, *Matthew: Storyteller*, 22, and Carter, *Matthew and the Margins*, 16–17.

Provided Syria is accepted, there is evidence for a more specific location, such as a larger city like Antioch. Matthew appears to demonstrate a preference for the "city" over the "village"—J. D. Kingsbury points out that Mark uses πόλις eight times and κώμη seven times, while Matthew uses κώμη only four times and πόλις no fewer than twenty-six times.[26] Based on this, Kingsbury suggests that the Matthean community was urban, not rural. In addition are historical factors. Antioch recognized the citizenship of its Jewish population,[27] and the place outside Palestine with the most concentrated Jewish population was Syria, especially Antioch.[28] If Matthew's audience consisted largely of Jews (see below) then Antioch is a strong possibility.

While Antioch in Syria presents itself as the most popular candidate for Matthew's recipient location amongst contemporary scholars, this is far from immune to challenge. For instance, it is not at all clear that Kingsbury's assertion of an urban destination for Matthew such as Antioch is correct—most of Matthew's parables reflect the lives of rural peasants, those exploited within the agrarian economy, and we would expect that such people make up at least some of the audience. More comprehensive is the challenge offered by Andrew Overman, who suggests that the Matthean community was located in Galilee.[29] Overman questions whether Ignatius actually quoted Matthew or whether he referred to another source, and also whether Ignatius' supposed knowledge of Matthew's Gospel should in any case suggest Antioch as the place of the text's intended destination.[30]

There are a number of good reasons to commend Galilee as the intended destination of Matthew. First, Matthew's Jesus never leaves Galilee until his final pilgrimage to Jerusalem and this could reflect the social setting of the recipient community.[31] Moreover the fact that Matthew expends so much time and effort denouncing the Pharisees suggests a Galilean audience; the most likely place for Matthew's community to be confronted by "Pharisees" is Galilee since they were forced from Jerusalem after 70 CE and Galilee became a prime location for them.[32] This is not to say that the Pharisees were not

---

26. Kingsbury, *Matthew as Story*, 152.

27. Josephus, *Ag. Ap.*, 2.39; Keener, *Gospel of Matthew*, 41.

28. Josephus, *J.W.*, 7.43; Keener, *Gospel of Matthew*, 41.

29. Overman, *Church and Community*,

30. Overman, *Church and Community*, 16. In any case, Matthew is quoted in 1 Clem. 46:6–8. Assuming 1 Clement originates from Rome, and that it dates from around the time of Ignatius (if not earlier), the argument for a Syrian destination based on Ignatius is moot.

31. Overman, *Church and Community*, 17.

32. Segal, "Matthew's Jewish Voice," 27.

found beyond Galilee—one only need look to Saul of Tarsus to remedy such a misapprehension—but Matthew is dealing with what appears to be a strong community of Pharisees, a community certainly to be found in Galilee. It is also the case that the pressing issues which faced early rabbinic Judaism are also issues in Matthew's Gospel. Overman writes:

> Issues of ritual purity and legal interpretation, followers and disciples depicted as teachers, struggles over authority, who will work with the imperial powers, and how to structure the community in the post-destruction years are examples of the issues found both in Matthew and early rabbinic literature. These conversations and developments were taking place largely in the north of Israel after 70.[33]

The arguments for and against certain locations could continue to extend back and forth, but they would inevitably be unhelpful since there is no definitive case to be made. Further, a problem with the insistence on a single destination and a single Matthean "community" is that it implies clearly delineated first-century territoriality as with modern nation-states, sedentary community members, and a narrow intended audience. Each of these points requires attention.

First, though there is no doubt that territory was bounded in the ancient Near East, how these delineations functioned, and how they affected the lives of communities like that addressed by Matthew, is often unexamined by exegetes. Anthropologist Monica Smith outlines some important matters regarding the cartography of the ancient world:

> Historical and archaeological data illustrate that ancient states and empires are more effectively depicted and understood as networks rather than as homogenous territorial entities. . . . Mappers of ancient polities face a double challenge to cartography: premodern states and empires were behaviorally more complex than a simple territorial outline would imply . . . we need to recognize that territorial maps of ancient states are an idealized projection of state authority rather than a depiction of the way in which ancient political domains were actually governed. Simple territorial maps on the basis of site locations or artifact distributions obscure the multilayered processes of contact, interaction, domination, resistance, and tenuous integration that characterized premodern political systems. Even when absolute boundaries can be precisely defined and delineated,

---

33. Overman, *Church and Community*, 18.

> the presence of numerous competing claims may make state
> boundaries porous and meaningless.[34]

In short, though we may find that the Roman authorities divided up their empire into provinces for the sake of administration, this delineation was not necessarily the territorial framework in the minds of the majority of those who lived under the Empire, particularly those at its edges. Alan Segal points out that Jewish Christian refugees had settled within an arc that included Galilee, Pella, and parts of Syria, including Antioch and Edessa,[35] and it would not be surprising if these congregations were in regular contact. He argues also that the Jewish community of Syria was in good communication with Galilee, except during the rebellions,[36] strengthening the case that Galilee and Syria are to be viewed, at least in some ways, as a single geographical region. Travel between provinces, unhindered as it was by modern national borders, was common for trade and, in the case of the early church, ministry and mission.

This leads to our second point: it is clear that Matthew's community included itinerants.[37] For these figures, Galilee and Antioch were "merely two fixed points in a rather loosely confederated group of congregations, united by missionaries who were more or less constantly on the move at first."[38] Internal to Matthew are elements of rhetoric that seem to reflect the interests of such missionaries, such as in Matt 10:5–15, a passage which serves not only as instructions for such itinerants, but also for those who are to show them hospitality. No doubt there were many in the Matthean community who led sedentary lives in urban or near-urban areas. Even so, the audience as a whole is expected to be missional and, judging by Matthew's universalizing predictions in Matt 24:14 and 26:13, as well as the final command in 28:19–20,[39] there were some in the community who acted itinerantly. That itinerants were apparently moving frequently from community to community should lead us to be suspicious of the functional isolation often inherent in conclusions about early Christian communities.

That the author of Matthew would have known his writing could have been circulated easily and rapidly due to itinerants (perhaps he himself was one) leads us to our third point, namely, that the author's intended audience need not be as narrow as has typically been thought. That Matthew's Gospel

---

34. Smith, "Networks, Territories, and the Cartography of Ancient States," 845.

35. Segal, "Matthew's Jewish Voice," 26.

36. Segal, "Matthew's Jewish Voice," 26.

37. Schweizer, "Matthew's Church," 162–67; Luz, Studies in Matthew, 151–53.

38. Segal, "Matthew's Jewish Voice," 27.

39. Ulrich, "Missional Audience," 66–73.

was widely circulated is well established; Matthew is widely quoted in writings dating from the early centuries of the church.[40] What is crucial is the author's intent—did he expect the text to circulate and was it written with this in mind? While claims of authorial intent should generally be avoided, some conclusions can be drawn.

The Gospels for All Christians,[41] edited by Richard Bauckham and published in 1998, marked a radical departure from the dominant paradigm that the Gospels were composed for individual local Christian communities. In Bauckham's view, the "Matthean community" (and indeed the Markan, Lukan, and Johannine communities) are scholarly constructs, all too often assumed but rarely evidenced. On the contrary, the Gospels, he claims, were intended for a broad audience, having been written to those communities to which they may have circulated. For Bauckham, Matthew and Luke used Mark's Gospel, which indicates it had already circulated widely. This, he says, would have led to the expectation of the authors that their writings would also circulate in a similar way.[42] Bauckham argues that there would be no need to write the Gospels if the messages therein could have been orally communicated to those near where the authors resided; the very reason for writing was to communicate over distance (and, I would add, time).[43]

Graham Stanton has agreed with Bauckham, pointing out that "Many redaction critics have assumed that Matthew's relationship with his readers was rather like Paul's intimate relationship with the Christian communities to whom he wrote. That view needs to be reconsidered."[44] Stanton goes on to ask, in light of the fact that first-century followers of Jesus met in houses and could not have numbered more than fifty in any single group, whether it is likely that Matthew would have "composed such an elaborate gospel for one relatively small group."[45]

David Sim, whose work *The Gospel of Matthew and Christian Judaism: The History and Social Setting of the Matthean Community*[46] was potentially compromised by Bauckham's claims, has subsequently dismissed the broad-audience hypothesis. While this is not the space to outline this debate in detail, a few relevant points are worth noting. Sim takes Bauckham's point

40. See Metzger, *Canon of the New Testament*, esp. 39–73. See also Stanton, *Gospel Truth?*, 98.

41. Bauckham, *Gospels for All Christians*. In particular Bauckham's essay within, "For Whom Were the Gospels Written?" (*Gospels for All Christians*, 9–49).

42. Bauckham, *Gospels for All Christians*, 12–13.

43. Bauckham, *Gospels for All Christians*, 28–30.

44. Stanton, *Gospel for a New People*, 50.

45. Stanton, *Gospel for a New People*, 51.

46. Sim, *Gospel of Matthew and Christian Judaism*.

about Matthew and Luke expecting their Gospels to circulate in the same
fashion as Mark's and turns it on its head—Matthew and Luke radically al-
tered Mark's text for their own purpose and would have learned from doing
this that their own texts would have been equally at the mercy of others who
did not share their viewpoint:[47]

> They would therefore have been very mindful of the inherent
> dangers associated with writing for a general audience and ex-
> pecting their message to be preserved intact; either their Gos-
> pels could be re-written (as happened with Mark) or they could
> be misinterpreted, either deliberately or accidentally, by those
> Christians who belonged to an alternative tradition.[48]

Sim, moreover, argues that the lack of identification in the Gospels of a specific recipient[49] is not evidence of an open audience but, on the contrary, is
more likely to indicate "the proximity between the author and the Christian
group for whom he was writing."[50] For Bauckham, the Gospel authors were
not so concerned about how different audiences might understand their
texts,[51] though Sim views this proposition as difficult to accept since the
texts were written, implicitly or explicitly, to discredit other views.[52] On the
last point Sim's argument is most logical, but this is not to say it is mutually
exclusive to Bauckham's overall case. In truth, there is no definitive way of
deciding between these two hypotheses as both are possibilities and there
is a shortage of primary evidence.

A major flaw in Sim's rebuttal against Bauckham is his understanding
of Bauckham's case: "the Gospels were written for all Christians in each and
every Christian church."[53] This is not Bauckham's argument. Bauckham suggests that the Gospels "were designed for any and every Christian community
to which they may have circulated."[54] The difference is significant and Bauckham's case need not exclude that the authors wrote with a particular audience
in mind even if they did not deem their text limited to that audience. While
it is unlikely that Matthew intended his Gospel to be read by *all* Christians,
Bauckham's assertion that the text was expected to circulate is convincing.

47. Sim, "Gospels for All Christians?," 16. A point also made by Esler, "Community
and Gospel in Early Christianity," 241.

48. Sim, "Gospels for All Christians," 16.

49. Sim does not mention Theophilus (Luke 1:3).

50. Sim, "Gospels for All Christians," 17.

51. Bauckham, *Gospels for All Christians*, 48.

52. Sim, "Gospels for All Christians," 17–18.

53. Sim, "Gospels for All Christians," 27.

54. Bauckham, *Gospels for All Christians*, 10–11.

This need not exclude the possibility that the author had particular communities in mind, but it does mean that in writing they had an awareness of an expectedly broad audience. What is most important for us is that the concept of a single Matthean community is at least suspect, and it is probable that Matthew's intended audience was to be found in multiple locations, including popular suggestions such as Antioch and Galilee.[55]

In light of these considerations, I must express substantial doubt about the majority view that Matthew's Gospel was directed only to Antioch. There is no reason to assume that Matthew wrote to only one community and, as discussed, it is more likely that he did not. Galilee and Antioch provide two compelling candidates and the connection between the early Christian communities in these places makes likely a compound of the two as Matthew's destination. This does not discount the possibility or even likelihood that other locations and communities, especially in Judea and the Transjordan, were addressed, but if they were there are few indicators. What should be clear is that the destination for Matthew's Gospel, wherever that may be, included a large Jewish population, contained synagogues, was a center of the rising sphere of rabbinic influence, and spoke Greek. Until better evidence is discovered, a range of communities in Syro-Palestine, possibly a mix of urban and rural, remains the best guess.

The implications of this conclusion for the interpretation of Matthew are significant. That Matthew was not intended for a single community does not suggest that it should be seen outside of a historical context. While Bauckham says "the context is the late first-century Christian movement in general and not the Evangelist's particular community,"[56] this creates an unnecessary dichotomy between two deficient options. On the one hand, we need not posit a single Matthean community, but on the other, we need not spread the net so widely as to encompass a defined and unified but historically questionable late first-century Christian movement.[57] The truth is more likely somewhere in the middle, with a potential range of communities finding themselves in some way entwined in similar issues addressed by Matthew. These issues, as best as we can reconstruct them from both

55. It is noteworthy that other texts within the NT were written with the apparent intention of broad circulation, for example 1 Peter and Revelation.

56. Bauckham, *Gospels for All Christians*, 46.

57. It is unlikely that there was a single and unified Christian movement in the late first century. See Sim, "Gospels for All Christians," 10: "It is well known that in the initial decades the early Christians were divided into at least two distinct and very different groups that were often in conflict with one another. At the very heart of this dispute was the issue of Christian identity. To put the matter in simple terms, one faction required all followers of Jesus the Christ to belong to the people of Israel and to follow the Torah, while the other did not."

internal and external evidence, are a large part of Matthew's historical context. This raises the question as to what issues the communities may have been facing, though this will be considered below in the discussion about Matthew's *Sitz im Leben*. For now, it is sufficient to say that it is problematic to appeal to our sizable knowledge of first-century Antioch in order to determine the context of Matthew's Gospel since this may not be the only or even primary intended destination for the text.

1.3 Intended Audience

In terms of the actual recipients of Matthew, it has already been pointed out that they are largely Jewish. Matthew's Gospel leaves many Jewish terms and customs unexplained, including handwashing (15:1), the "two drachma tax" (temple tax; 17:24–27), the seat of Moses (23:2), phylacteries and fringes (23:5), and flight on the Sabbath (24:20).[58] The author simply assumes that his audience understands these references. Matthew's positive stance toward the mission to the nations may suggest that there are also gentiles among the recipients, but not necessarily since he may simply be affirming this mission in the absence of gentiles. Still, that Matthew three times translates Semitic words (1:23; 27:33, 46) suggests a partly gentile, non-Semitic-speaking audience.

That Matthew wrote in Greek has been used to suggest that a gentile audience is in view but, in light of other considerations above, this does not seem likely. Donald Hagner has proposed that the use of Greek could suggest an audience of Hellenistic Jews and Jews of the diaspora.[59] This may indeed be the case but, given that we have argued for a wider range of destination than is typically imagined, it may be that Matthew's Gospel was written to communities of diaspora Jews as well as Palestinian Jews, to communities with gentile converts and to those without. In the first century, Greek was simply the most universal language and it makes sense for the author, who has circulation of his narrative in mind, to prefer it.[60]

We have already pointed to Kingsbury's suggestion that Matthew's audience is situated in urban or near-urban areas. Kingsbury adds that the

---

58. Garland, *Reading Matthew*, 2.

59. Hagner, *Matthew 1–13*, lxv.

60. Martin Hengel's well known study of Hellenism in Palestine suggests that the region was deeply Hellenized well before the first century CE. Hengel, *Judaism and Hellenism*.

audience is probably well-to-do and provides a number of reasons for this assertion:[61]

1. Luke pronounces blessing for the "poor" (6:20) but Matthew on "the poor in spirit" (5:3).[62]

2. Mark's Jesus commands disciples to take no "copper coin" on their missionary journey (6:8) but Matthew's Jesus says to take no "gold, nor silver, nor copper coin" (10:9).

3. Luke tells a parable about minas (19:11–27) but Matthew about talents (25:14–30), the latter worth around fifty times that of the former.

4. In relation to the great supper, Luke instructs, "bring in the poor and maimed and blind and lame" (14:21). Matthew alternatively has the instruction to bring in as many as can be found, with no explicit reference to the marginalized (22:9).

5. In Mark (15:43) and Luke (23:50–51), Joseph of Arimathea is a member of the Council looking for the kingdom of God. In Matthew he is a rich man and a disciple (27:57).

6. Luke makes four references to silver, Mark has only one. Matthew on the other hand mentions the terms silver, gold, and talents no fewer than twenty-eight times.

7. Matthew (13:22; 19:23) redacts Mark's warnings against wealth (Mark 4:19; 10:23).

Though the weight of these points together seems formidable, a number are problematic[63] and they are not at all sufficient to show that Matthew's audience was well-to-do. In any case, these observations prove little—they could as easily reflect an aspect of the wider world of Matthew's audience with which they were only distantly familiar. That is to say, the frequent mention of money in no way necessitates an audience who are themselves rich or an author who is supportive of wealth.

If we were to accept Kingsbury's method, then other material within Matthew might point to an entirely different sketch of the audience from that which Kingsbury proposes. Matthew 18:23–35 has a parable based on the tributary economy, Jesus' disciples are sent out amongst "involuntary

---

61. Kingsbury, *Matthew as Story*, 152–53.

62. I disagree with Kingsbury that there is a sharp distinction between the poor and the poor in spirit. The meaning of the latter will be explored in chapter 4.

63. Though this is not the place to detail these problems and the related debates.

marginals"[64] (10:7–8; 25:31–45),[65] and tax collectors from the retainer class are called to discipleship alongside outcasts (9:9–13). Indeed, most of the parables in Matthew seem to reflect the lives of those living in rural village settings, those majority peasants systematically exploited in an agrarian economy. Matthew speaks of both the wealthy and the poor and the mention of either group does not constitute a sign of their being his intended audience.

Carter, appealing to Pauline material regarding the constitution of the early Christian movement, concludes with Wayne Meeks that these Christian communities represented a cross-section of society.[66] While Matthew's audience may well reflect a similar cross-section to that of the Pauline communities, as Carter argues, appealing to Pauline evidence does not guarantee this. After all, Paul's communities were found in cities at least as far west as Rome; they were not living in agricultural villages in Syro-Palestine. More helpful is the work of Evert-Jan Vledder in mapping the social stratification in advanced agrarian societies, such as that of first-century Palestine and Syria.[67] Such a project is fraught with obvious issues, not least whether such modern social-scientific models can adequately describe ancient societies about which we have limited data. In light of this, it is worth noting that Vledder is heavily reliant on the work of Gerhard Lenski, who has often used the Roman Empire as a test case for advanced agrarian societies.[68] That is to say, a model derived from contemporary cross-cultural case studies is not simply imposed on ancient Roman Palestine. The levels of stratification described by Vledder are as follows:[69]

---

64. A term taken from Duling, "Matthew and Marginality," 642–71. Duling defines involuntary marginals as those who are unable to "conform to expected social roles with respect to sex, age, civil life, occupation, and social life in relation to levels of status in the social system" because of the unavailability of objective resources (e.g., education, jobs, purchasing power, housing) and a lack of personal conditions (psychological features) needed to exercise those social roles.

65. Carter, *Matthew and the Margins*, 24–25.

66. Carter, *Matthew and the Margins*, 26.

67. Vledder, *Conflict in the Miracle Stories*.

68. Lenski, *Power and Privilege*, esp. 189–242.

69. Vledder, *Conflict in the Miracle Stories*, 117–67. Lenski's model is far more detailed and convincing, but it is too complex to discuss here and Vledder's typology is sufficient. Lenski's model is helpfully depicted in graphic form in Lenski, *Power and Privilege*, 284.

Urban elite	Ruler and governing classes; Caesar, rulers of the gentiles, high officials, Herod, scribes, Sanhedrin
Retainer class	Those who served the elite as professional functionaries; e.g., Pharisees, Sadducees, scribes, centurions, tax collectors, Herodians
Urban nonelite	Merchants, artisans etc.; Joseph, Mary, Jesus and his brothers (and sisters), money-changers, fisherman (such as Peter, Andrew, James and John)
Peasants	Slaves and tenants
The degraded, unclean and expendable classes	Lived outside the city walls; tanners, lepers, beggars, robbers, low-status prostitutes, poor laborers, some merchants

For Vledder, the criteria of social stratification in advanced agrarian societies is not merely wealth, as might be argued of modern industrial societies, but also health, friendship and love, honor, respect and status, power and influence, and security and safety.[70] This means that defining Matthew's audience as "well-to-do" or "poor" in purely economic terms is to impose a modern industrial social scheme—it is quite possible that people of variant levels of economic well-being were to be found within the same non-elite social strata, for example.[71] That in Matthew Jesus himself comes from a lower "artisan" strata and ministers mainly among the lower classes[72] should

70. Vledder, *Conflict in the Miracle Stories*, 118–19.

71. Saldarini, *Pharisees, Scribes, and Sadducees*, 28: "Status was determined by a variety of social criteria, including citizenship and family. Wealth was necessary to the upper class person, but its possession did not make one a member of the upper class."

72. I am aware of the complexities in the use of a term such as "class." Rohrbaugh notes "that popular and nontechnical use of [class terminology] abounds." Rohrbaugh, "Methodological Considerations," 528. Weber associated *class* with economic situation vis-à-vis *status* which refers to one's social standing according to law and prestige, what could be called social honor (*Economy and Society*, 302–10). Lenski, on the other hand, viewed class as being best understood according to the underlying question: *who gets what and why?* (what he calls the distributive process; *Power and Privilege*, 2–3). Class, according to Lenski, is "an aggregation of persons in a society who stand in a similar position with respect to force or some specific form of institutionalized power" (*Power and Privilege*, 75), thus his concept of *class* included aspects of Weber's *status*. Rohrbaugh suggests that this kind of defining class according to social positions, or "gradations," is problematic, and "not just that they are simple while societies are complex . . . statistical pictures of income level in Roman society bear no relation to the dynamics of the social situation. Few such variables do . . . a person in antiquity may have been poor and honored or rich and despised" ("Methodological Considerations," 529–30). For Rohrbaugh, ranking by status group is "synthetic." Over against "gradational conceptions of social class," he suggests relational conceptions: "instead of

not be overlooked, nor should the fact that a vast majority of disciples in the text are of the same or similar lower classes. From this we could conclude that Matthew's implied audience is meant to identify with these lower strata, perhaps a signal that a good number of them hail from there.

A major exception in Matthew is the implication at several points that scribes make up a segment of the Matthean audience. Whether the author himself was a scribe, a proposal advanced by Dennis Duling, is not of concern here.[73] Duling does, however, show that scribes, as educated and literate, came from the elite classes, though they were not in the top tier and are best described, at least generally, as retainers.[74] This is in agreement with Vledder and Lenski. Even so, scribes held a special prestige or honor owing to their religious functions throughout Jewish history.[75] In Matthew, of the twenty-two references to scribes, sixteen have them bound with opponents of Jesus.[76] Far from Matthew confusing these groups, in the Gospel, "the scribes *per se* never stand alone as opponents of Jesus. They are tainted by the company they keep."[77] It is no coincidence that this company is typically Pharisaic in Matthew. In contrast, there are passages in Matthew that portray scribes positively (e.g., 8:19; 13:52; 17:10–13; 23:34). Based on these passages, particularly 13:52, it is reasonable to think that some of the members of the Matthean audience may have been scribes. This, in conjunction with the assertion above that Matthew's audience included members from the lower classes, leads us to believe that Matthew's audience was a cross-section of the social stratification present in Roman

---

looking at how much money a person has, and thereby classifying him in relation to his neighbors, we must look at a person's position in relation to others that enabled him to acquire the money in the first place. Position is the key . . . for example, people are understood as either owners or non-owners of the means of production. That is, they stand in a particular social relation in which the position of each defines the other." ("Methodological Considerations," 531). In other words, social relations demarcate and produce social position; studying social relations should be preferred over studying the characteristics of social positions, produced by relations as they are. All of this raises the problem, inherent in sociological studies of ancient societies, of which model to adopt. This is a reason why this study has opted for a socio-historical approach over a purely sociological one. Though social-scientific methods can help elucidate the data, I treat them mainly as a heuristic tool in social historical research. In this specific case I have opted for the model of Lenski, with its more conventional understanding of class, but I am conscious of the issues involved.

73. Duling, "Matthew and Marginality," 642–71.

74. Duling, "Matthean Brotherhood," 175–78.

75. Duling, "Matthean Brotherhood," 176.

76. Duling, "Matthew as Marginal Scribe," 524.

77. Orton, *Understanding Scribe*, 28.

Palestine and beyond. To reduce this to a discussion of mere wealth is to misunderstand the nature of this social stratification.

The connection between those in the Matthean communities could be called, according to Duling, a fictive kin group, or brotherhood.[78] Like the Pharisees,[79] this was a voluntary association and social movement. That Matthew's audience was a "brotherhood" is best demonstrated by the numerous passages in Matthew that speak openly about familial relationships (i.e., 5:21–26; 7:1–5; 12:46–50; 18:15–22, 35; 23:8–10; 25:40; 28:10).[80] Unlike the Pharisees, the Matthean brotherhood did not hail from a narrow band of social strata; this is significant for the way in which we define the nature of the Matthean communities, especially in regard to insider and outsider labeling.

The final thing that needs to be mentioned here, given its centrality to the study, is the presence of prophets in the Matthean audience. Whereas γραμματεὺς is used twenty-two times in Matthew, προφήτης is used thirty-seven times. That the author warns his audience of false prophets (7:15–23) is probably an indication that "true" prophets were not only present in the communities, but seen as legitimate and important, hence the need to give warning. It may be that the "brotherhood" of Matthew's audience was led by scribes and prophets, though there is no way to prove this at present.

To sum up, Matthew's audience was mostly Jewish, with some gentiles in at least some of the communities. They represented a cross-section of the stratification within Roman society, some from the lower peasant and non-elite classes, with others from the elite retainer class, and perhaps even higher. The communities were fictive kin groups, or brotherhoods, with an openness to outsiders. Included in this cross-section were likely scribes not aligned with the Pharisees and other opposition groups. There were also prophets in the Matthean communities and they, potentially along with scribes, probably made up an important section of the community.

1.4 The Date of Matthew, the Problem of Yavneh, and the Identity of the Pharisees

The window typically given for Matthew's date is between 70–110 CE. A good reason for the upper limit is the possible references to Matthew found in 1 Clement, Ignatius, and the Didache, as well as in the work of Papias

---

78. Duling, "Matthean Brotherhood," 161–72.

79. Saldarini, *Pharisees, Scribes, and Sadducees,* 281.

80. Each of these is looked at in detail in Duling, "Matthean Brotherhood," 164–72.

as recorded in Eusebius.[81] These texts are all normally dated no later than the early second century CE. Even if only one of these references were actually taken from Matthew, it would suffice to show that the Gospel was written prior to the early second century.[82] Moreover, the effects of the fall of Jerusalem can still be felt in Matthew as a relevant issue, especially in 23:37—25:46, suggesting the event was not far in the past. For these reasons, I suggest the date of Matthew must be before the end of the first century CE.

In attempting to provide a boundary on the lower end of the 70–110 CE window, redaction critics have tended to rely on the insistence that Matthew used Mark as a source to narrow the possibilities. Mark is typically dated from the late 60s to the mid-70s CE and, since it is thought that Matthew describes the destruction of Jerusalem in more detail than Mark, the conclusion follows that Matthew came later. But the dating of Mark is equally as perilous as that of Matthew, and there are a range of opinions on the matter. In short, we do not have a definite date for Mark. R. T. France, a scholar who cautiously asserts a pre-70 CE date, rightly points out that our assertions "depend on a relative dating of various writings and events . . . there are very few fixed points."[83]

This study is not the place to engage the dating of Mark except to say that some scholars date it to the early 60s CE, leaving room for Matthew to have been written before 70 CE. Some scholars claim that since Matthew's Gospel seems to allude to the burning of Jerusalem (Matt 22:7), unlike Mark, it must have been composed after that event, that is, after 70 CE.[84] However, this conclusion rests on a number of assumptions, not least an a priori rejection of the possibility of foretelling the future, either through divine revelation or by reading the signs of the times.[85] The tendency to consider

81. Craig Keener points out that Graham Stanton adds 5 Ezra as a text whose author utilized Matthew (*Gospel of Matthew*, 44). Keener implies that this is evidence that the Gospel should not be dated too late in the first century CE. However, since Stanton himself dates 5 Ezra to the mid-second century (probably after the Bar Kokhba rebellion; Stanton, *Gospel for a New People*, 256–77) it seems unlikely that the text can give weight to a pre-90 CE date.

82. Earlier we briefly discussed the issues surrounding the source of these references, and also Overman's doubts as to whether Ignatius had actually quoted Matthew; Overman, *Church and Community*, 16.

83. France, *Matthew*, 30.

84. Perhaps most notably see Carter, *Matthew: Storyteller*, 22, and Carter, *Matthew and the Margins*, 16–17.

85. If Mark was written pre-70 CE, as is argued by a strong minority, then the author there predicted the destruction of Jerusalem prior to this event (Mark 13). The only significant difference between this account and that of Matthew is that the latter refers to the burning of the city (Matt 22:7), a prediction that could feasibly rest on knowledge of previous Roman conquests.

as authentic prophecy that which went unfulfilled while insisting on the *ex eventu* nature of all fulfilled prophecies is a hallmark of such an assumption, and it deserves scrutiny for its potential to skew our conclusions. With Hagner we must say, "Far too much weight has been put on [Matthew 22:7] in the confident post-70 dating of Matthew,"[86] though this does not preclude the possibility of a post-70 date on account of other evidence.

A pre-70 CE date for Matthew, while still a minority position, is asserted by a number of mainly conservative scholars.[87] Some of the points raised by the proponents of this position are valid but inconclusive, while others are simply debatable or irrelevant. Points include: patristic witness, that anti-Pharisaism could just as likely date to a time pre-70 given widespread Pharisaic influence in that period, the vagueness of Matt 22:7 regarding details of the Roman war (66–73 CE),[88] problems related to the fulfillment of the apocalyptic predictions in Matt 23–25, the apparent lack of influence of the Pauline literature,[89] and the occurrence of synagogue expulsion prior to 70 CE. In my view these points are affected by the pitting of mere historical possibilities against more likely scenarios, too-literal interpretations of parables, the misreading of Jesus' apocalyptic discourse, and the rejection of the possibility that Matthew knew of Paul but disagreed with him.

One problem raised by Gundry and Carson and Moo for the post-70 CE position that warrants more attention is the presence of the temple tax in Matt 17:24–27.[90] With the temple no longer standing, goes the argument, this story is irrelevant to a post-70 CE audience, even despite the fact that

86. Hagner, *Matthew 1–13*, lxxiv.

87. Robinson, *Redating the New Testament*, 86–117; Gundry, *Matthew*, 599–609; Carson and Moo, *Introduction to the New Testament*, 152–57; Nolland, *Gospel of Matthew*, 16–17; France, *Gospel of Matthew*, 18–19.

88. This is said to be an indication that Matthew was not written after 70 CE since if it had the details of the war would be much more detailed. Gundry, *Matthew*, 600. As described above, the exact same verse is used as evidence for precisely the opposite argument.

89. It is thought that a lack of interaction with the Pauline corpus would have been impossible after 70 CE (Carson and Moo, *Introduction to the New Testament*, 156–57). This is essentially an adaptation of Kilpatrick's argument of the same logic that Matthew cannot have been written after 90 CE: Kilpatrick, *Origins of the Gospel According to St. Matthew*, 129–30. It is thought that Matthew, for example, would not have written his Resurrection account in chapter 28 had he known about 1 Cor 15. Moreover, his view of the law is vastly different from that of Paul, with the implication being that Paul's view is superior and Matthew would certainly have reflected Paul's doctrine of χάρις had he known of it.

90. Gundry, *Matthew*, 606; Carson and Moo, *Introduction to the New Testament*, 155–56.

after the war Roman authorities continued to collect the tax (the *fiscus Judaicus*) in order to fund the temple to Jupiter Capitolinus in Rome.[91] Gundry, referring to Jesus' comment that "the sons are free" in Matt 17:26b, suggests that if the passage were a later adaptation addressing the Roman temple tax then it "implies that the disciples are sons of a pagan god!"[92] But Matthew has Jesus making no claim that "the sons" (17:26) refers to the disciples. On the contrary, these sons are those of the "kings of the earth" (17:25), that is, the Roman authorities. It is quite possible the whole form of the discourse is purposefully subtle given the domination of Rome and its near-guaranteed retaliation against any notion of rebelliousness. As Warren Carter acknowledges, to pay the tax was a pragmatic necessity. The miraculous procurement of the drachmas does not represent voluntary payment, but God's provision.[93] The episode is a kind of resistance literature taking on the form of a harmless, "irrelevant" story. This is discourse from the bottom, from people who cannot simply say what they mean (no wonder it is lost on Western interpreters, hailing from low-context cultures[94] as they do). While this interpretation does not prove the story is not intended to refer to the pre-70 CE Jerusalem temple, it does show that the pericope is not nearly as difficult for a post-70 CE dating scheme as Gundry and others suggest. Overall, along with the majority of scholars, I find the pre-70 CE dating of Matthew to be unlikely given the lack of convincing evidence.

The majority of recent scholars who posit a post-70 CE date for Matthew argue for a more specific date, somewhere between 85–90 CE, because they see in Matthew evidence that a final break between church and synagogue had already occurred.[95] This break is often associated with the hypothetical decisions at Yavneh (Jamnia) around 85 CE. Most notable is the insistence that a decision was made by rabbis in Yavneh at this time to evict Christians from the synagogues, a decision enshrined in the *Birkat ha-Minim*, a curse against the "heretics" (*minim*). This curse was incorporated into the liturgy of the synagogue, the twelfth of the Eighteen Benedictions

91. Josephus, *J.W.* 7.216–18; Dio Cassius 65.7.2.

92. Gundry, *Matthew*, 606.

93. Carter, *Matthew and the Margins*, 359–60.

94. Low- and high-context refer to the nature of communication in any culture, whether its communicators use high-context messages suited to an in-group to communicate complex meaning, thus requiring fewer words in order for the in-group to comprehend that meaning (high-context), or whether they must be more explicit and verbose in communicating their message (low-context). See Hall, *Beyond Culture*.

95. For example, Meier, "Locating Matthew in Time and Space," in *Antioch and Rome*, ed. Brown and Meier, 15–27; Stanton, *Gospel for a New People*, 113–45; Luz, *Theology of the Gospel of Matthew*, 15; Sim, *Gospel of Matthew*, 150–51.

entitled *Shemonah Esreh*. It has been claimed that Matthew must have been written around the time of the formulation of the *Birkat ha-Minim*, a measure that significantly influenced Jewish–Christian relations at a time when Judaism was being reconstructed post-70 CE.[96]

There are, however, a number of reasons to contest this claim. If the *Birkat ha-Minim* was truly a formalizing of the hostility between some Jews and Christians it is highly improbable that it was a sudden development. More likely is that such hostility boiled over into this formalizing process, not the other way around. Such would not imply a specific date for the composition of Matthew since the *Birkat ha-Minim* documents feelings that pre-existed over a period of time. Further, those rabbis at Yavneh were a tiny portion of the population[97] and it is unclear that Matthew's communities were aware of the curse. That is to say, the *Birkat ha-Minim* does not necessarily reflect the feelings of the author and audience of Matthew, nor of other Jews. In the case of Matthew's author, it would appear from his writing that relations with *some* form of "Judaism" had become strained to the point that he disassociated himself and his audience from it, referring to "*their* synagogues" (Matt 4:23; 9:35; 10:17; 12:9; 13:54), "*your* synagogues" (23:34), "*their* scribes" (7:29), and "the Jews to this day" (28:15).[98] But for all we know this self-image, of separation from these Jews, may have pre-dated any such reciprocal identification by a rabbinic group. Further, there is no evidence that the *Birkat ha-Minim* was seen as universally binding for Jews not associated with the early rabbis, as if it were some kind of medieval papal decree.[99] It is likely that other Jews did not share the sentiments of the *Birkat ha-Minim* at all.[100] Alternatively, it may be that exclusion of Jewish Christians from synagogues was common prior to the curse. In reality, it may have been a mix, and we at least know from the Pauline corpus that the earliest Christians experienced at least some exclusion from and persecution by some Jewish communities (e.g., 2 Cor 11:23–26; Gal 1:13; 4:29; 5:11; Phil 3:6). In any case, we do not know precisely when the *Birkat ha-Minim* was composed or whether the Egyptian form of it discovered in 1898 is in fact original.[101] We cannot justifiably link the date or *Sitz im Leben* of Mat-

96. So Davies and Allison, *Matthew 1–7*, 136–38.

97. Lapin, "Origins and Development," 222. Lapin argues that the rabbis, as a "movement," were a "miniscule proportion of the urban population" even in the third and fourth centuries.

98. Hagner, *Matthew 1–13*, lxvii (emphasis original).

99. This simile comes from Stanton, *Gospel for a New People*, 143.

100. For more on the *Birkat-ha Minim*, see Marcus, "*Birkat Ha-Minim* Revisited," 523–51.

101. Alexander, "'Parting of the Ways,'" 143.

thew to the *Birkat ha-Minim*. This does not, however, exclude the possibility of Matthew being related to the early rabbis more generally. What we must establish is what influence the rabbis might have had in the first century and how, if at all, this affects our understanding of Matthew's date.

While it is not clear when the title "rabbi" came into usage in the official sense expressed in rabbinic literature, it is reasonably clear that Matthew denounces the use of the title (Matt 23:7–8). That Matthew is opposed to "rabbis" is further evidenced by the fact that the only character within his Gospel to refer to Jesus as ῥαββί is Judas Iscariot. It is possible that the placing of the title on the lips of Judas is a literary device to incite comparisons between the betrayer and some opposition group. In all other cases, without exception, Matthew avoids this term and even when Jesus is called "teacher" he is addressed as διδάσκαλος. Whatever is the case historically, Matthew seems to be highly critical of some group of "rabbis."

If ever there was a typical account about what occurred at Yavneh it is well summarized by Katz: "Judaism under the leadership of R. Yohanan ben Zakkai and his circle at Yavneh sought to reconstitute itself and to find a new equilibrium in the face of the disaster of 70."[102] The problems that would have resulted from this disaster are difficult to overstate:[103]

- Theological difficulties stemming from the end of the sacrificial cult, the loss of the temple and thus the symbols of God's protective presence, the power displayed by Rome and its gods and the impotence of Israel and her god, and the failure of apocalyptic dreams and prophecies.

- Economic difficulties caused by the massive destruction and confiscation of Judean land and property.

- Social difficulties caused by massacre, enslavement, and the loss of national institutions.

In the aftermath of this crisis, it is said the party at Yavneh sought to reconstruct Judaism. It is often thought that this movement, dominated by Pharisees, forged the way for the emergence of rabbinic Judaism and that this group would become both the leaders of the Jewish community and major opponents of Jewish Christians. This is the reason typically given for Matthew's preoccupation with Pharisees. This narrative is, however, often asserted without any reference to primary sources. Indeed, there are problems with this narrative given the limited evidence regarding a

102. Katz, "Issues in the Separation of Judaism," 44.
103. Cohen, "Significance of Yavneh," 27–28.

"Council" of Yavneh. In actuality, we have only the Mishnah, or works that appeared later. Such later works were redacted more than a century after the event and were affected by later crises, not least the Bar-Kokhba Rebellion of 132–35 CE.

The first problem with the standard narrative about Yavneh is that the focus on Yavneh itself as the location of early rabbinic Judaism is probably overstated. Yavneh may have been only one gathering point among many for early rabbis. If there was a Council of some kind at Yavneh, it almost certainly did not make the monumental decisions attributed to it throughout the twentieth century. Even so, Yavneh was likely an important location for the early rabbis, a major gathering point as attested to by the near-mythical status of Yavneh in some Tannaitic writings. This would be understandable since Jerusalem had been destroyed.

Second, it is unclear what role the Pharisees played amongst the early rabbis. Sim claims that, "[W]hatever the precise composition of this post-war coalition, it is clear that the real power and influence lay with the scribes and Pharisees."[104] Yet in Sim's study there is no primary evidence cited in support of such a claim. In fact, the (much later) Mishnah rarely mentions Pharisees, and indeed none of the figures listed in *m. 'Abot* 1 are identified as Pharisees in the text itself. The only exceptions that we know of are Gamaliel I and Simon ben Gamaliel, and even then, it is only Acts (Gamaliel) and Josephus (Simon; *Life* 190–91) who refer to them as Pharisees.[105] These figures are, however, not rabbis but proto-rabbinic figures claimed as rabbis in the later rabbinic literature. In truth, rabbinic literature never identifies the rabbis with the Pharisees. The early leader at Yavneh, Yohanan ben Zakkai, is not identified as a Pharisee in any sources, and *m. Yad.* 4:6 would suggest that he was *not* one.[106] According to E. P. Sanders, by the time of the second century CE it seems that "The Rabbis of that period seem to have had no consciousness of being 'Pharisees.'"[107]

Nonetheless, there are reasons to believe that many of the rabbis of the period were from a Pharisaic background and that, while they did not identify as Pharisees *per se*, the later rabbis and authors of the rabbinic literature did view the Pharisees as their predecessors. Josephus recounts a conflict between John Hyrcanus and the Pharisees (*Ant.* 13.288–96) and this same episode is retold in the Babylonian Talmud, though the characters

104. Sim, *Gospel of Matthew and Christian Judaism*, 113.

105. Sigal, *Halakhah of Jesus*, 48.

106. *m. Yada.* 4:6D: "And do we have against the Pharisees only this matter alone?" From Neusner, *Mishnah*, 1130.

107. Sanders, *Paul and Palestinian Judaism*, 153.

are replaced by Yannai the King and the sages of Israel (*b. Kiddushin* 66a). From this we can infer that the rabbis identified the proto-rabbis (sages) with the Pharisees. Moreover, Josephus makes the claim that the Sadducees were afraid to implement their doctrines due to fear of the Pharisees and their followers (*Ant.* 18.15–17); according to the rabbinic account this occurs with the Boethusians (Sadducees[108]) and the sages (*t. Yoma* 1:8; *t. Parah* 3:8; *m. Nid.* 4:2; *t. Nid.* 5:3; *t. Sukkah* 3:1, 16).[109] In addition, certain beliefs that are ascribed to the Pharisees by Josephus and the New Testament (indeed, Matthew) are shared by rabbinic Judaism, and these are listed by Shaye Cohen: "the belief in a combination of fate and free will, the belief in the immortality of the soul and resurrection, the acceptance of ancestral traditions in addition to the written law, and the meticulous observance of the laws of purity, tithing, Shabbat, and other rituals."[110] It is also worth noting that Gamaliel II, almost certainly a Pharisee, eventually wrested the leadership at Yavneh from Yohanan ben Zakkai. It is of course precarious to use such late literature as a historical source for first-century rabbinism, but, with sufficient caution, doing so contributes to the case that the early rabbis were at least partly from a Pharisaic background.

That the Mishnah does not directly identify any rabbis as Pharisees is not necessarily a problem. Indeed, it is not clear whether *any* Jewish group at any time referred to themselves as "Pharisees" ("the separated ones")— the rabbinic evidence can be read to suggest it was a title or label used by outsiders such as the authors of the New Testament, Josephus (qua Hellenistic historian), and the later sages.[111] We can, however, make several likely deductions. The Pharisees were a distinct party pre-70 CE in an environment of multiple groups and sects.[112] While it is difficult to know much about the pre-70 CE Pharisees, and indeed it may be that we inflate their importance in Jewish society based on the scarcity of evidence about other groups, we can probably assume that they were quite scrupulous about purity and ritual laws since this is the picture given both in the New Testament and in later rabbinic Judaism. In the aftermath of 70 CE, however, such

---

108. Saldarini shows that though the Boethusians and Sadducees were probably distinct groups in the first century CE, they were later unhistorically conflated in the rabbinic literature. *Pharisees, Scribes, and Sadducees*, 227–28.

109. I owe these references to Cohen, "Significance of Yavneh," 37.

110. Cohen, "Significance of Yavneh," 37.

111. Saldarini, *Pharisees, Scribes and Sadducees*, 221. For a contrary view, see Deines, "Pharisees Between 'Judaisms' and 'Common Judaism'" 443–504 (esp. 491–504). Deines argues that there were those who called themselves "Pharisees."

112. For an overview of Jewish sectarianism see Blenkinsopp, "Interpretation and the Tendency to Sectarianism," 1–26.

sectarianism was apparently not well accepted.[113] It is also possible that, given that much group self-definition seems to have revolved around competing sects and the temple, both of which had either become powerless or non-existent, sectarianism was temporarily superseded. Anthony Saldarini, based on the work of Jacob Neusner, asserts of the later rabbis: "They were most probably not a sect, as the Pharisees had been before 70 CE. Rather, they were a coalition of scribes, Pharisees, priests, and landowners seeking to define Judaism in new circumstances."[114] Such new circumstances may have included a sense that Judaism needed to be rebuilt after the devastation of the war. Whatever the case, there is no real evidence that the early rabbis held an exclusivist ethic, often supposed in a way that results in the hypothetical "synod" of Yavneh looking like the Council of Nicea.[115] Cohen claims of the Mishnah (inasmuch as we can take for granted that it paints an accurate picture of early rabbinic Judaism):

> No previous Jewish work looks like the Mishnah because no previous Jewish work, neither biblical nor post-biblical, neither Hebrew nor Greek, neither Palestinian nor diasporan, attributes conflicting legal and exegetical opinions to named individuals who, in spite of their differences, belong to the same fraternity. The dominant ethic here is not exclusivity but elasticity. The goal was not the triumph over other sects but the elimination of the need for sectarianism itself.[116]

The rabbis behind the later literature sought to distance themselves from any perceived sectarianism. They never identify their predecessors with any post-destruction sect. It is not immediately clear why this might be so. Cohen suggests that the rabbis had a large vision for a grand (rabbinic) coalition and wished to emphasize that "rabbinic Judaism" was a new entity free from sectarian rifts.[117] It is unlikely that early rabbinic Judaism was so harmonious—it may be that later rabbinic authors created this image in response to actual tensions between internal groups—though any conflicts were unlike the sectarian rifts of the past.

113. By "sect" I do not mean a strange minority group withdrawn from society and politics as in popular usage. On the contrary, I understand a sect to be a distinct group seeking change as a reaction against a society. This especially applies to religious groups which are active politically. This is certainly true of the Pharisees, who were highly engaged with society and politics. See the typology of Wilson, *Magic and the Millennium*, 16–26. I owe this reference to Saldarini, *Pharisees, Scribes, and Sadducees*, 71.

114. Saldarini, "Delegitimation of Leaders in Matthew 23," 663.

115. A comparison drawn by Cohen, "Significance of Yavneh," 28.

116. Cohen, "Significance of Yavneh," 29.

117. Cohen, "Significance of Yavneh," 41, 45.

The character of such rifts is important. In regard to pre-70 CE sectarian conflicts, the primary sources never give the sense that they were motivated by doctrinal purity. On the contrary, conflict typically arose regarding the ability of groups (or individuals) to implement their doctrines (policies) within society. The rivalry between the Pharisees and Sadducees during the reigns of John Hyrcanus, Alexander Jannaeus, and Alexandra was, at least according to Josephus' account, motivated by their shared desire to gain power and influence, usually by way of seeking a patron-client relationship with the ruler.[118] The Gospel of Matthew presents the conflict between Jesus and the community leaders in a similar light; the conflict is not primarily concerned with doctrine *per se*, but with the practice of the law in the life of the community. The post-70 CE political environment had in many ways changed. The temple no longer stood, and thus the power of the temple cult in Palestine's religio-political life had ended. There was no longer a need to gain the patronage of those in the temple cult, those with the power to sanction official legitimating doctrines. This left some room for new groups to step in to the cult void and to reimagine Judaism and its implementation, though in truth the rabbis would have held very little power at the time of Matthew, even in terms of the cult (see below).

Still, the way to influence had been opened and later rabbis would have good reason for not characterizing their predecessors as former sectarian groups: they wished to portray the rabbis as being of one mind in speaking "to and for all Israel."[119] At the time of Matthew, however, this unity was probably not so developed.[120] Hayim Lapin suggests that it is possible the rabbinic connection with Pharisees was fairly weak early on and was later amplified in the history the rabbis constructed for themselves.[121] In my view, the inverse seems far more likely: there was a strong connection early on and this was minimized in the later literature by those wanting to portray a universal and harmonious rabbinic Judaism. At the time of Matthew, Pharisaic rabbinic groups were probably quite distinct from other strands in a fragile post-war coalition. These were Matthew's main opponents. This makes the most sense of Matt 23:7–8 which, while addressing Pharisees

118. See Book 1 of *Jewish War* and Book 13 of *Antiquities*.

119. Lapin, "Origins and Development," 222.

120. So Hezser, *Social Structure of the Rabbinic Movement*, 77: "We do not know whether 'sectarian' affiliations continued to exist among post-70 rabbis. In all likelihood they did, at least for a certain time. . . . Rabbinic literature has a tendency to suppress rabbis' individual traits in order to create the image of rabbinic 'society' as a 'grand coalition' which tolerated disputes and lived in utter harmony. This image seems to be a literary creation which hides the actual diversity which existed amongst rabbis."

121. Lapin, "Origins and Development," 222.

and associated scribes, appears to be anachronistically referring to a kind of post-70 CE formal rabbinic status.

The third problem with the standard narrative about early rabbinic Judaism is that there is no evidence that the early rabbis were meaningfully influential amongst the larger Jewish community in the Syro-Palestinian region, much less inter-regionally. Saldarini declares,

> The group of teachers and leaders who gathered at Jamnia were not in charge of the Jewish community, as is often claimed in traditional treatments of Rabbinic Judaism. The rabbis gained control of community life and the synagogue *only gradually from the second to seventh centuries in Palestine.*[122]

And, elsewhere he writes,

> The early rabbinic group was struggling to gain influence and power in the Jewish community and only began to gain widespread power at the end of the second century under Rabbi Judah the Prince. The process whereby rabbis became judges, officials, and village leaders continued with varied results in Galilean villages and cities throughout the third, fourth, and early fifth centuries.[123]

Any supposed power vacuum following 70 CE that might have allowed for this group to emerge as influential community leaders may not have even existed. Again, we turn to Saldarini:

> King Agrippa II, who had remained loyal to Rome during the revolt, continued to rule parts of Galilee, the provinces east of the Sea of Galilee and areas to the north. Local rule probably remained relatively unchanged. Jewish villages and urban communities would have continued to be led by their traditional leaders, wealthy landowning families, upper-class priests who had not been caught up in the destruction of Jerusalem, and learned officials and educators employed by the wealthy. A number of groups competed for the highest levels of power and influence within the Jewish communities in Judea, Galilee, and beyond, among whom the most prominent were the surviving priests, the members of the Herodian family, and the Pharisees.[124]

122. Saldarini, "Delegitimation of Leaders in Matthew 23," 663 (emphasis mine). See also Cohen, *From the Maccabees to the Mishnah*, 221–24.

123. Saldarini, *Matthew's Jewish-Christian Community*, 15.

124. Saldarini, "Delegitimation of Leaders in Matthew 23," 662.

In the midst of a power vacuum, there is no reason to believe that a small, geographically-spread community of rabbis was able suddenly to step in and wield widespread influence. But, of course, holding such power is not a prerequisite for Matthew to be in conflict with this community; a group of rabbis with an alternative plan for the restoration of Judaism and gaining support from parts of the population of Syro-Palestine could represent a significant competitive threat, particularly if that group was winning over members of Matthew's communities. For Matthew, this was, at least in part, a conflict over differing interpretations and expressions of Judaism. This is reflected in the strong focus on Torah in Matthew. Indeed, Jesus is the authoritative teacher in Matthew, and more—he is κύριος, and he is "chosen and authorized by God to give the correct interpretation of Torah."[125] He is also a προφήτης, one who can authoritatively express the will of God beyond Torah study. Such a focus suggests a polemical intent against rival interpreters. It may also be that the Pharisees, who had been popular in some communities prior to 70 CE, had retained their social positions in the aftermath of the war and were able to thrive after the razing of the temple, a possibility supported by the fact that the Pharisees had developed an expression of Judaism that was not entirely centered on the temple.[126] In the case of Galilee and beyond, where the forms of Judaism had never been centered on the temple, it may have been that the Pharisees, with their Torah- and tradition-centered practices, came into a position of increased prominence in the new situation. Even amongst communities that had held the temple in esteem, the Pharisees would have provided a viable and pre-existing alternative. This would no doubt have helped those Pharisees aligned with rabbis to gain an initial foothold of influence amongst some communities of Syro-Palestine at the time of Matthew. We should be clear, however, that this influence does not equate to the immediate reconstruction of "Judaism" upon the founding of a Yavnean "academy," nor to the meaningful or lasting prominence of Pharisaic identity.[127] The rabbis themselves in the first century were, at best, prominent as individuals in a local setting, and perhaps notable when they gathered; overall they were invisible as a "movement."[128]

While what has been presented thus far may be a potential summary of the connection between the Pharisees and the early rabbis, it does not necessarily prove any connection between the specific Pharisees signified in Matthew's Gospel and the early rabbis, thus leaving us still without a date for

125. Squires, "'To the Lost Sheep of Israel,'" 45.

126. See Deines, "Pharisees," 495–98.

127. Sim, *Gospel of Matthew and Christian Judaism*, 114.

128. Lapin, "Origins and Development," 221–22.

the Gospel. Indeed, it is not at all clear that all Pharisees were herded into the early rabbinic movement; such is unlikely. However, with the demise of sectarianism described above, it would not be surprising for any Pharisees detached from the rabbinic coalition to have become less and less prominent as time went on. Certainly, by the time of the mid-second century CE the Pharisees seem to have become non-existent. Hegesippus the Chronicler, from whom we have only snippets of material as quoted in other Patristic writings, speaks of Pharisees among other sects of the past:

> The same writer also records the ancient heresies which arose among the Jews, in the following words: There were, moreover, various opinions in the circumcision, among the children of Israel. The following were those that were opposed to the tribe of Judah and the Christ: Essenes, Galileans, Hemerobaptists, Masbothaeans, Samaritans, Sadducees, Pharisees. (Eusebius, *Church History*, IV 22.6)

Matthew seems to reflect that the Pharisees in his Gospel have a position of community influence, probably as retainers. It is not clear how many rabbis there may have been at the time of the Gospel, but the number could not have been large, and, as stated above, certainly not large enough to constitute a highly visible "movement."[129] But as Lapin suggests, individual rabbis may have enjoyed local prominence as sages and, even in small numbers clustered in cities, may have been sufficiently visible to have made a cultural impact and carry some influence, particularly in any educational sphere.[130] Such an impact would have been felt strongly by a small burgeoning movement with a unique program for the restoration of Judaism at odds with that of these rabbis.

It is possible that Matthew has in view a Pharisaic group not aligned with the rabbinic community. What is more likely, however, is that Matthew is addressing the Pharisaic rabbinic group (cf. Matt 23:7–8), a retainer group holding a small amount of continually growing influence, referring to them by the name of the sect from which many of them had come. This was a label from which the rabbis had probably wished to appear detached.[131] In this construal, Matthew's use of the term "Pharisees" may be polemical, connecting some Pharisaic rabbis with those figures of the past that he depicts so

129. Lapin, "Origins and Development," 222.

130. Lapin, "Origins and Development," 222.

131. Cohen, "Significance of Yavneh," 45, hypothesizes that the developments after the fall of the Jerusalem temple, whereby the focal point of sectarianism was destroyed, facilitated "the end of sectarianism and the creation of a society marked by legal disputes between individual teachers who nevertheless respected each other's right to disagree."

negatively. Indeed, throughout Matthew the Pharisees are depicted as having created or perpetuated problems for communities in recent history, particularly the poor and lower classes, and even, according to Matthew 23, as being largely responsible for the war/apocalyptic judgement of 66–73 CE.

This leads us to suppose that Matthew's main opponents are in fact those Pharisees (and their scribes) who were associated with the rabbinic coalition after 70 CE. This need not preclude the possibility that the Matthean audience was in conflict with the Pharisees even before 70 CE and that this conflict may have continued right up to the time of the Gospel. It also does not preclude the likelihood that Matthew was in conflict with other strands of early rabbinic Judaism, such as those connected to landowners or former religious elites. The conflict was, at its core, a struggle over which community had a faithful interpretation and practice of Judaism. For Matthew, the correct "Judaism" was that espoused by Jesus and expressed in Matthew's communities.

To summarize, a precise date for Matthew is not yet possible to determine with certainty. A date prior to 70 CE seems to be based mostly on unproven historical possibilities and debatable interpretations of texts. A date after the close of the first century CE ignores possible later quotations of Matthew's work from no later than the early second century CE. The best we can say at this point is that Matthew was written somewhere between the aftermath of the war ending in 73 CE and 100 CE. Leaving enough room for the early rabbis to have established themselves post-70 we could narrow the possible date to between 80 and 100 CE. Whatever the exact date, Matthew's Gospel is written in part to confront Pharisees involved with the burgeoning rabbinic movement that has begun to gain influence among some communities in Syro-Palestine. One of the positive elements of this treatment is that it does not rely on the assumed dating of any other New Testament books, especially Mark (as with many commentators) or Luke (as with Gundry). It also makes sense of Matthew's fierce opposition to the scribes and Pharisees, who are apparently to be equated with "rabbis" in an official sense of the word (Matt 23:7–8).

In terms of the implications on Matthew's social setting, Matthew includes as a focus an ongoing conflict with an emerging group within Judaism, the early rabbis. This community finds its ancestry at least partly in the scribes and Pharisees of the pre-70 CE era. Following the war of 66–73 CE many of the Pharisees, together with the remnants of other unknown groups, came together to reformulate Judaism in the aftermath of the destruction of Jerusalem and its temple. It was a Pharisaic element of this group with whom Matthew's communities came into conflict over a range of issues related to the understanding and practice of Judaism.

Simply put, these groups had opposing programs for the restoration of Judaism. If this understanding of Matthew's setting is correct, then it adds further credence to the suggestion that Syro-Palestine is the location of the Matthean communities.

1.5 The Parting of the Ways?

The rabbis by no means dominated "Judaism" at the end of the first century CE. That Matthew was in conflict with the burgeoning rabbinic movement has often been used as a stepping stone on the way to the assertion that Matthew's community had completely parted ways with all of "Judaism." Sjef van Tilborg argued that Matthew and his community had little to no contact with their local Jewish community:

> Mt lived in a world in which Judaism was no longer a serious competitor. If one wishes to call Jews who have refused to be converted hypocrites, evil people, murderers and imposters, there must be a fairly great and satisfactory distance on a historical level. This idea held by Mt can only be explained as being held by someone who, if he happened to come face to face with them, was still so absorbed in his own ideas that he had lost sight of reality.[132]

Stendahl shared a similar view: "Matthew's community now existed in sharp contrast to the Jewish community in town. For in this church things Jewish meant Jewish and not Jewish Christian versus Gentile Christian."[133] Other scholars who have echoed this view—that Matthew's audience had decisively broken with Judaism—include Meier, Meeks, Stanton, and Hagner.[134] It is not at all clear that there was such a *thing* as "Judaism" from which to break, but this has not deterred some from arriving at such a conclusion. By this I mean that there was no centralized form of Judaism or synagogue authority from which to secede. On the contrary, one of the difficulties of modern scholars has been to posit what characteristics early Judaisms shared. For example, James Dunn mentions four elements that all Jewish groups held in common: monotheism, election, Torah, and temple.[135] Whether Dunn is accurate is unimportant, as is what precisely

132. Tilborg, *Jewish Leaders*, 171.

133. Stendahl, *School of St. Matthew*, xiii.

134. Brown and Meier, *Antioch and Rome*, 49; Meeks, *Moral World of the First Christians*, 137; Stanton, *Gospel for a New People*, 124–31; Hagner, "*Sitz im Leben* of the Gospel of Matthew," 27–68.

135. Dunn, *Partings of the Ways*, esp. 24–48.

Judaism held in common—what is important is that we understand Judaism as a large body that contained room for many interpretations and variations. As Bruce Chilton and Jacob Neusner point out:

> Most knowledgeable people now reject the conception of a single Judaism, everywhere paramount. A requirement of theology, the dogma of a single, valid Judaism contradicts the facts of history at every point in the history of Judaism, which finds its dynamic in the on-going struggle among Judaisms to gain the position of the sole, authentic representation of the Torah.[136]

This was the reality with what we know of the Qumran community. Interestingly, Stanton compares Matthew's polemic against the Pharisees with a similar polemic in the *Damascus Document* (CD) from Qumran: he claims both reflect a "sharp distancing of the minority group from the parent body."[137] It is a mistake for Stanton to use this as an argument for his belief that Matthew's communities stood *extra-muros* to Judaism; it is not at all clear that the Pharisees are meant to represent all of Judaism. Moreover, what Stanton notes about the community behind CD is true— they had "parted company with the Temple authorities in Jerusalem."[138] This, however, is a far cry from parting with Judaism altogether. On the contrary, the community behind CD would appear to have viewed itself as a kind of protest movement, opposed to Israel's corrupt leadership, but nonetheless perceiving itself existing firmly as Israel. CD includes references to such things as the voice of Moses, God's laws and covenant, and the need to conduct one's life according to these laws in order to be given the life promised in said covenant. This is clearly a conflict internal to Judaism, much like that of Matthew and his opponents.

On a related note, it seems that some scholars have confused Matthew's polemic against "synagogues" with a polemic against Judaism generally. It may have been that members of Matthew's communities were being persecuted and excluded, possibly even expelled, from synagogues (Matt 10:17; 23:34). But to think that Matthew's community members saw this as a separation from Judaism itself is to apply anachronistically a

136. Chilton and Neusner, *Judaism in the New Testament*, 5–6.

137. Stanton, *Gospel for a New People*, 91–98 (esp. 96). Riches argues that this *distancing* is "precisely a move made by those who have not yet fully *parted* ways with the parent body." Riches, *Matthew*, 60 (emphasis original). This argument falls down when both Matthew and the Damascus Document are seen as documents legitimating an *earlier* separation, a view taken by Stanton: "In its final form the Damascus Document is a foundation document for a new community: it functioned as legitimation of the separation from Essenism" (*Gospel for a New People*, 93).

138. Stanton, *Gospel for a New People*, 91.

modern concept of "religion." On this problem Horsley is forthright, and worth quoting at length:

> We have been assuming for some time that what the Gospels refer to as *synagogai*, "synagogues," were religious buildings. That assumption, enshrined in Jewish history books, Gospel commentaries, and reconstructions of Jesus' ministry, is solidly rooted in the standard modern presuppositions . . . that rabbinic and New Testament literature are basically about religion, in particular about Judaism and a new "Christian" religion that broke away from it. . . . The retrojection of modern European or American urban experience back into biblical times is most dramatic, perhaps, in the interpretation current not long ago that the Gospel of Matthew was written for a church in competition with "the synagogue down the street." . . . A closer look at [recent] archaeological finds, however, indicates that there is little or no solid evidence for the existence of synagogues as religious buildings in Galilee before the third century C.E.[139]

Horsley goes on to show that synagogues were not religious edifices but rather community assemblies that had socio-economic and political dimensions at least as significant as their so-called "religious" dimension.[140] Cohen argues that the Greek συναγωγή is different from the English "synagogue" in at least three ways, namely, that unlike the English the Greek implies "community," that unlike the Greek the English implies a building, and that the English implies a gathering of Jews for communal prayer or Torah study whereas the Greek implies gatherings of various sorts.[141] Cohen shows elsewhere that synagogues had a wide variety of forms, but were often used for reading the law, teaching, and municipal organization.[142] They could, however, also be "private affairs, just like clubs or associations . . . the private foundations of the dedicators."[143] Indeed, rabbinic narratives often portray rabbis or their families as having gifted synagogues or houses of study.[144] It is not surprising then that Matthew polemicized against "their" synagogues—they were assemblies, possibly the private associations of a competing "brotherhood," likely rooted in the life of the wider community, that taught an opposing interpretation of the law from that of

139. Horsley, *Galilee*, 222.

140. Horsley, *Galilee*, 222–37.

141. Cohen, "Were Pharisees and Rabbis the Leaders," 267–68.

142. Cohen, *From the Maccabees to the Mishnah*, 107–8.

143. Cohen, *From the Maccabees to the Mishnah*, 108–9.

144. Lapin, "Origins and Development," 219.

Jesus and organized the socio-economic affairs of the community in a way unsatisfactory to Matthew and his audience.

It is not difficult to conclude why Matthew might have used ἐκκλησία to describe his communities. The word is used in the LXX as a synonym for συναγωγή.[145] Both are used, among other nuances, to describe the assembly of Israel. Ἐκκλησία was also used by Greek voluntary associations in relation to their meetings.[146] It seems Matthew wished to differentiate his communities from those leaders whose assemblies were called synagogues. This was a counterclaim against their insistence that they were the assembly (συναγωγή) of Israel; Matthew's communities were the true assembly (ἐκκλησία) of Israel according to the teachings of Jesus.[147]

A point often used in favor of Matthew's *extra-muros* standing vis-à-vis Judaism is that the Gospel refers to *"their* synagogues" (Matt 4:23; 9:35; 10:17; 12:9; 13:54), *"your* synagogues" (23:34), *"their* scribes" (7:29), and "the Jews to this day" (28:15), thus creating distance between the Matthean communities and the Jews and their institutions. But these references can be explained better and more consistently without having to divorce Matthew from "Judaism." In two cases (12:9; 23:34), the narrative context has Jesus in conflict with the Pharisees, referring to "their synagogues." This need not be a negative reference to Judaism, but merely to the assemblies affiliated with those Pharisees.[148] In 4:23, "their synagogues" refers to the assemblies of the people living in Galilee, that is, it is a geographical designation, in no way malicious. Matthew 7:29 refers to "their scribes," those associated with the crowds present at the Sermon on the Mount, not to Israel's scribes generally. In 9:35, "their synagogues" refers to those belonging to "all the cities and villages," thereby specifying a geographical boundary, not a sociological one. In 10:17, "their synagogues" refers to those belonging to the "men," characterized as wolves, of whom the disciples should beware. This need not be seen as a condemnation of all synagogues, but of these specific men and their affiliates. In 13:54, "their synagogue" refers

---

145. Good examples are Judg 20:1–2; 21:5–16; Ps 40:9–10; Prov 5:14.

146. Sim, *Gospel of Matthew and Christian Judaism*, 146.

147. So Saldarini, *Matthew's Jewish-Christian Community*, 119.

148. In Matt 12:9 the synagogue is referred to as "their synagogue," with "them" referring to those in the previous pericope who challenged Jesus about Sabbath, and who attempt to set him up in 12:10 and conspire against him in 12:14 (i.e., the Pharisees). Cohen, "Were Pharisees and Rabbis the Leaders?" 269, argues to the contrary, though I find his argument unconvincing since it implies an arbitrary distinction between the pericopes of 12:1–8 and 12:9–14. It also ignores that the third person plural throughout 12:1–14 is consistently a reference to the Pharisees, both before and after 12:9—the "they" that intend to accuse him (12:10) are clearly the Pharisees who, in response to Jesus' words and deeds in the periscope, later conspire to destroy him (12:14).

to that belonging to Jesus' hometown in which he no longer lived (4:13), hence it is *theirs*. In 28:15, the reference to the story being spread among "the Jews to this day" need not be read as antagonistic, but simply as an acknowledgement of what has continued to occur. There is no indication that all the Jews believe the story, that they should be condemned for doing so, or that Matthew's communities are not included amongst "the Jews." Given that there is no indication that Matthew uses *synagogue* as a synonym for "Judaism,"[149] the most we can say is that the Evangelist is antagonistic to *some* synagogues that are affiliated with his opponents.

Another passage that requires attention is Matt 27:25—"His blood be upon us and on our children." Hagner includes this passage amongst those speaking of "the judgement of unbelieving Israel" and the transference of the Kingdom from Israel to the church.[150] Narratively, however, this interpretation is not decisive. Following Jesus' entry into Jerusalem (21:1–11) and his judgement of the city and its temple (esp. 21:12–22, 28–46; 23:1–39), we find that his judgement is not leveled against all Israel, but the corrupt leaders, the chief priests, and Pharisees (cf. 21:45). It is the scribes and Pharisees who have "murdered the prophets" (23:31). Matthew reiterates the scene in which this judgement takes place—"O Jerusalem, Jerusalem, the city that kills the prophets" (23:37). By the time we reach Jesus being delivered to Pilate, we find the chief priests and elders persuading the crowd against the prophet (27:20). The willingness of the people to have Jesus' blood be on them and their children is a result of their willingness to conform to the wishes of the Jerusalem leadership; again, like the scribes discussed above, the people are tainted by the company they keep. The blood of Jesus being on their children is probably Matthew's thinly veiled allusion to the destruction of Jerusalem that would come a generation later. In this reading, Matthew seeks not to condemn Israel, but rather the scribes, Pharisees, and Jerusalem elite. This is another example of Matthew's polemic against his opponents, a limited group made up of certain leaders who do not represent the entirety of "Judaism."

What all this means is that we cannot simply conclude that Matthew's Gospel, in its polemic against the synagogue, reflects a split from "Judaism." Even if those associated with early rabbinic Judaism were driven to expel the Matthean community from their synagogues—an unclear assertion—there is no reason to go further in claiming that Matthew's mainly Jewish Christian audience thought they should abandon ethnic and cultural ties at the behest of this group whom in any case they believed to be

---

149. So Sim, *Gospel of Matthew and Christian Judaism*, 147.

150. Hagner, "*Sitz im Leben*," 30–31.

illegitimate spokespersons of Judaism. As Sim argues, what best explains the sheer intensity of Matthew's polemic is that he is describing contemporary opponents with whom he still has frequent contact.[151] In addition, Saldarini states:

> Being treated as deviant, far from driving a group out of society, often keeps it in. Social theory has established that nonconformity, resistance to social structures, and deviance are, paradoxically, always part of any functioning society. Thus the hasty conclusion that evidence of conflict implies a complete break with the Jewish community is contrary to normal sociological processes.[152]

In short, Matthew's communities are fighting to remain part of their local "synagogues," that is, community assemblies.[153] The remainder of this study will proceed according to the view that the so-called parting of the ways between Matthew's communities and "Judaism" is a flawed reading of the evidence. On the contrary, Matthew's communities were mostly made up of Jewish Christians who had not abandoned their Jewish heritage but who believed that they represented the truest form of "Judaism" based on the Torah interpretation of Jesus. They were, in their own view, and over against their opponents, the ἐκκλησία—the continuation of the assembly of Israel.

1.6 The *Sitz im Leben* of Matthew's Communities

So far, we have already detailed much in the way of Matthew's social setting. Following a number of studies, particularly those of Sim, Saldarini, and Overman, we have outlined the conflict between Matthew's audience and a particular Pharisaic group within the movement we have called formative or rabbinic Judaism. It should be stated clearly, however, that it would be a mistake to think that such a conflict comprises the only major element of Matthew's social setting and purpose for writing—such a conflict merely served as the most helpful aspect of Matthew's *Sitz im Leben* from which to make a judgement about the approximate date of writing. Matthew's text reflects a range of social and rhetorical concerns; we ought not reduce them down to a single focus.

---

151. Sim, *Gospel of Matthew and Christian Judaism*, 120–21.

152. Saldarini, *Matthew's Jewish-Christian Community*, 1–2.

153. In agreement with Keener, *Matthew*, 49.

On a separate but related note, the sense one gets of Matthew's community from reading some recent studies is of a bitter and twisted group, unable to cope with their own marginality, calling for love of enemy on the one hand while on the other savagely and abusively attacking opponents without much in the way of reasonableness.[154] It is of course true that Matthew is intense in his criticism of his opponents, but to argue that this polemic is simply a reflection of the group's marginality is an unsatisfying reading of the text's story. At different points Matthew has Jesus teaching that marginalization and even persecution are inevitable (7:13–14; 10:5–40; 13:1–9, 18–23), though there is no directive that encourages Matthew's audience to retaliate. By reducing Matthew's attack to a struggle against marginalization we ignore that the author seems to think such a state of affairs is indicative of larger issues—we miss the proverbial forest for the trees. Throughout Matthew, the dominant message of the prophetic Jesus is that of ἡ βασιλεία τῶν οὐρανῶν. Matthew's narrative paints pictures for his readers of what this kingdom entails: "Your will be done, on earth as it is in heaven" (Matt 6:10). The sustained critique of enemies in Matthew could perhaps be summarized as concerning their unwillingness to follow the way of the kingdom of heaven, the central teaching of the story's central figure. For Matthew, the way of the kingdom is characterized by justice, mercy, and faithfulness (23:23). The Pharisees, scribes, and religious leaders are said to act contrary to this way. This is demonstrated most poignantly in Matthew 23 and Jesus' woes against the scribes and Pharisees. The central issue at hand in such passages is not the bitterness of marginalization but disagreement over the interpretation of Torah. More specifically, although fallout over Torah interpretation was not a problem *per se* (as we have seen, Judaism made way for multiple views after 70 CE), it was the *enacting* of these interpretations and the effects on community life that made for conflict. For Matthew, and indeed for Jesus within his story, the issue is that the scribes and Pharisees, representing a strand of early rabbinic Judaism, have not enacted the central aspects of the law—justice, mercy, and faithfulness—summarized by Matthew as love for God and neighbor (22:34–40). Within Matthew, the failure of the community leaders to love by way of justice, mercy, and faithfulness is demonstrated in narrative depictions of major interpretive issues of the time such as divorce, Sabbath, and food laws. Whether Matthew's perspective is historically accurate in every sense is largely irrelevant—this is the perspective of the author and probably the audience, and it gives shape to the narrative.

154. So Sim, *Matthean Community and Formative Judaism*, 160.

It is worth noting that some recent studies have gone into great detail regarding the socio-economic status of the rabbis, an area of research that could reap important results for the study of Matthew. Though some have questioned rabbinic wealth,[155] others have shown that rabbis were, on average, better off than the rest of the population. This does not necessitate all rabbis having been prosperous landowners, only that they were not living in poverty. Indeed, Cohen points out that the only tannaim exception to this rule is the story of Rabbi Akiba in 'Abot R. Nat., though he eventually becomes learned and rich.[156] Overall the rabbis "share not only the prejudices but also the concerns of the landowning class," with the Mishnah and other legal traditions treating the problems faced by the landowner.[157] Such people could have been anything from barely comfortable to very wealthy, but most were probably closer to the latter.[158] Relying less on later rabbinic literature, we can say that literacy is presumed for scribes and rabbis, and this implies the opportunity of education. The general wealth of the rabbis seems to be a fair assumption. If the rabbis were largely wealthy landowners, then this lends weight to the above portrayal of Matthew's critique of his opponents for their failure to enact what he viewed as central aspects of the law.

While it would be interesting to immerse ourselves in the ongoing contemporary debate about the place of Torah in Matthew's theology and community life, this is simply outside the scope of this study, except where relevant in later chapters. Nonetheless, it is important to state that the view taken here is that the author of Matthew in no way annuls Torah, but rather defends his own interpretation of it. It is also worth noting that the interpretation of Torah was not, for Matthew and his contemporaries, simply an issue of religious concern as it might be in our modern context. In the same way that we have anachronistically applied modern religious concepts to συναγωγή, so too have modern Christians imagined ancient interpretive disputes almost exclusively in terms of doctrine. But as Saldarini has said, one's interpretation of biblical law in the first century CE was an articulation of "a particular vision of life under God" and thus interpretation was "a political act in which the control of society was at stake."[159] Matthew, by entering into a wider debate about interpretation, is a text deeply political in nature. That

---

155. Such as Hezser, *Social Structure*, 257–66.

156. Cohen, "Rabbi in Second-Century Jewish Society," 931–32.

157. Cohen, "Rabbi in Second-Century Jewish Society," 931; Lapin, "Origins and Development," 219.

158. Cohen, "Rabbi in Second-Century Jewish Society," 931.

159. Saldarini, *Matthew's Jewish-Christian Community*, 124.

Matthew is concerned with issues of "justice and mercy and faithfulness" (τὴν κρίσιν καὶ τὸ ἔλεος καὶ τὴν πίστιν) and righteousness (δικαιοσύνην) gives us a sense of both his politics and his social situation. Indeed, the kingdom of heaven is the desire of those who are ultimately dissatisfied with the current order of things, either because of their social vision (stemming from Torah) or their current lot in life—perhaps both.

The imperative of the kingdom of heaven as a central theme in Matthew also provides grounds on which to discuss other aims and issues addressed by the Gospel, not least tensions with groups other than the early rabbinic movement. Such an issue is that of Roman imperialism. For some, this is a contestable assertion. Witherington states:

> Just as I am unconvinced of the Antiochian provenance of this Gospel, I am even more unconvinced that its primary focus of animus is on the Roman Empire and the imperial cult. While it is true that the dominion of God is being asserted over against other possible dominions, Rome's is not singled out for special contumely; rather there is more concern with the client king Herod Antipas and his misdeeds.[160]

There is little doubt that Matthew addresses Herod and his establishment, though the nature and meaning of this attention needs to be further teased out since Herod was no longer king at the time of Matthean composition. This will be addressed shortly. For now, it is important simply to note that Herod was a client king under the auspices of Rome. Additionally, while we have focused mainly on the intra-Judaic conflict with rabbinic Judaism thus far, it is noteworthy that this conflict arises partly due to the destruction of the Jerusalem temple, a crucial event in the emergence of rabbinic Judaism. The destruction of the temple, an event sparking a crisis in various strands of Judaism, forms an important theme in Matthew, particularly in the book's second half, and it should not be forgotten that this devastation occurred at the hands of Rome (as did the crucifixion of the book's main character).

Witherington's assertion that Matthew does not address Rome in any meaningful fashion is to take for granted the communicative *modus operandi* of a low-context culture, such as that of his American location. Such low-context reading of Matthew (and indeed many other biblical books, particularly in the New Testament) has been challenged by the emergence of liberation hermeneutics[161] and post-colonial and empire-critical

---

160. Witherington, *Matthew*, 35n29.

161. The task of liberation hermeneutics is to amalgamate "two horizons"—that of the original author and audience, and that of the interpreter. "We reinterpret the Bible from the viewpoint of our own world—from our personal experience as human beings,

readings,[162] all of which recognize, whether implicitly or explicitly, the high-context situation of the New Testament writings. In any case, for Wither-ington to reject the notion of bringing Rome to the forefront of interpreting Matthew is to overlook large amounts of data in the Gospel itself. It is not so difficult to believe that the Matthean communities saw themselves liv-ing in a world of conflict on *numerous* fronts, with formative Judaism, with imperial Rome, and perhaps other opponents. Indeed, any framework for Matthew's social setting must account for the violent execution of Jesus by Rome as a political dissident in the story.

In terms of the study of the Gospel of Matthew's Roman imperial context, there is perhaps no more prominent voice than Warren Carter.[163] In *Matthew and Empire*, Carter outlines some of the major elements of the Roman imperial system, including its political network, socio-economic structure, military strength, and imperial theology/mythology.[164] Carter then goes on to show that "Matthew's Gospel assumes this experience of Roman imperial power on every page,"[165] and that it is a form of resistance literature. The imperial realities are not always explicit, and this is a fair expectation given Matthew's imperial context, though the audience will

---

as believers, and as church." Gutiérrez, *Power of the Poor in History*, 4. As Assmann has described, liberation hermeneutics understands theology as "critical reflection on action." Assmann, *Theology for a Nomad Church*, 59. Of the locus of liberation theology, Jon Sobrino writes: "Oppression is not just one of many hermeneutical situations from which to approach faith in the Son of God. It is the situation that is de facto the most apt for the Third World today, and de jure the one that appears throughout Scripture for understanding the message of salvation. Any Christian theology that is biblical, and therefore historical, must take full account of the signs of the times in its reflection. These are many, but one recurs throughout history. This sign is always the people cruci-fied in history." Sobrino, *Jesus in Latin America*, 159.

162. Empire-critical (or imperial-critical) studies of the Bible, approaches that seek to read the biblical text in the shadow of imperial realities, have become increasingly popular in recent decades. The landmark work, at least in a Western context, is prob-ably Myers, *Binding the Strong Man*. Empire-critical studies are built on social history, politico-economic culture, archaeological data and anthropological modelling. Such studies are, generally speaking, an amalgamation of historical-critical approaches, in-tertextuality, liberationist approaches, narrative and literary criticism and postcolonial theory. In this sense empire-critical studies can include a wide variety of specific meth-odologies. Some major Western figures adopting this approach in biblical studies (not necessarily explicitly) include Ched Myers, Warren Carter, Richard Horsley, Walter Brueggemann and Wes Howard-Brook.

163. See especially Carter, *Matthew and the Margins*, and Carter, *Matthew and Empire*.

164. It would be ideal to summarize Carter's findings, but this is simply outside the limitations of this study. I will simply outline elements of the Roman imperial machine as required when studying particular texts in later chapters.

165. Carter, *Matthew and Empire*, 35.

recognize these realities and understand the Gospel in relation to them.[166] "The empire claimed a universalism in bringing the whole world under Roman rule,"[167] says Carter, and it is no coincidence to find that Matthew's central theme, over against the βασιλεία of Rome, is the βασιλεία of heaven, a challenge to the sovereign claims and performance of Rome. In addition, there is a striking similarity between the claims of Roman imperial theology regarding the emperor and empire on the one hand and Matthew's presentation of Jesus on the other. In the face of dominant explanations of Matthean Christology, Carter's construal of Matthew's presentation of Jesus asserts that titles such as "Emmanuel," "Christ," "King," and "Son" all present a poignant challenge to imperial theology,[168] particularly the claim that the emperor and empire are the agents of the gods. For Matthew, the "divine presence is manifested in Jesus and the community of disciples."[169] According to Carter, this challenge is perhaps nowhere better imaged than in the episode of Jesus throwing demons into pigs that then charge over the side of a cliff (8:28–34):

> The pig was the mascot of Rome's Tenth Fretensis Legion that was stationed in Antioch and that played a prominent part in the destruction of Jerusalem in 70 C.E. The exorcism represents, among other things, Jesus' victory over the demonic forces, the throwing out of Rome.[170]

Roman power is also confronted by the social challenge offered by Matthew's Gospel. If Rome boasted about its bringing wellbeing into the world,[171] Matthew's Jesus proclaims the turning upside down of social values (5:3–12) and expresses "a desire for God's transforming work to

---

166. Carter, *Matthew and Empire*, 35.

167. Carter, *Matthew and Empire*, 50.

168. Domitian, who may have been emperor (81–96 CE) during the time of the authorship of Matthew, was called *deus praesens* (θεὸς ἐπιφανής), the manifestation of Jupiter's presence amongst humankind (Statius, *Silvae*, 4.3.128–29, 139–40; 5.1.37–39; 5.2.170); "Lord of the earth" (*Silvae*, 3.4.20); "Ruler of the nations and mighty sire of the conquered world, hope of men and beloved of the gods" (*Silvae*, 4.2.14–15); "The world's sure salvation" (Martial, *Epigrams*, 2.91.1); "Blest protector and savior" (*Epigrams*, 5.1.7). Carter, *Matthew and Empire*, 20–34.

169. Carter, *Matthew and Empire*, 57–74 (67).

170. Carter, *Matthew and Empire*, 71. Following the war of 66–73 CE the Tenth Fretensis Legion was permanently garrisoned near the ruins of Jerusalem; Schwartz, "Political, Social and Economic Life," 25.

171. "The gods through the emperor have gifted peace, corn, harmony, well-being, safety, and protection to humans." Carter, *Matthew and Empire*, 70.

be completed."[172] When God's kingdom is manifested it creates wellbeing amongst those who are marginalized, not through the emperor, but
through the miracles, deliverance, and healings performed by Jesus. In this
way Jesus offers the possibility of "new physical, social and economic life,"[173]
a sign of the turning upside down of social values, and of God's power of
new creation.[174] God's new social vision and alternative to Rome offered in
Jesus takes shape in his words and actions. In terms of specific examples,
this vision looks like the rejection of domination and hierarchy (20:25–26;
23:8–12), practices of indiscriminate mercy and social inclusion (5:43–48;
9:12), rejection of violent resistance (5:38–48), the alleviation of economic
misery (5:42; 6:1–4), and prayer for God's empire to come in full (6:10).[175]
If Matthew is concerned about justice, mercy, and faithfulness in regard
to Torah and his conflict with a budding rabbinic Judaism, this concern
applies equally to Roman domination.

In light of the limitations of this study it is unnecessary to explore this
issue further since greater detail will accompany relevant texts as needed
in later chapters. Nonetheless, it is important to point out that Matthew's
Gospel does not simply offer the above social vision in a vacuum; it is a
challenge to a dominant order that was all too real in the first century CE.
We simply cannot ignore that the overarching social setting of Matthew's
Gospel is the Roman Empire. Even the conflict between Matthew's communities and formative Judaism is to be located within this setting. Jesus'
conflict with the community leaders throughout Matthew, while representing a conflict with formative Judaism, is not limited to them. As we have
explored above, those involved with the early rabbinic movement, largely
made up of scribes and former Pharisees as it was, occupied positions in the
retainer class of the agrarian social hierarchy of Syro-Palestine. The community leaders in Matthew's story represent this specific rabbinic group (or
groups), yes, but simultaneously represent that part of the social elite that
benefit from the stagnation of the social order. In other words, these leaders in the narrative are intertwined with the social, political, and economic
structures of the empire, and they benefit from its continuation. Whether or
not we can justifiably link the early rabbinic movement with such a retainer
class in historical terms is not clear, though there is reason to suggest the

172. Carter, *Matthew and Empire*, 71.

173. Carter, *Matthew and Empire*, 72.

174. Matthew 1:1 opens with Βίβλος γενέσεως Ἰησοῦ Χριστοῦ υἱοῦ Δαυὶδ υἱοῦ
Ἀβραάμ. The word γένεσις, translated "genealogy," can also mean "beginning." It is the
title of the LXX version of the book of Genesis.

175. Carter, *Matthew and Empire*, 72–73.

probability of this connection.[176] Either way, Matthew makes such a connection, and in light of narrative-critical considerations we take him at his word whilst acknowledging the socio-historical dimensions of the query. Within Matthew's story we find community leaders within the retainer stratum, representing Matthew's opponents. They have, by way of acting in a fashion loyal to Rome and benefitting from this state of affairs, proliferated the seeming immutability of the social order. The result is the condemnation of the majority of the population to an existence of domination and daily struggle for subsistence. If this is the case within Matthew's story, it is not out of place to think that is also the case in Matthew's social world external to the text, at least from the author's perspective.

If Matthew draws a connection between his Jewish opponents and the Roman powers, then the connection between the Herodian regime and Rome is even more pointed. We need not say much on this, except that Witherington's marked distinction between Matthew's focus on Herod and his (non-)focus on Rome is debatable. As mentioned above, the Herods ruled under the auspices of Rome. That is to say, Herod was not a ruler in his own right but a client of the emperor. Brown describes Herod Antipas' relationship to Rome:

> The original meaning of *tetrarches*, "ruler of the fourth part," had been lost, and it now marked its holder as ruling a Roman protectorate in a status inferior to that of a nominally independent king. . . . Herod held his realm by favor of Augustus and Tiberius, and was removed by Caligula. . . . We can be sure that he paid the emperor tribute, but our sources give no figure.[177]

In terms of Herod Antipas' rule, the peasantry bore the brunt of his ambition. Horsley writes:

> Estates grew and tenancy increased as economics of scale for cash crops were created. More currency in the Galilean economy facilitated taxation, which funded Antipas' urbanization. . . . Architectural grandeur increased at one end of Galilean society by making poverty increase at the other.[178]

---

176. The early rabbinic movement being constituted largely by scribes and former Pharisees is an important point of probable connection. The chief priests were, according to Josephus, pro-Roman leading up to the war of 66–73 CE (*J.W.*, 2.320). At one point he has the Pharisees allied with the chief priests in attempting to calm seditious intent (*J.W.*, 2.411) though we cannot know if this is a reliable account given Josephus' apologetic motives vis-à-vis the Roman victory.

177. Brown, "Techniques of Imperial Control," 360–61.

178. Crossan and Reed, *Excavating Jesus*, 70. See also Horsley, "Ancient Jewish

Of course, Herod Antipas was no longer ruler at the time of Matthew. Why did Matthew include Herod Antipas (and Herod the Great) in his story? Herod was the local face of Roman rule at the time of Jesus and Matthew's audience would have been aware of this. Moreover, a Herod still held power in parts of Galilee and Syria, namely Herod Agrippa II.[179] In truth, any of the Herodian kings could have come to mind when using the designation "Herod" and it is likely that Matthew is making use of the multi-referential nature of the name—for Matthew they are all the same. Matthew is speaking about a local expression of the empire that has existed for over a century. Indeed, toward the beginning of his story, Matthew characterizes Herod the Great as a type of Pharaoh, employing infanticide to eliminate a perceived threat (Matt 2:13–18). These are imperial echoes. For Matthew, Herod's character is an extension of the Roman Empire, representing a high stratum of the social order that stands contrary to the way of the kingdom of heaven. Matthew's communities included those who hailed from the bottom of this social order and the Gospel's insistence that Rome (whether emperors, client kings, or centurions) was not ultimately sovereign would have been meaningful to them.

We must be cautious not to overstate the empire-critical angle.[180] At times, Matthew may allude to imperial realities without seeking to subvert them in any purposeful way. Indeed, the realities of Matthew's social world may find their way into his narrative without being its primary focus. Still, there is reason enough to think that at times Matthew did offer a critique of the Roman Empire and the daily realties therein. But more than this, he offered a picture of an alternative to Rome's empire which, by its very nature, took on a subversive character.

Another issue in Matthew's social world that appears a number of times in the Gospel is that of the tension between universalism and particularism. In other words, what is the place of gentiles in Matthew's communities and, more widely, in the kingdom of heaven? On the one hand, some pericopes in Matthew's Gospel suggest a very open stance toward the inclusion of and mission to gentiles: Matthew's narrative begins with a reference to Abraham, perhaps an allusion to God's call to him and its bearing on the "families of

---

Banditry," 416–17; Eck, "Prophet of Old," 49–50.

179. Agrippa II ruled the former tetrarchy of Philip from 53 CE, and in c. 61 CE was given further territory in Galilee and Perea by Nero. After the Roman–Jewish war, in which he actively supported the Romans, he was again given more territory. He died in c. 93 CE, meaning that he was likely still ruling when Matthew was written, or (if Matthew was written post-93 CE) was at least present in very recent memory.

180. See Willitts, "Matthew," 82–100.

the earth" (Gen 12:1-3); gentiles are specially mentioned[181] in the genealogy of Jesus (1:3, 5)[182]; the positive account of the Magi (2:1-12); the story of the centurion's faith (8:5-13); the use of the Isaianic passage, including the phrase "in his name the Gentiles will hope" (12:21); the Canaanite woman (15:21-28); the parable of the wedding feast (22:1-10); the claim that the gospel will be preached throughout the whole world (24:14); the confession of the Roman soldier (27:54); and the commissioning to make disciples of all the nations (28:19-20). On the other hand, there are passages that, at least on the surface, seem to suggest a strict particularism: the command for the disciples to go not to the gentiles but only to the lost sheep of Israel (10:5-6); and Jesus' rebuttal of the request of the Canaanite woman by saying that he was "sent only to the lost sheep of the house of Israel" (15:24).

Of Matthew's particularism and universalism, the latter is comparatively straightforward; there are no major scholars today who would argue, contrary to all the evidence within the Gospel's narrative, that Matthew was uninterested in the mission to the gentiles. Matthew's particularist statements, on the other hand, difficult to understand as they are, have garnered more debate. For some, the particularist strand of Matthew represents a period, now past, in which there was a determined mission amongst the Jews. Hare explains:

> Because of the failure of Matthew's Christian Jews to win many
> Jewish converts (the unifying theme of the missionary chapter,
> Matthew 10, is pessimism concerning the mission to the lost
> sheep of the house of Israel), Matthew believes that the church's
> future is intimately bound up with the mission to the Gentiles.[183]

This explanation is unsatisfactory given that it relegates sections of Matthew to functional irrelevance, even for the original audience. A literary approach, as in this study, denies this possibility as a satisfactory option because it

181. The three gentile women mentioned, as well as Bathsheba, the daughter of Eliam the Gilonite, are unnecessary inclusions, since the genealogical line is recounted through males, except for Mary. These women are mentioned secondarily, breaking the "X father of Y" pattern. This suggests a purposeful hand in composition, seeking to make a positive point about both women and gentiles. See Hood, *Messiah, His Brothers, and the Nations*, 88-118, who cautions against seeing the four women as functioning together as a unit and interpreting them in the same way.

182. I have not included Bathsheba, since it seems unlikely that she was a gentile— her father was Eliam the Gilonite and her grandfather was Ahithophel the Gilonite. There is no reason to suggest that Matthew thought otherwise. I recognize that it is not clear in Gen 38 whether Tamar was in fact gentile. There were divergent views among Jewish exegetes, though it is outside the scope of this study to explore this here. See Bauckham, "Tamar's Ancestry and Rahab's Marriage," 313-29.

183. Hare, "How Jewish Is the Gospel of Matthew?," 276.

overestimates discontinuities in the text on the basis of a questionable historical reconstruction; the text itself should be the primary framework of interpretation, albeit with the aid of historical knowledge.

For Hare, Matthew reflects that the mission is no longer to Israel, but only to gentiles.[184] However, against this view, the Matthean contrast of "unbelieving" Israel with "the nations who will produce the fruit of the kingdom" is not a form of supersessionism; on the contrary, it is in keeping with the prophetic tradition of critiquing Israel with the aim of repentance. As we have already seen, the Jewish opponents in Matthew are not the Jews generally, nor are the judgements simply meted out to all Israel. Instead, Matthew critiques Jewish community leaders, those we have identified primarily as those involved in the early rabbinic movement, not because Israel is being replaced by the church, but because these particular Jewish groups are considered by the author to be acting contrary to imperatives of the authoritative interpretation of Torah given by Jesus. Ultimately Matthew applies the same criteria of membership to all who would seek to enter the kingdom of God, whether Jew or gentile— "There is . . . no rejection of Israel as a whole."[185] The idea of supersession finds no grounding in Matthew. There is no indication that the mission to the "lost sheep of the house of Israel" is to cease; indeed, the presence of particularist commands suggests that the mission had not ended, that a mission to the Jews was still important in Matthew's communities. If anything, the story of the Canaanite woman (15:21–28), in which the phrase "lost sheep of the house of Israel" reappears, moves the narrative in a more *universalizing* direction inclusive of both the initial lost sheep (Israel) and those gentiles of faith. The commission of 28:19–20 is at no point said to replace the concern for the lost sheep of Israel. In fact, it is more likely that πάντα τὰ ἔθνη is inclusive of Israel.

What, then, does this tension between particularism and universalism mean for Matthew's *Sitz im Leben*? At the very least we can say that Matthew has made the mission to the gentiles an imperative in his story. Whether this is because his communities needed encouragement to continue doing this or because they needed to be convinced to do this at all is unclear. I tend to favor the former option given the hints in the Gospel that there were at least some gentiles in Matthew's communities. It is also very likely that the mission to the Jews was, in Matthew's view, to continue. Indeed, if the social setting of Matthew painted so far is at all correct, the conflict with certain Jewish groups was engaged partly on the basis of what was at

---

184. Hare, *Theme of the Jewish Persecution of Christians*, 148.
185. Saldarini, *Matthew's Christian–Jewish Community*, 71.

stake—influence among and the loyalty of Jewish people in Syro-Palestine. More than this, the inclusion of sayings about the importance of the mission to the lost sheep of the house of Israel likely played a role in reinforcing the significance of the Jews in early Christianity. This would have been a vital identity-bolstering message for those in Matthew's communities who were flanked by unbelieving Jews representing the failure of the Jewish mission on one side, and Torah-free gentile Christianity on the other. By holding in tension particularist and universalist sayings, Matthew was able to affirm delicately the continuing validity of Jewish Christianity and the essentiality of the gentile mission in discipleship.

There are of course other themes in Matthew that may well reflect on its *Sitz im Leben* such as salvation history, the role of women in the communities, particular issues of Torah interpretation, dealing with conflict in the communities, antinomianism, and understanding eschatology, though these could probably be subsumed under one or more of the decidedly "major" themes already addressed. In any case, the scope of this study limits such discussion. What has been raised, though, brings into focus a crucial question, one that is relevant to our study here: what concern unites these superficially disjointed aspects of Matthew's social setting? What is Matthew's Gospel trying to *do* overall?

1.7　The Structure of Matthew

Before we discuss such central questions, a short detour to discuss the structure of Matthew's Gospel is necessary. This is to better understand Matthew's narrative arc, and thus how we might read it. As with other aspects of the study of Matthew's Gospel, there is no consensus and a range of suggestions as to its structure. Two main suggestions have garnered the most support. The first is that of Benjamin Bacon,[186] who suggested that Matthew's structure is based on five discourses (5–7; 10; 13:1–52; 18; 24–25), each of which is tied to a preceding narrative formula "which in every case appropriately leads up to the discourse and furnishes its historical setting."[187] Thus Matthew is, according to Bacon, made up of five "books," each a discourse and its preceding narrative (3–7; 8–10; 11:1—13:52; 13:53–18; 19–25), plus a prologue (1–2) and epilogue (26–28). The narrative device used to couple the end of a discourse to a new narrative introduction is the formula, "Now it came to pass when Jesus had ended these words, etc."

186. Bacon, "'Five Books,'" 56–66.
187. Bacon, "'Five Books,'" 65.

(7:28; 11:1; 13:53; 19:1; 26:1).[188] Matthew's intention with this structural plan, according to Bacon, was "to give his work this symmetrical, typically Jewish form of a fivefold *torah* of Jesus."[189] In other words, Matthew's Gospel is a new Torah ("the great apostolic refutation of the Jews"[190]), and Jesus the new Moses. This theory, in some form at least, continues to be espoused today, by no less than Davies and Allison,[191] though it is far less popular than it once was. Such waning popularity is for good reason since there are a number of issues with this structure. For example, the coupled narratives and discourses do not always share consistent content, such as Matt 11–12 not having any particular attachment to Matt 13.[192] Moreover, the inclusio marked at 4:23 and 9:35 suggests that chapters 5–7 belong with 8–9, not 3–4, and this suggests that the refrain ("Now when Jesus had finished saying these things . . .") may connect a discourse and narrative rather than concluding a block.[193] Moreover, Bacon's structure, having reduced the birth, death, and resurrection of Jesus to prologue and epilogue, does not adequately reflect the significance of these events in the narrative. This is especially the case with the death and resurrection of Jesus, which the narrative seems to build toward as its climax. Most problematic is Carter's contention that Bacon's scheme pays little attention to the actual story of the Gospel.[194] Still, the five discourses are prominent in Matthew's plot and the five structural markers are noticeably similar. This suggests that the five discourses may contribute a major structural form, even if it should not be thought of as defining the narrative as a whole.

The second main suggestion as to Matthew's structure is that most often associated with J. D. Kingsbury who claims Matthew's story unfolds in three broad parts. These parts are separated by the formulaic phrase, "From that time Jesus began to [proclaim/show his disciples . . .]," found in 4:17 and 16:21.[195] Each block is a separate phase in the ministry of Jesus. For Kingsbury, the broad outline of Matthew's Gospel is: (1) The presentation of Jesus Messiah (1:1–4:16); (2) The ministry of Jesus Messiah to Israel and Israel's repudiation of Jesus (4:17—16:20); (3) The journey of Jesus Messiah

---

188. Bacon, "'Five Books,'" 65. The quotation is the translation used by Bacon.

189. Bacon, "'Five Books,'" 66.

190. Bacon, "'Five Books,'" 65.

191. Davies and Allison, *Matthew 1–7*, 61.

192. Luz, *Matthew 1–7*, 3.

193. Garland, *Reading Matthew*, 8–9. Luz, *Matthew 1–7*, 3 makes a similar point, but seems to have a typographical error when he identifies the inclusio as 4:25/9:35.

194. Carter, *Matthew: Storyteller*, 133.

195. Kingsbury, *Matthew as Story*, 40.

to Jerusalem and his suffering, death, and resurrection (16:21—28:20).[196] Like the previous suggestion, this structure is not without its problems. The rare appearance of what is claimed to be a defining phrase in the Gospel is an obvious issue, as is the difficulty in separating 4:17 and (particularly) 16:21 from their preceding verses. Moreover, it is not at all clear why 1:1—4:16 more strongly presents Jesus as Messiah than, for example, 16:13–28, or why 4:17—16:20 presents Jesus' ministry and rejection more prominently than, say, 21:1—27:56. In other words, the themes apparently characterizing certain sections are to be found elsewhere in possibly more potent forms. The strength of Kingsbury's scheme is that it pays much greater attention to Matthew's story than does Bacon's. As Hagner notes, Kingsbury's divisions are indeed found at critical junctures that are important to the shape of the narrative. Like the previous scheme, it may be that these phrases contribute markers to Matthew's story but are not definitive for the narrative as a whole.

Other suggestions as to Matthew's structure have been made, but they have proved less popular. A range of chiastic structures for the Gospel have been proposed, but scholars who have espoused such structures have not been able to agree on what parts of the Gospel should constitute distinct sections, or even the center of the concentric ordering.[197] Frank Matera and Warren Carter have both raised the concept of "kernels" (the crucial "branching points" of the story) and "satellites" (minor events that extend from and elaborate kernels), which together form narrative blocks, each composed of one kernel and a series of satellites.[198] In regard to Matthew, Carter identifies six kernels (1:18–25; 4:17–25; 11:2–6; 16:21–28; 21:1–27; 28:1–10) and thus six narrative blocks extending from them (1:1—4:16; 4:17–11:1; 11:2—16:20; 16:21—20:34; 21:1—27:66; 28:1–20).[199] Matera also identifies six kernels (2:1a; 4:12–17; 11:2–6; 16:13–28; 21:1–17; 28:16–20),[200] and six narrative blocks (1:1—4:11; 4:12—11:1; 11:2—16:12; 16:13—20:34; 21:1—28:15; 28:16–20).[201] While Matera and Carter's schemes are similar, they are not identical, and this raises problems with their method—who

196. Kingsbury, *Matthew as Story*, 40.

197. See, for example, Lohr, "Oral Techniques in the Gospel of Matthew," 403–35; Green, "Structure of St Matthew's Gospel," 47–59; Ellis, *Matthew*, 12; Combrink, "Structure of the Gospel of Matthew as Narrative," 61–90 (esp. 71).

198. Matera, "Plot of Matthew's Gospel," 233–53; Carter, *Matthew: Storyteller*, 137–53. This language of "kernels" and "satellites" is borrowed from Chatman, *Story and Discourse*, 43–95.

199. Carter, *Matthew: Storyteller*, 140.

200. Matera, "Plot of Matthew," 244–45. Matera's paper has a typographical error, identifying this last kernel as "28:20–16." I assume the verses are reversed accidentally.

201. Matera, "Plot of Matthew," 238.

can be certain as to the definition of a kernel? What defines the boundaries of a narrative block? How are transitional pericopes to be treated? This last question is particularly relevant given the differences between Matera and Carter's narrative blocks. For example, is the important pericope about the beginning of Jesus' ministry in 4:12–17, whose position is disputed in the schemes of Matera and Carter, to be thought of as an extension and result of Jesus' temptation, or the prelude to his calling of disciples? It is most likely both. Perhaps thinking of structure in rigid terms is itself a problem. The strength of the kernel/satellite approach is its focus on narrative elements rather than mere verbal markers, though of course narrative elements are, to a certain extent, constructions resulting from the worldview of the reader. Some would no doubt welcome such subjectivity, and I would have no complaint except that such an approach makes determining an agreed-upon structure for the narrative an impossibility.

There are also those who structure Matthew according to the narrative pattern of Mark. Ulrich Luz, for example, advocates this approach.[202] The most obvious problem with this model is that it relies on one's scheme for structuring Mark, which trades one problem for another. If one has a convincing structure for Mark, however, there is the potential to move forward. R. T. France thinks that Mark's narrative is structured geographically—Mark systematizes his Gospel according to the movements of Jesus from Galilee to Jerusalem.[203] Matthew begins with a longer prologue than Mark, but from 4:17 onward Jesus' ministry is, like in Mark, focused totally in Galilee until he announces his intent to travel to Jerusalem (16:21). France ultimately identifies six sections (1:1—4:11; 4:12—16:20; 16:21—20:34; 21:1—25:46; 26:1—28:15; 28:16–20).[204] This structure has the same strength as the kernel/satellite approach in that it focuses on narrative elements (in this case, the setting) rather than verbal markers. Its advantage over the kernel/satellite approach in determining a narrative structure is its reliance on what the text says rather than on our subjective judgements about it. Moreover, the weakness already outlined for this approach—the need for a prior structure for Mark's Gospel—is not necessarily a problem in the case of France's geographical structural model; it could simply be argued that a geographical

202. Luz, *Matthew 1–7*, 3–4.

203. France, *Gospel of Matthew*, 3–4.

204. He describes these as: Introducing the Messiah (1:1—4:11); Galilee: The Messiah revealed in word and deed (4:12—16:20); From Galilee to Jerusalem: The Messiah and his followers prepare for the confrontation (16:21—20:34); Jerusalem: The Messiah in confrontation with the religious authorities (21:1—25:46); Jerusalem: The Messiah rejected, killed, and vindicated (26:1—28:15); Galilee: The Messianic mission is launched (28:16–20). France, *Gospel of Matthew*, vii–xv.

structure for Matthew's Gospel need not be reliant on Mark. In fact, I am convinced that a geographical approach to Matthew's structure need not refer to Mark at all since all the necessary resources are present in Matthew's narrative.[205] This is preferable from a narrative-critical perspective since it does not rely on external sources.

Wim Weren has more recently offered a similar proposal that blends ideas from Matera and Carter, utilizing the language of kernels, with the geographical approach of France.[206] Weren, however, adds temporal information to topographical information in order to determine the "hinge texts" (his preferred term for "kernels") of the story. Such hinge texts have "a macro syntactical function: they bring about a turning point in the plot, a turning point that is fleshed out in a large number of the subsequent pericopes."[207] Weren also asserts that these texts refer, at the same time, to the preceding block and thus have a double function. For Weren, there are two main hinge texts (4:12–17; 26:1–16) between which there is a "corpus" (4:18—25:46), and this large unit is contained within an overture[208] (1:1—4:11) and a finale[209] (26:17—28:20).[210] The corpus contains hinge texts, a primary one at 16:13–28 which splits the corpus in two, and secondary hinges at 11:2–30 and 21:1–17. The great strength of Weren's approach is that it takes seriously the fluidity of narratives. His approach allows multiple levels of structure, with the first level being quite coarse, the second splitting the corpus in two, and the third presenting the corpus in more detail.[211] Moreover, in addition to the size of sequences becoming gradually smaller through these levels rather than being uniform in size, Weren's approach also makes room for hinge texts to refer to previous pericopes and not merely those that follow. This is important, since it may well offer

205. Of course, Matthew *does* follow Mark's plot closely in regard to the Markan material he uses. Still, it could be argued that discussion of Matthew's plot should remain independent of Markan considerations, notwithstanding his use of Mark as a source. From a narrative-critical standpoint, whatever sources Matthew used are irrelevant since we are concerned with the final form of the text.

206. Weren, "Macrostructure of Matthew's Gospel," 171–200.

207. Weren, "Macrostructure of Matthew's Gospel," 188.

208. Weren rejects the use of the term "prologue" since, he says, it gives the impression that 1:1—4:11 "is a non-narrative introductory section, like the prologue in John 1,1–18. The term 'overture' does more justice to the fact that Matthew's story about Jesus already begins in 1,18." Weren, "Macrostructure of Matthew's Gospel," 189.

209. "The term 'finale' has been chosen in order to express that the passion narrative is an integrated constituent that forms the climax of the entire book." Weren, "Macrostructure of Matthew's Gospel," 189.

210. Weren, "Macrostructure of Matthew's Gospel," 188–89.

211. Weren, "Macrostructure of Matthew's Gospel," 198.

a satisfactory solution to an issue such as the deadlock between Matera and Carter over whether 4:12–17 belongs with the preceding or following pericope—it can simply belong to both. In this way, we are not overly focused on caesuras and are free to underline the continuity of Matthew's story.[212] I find the less rigid approach of Weren, which fluidly moves along with the rhythm of Matthew's geography and chronology, convincing.

It is also the perspective of some scholars that there is simply no cohesive structure to Matthew as a whole, but only substructures that make up a larger story. Robert Gundry is of this opinion, as are Stanton and Hagner.[213] It certainly appears that Matthew is organized topically (rather than strictly chronologically),[214] and there are good reasons to think that an overarching structure may not have been in the mind of the author.

Which model best reflects the structure of Matthew? In truth, Matthew's overall plot is difficult to outline in terms of a structure. As Luz says, "it is easier to recognize the evangelist's work in arranging shorter sections of the text than to see a disposition of the entire Gospel."[215] Still, there are ways forward. I am persuaded that the geographical structural model holds much value, since it both focuses on the actual story of the Gospel rather than imposed schemes and relies on concrete elements in the text (geographical setting) rather than questionable textual cues. I am, however, not convinced that geography is the only narrative element worthy of forming markers in the story, nor that we should be bound to a rigid structure. I find Weren's macrostructure for Matthew to be a helpful and convincing approach, offering as it does a multi-leveled and fluid structure for the narrative. I think, then, following Weren, that the structure of Matthew is as such:[216]

---

212. Weren, "Macrostructure of Matthew's Gospel," 199.

213. Gundry says Matthew is "structurally mixed." Gundry, *Matthew*, 11. Stanton, "Origin and Purpose of Matthew's Gospel," 1905; Hagner, *Matthew 1–13*, liii. Hagner agrees with Davies and Allison that Matthew alternates between narrative and discourse, though he does not appear to think this constitutes an overall structure.

214. Keener, *Gospel of Matthew*, 36; Davies and Allison, *Matthew 1–7*, 87–88.

215. Luz, *Matthew 1–7*, 5.

216. Weren, "Macrostructure of Matthew's Gospel," 200.

1:1–4:11 Overture (Origin, identity and mission)

4:12–17 Hinge

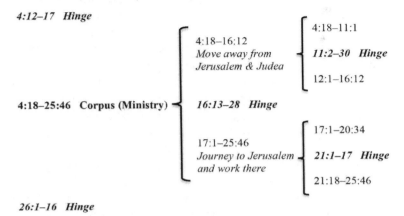

4:18–16:12
*Move away from
Jerusalem & Judea*

4:18–11:1

11:2–30 Hinge

12:1–16:12

4:18–25:46 Corpus (Ministry)

16:13–28 Hinge

17:1–25:46
*Journey to Jerusalem
and work there*

17:1–20:34

21:1–17 Hinge

21:18–25:46

26:1–16 Hinge

26:17–28:20 Finale (Suffering, death, resurrection, mission to the world)

I am also convinced that there is some merit in the five-discourse form. As mentioned, however, I do not think this scheme is appropriate as a definitive structure for the entire narrative. Rather, the five discourses punctuate the overall structure of the story with teaching that applies as direct commandment for the readers.[217] They may also be an element in Matthew's new Moses theme. Whatever the case, finding significance in Matthew's five discourses as a structural element need not be an approach in discord with the larger structural approach settled on above—they can be viewed as complementary. As a final note, it should be said that since Matthew's structure is far from clear, we should not allow our exegesis to rely too heavily on structural considerations.

1.8 The Genre[218] and Purpose of Matthew

Moving back to a discussion of what Matthew is trying to do, we ought to recognize that the book is presented in the form of a story. Matthew is not

217. So Luz, *Matthew 1–7*, 12.

218. I am aware that the term "genre" should be used with caution. "The text of Matthew provides no direct access to Jesus. His words and deeds had already been interpreted by the sources incorporated in it; and these sources were in turn arranged and molded afresh to offer further interpretation. Still, that text always presupposes an historical figure, Jesus, as its *raison d'être*. If it be legitimate to use the literary term, 'genre', for our canonical gospels—an uncertain issue—this should not prevent us from

a set of frequently asked questions about early rabbinic Judaism, Roman domination, or the tension between particularism and universalism, nor is it a systematic theology. But Matthew is not merely a "story" in some general sense either. It is a particular kind of story, centered on a significant individual. What kind of story, exactly? Throughout the centuries the dominant view has been that Matthew is a biography. This changed in the twentieth century, however, as scholars, notably Bultmann,[219] asserted that the Gospels were expressions of early Christian proclamation and were not historical accounts. Bultmann followed Schmidt's form-critical distinction between *Hochliteratur* and *Kleinliteratur* and the assertion that the Gospels were the latter, a collection of folk stories with no overarching literary intention.[220] Bultmann insisted that, "while we need analogies for understanding the individual components of the Synoptic Tradition we do not need them for the Gospel as a whole."[221] But, as later scholars have tended to agree, the dichotomy between *Hochliteratur* and *Kleinliteratur* is artificially rigid, finding no empirical basis in ancient literary studies. Moreover, such an approach is flawed on account of ignoring the creative redactional and compositional role of the author. In other words, the background of material, oral or written, says little about the author's role in selecting and structuring that material or the overall genre of the final work.[222] The Gospel authors are not simply robotic collectors of traditions. Bultmann may have been correct to discern a range of genres in different components of the Gospels, but to conclude that the Gospels were therefore merely "unliterary" is to go beyond what this observation permits. To conclude such is to exclude the possibility that the authors utilized a range of genres, such as apocalyptic or catechism, in a mixed-genre work. Equally neglected is the potential for genres to form sub-types within an overall genre construct adopted by the author.

In more recent decades the trend of seeing the Gospels as not having a historical character has largely been reversed and many scholars now

---

recognizing that they are not 'art for art's sake': their aims, even those of Luke, are not primarily literary so that from a classical point of view 'gospel' is not a literary genre; rather do they intend to point to the manifold significance of Jesus of Nazareth for the communities within which they wrote and for humankind and his *mysterium tremendum*." Davies and Allison, *Matthew 1–7*, 4–5.

219. "There is no historical-biographical interest in the Gospels." Bultmann, *History of the Synoptic Tradition*, 372. Bultmann argued that Hellenistic biographies provided no analogy for the genre of the Gospels, though Stanton has called this "surprisingly inaccurate" (*Gospel for a New People*, 63).

220. Schmidt, *Place of the Gospels*.

221. Bultmann, *History of the Synoptic Tradition*, 373.

222. Burridge, *What Are the Gospels?*, 12.

conclude that Matthew and the other Gospels are indeed to be seen as ancient biography.[223] Within this movement there have been a number of approaches to defining genre itself and, by extension, to determining the biographical nature of the Gospels. In a 1986 volume of *Semeia*, for example, Adela Yarbro Collins, David Hellholm, and David Aune all define genre as the interplay between form, content, and function.[224] Using this framework, Aune shows convincingly that the Gospels are not to be seen as conforming to kerygmatic or liturgical genres.[225] Using the same framework, he goes on to give a coherent account of the biographical character of the Gospels.[226] Aune says, "A biography relates to the significance of a famous person's career (i.e., his [*sic*] character and achievements), optionally framed by a narrative of origins and youth, on the one hand, and death and lasting significance on the other."[227] He lists four important characteristics of ancient biography, three of which are important in the present case: (1) ancient biographies tended to be host genres serving as a literary frame for a range of shorter forms; (2) they focused on the public life of an individual and emphasized the stages of professional life; (3) individuals are stylized as *types*, those who represent group norms and values, not in terms of their historical particularity.[228] Each of these is clearly applicable to Matthew.

Still, the form-content-function typology of genre offered by Aune and others is not without its problems. Burridge notes that some

223. For example, see Aune, *New Testament*, 46–76; Burridge, *What Are the Gospels?*; Davies and Allison, *Matthew: A Shorter Commentary*, xxvi–xxviii; Garland, *Reading Matthew*, 5; Hagner, *Matthew 1–13*, lvii; Keener, *Matthew*, 16–24; Stanton, *Gospel for a New People*, 59–71; Talbert, "Once Again," 53–73. See also Neyrey, *Honor and Shame* and Schuler, *Genre for the Gospels* who both, probably too narrowly, identify Matthew as an encomium.

224. Yarbro Collins, *Early Christian Apocalypticism*, 2–7, 17–18, 65–96; repr. from Collins, "Introduction," 2–7. Hellholm, "Problem of Apocalyptic Genre," 17–18; Aune, "Apocalypse of John and the Problem of Genre," 65–96. See also Aune, *New Testament*, 24.

225. Aune, *New Testament*, 23–27. Kerygma, he says, is typically in the *form* of a speech, with *content* that tends away from the ministry of Jesus but toward the exaltation and return of Jesus and appeals to repentance and faith as strong motifs (unlike the Gospels); and *functioning* evangelistically to evoke repentance and faith (also unlike the Gospels). In regard to the possibility of Matthew being a liturgical work, Aune outlines several theories before acknowledging that the scarcity of evidence for Jewish lectionary practice in the first century permits very few conclusions.

226. Aune, *New Testament*, 46–76.

227. Aune, *New Testament*, 27.

228. Aune, *New Testament*, 27–28. The fourth characteristic of ancient biography that Aune mentions is that obituaries were important to their development, such as found in dirges, eulogies and epitaphs. Given Matthew's insistence that Jesus did not remain dead, this characteristic seems less crucial in our case.

characteristics could span two or more of the groupings. For example, a vision could be a formal characteristic as well as an aspect of content.[229] Burridge goes on to say that function is often hypothetical unless we have other evidence about a work's purpose or social setting.[230] It is thus not a firm basis for determining genre. Such is a fair critique, though it does not completely negate the value of Aune's approach.

Burridge contributes an alternative typology of genre, one more refined and precise:[231]

Opening features

Title

Opening words

Prologue

Subject

Analysis of the Verbs' Subjects

Allocation of Space

External Features

Mode of Representation

Meter

Size and Length

Structure

Scale

Literary Units

Use of Sources

Methods of Characterization

Internal Features

Setting

Topics

Style

Tone/Mood/Attitudes/Values

Quality of Characterization

---

229. Burridge, *What Are the Gospels?*, 106.

230. Burridge, *What Are the Gospels?*, 106.

231. Burridge, *What Are the Gospels?*, 104–48.

Social Setting and Occasion

Authorial Intention and Purpose

According to Burridge, these elements are a "set of expectations," a contract between the author and reader.[232] Whatever the differences in Burridge's typology may be, he arrives at the same destination as Aune and others, namely, that the Synoptics are to be understood as Graeco-Roman biographies, what Burridge prefers to call βίοι. Indeed, a large number of features of Matthew's Gospel make for a persuasive case that it is in fact an ancient biography. Matthew's prologue (genealogy), large allocation of space to and focus on the main subject, its overall length,[233] insertion of topical material into chronological structure, combination of stories, sayings and speeches, the selection and editing of sources, depiction of Jesus at times in a stereotypical role (e.g., new Moses), and the use of Jesus as exemplar are all in keeping with standard characteristics of ancient biographies.[234] Given the potential for this subject to become a lengthy tangent, it suffices to say that, with Burridge and the majority of contemporary scholars, I agree that Matthew is a βίος.

Far more important for our study are the implications of Matthew's biographical nature. Paramount in this is a discussion of function. Though Burridge's critique of function in determining genre was previously noted, such does not apply to the discussion of a text whose genre has already been judged. Speaking of function, Aune suggests ancient biography could have both obvious and latent functions.[235] Of the conscious functions, the demonstrative (epideictic) is most common in ancient biography, but could be mixed with deliberative and forensic elements.[236] Epideictic rhetoric, usually praise or blame, was a category concerned with persuading an audience to take on or uphold a certain point of view in the present. Deliberative rhetoric sought to persuade an audience to take a future action. Forensic rhetoric used apologetic or accusation to persuade the audience to make a decision about past events. In regard to the latent, or unconscious, function of biography, such typically involved the historical legitimation or discrediting of a social belief or value system personified in the biography's subject.[237] In other

---

232. Burridge, *What Are the Gospels?*, 33–34.

233. Around 18,300 words. Burridge argues that this would make it a "medium-length" work (10,000–25,000 words), and this was normal for βίοι. Burridge, *What Are the Gospels?*, 114, 194.

234. Burridge, *What Are the Gospels?*, 185–212.

235. Aune, *New Testament*, 35.

236. Aune, *New Testament*, 35–36.

237. Aune, *New Testament*, 35.

words, ancient biography was an effective propaganda tool, as well as a way to aim direct or indirect criticism at an established order.[238] Equally important, however, was that ancient biography could function didactically, with the subject as a model of virtue;[239] this was an encomium. With an encomium, the audience was more interested in the person as a model for virtue rather than for their historical particularity. Thus, there was a tension between historical and paradigmatic elements in ancient biographies.

That Matthew utilized the genre of βίος gives us a clue as to his overall purpose. Functionally, Matthew utilizes epideictic and forensic forms of rhetoric at different stages: the audience is urged to maintain a particular perspective in the present regarding Jesus and the way of life he commands and are expected to have come to a decision about the meaning of past events (i.e., the ministry, death, and resurrection of Jesus). It could also be suggested that there are certain deliberative rhetorical elements in Matthew, such as the suggestion that disciples will need to make decisions in an ongoing sense in the face of persecution. Moreover, Matthew functions to both legitimate and discredit particular social views, as we will see in later chapters. It would be one thing for Matthew to use a systematic approach to discrediting his opponents, but it is quite another for him to use a biographical narrative of Jesus. By doing so, Matthew does not merely counter the claims of his enemies, he also offers a positive contribution to the lives of his readers. As with other Graeco-Roman biographies, Matthew puts forward a didactic and rhetorical object of crisis—the audience must take a side in the present based on the meaning of the past. Through the story of Jesus, the progenitor and object of the audience's loyalty, Matthew is able to offer a persuasive worldview. The strong imperatives to and examples of discipleship throughout the Gospel are not merely teachings but are a way of looking at the world contra internecine Jewish claims and Roman domination. In the midst of such a world, Matthew offers what Carter calls "a compelling alternative social experience," which provides a meaningful answer to the question, "To what society do I belong?" and, even more importantly, "To whom does the world belong?"[240] For Matthew the answers are bound up in the claim of Jesus that God reigns. The audience is invited to live in light of the implications of this claim, as are the disciples portrayed in the story. In

---

238. Aune offers a number of examples. Aune, *New Testament*, 35–36.

239. On the Gospels as virtue-forming, see Pennington, *Reading the Gospels Wisely.* Pennington rightly warns against reducing the Gospel's vision of Jesus to a model of virtue at the expense of the Evangelists' Christological aims.

240. Carter, *Matthew and Empire*, 51.

this way, Matthew's story is, as Carter argues, a counternarrative in the form of a biography about an executed prophet from Galilee.[241]

In my view, this suggestion makes the most sense of all the elements of Matthew's *Sitz im Leben* that have been explored above. Matthew's Gospel, a βίος, seeks to persuade its audience of its view of the present on the basis of the past, and in doing so to answer the questions "Who are we?" and "Whose world is this?" in the face of present distress: early rabbinic opposition, Roman power, and ethnic tensions. The question of the identity of Matthew's audience necessarily has ramifications for its community life, ethics, and mission, as personified in the Matthean Jesus.

1.9 The Prophetic Vocation and Matthew's Social Setting

All of this leads us to a discussion of our central concern—Matthew's portrayal of Jesus' prophetic vocation—in light of Matthew's social setting and narrative structure. Matthew depicts Jesus as a prophet at numerous points. Many of his words and deeds are prophetic in a way that resembles Old Testament prophetic episodes, particularly those of Moses (e.g., Matt 1:18—2:23; 5–7), Jeremiah[242] (e.g., Matt 21:12), and Elijah (e.g., Matthew 8–9) and the crowds perceive him to be a prophet (cf. Matt 16:14; 21:8–11, 46). Jesus himself alludes to his own prophetic identity (Matt 13:57; 23:29–32). Our aim here is not to discuss these episodes and their meaning. Such a discussion would require first attending to those first-century Jewish prophets and the coexistent popular understanding of prophecy and prophets around the time of Jesus. This topic will receive our attention in the next chapter and will give an insight into the prophetic milieu of the time, which would no doubt have influenced Matthew's understanding of prophecy. For now, our question is why Matthew would so adamantly depict Jesus as a prophet in his narrative. What would be the aim in light of Matthew's purposes and social setting?

That Matthew contains apologetic and polemical elements is clear. One way to understand his depiction of Jesus as prophet is as apologetic for the legitimacy of his communities and polemic against his opponents. Unfortunately, in turning our attention to Matthew's opponents, it is impossible to know what were the views on prophecy held by the early rabbinic movement of the late first century CE since they left no evidence

---

241. Carter, *Matthew and the Margins*, 1; Carter, *Matthew and Empire*, 35–53.

242. For an excellent treatment of Jesus and Jeremiah in Matthew, see Zucker, "Jesus and Jeremiah in the Matthean Tradition," 288–305.

relating to the matter.[243] The later authors of the rabbinic literature did, however, discuss the topic. We cannot be certain, though, that the views of the later rabbis were the same as their first-century counterparts.[244] Granted, any investigation of ancient Judaism is "bound to rely heavily on the vast corpus of early rabbinic literature."[245] Still, there are many problems with reading the later rabbinic sources back into the first century, even those which claim to report historical incidents from that period. Of these instances, Saldarini is correct:

> Because each of the rabbinic sources tells stories of earlier times to accomplish its own religious purposes, these stories cannot be taken as history. If they are, they produce an illegitimate and unhistorical retrojection of second through seventh century Rabbinic Judaism on the first century.[246]

That is, the task of historical investigation is made even more complicated by the fact that the rabbinic passages with which we are concerned are not even intended as retrospective history, but rather as the contemporary teachings of the authors. Still, though the relevant texts do not attempt to "do" history, they do give an indication of the eventual trajectory that begins with first-century rabbinic belief.[247] There are also some sources roughly contemporary with the early rabbis that may offer insight.

Josephus, for instance, includes a pericope that provides some detail about the prophetic practices of the Pharisees in *Ant.* 17.41–45:

> Pheroras' wife paid the fine for them [the Pharisees]. In return for her friendliness they foretold—for they were believed to have foreknowledge of things through God's appearances to them—that by God's decree Herod's throne would be taken from him, both himself and his descendants, and the royal power would fall to her and Pheroras and to any children that they might have.[248]

From this, and also *Ant.* 14.172–76 and 15.3–4, Webb concludes that these Pharisees were perceived as functioning in a sapiential form of prophetic

---

243. There is likely no such united belief to be discovered, but rather a range of views.

244. Goldenberg, "Destruction of the Jerusalem Temple," 191.

245. Goldenberg, "Destruction of the Jerusalem Temple," 191.

246. Saldarini, *Pharisees, Scribes and Sadducees*, 200.

247. I stress the word "indication" since historical trajectories are rarely as simple as a straight line between points A and B.

248. Josephus, *Ant.* 17.42–43.

role, that is, as a wise person normally associated with a sectarian group.[249] Such prophets were intellectuals and elites whose prophecy came in the form of predictions about events related to political leaders with the method primarily being the interpretation of scripture, but also the reception of visions and dreams.[250] Josephus, a Pharisee, records that he himself performed such a prophetic act in *J.W.* 3.400–402, where he describes his prediction of Vespasian's ascension to the Roman Emperorship. This appreciation for prophecy is in contrast to other forms of what Josephus calls "pseudo-prophecy" as enacted by popular prophets who, according to Josephus, sought miraculous acts of divine deliverance and who consequently brought their followers to ruin. Such prophets, as we will see in chapter 2, embody Mosaic characteristics in their actions. For now we can say that the Pharisaic understanding and practice of prophecy, at least as far as we can tell from the scant evidence, was quite distinct from much of the practice of the earlier canonical prophets, of first-century popular prophets, and of Matthew's Jesus. Moreover, Josephus seems to assess positively such sapiential forms of prophecy, in contrast to his dismissive attitude to what we will call popular prophecy (see chapter 2).

From later rabbinic literature we see how Palestinian[251] rabbinic thought had developed by the third century:[252]

> When the last of the prophets—i.e. Haggai, Zechariah and Malachi—died, the holy spirit ceased in Israel. Despite this they were informed by means of oracles.[253] (*t. Sotah* 13:2)

Aune claims that in rabbinic Judaism the holy spirit was "virtually synonymous" with prophecy,[254] a point agreed upon by Greenspahn who says that in Jewish tradition *rûaḥ nĕbûʾâ* (spirit of prophecy) and *rûaḥ qûdšâ* (holy spirit) are used almost interchangeably.[255] Though there is much complexity regarding the perception by different groups concerning the continuation of prophecy and the nature of oracles in the late Second Temple

---

249. Webb, *John the Baptizer and Prophet*, 322, 326–32. Webb's typology of prophets is explored in greater detail in chapter 2.

250. Webb, *John the Baptizer and Prophet*, 331.

251. Mandel, "Tosefta," 320, claims there is "no doubt that the Tosefta is a Palestinian work."

252. This is the probable date for the Tosefta, and the majority view, though it is not definite. Equally unclear is the date of the traditions and pericopes that make up the Tosefta.

253. That is, *Bat Qol*.

254. Aune, *Prophecy in Early Christianity*, 104.

255. Greenspahn, "Why Prophecy Ceased," 37.

period, what we can say with reasonable confidence is that the conviction of rabbinic Judaism at the time of the Tosefta is that the inspired prophet was no longer the channel of divine revelation. Still, revelation continued to be mediated through "oracles," or *Bat Qol* ("the daughter of a voice"), which was believed to be a heavenly voice distinct from the revelations given to the classical prophets.[256] The Tannaitic literature, most probably dating from earlier than the Tosefta, says:

> Until then, the prophets prophesied by means of the holy spirit. From then on give ear and listen to the words of the sages. (S. *'Olam Rab.* 30)

This seems to suggest that the rabbis (sages) saw themselves as the successors of the canonical prophets. The prophets themselves were viewed as the interpreters and expositors of the Mosaic law, in a sense the successors of Moses;[257] Moses had spoken the words of Torah, and everything prophesied later was derived from him:

> Moses received Torah from Sinai and gave it to Joshua; Joshua gave it to the elders, and the elders gave it to the prophets, and the prophets gave it to the men of the Great Assembly . . . (*m. 'Abot* 1:1)

By asserting their own connection to the prophets of old, the rabbis held claim to be the true successors of Moses himself, those who interpreted Torah legitimately. This does not equate to the rabbis believing that they themselves were prophets. True, there are a small number of cases in Tannaitic rabbinic literature in which rabbis claim visions and other forms of revelation by the holy spirit,[258] but the general consensus among the rabbis seems to have been that there was a qualitative difference between past prophecy and contemporary *Bat Qol*, and that the former had ceased.[259] For the rabbis, the prophet was a figure similar to the sage, differing in degree but not in kind. The age

---

256. Boring, *Continuing Voice Of Jesus*, 53.

257. According to the Babylonian Talmud, "Our Rabbis taught: 'Forty-eight prophets and seven prophetesses prophesied to Israel, and they neither took away from nor added aught to what is written in the Torah save only the reading of the Megillah.'" (*b. Meg.* 14a). While it is anachronistic to assume that the later authors of this text represent the views of the late-first century rabbinic movement, it does give us an indication of the importance given to the Torah by the rabbis and the place of the prophets in history. It is not unreasonable to assume that this same view was taken by the earlier rabbis.

258. See Erik Sjöberg, "πνεῦμα, πνευματικός: רוח in Palestinian Judaism," *TDNT* 6:386.

259. See R. Meyer, "προφήτης," *TDNT* 6:816–23, for a more in-depth study of many of the statements made in rabbinic literature regarding prophecy.

of the inspired prophet was finished, and this belief would have legitimated their role as successors of Moses.[260] It is quite possible that this was a development of the Pharisaic understanding of prophecy presented in Josephus: the Pharisaic mode of prophecy was essentially sapiential prediction using scripture and dream interpretation as its method. The two understandings of prophecy are strikingly similar. It is not difficult to envision a development of prophecy from the time of the first-century Pharisees to the later authors of the rabbinic literature.

Meyer is probably correct when he makes the judgement that in rabbinic tradition, "one finds sophisticated theological deliberation aimed at restricting the rise of legitimate prophecy to an ideal classical period in the past."[261] The presence of the *Bat Qol* was not simply a replacement of the absent spirit of prophecy; on the contrary, it was seen as an authentic continuation of prophecy, albeit less prestigious and in a different form, that legitimated the sages as being in the line of the prophets of old. "R. Abdimi from Haifa said: Since the day when the temple was destroyed, prophecy has been taken from the prophets and given to the wise" (*b. B. Bat.* 12a). People were now to incline their ears to the sage, not the prophet. This shift may have been motivated by the desire of the rabbis to avoid future cataclysms, such as the destruction of the temple, which was no doubt exacerbated by the resistive activities of popular prophetic movements (discussed in chapter 2). Indeed, *b. B. Bat.* 12b suggests that the rabbis were far from tolerant of more charismatic competition: "Since the Temple was destroyed, prophecy has been taken from prophets and given to fools and children." While we cannot know definitively that the earliest rabbis held the same views as that presented in the later rabbinic literature, there is a resemblance between these later views and what we can gather about the views of the first-century Pharisees as reported by Josephus—prophecy rooted in wisdom, interpretation, and occasionally visions—and this suggests similarities in belief.

If this is how the early rabbis of the late first century viewed prophets and prophecy, we can begin to see why Matthew might have portrayed Jesus so intentionally as a prophet. By depicting Jesus in numerous narrative episodes as a type of Moses, Elijah, and Jeremiah, a polemical purpose becomes apparent—the true spirit of prophecy lies not with any Pharisaic rabbis but with Jesus of Nazareth. This is anything but an innocuous assertion given that the claim of the rabbis to stand within the tradition of the prophets was a *legitimating* one. The *Bat Qol* is a signal that their interpretation of Torah is true and that ears should be inclined to their

---

260. Aune, *Prophecy in Early Christianity*, 104.

261. Meyer, "προφήτης," 6:816.

words. Such a claim is not merely related to doctrinal matters, but works itself out in terms of power, influence, and the ability to implement one's policies within the local community. For Jesus to be portrayed as one like the prophets of old is essentially to outstrip the claims of Matthew's opponents. Jesus being portrayed as prophet legitimates the claims of the Matthean communities over against their local opponents and affirms the identity of Matthew's audience in a turbulent time.

We must also pay attention to the other major social consideration of Matthew and his audience that has a strong bearing on his portrayal of the prophetic vocation, namely, the presence of the Roman Empire. It is not necessary to enter here into a discussion of widespread prophetic activity in light of Roman power—that will be explored in detail in the next chapter—though it is important to provide a basic sketch of the long tradition of prophetic resistance to empire in Israel. For Jesus to be characterized as a type of Moses, Elijah, and Jeremiah at different points in the Matthean story is almost necessarily to set Jesus as an anti-imperial figure. The Israelite prophets of old had, each in their own ways, proclaimed God's sovereignty over all other claims, whether from Egypt, Babylon, Greece, or indeed Israel's leaders themselves. Jesus, by echoing the prophets in his words and actions, stood in their resistive tradition. We ought not get ahead of ourselves, but we can say in a general sense that Jesus' range of prophetic expression—everything from parables and social teachings to signs, miracles, and healings[262]—provides a critical lens through which to view empire and oppression.[263] Moreover, the Matthean Jesus' use of apocalyptic themes,[264] and indeed his self-identification with Daniel (Matt 16:27–28; 24:30), places him squarely in the apocalyptic tradition that, in the words of Portier-Young, "answered the empire."[265] At times in this study we will see

262. These are all activities of the classical prophets. Prophecy has too often been narrowly defined as forms of verbal utterance, but this narrow understanding is by no means comprehensive. In Matthew, John is said to be a prophet (11:9; 14:5), despite his primary activity being baptism. Moreover, it is said that Jesus is thought by some to be Elijah (16:14), and narratively this can only be inferred from his healings and signs earlier in the story. See ahead to my chapter on "Which of Jesus' Words and Actions are 'Prophetic'?"

263. On the subversive nature of parables, see Herzog, *Parables as Subversive Speech*. On the state of daily life in the empire for the lower classes, see Stark, *Rise of Christianity*, 147–62. Stark does not explore healings, but the material does provide an obvious groundwork for how healings might have subverted the empire.

264. In the next chapter I explore "apocalyptic" in greater depth.

265. Portier-Young, *Apocalypse Against Empire*, 217. Portier-Young's book is a fine study of the resistive nature of apocalyptic, as is Horsley, *Revolt of the Scribes*. See also Hanson, *Dawn of Apocalyptic*. Hanson is right to point out that there were, *very* broadly speaking, two primary religious orientations throughout Second Temple Judaism, the

that Matthew's portrayal of Jesus' prophetic vocation is a powerful challenge to the sovereign claims of Rome, its legitimating myths and stories, and the resultant social world in which the majority of people suffered day-to-day oppression and domination. In sum, if Matthew's portrayal of Jesus' prophetic vocation is meant to affirm the identity of his communities vis-à-vis the competing claims of rabbinic Judaism ("who are we?"), then it is also meant to proclaim the sovereignty of God over against the competing claims of Rome's empire ("whose world is this?").

This conclusion regarding Jesus' prophetic vocation is described well by the classic paradigm of Walter Brueggemann in *The Prophetic Imagination*. For Brueggemann, "The task of prophetic ministry is to nurture, nourish, and evoke a consciousness and perception alternative to the consciousness and perception of the dominant culture around us."[266] Simply put, the twofold task of the prophet is to *criticize* and dismantle the dominant consciousness and present order, and to *energize* persons and communities by its promise of a new way that God will give.[267] In my view, this impeccably explains the way in which Matthew describes the prophetic ministry of Jesus.

Ultimately, Jesus' prophetic vocation as depicted by Matthew is not only a form of polemic and apologetic—it is also an example to the prophets that were present in Matthew's communities, and to all believers. The imperative to take up one's cross, for example, is an implicitly prophetic one (Matt 16:24–28; cf. 23:31–36). This suggestion is important because it frames not only the discipleship expectation on Matthew's audience, but also all subsequent readers.

---

priestly-hierocratic perspective and the prophetic-visionary perspective, though this likely an oversimplification. Where he is mistaken is in the assertion that apocalyptic, undertaken by those of the prophetic-eschatological perspective who are oppressed and powerless, is apolitical, having given up on the transformation of the present order. Hanson says, "When separated from realism, the vision leads to a retreat into the world of ecstasy and dreams and to an abdication of the social responsibility of translating the vision of the divine order into the realm of everyday earthly concerns" (30). While not addressing the same texts as Hanson, Portier-Young shows convincingly that later apocalyptic texts do anything *but* retreat, that in fact they were highly subversive texts, not retreating from realism, but challenging readers to engage reality.

266. Brueggemann, *Prophetic Imagination*, 3.

267. Brueggemann, *Prophetic Imagination*, 3.

1.10 Conclusion

Matthew was written by a well-educated Jewish Christian, well acquainted with the wider Graeco-Roman world, to an audience of multiple communities that were mainly Jewish but containing a minority of gentiles. These communities represented a cross-section of the social strata present in Roman society—some were from the lower strata, with others from the elite—and almost certainly included some scribal and prophetic figures. These communities were located in a range of areas across Syro-Palestine, most probably Antioch and Galilee, and quite possibly elsewhere in the Transjordan. Matthew's Gospel was probably written sometime between 80 and 100 CE, and was partly a response to the competing claims of Pharisaic elements of the nascent rabbinic movement.

With the destruction of the temple, the religio-political situation in Palestine had changed, and in this new situation Matthew's communities found themselves in tension with sections of the early rabbinic movement. This tension related to conflict over their place in the synagogue and the life of their wider communities, and to certain interpretive conflicts. Such interpretive conflicts, far from being merely doctrinal disagreements, constituted competing claims regarding the vision and practice of the life of the community.

For Matthew and his audience, the definitive interpretation of Torah came from Jesus of Nazareth, with one of the primary issues being the nature of "the kingdom of heaven." For Matthew, the kingdom of heaven is intertwined with issues of justice, mercy, and faithfulness, as demonstrated in the life and teachings of Jesus. It seems that Matthew and his audience were opposed to certain Pharisaic elements of the early rabbinic movement, those which were growing in local influence, for what they perceived as an unfaithful interpretation and practice of God's will expressed in Torah.

Another central aspect of the social setting of Matthew is the presence of Roman power. In light of the empire's claims of sovereignty and its military power, economic oppression, and legitimating myths, Matthew has Jesus declaring the presence of a new kingdom/empire, God's new creation, the promise of a new physical, social, and economic life as an alternative to Rome. In answer to Rome's sovereign claims and imperial theology Matthew has Jesus declare, in word and deed, God's sovereignty over the whole world.

As an extension of this new life declared by Jesus, Matthew confronts tensions between Jews and gentiles in Christian communities that likely arose from the apparent failure of the mission to the Jews and the success of gentile Christianity. For Matthew and his audience, there is to be no end to the mission to the Jews, and indeed he strongly affirms Jewish Christianity. At the same time, the gentile mission is viewed as an essential element in Christian discipleship.

Finally, Jesus' prophetic vocation is a key element in Matthew's narrative challenge to his Jewish opponents and to Roman imperial power. By portraying Jesus as standing in the line of the prophets of old, Matthew both challenges the authority of the Pharisaic rabbis and depicts the central figure of the early Christian movement as one who resists and subverts unjust imperial power. This not only has the effect of providing a new and alternative way of life for his communities, it also affirms their marginal identity in light of competing rabbinic claims ("who are we?") and proclaims the sovereignty of the God of Israel in the face of Roman claims ("whose world is this?"). In other words, it embodies the prophetic imagination described by Brueggemann—criticism of the current dominant consciousness and the nurturing of a new energizing consciousness that promises an alternative to it. Jesus' prophetic vocation in Matthew also provides a pattern for ongoing discipleship.

This leads us to consider in greater detail the nature, form, and function of prophetic expression at the time of Jesus and Matthew, and how it might have achieved the purposes that have been outlined for it here.

Chapter 2

Understanding Jewish Prophecy in the First Century CE

2.1 Introduction

IN THE PREVIOUS CHAPTER we discussed Matthew's use of prophetic themes, mostly in relation to his Pharisaic/rabbinic opponents. As noted, such a task is not without problems since we must rely so heavily on rabbinic literature from a later time to determine the views of Matthew's opponents. An alternative and complementary area of study—one that promises to give us greater insight into Matthew's understanding of the prophetic vocation—is that of prophets in the late Second Temple period in Syro-Palestine. This area of study is less concerned with the social phenomena to which Matthew is responding (such as his opponents) and more concerned with the historical traditions and forces that inform his concepts and symbolic universe.

While the central subject matter of this study's analysis of Jesus' prophetic vocation is to be found within the narrative of the First Gospel, it is necessary for us to detail some of the socio-historical background of prophecy at the time of Jesus that informs this narrative. Narratives exist within a sphere of social history, and it would be naïve to assume that Matthew's story is in any way dissimilar. For us to do justice to Matthew's depiction of Jesus' prophetic role we must understand the social history that informs the content of the story being told.

Problems of Studying Prophecy around the Time of Jesus

The study of prophets and prophetic activity in and around the time and geography of Jesus of Nazareth suffers from at least several problems that should initially be acknowledged. The first of these is simply the relative lack of primary sources. In his seminal work, *Bandits, Prophets and Messiahs*,[1] Richard Horsley attempts to set out a social history of Palestine up to the Bar Kokhba revolt of 132–35 CE, focusing on the role of the peasantry in the first and early-second centuries CE. One of the key movements occupying Horsley's attention is that of popular prophets, though Horsley acknowledges the lack of primary evidence in researching this social phenomenon.[2] Much of the book's first-century history is reliant on the work of Josephus, which Horsley acknowledges is problematic, in part due to Josephus' aristocratic perspective.[3]

The second issue that has hindered study of prophecy at the time of Jesus is the widespread belief that prophecy ceased during the so-called "Intertestamental period."[4] This single assumption has left studies of post-Exilic prophecy up to the time of the origins of Christianity severely wanting. While in recent decades the body of material investigating this issue is growing, it is far from comprehensive. Unfortunately, this is not the setting to consider the issues of the continuation of prophecy during the Second Temple Period.[5] For our purposes it is sufficient to say that there are a number of texts, not least in Josephus' writings, that seem to demonstrate the existence of prophecy, and that this was not a surprising or sudden state of affairs.[6] Moreover, the texts that have tended to be adopted in making the case that prophecy ceased are questionable at best; there seems to be no universal dogma in Second Temple Judaism that such cessation had occurred, but rather a "nostalgic belief that there were no longer any prophets *like the prophets of old*."[7]

---

1. Horsley with Hanson, *Bandits, Prophets and Messiahs*.

2. Horsley with Hanson, *Bandits, Prophets and Messiahs*, xxx–xl (esp. xxxiv–xxxv).

3. Horsley with Hanson, *Bandits, Prophets and Messiahs*, xxxi–xxxii.

4. At a more popular level is Grudem, *Gift of Prophecy*, who argues that prophecy ceased when the Old Testament was completed (he assumes this was around the time of Malachi). This is due to his assumption that prophetic utterances by OT prophets always had the same authority as Scripture, and so when OT Scripture was no longer being written prophecy must have ceased. This conclusion misrepresents prophecy during the OT period, and also mistakes the dating of a number of OT books (an error that effectively undermines a large portion of Grudem's case). A more scholarly treatment of this subject is Sommer, "Did Prophecy Cease?," 31–47, who argues that the more recent attempts to show that prophecy continued after its supposed post-Exile demise are unconvincing.

5. See Aernie, *Is Paul Also Among the Prophets?*, 28–51, for an overview of the prophetic tradition in Second Temple Judaism.

6. Josephus, *J.W.* 1.78–80; 2.112–13, 159, 259–63; 6.283–88, 300–309; *Ant.* 13.311–13; 14.172–76; 15.3–4, 370; 17.345–48; 20.97–99, 168–72.

7. Hooker, *Signs of a Prophet*, 6.

The third problem for our task is the definition of the terms "prophet" and "prophecy." Such definition is a treacherous task in light of the dialectic between, on the one hand, requiring a working definition to engage with the Matthean text and, on the other hand, allowing the narrative to construct the definition. In this chapter, the approach taken will be to study some of those Jewish figures in the first century expressly named as προφήτης or ψευδοπροφήτης. Such figures are recorded in Josephus because they were held by some to be prophets. This of course runs a risk of binding prophecy to a particular vocabulary,[8] a potential semantic, methodological, and historical fallacy. Still, such figures provide the groundwork for what was considered a prophet or prophecy at the time and, by extension, a working definition.

Types of Jewish Prophets and Prophecy in the First Century CE

A consideration that must be addressed before launching into a study of historical occurrences of prophets is that of categorization: what types of prophets existed, and on which will this study focus? A range of opinions exist.

R. Meyer notes the distinct perspectives on prophecy that arise from Palestinian and Alexandrian sources.[9] For Meyer, seers and prophets are interchangeable references, while the figure of John Hyrcanus merits his own category ("The Ruler with the Threefold Office"), though for both assertions no justification is given.[10] Meyer also creates the category of messianic prophet,[11] a reference to two distinct identities combined that, though conceivably residing within a single figure, should probably be studied separately. According to Meyer, each of these categories falls within his broader category of "historical manifestations," which he distinguishes from apocalyptic literature.

Jürgen Becker discerns four types of prophet in early Judaism:[12]

1. The prophet who knows God's will in cases unforeseen by the law through charismatic endowment by the Spirit

---

8. So Boring, *Continuing Voice of Jesus*, 54.

9. See Meyer, "προφήτης," 6:819–23.

10. Meyer, "προφήτης," 6:823–26.

11. Meyer, "προφήτης," 6:826–27.

12. Becker, *Johannes der Täufer und Jesus von Nazareth*, 44–60.

2. The political-nationalistic prophet without eschatological understanding

3. Eschatological prophets

4. The charismatic prophet who represents God and demands repentance for Israel to escape judgement

Such a typology is problematic. The rigid lines of distinction between Becker's "types" are largely blurred in light of the primary evidence, particularly when viewed within the social context in which the prophets functioned. What, for example, is the difference between an eschatological prophet and a charismatic prophet who demands repentance if Israel is to escape judgement? Moreover, in Becker's schema there is no way to distinguish between historical prophets and theoretical prophets (such as an ideal but non-historical eschatological prophet).[13]

Aune provides a more developed framework for categories of prophecy and prophets:[14]

1. Apocalyptic literature

2. Eschatological prophecy

   a. Within a millenarian movement

   b. Unrelated to a millenarian movement

3. Clerical prophecy

4. Sapiential Prophecy (both Palestinian and diaspora)

Aune's framework is, overall, quite sound, though Webb raises questions around the second category and Aune's failure to distinguish between messianic and prophetic expectation.[15] Webb himself sets out three categories of prophet, similar to Aune, namely:[16]

1. Clerical prophets

2. Sapiential prophets

3. Popular prophets

The absence of apocalyptic literature in Webb's typology is unexplained, though it probably has to do with the fact that Webb focuses on prophets

13. For more discussion on Becker's typologies, see Aune, *Prophecy in Early Christianity*, 107.

14. Aune, *Prophecy in Early Christianity*, 103–52.

15. Webb, *John the Baptizer and Prophet*, 315.

16. Webb, *John the Baptizer and Prophet*, 307–48.

rather than prophecy and, though these are necessarily linked, apocalyptic literature, which is not a focus for Webb, falls into the latter category.[17] In our case the focus is also on prophets. Still, it is worth noting that I believe the old contrast of "apocalyptic" with "prophetic" to be mistaken, assuming as it does that "prophecy" (i.e., "OT prophecy," most notably during the monarchic period) is basically a static phenomenon. I understand prophecy to be a broader concept that is able to accommodate the literary genre "apocalyptic." N. T. Wright says it well: "'Apocalyptic' . . . represents what happens to prophecy under certain historical and theological circumstances, notably continued oppression and the puzzle of what God is going to do about it and how."[18]

Webb's categories seem most helpful since eschatological orientation is not excluded from any typology, as it is with Aune. This is important since eschatological elements can be detected in at least one Pharisaic example of sapiential prophecy.[19] Further, Webb's typology is helpful in that it is based not on the content, form, or nature of prophecies, but on the social role of the prophets themselves. This makes most sense for us in seeking to study Jesus' prophetic vocation in light of social history and the Matthean narrative.

In order to narrow our study here it is important to determine which of these categories warrant further investigation. This choice does not need to be made complicated since Webb's astute analysis convincingly shows that clerical, sapiential, and popular prophets were each found among particular classes of people. Clerical prophets were affiliated with the temple priesthood and the ruling class, while sapiential prophets came from sectarian groups, mainly the Essenes but also the Pharisees, and functioned as recognized wise persons, forming part of the "small, intellectual elite of Palestine."[20] Popular prophets, however, functioned within "the social milieu of . . . the common people or populace."[21] The tag "popular" designates not universal acceptance, but rather that their primary social sphere was the common populace, that

17. The topic of apocalyptic, its meaning and nature, is of course complex and contested. See Bauckham, "Rise of Apocalyptic," 39–64; Rowland, *Open Heaven*; Collins, *Oxford Handbook of Apocalyptic Literature*, esp. 1–16.

18. Wright, *Paul*, 50. See also Grabbe, "Prophetic and Apocalyptic," 107–33: "apocalyptic writing should be seen simply as a species of the broader category of prophetic writing" (129).

19. Josephus, *Ant.* 17.41–45.

20. Webb, *John the Baptizer and Prophet*, 317–32. Webb's discussion on these types of prophecy is a worthwhile summary of the primary literature, though such a summary is too detailed for this study.

21. Webb, *John the Baptizer and Prophet*, 333.

is, the peasantry. Here it could be said that the nature and methods of the prophetic gift associated with clerical and sapiential prophets was quite similar—according to Webb's analysis of the primary sources, they heard voices and interpreted dreams, signs, and scripture and predicted events, most often political in subject.[22] Popular prophets were a different phenomenon altogether, a divide acknowledged by Horsley's differentiation of clerical and sapiential prophets as "seers" (μάντεις; i.e., diviners) and popular prophets as "prophets."[23] Popular prophets conform broadly to the pattern set by OT prophecy and prophets, such as Moses, Joshua, and the classical prophets. According to Webb, popular prophets can be divided into leaders of movements and solitary figures and, for all their differences, both types shared an eschatological orientation to deliverance.[24]

There is no doubt in Matthew that Jesus is, among other roles, presented as a prophet. But which kind? There are several factors in the First Gospel to suggest that Jesus is portrayed as a popular prophet, including: (1) the primary social setting of Jesus' ministry among the peasantry; (2) the testimony of common people throughout Matthew expressing belief in Jesus' prophetic identity; (3) the people's recurring expectation of socio-political liberation by way of his action; and (4) the apparent lack of intellectual, elite, and sacerdotal support for Jesus' ministry. It would seem natural to associate Jesus with other popular prophets of his time rather than with clerical or sapiential figures. We will soon return to discussing instances of popular prophets in greater detail. For now, two detours are required: the first relates to how we might understand prophetic eschatology in the first century, and the second is a lengthier discussion of the socio-political and economic conditions of that period.

Prophetic Eschatology in the First Century CE

As the above typologies may have indicated, eschatological expectation was an important ingredient in some prophetic movements. Already, numerous references have been made in this chapter to an "eschatological orientation," but what exactly do we mean by "eschatology"? Such a question forces a reasonable and necessary detour.

The term "eschatology" is of course a relatively modern one,[25] coined to describe the systematic theological study of and reflection on

22. Webb, *John the Baptizer and Prophet*, 317–32.

23. Horsley, "'Like One of the Prophets of Old,'" 435–63.

24. Webb, *John the Baptizer and Prophet*, 347.

25. Borg suggests the first use of the term was by Lutheran theologian Abraham

the "last things." In other words, "eschatology" is a theological concept, not a historical one *per se*. As an ongoing theological pursuit, such study has its place. However, problems arise when contemporary eschatological schemes are imposed onto ancient Jewish and Christian texts which may not have been intended to deal with "last things" in the sense of systematic theology. This is not to say that the language of "eschatology" cannot be applied in biblical and historical studies legitimately, but that there are inherent problems since anachronistic systematic theological concepts may distort our readings of the relevant texts.

Dating back at least to Albert Schweitzer, "eschatology" has commonly been associated with apocalyptic. This is understandable since apocalyptic literature is perhaps the most important source in ancient literature for determining the nature of Jewish and Christian eschatologies.[26] One of the most positive elements of Schweitzer's work was that Jesus' proclamation was identified as being historical and eschatological. This was in contrast to the earlier Enlightenment concept of Albrecht Ritschl and others in which Jesus was portrayed as the conveyor of an ahistorical liberal moral ethic. For Schweitzer, Jesus was the proclaimer of the imminent eschatological kingdom of God. Schweitzer's definition of eschatology, however, is difficult to pin down.[27] Overall, it seems to refer to the imminent arrival of the kingdom of God, what Schweitzer famously described as "that last revolution which is to bring all ordinary history to a close."[28] In this scheme, eschatology is a notion referring to the literal end of history, a view (or assumption) that has been taken up by many subsequent biblical scholars.

Other schools of thought emerged in the twentieth century. Rudolf Bultmann demythologized Schweitzer's eschatology, making it into a dramatic existential event for the individual:[29] "In every moment slumbers the

---

Calov in 1677. "[I]t was the title of the last section of his dogmatics, in which he treated death, judgment, consummation, hell, everlasting death and life everlasting." Borg, *Jesus in Contemporary Scholarship*, 70.

26. "[T]he apocalypses are our major source of information about the eschatological beliefs of Jews at the beginning of the Christian era." Rowland, *Open Heaven*, 29.

27. See Crossan, *Birth of Christianity*, 274–75, for a brief survey of this problem.

28. Schweitzer, *Quest of the Historical Jesus*, 370.

29. "The Reign of God is a power which wholly determines the present although in itself it is entirely future. It determines the present in that it forces man to decision: he becomes one thing or the other, chosen or rejected, his entire present experience determined by it. . . . The coming of the Kingdom of God is not therefore actually an event in the course of time, which will come within time and to which a man will be able to take up a position, or even hold himself neutral. Rather, before he takes up a position he is already revealed for what he is, and he must therefore realize that the necessity for decision is the essential quality of his being. Because Jesus so sees man as

possibility of being the eschatological moment. You must awaken it."[30] C. H. Dodd, on the other hand, rejected Schweitzer's imminent eschatology in favor of what he called "realized eschatology," the view that Jesus spoke of the kingdom of God as present rather than future.[31] Still, for Dodd, eschatology referred to the coming of the kingdom of God.[32] Dodd did not consider it to refer to the end of history but to a range of historical expectations within Judaism, most ultimately the coming of a new, transcendent age.[33] Despite their differences, each of these perspectives construes eschatology as an expected dramatic event of divine causation—for Schweitzer this event was in the near future, for Bultmann an existential decision forced by divine power and possible in the present and future, and for Dodd a previously expected event that has moved from the future to the present and that may be expected to occur in a fuller sense in the future.

That Schweitzer seems to have equated "eschatology" with "apocalyptic" (much of the time at least[34]), and that subsequent scholars have often

---

standing in this crisis of decision before the activity of God, it is understandable that in him the Jewish expectation becomes the absolute certainty that now the hour of the breaking-in of the Reign of God has come. If man stands in the crisis of decision, and if this is the essential characteristic of his being as a man, then indeed every hour is the last hour, and it is understandable that for Jesus the whole contemporary mythology should be pressed into the service of this conception of human existence and that in the light of this he should understand and proclaim his hour as the last hour." Bultmann, *Jesus and the Word*, 52.

30. Bultmann, *History and Eschatology*, 155.

31. "This declaration that the Kingdom of God has already come necessarily dislocates the whole eschatological scheme in which its expected coming closes the long vista of the future. The *eschaton* has moved from the future to the present, from the sphere of expectation into that of realized experience." Dodd, *Parables of the Kingdom*, 40–41.

32. "'The Kingdom of God' is a hope for the future. It is itself the *eschaton*, or 'ultimate,' with which 'eschatology' is concerned." Dodd, *Parables of the Kingdom*, 30.

33. Dodd notes that some expectations may be "temporal and political" while others may be "associated with the final and absolute state of bliss in a transcendent order." *Parables of the Kingdom*, 30–31. Dodd goes on to say that "[i]n all these forms of belief the common underlying idea is that of God's sovereign power becoming manifestly effective in the world of human experience." *Parables of the Kingdom*, 32.

34. "For Schweitzer, then, *eschatology* and *world-negation* are synonyms. Schweitzer, however, also interjects the term *apocalyptic* into this debate. On the one hand he uses *eschatological* and *apocalyptic* to mean the same thing, referring on subsequent pages to, first, 'the eschatology of the time of Jesus' . . . and, then, 'the apocalyptic movement at the time of Jesus.' . . . On the other hand, in between, he distinguishes between 'two eschatologies'—one prophetic, with Elijah as hero, and one apocalyptic, with Daniel as hero. He distinguishes them by claiming that apocalyptic eschatology is created by 'external events,' while prophetic eschatology is created by 'great personalities' . . . a distinction whose romanticism would probably not hold up well to close scrutiny. But,

continued to use the two interchangeably further obfuscates our definitional predicament. Marcus Borg is worth quoting at length regarding the
ongoing confusion:

> "Eschatology" and "apocalyptic" . . . were initially used in Jesus
> studies to refer to the end of the world of ordinary history. But
> subsequent scholarship in this century has given the terms many
> different senses. "Eschatological" can be used metaphorically in
> a non-end-of-the-world sense: as a nuanced synonym for "deci-
> sive," or as "world-shattering," or to point to the *telos* of history
> entering history but not in such a way as to end history. Even
> "apocalyptic," we are discovering, need not refer to the end of
> the world; some apocalyptic literature describes experiences of
> another world (visions or other-worldly journeys) and does not
> refer to the imminent end of the world of ordinary history.
>
> Thus, there is considerable terminological confusion in
> the discipline. For example, I have heard one scholar argue
> that Jesus' message was eschatological but not apocalyptic,
> that is, concerned with a decisive change in history, but not
> with the end of the world. I have heard another scholar argue
> that Jesus' message was apocalyptic but not eschatological;
> that is, grounded in the experience of another world, but not
> concerned with the end of this world. Despite the directly con-
> trasting language, at a fundamental level both scholars meant
> the same thing: Jesus did not proclaim the imminent end of the
> world of ordinary history.[35]

Indeed, it continues to be common for "eschatology" and "apocalyptic" to be used interchangeably to refer to the end of history. Borg is
right, however, to point out that apocalyptic and eschatology need not refer
to the end of history. Referring to J. J. Collins' well-known definition of
the literary genre "apocalypse"—which claims that apocalyptic "envisages
eschatological salvation"[36]—Richard Bauckham notes that such would be
disputed in recent study of the apocalypses.[37] Note that by "eschatological" both Collins and Bauckham imply the end of history.[38] For Bauckham,

---

leaving that explanation aside, we now have (1) *eschatology* used as a genus with at least
two species (*apocalyptic* and *prophetic*) and (2) *eschatology* as a synonym for one of
those species. That, I think, is the root of our definitional problem. You cannot have it
both ways." Crossan, *Birth of Christianity*, 275 (emphasis original).

35. Borg, *Jesus in Contemporary Scholarship*, 8–9.

36. Collins, "Introduction," 9.

37. Bauckham, *Theology of the Book of Revelation*, 6.

38. Speaking of Revelation, Bauckham goes on to say that, "John's apocalypse, [in

apocalyptic is not necessarily "eschatological" since it does not necessarily refer to the end of history. However, all apocalyptic is eschatological in the sense described by Borg, that is, as a metaphor for a decisive, world-shattering historical event. For John Howard Yoder, apocalyptic eschatology is not world-ending since it was rooted in God's past liberating actions for Israel, God's judgement of evil, and a continuation of human experience in space and time. He says of Jesus' apocalyptic predictions:

> We tend to think of "apocalyptic" promises as pointing "off the map" of human experience, off the scale of time, in that they announce an end to history. But the past deliverances of Israel had been recounted as having taken place within their own history and on their own Palestinian soil. The whole body of hermeneutic prejudices linked with the concept of the "interim ethic," as if what Jesus was predicting was an end to time and space, gets us off the track right at this point. Jesus' proclamation of the kingdom was unacceptable to most of his listeners *not* because they thought it could not happen but because they feared it might, and that it would bring down judgment upon them.[39]

The picture painted by Yoder of apocalyptic eschatology is one of hope for the kingdom of God to arrive *in history*, not to put an end to it. In a similar vein, speaking of apocalyptic language regarding the eschatological new age, N. T. Wright makes the following statement that, though not speaking of it by name, offers an explicit critique of a Schweitzerian concept of eschatology:

> When [first-century Jews] used what we might call cosmic imagery to describe the coming new age, such language cannot be read in a crassly literalistic way without doing it great violence. . . . Far more important to the first-century Jew than questions of space, time and literal cosmology were the key issues of Temple, Land, and Torah, of race, economy and justice.

contrast to other Jewish apocalypses,] is exclusively concerned with eschatology: with eschatological judgment and salvation, and with the impact of these on the present situation in which he writes." Bauckham, *Theology of Revelation*, 6. For Bauckham eschatology may have ramifications in the present, but it is ultimately in reference to a once-off, future event.

39. Yoder, *Politics of Jesus*, 85 (emphasis original). It would be remiss of me not to draw attention to the issues involved in quoting the work of Yoder. There is a tension inherent in the prolificacy of both his writing on reconciliation, nonviolence, and ethics on the one hand, and his acts of sexual abuse on the other. By quoting Yoder, I do not wish to dismiss the complexity of these issues, nor overlook his abusive legacy, especially given that the journey of healing and reconciliation continues for many of Yoder's victims.

When Israel's god acted, Jews would be restored to their ancestral rights and would practice their ancestral religion, with the rest of the world looking on in awe, and/or making pilgrimages to Zion, and/or being ground to powder under Jewish feet. . . . Within the mainline Jewish writings of this period, covering a wide range of styles, genres, political persuasions and theological perspectives, *there is virtually no evidence that Jews were expecting the end of the space-time universe.* . . . They believed that *the present world order* would come to an end—the world order in which pagans held power, and Jews, the covenant people of the creator god, did not.[40]

The reconsideration of "eschatology" is not simply a matter of opening the word up to a new, broader meaning; it is a matter of doubting the historicity of the prevailing understanding in light of Jewish apocalyptic texts. Apocalyptic, as a chief source of insight into Jewish and Christian eschatological thought, provides a window into our understanding of eschatology from a historical perspective. There is little doubt that the eschatological fervor present in much of first-century Palestine was influenced by apocalyptic. The key question that arises is the nature of the expected divine action ("eschatology") found in apocalyptic literature. Petersen's definition of eschatology, a rare case of a sustained attempt at a definition, is a good illustration of the standard view:

> [Biblical eschatology] refers to a time in the future in which the course of history will be changed to such an extent that one can speak of an entirely new state of reality . . . [it describes] the last things in a worldwide and historical sense, e.g., an apocalyptic, cosmic cataclysm, and a new age followed by utopian bliss.[41]

Here Petersen begins generally (eschatology as new state of reality) before becoming more specific (last things—apocalyptic cataclysm, new age, utopian bliss). But Petersen's "new age followed by utopian bliss" is itself open to numerous interpretations. Does "utopian bliss" denote a perfected future state, or simply a future in which Israel/the church is able to exist freely in a world that has been set right but that is still ontologically the same? Is this "utopian bliss" truly a final state of affairs, the "last things," or does history simply continue in a new and improved situation?

Aune seems to clear some of the confusion by arguing that the basic horizon of the apocalyptic worldview is that "the End should recapitulate

---

40. Wright, *New Testament*, 284–85, 333 (emphasis original). Cf. Crossan, *Birth of Christianity*, 258.

41. Peterson, "Eschatology (OT)," *ABD* 2:575–76.

the Beginning . . . which is understood as both perfect and paradigmatic."[42] In other words the future is a return to the ideal past. This idea seems basically correct based on the activities of the first-century Palestinian prophets which we will explore below. These figures sought a return to the ideal setting of Israel as a free peasantry, though unlike in Aune's proposed scheme this ideal setting is not Edenic in nature. Aune goes on to explore different themes characteristic of apocalyptic texts—restoration of the land, restoration of kingship, regathering the people, Jerusalem and the temple, the loss and return of Paradise, and the restoration of creation.[43] He notes that these themes seem contradictory, inconsistent, and disordered and concludes that eschatological thought is "resistant to consistency and coherence."[44] However this apparent incoherence may be a symptom less of the internally inconsistent eschatological expectations of apocalyptic writers and more of problems with modern interpretation. The irony is that we are rightly counseled not to take apocalyptic symbolism too literally in our work of interpretation, yet when it comes to apocalyptic imagery regarding time and the future such caution is largely abandoned. Perhaps such imagery has a meaning different from what has been assumed for so long.[45]

To what, then, does the eschatological symbolism of apocalyptic refer? In discussing apocalyptic eschatology, John Dominic Crossan says it is concerned with the imminent "end of the world," but not in a way that brings about the end of space-time or history. On the contrary, apocalyptic eschatology expects "a divine intervention so transcendentally obvious that one's adversaries or enemies, oppressors or persecutors, would be forced to acknowledge it and to accept conversion or concede defeat."[46] This accords well with the function of apocalyptic texts: apocalyptic texts are counterdiscourses designed to change the minds and actions of the audience in the

---

42. Aune, *Apocalypticism, Prophecy and Magic*, 13.

43. Aune, *Apocalypticism, Prophecy and Magic*, 16–36.

44. Aune, *Apocalypticism, Prophecy and Magic*, 36.

45. "Despite the inclusion of occasional mythological elements in the eschatological descriptions, whether it be a belief in a new creation or the intervention of supernatural beings, the apocalypses indicate a view of the future which stresses the outworking of God's purposes within history. A glance at the contents of the apocalypses reveals that other-worldly eschatology is by no means as typical as is often suggested. Indeed, when it is to be found, it is not usually at the expense of the vindication of God's ways within the fabric of history. The eschatology of the apocalypses may have looked to God at work in history as the only means of final salvation, but their authors expected a vindication of their righteousness within the world of men, not in some intangible existence beyond the sphere of history." Rowland, *Open Heaven*, 38.

46. Crossan, *Historical Jesus*, 238.

present.[47] Certainly those apocalyptic texts most influential for early Christians such as Daniel and 1 Enoch critique current ruling empires by "exposing their character (as demonic, monstrous, violent, destructive, or rapacious), revealing their transience, and asserting that they are subject to the greater power of God and accountable to divine judgment."[48] The Christian book of Revelation functions in the same way, that is, it deals less with the future and accurate predictions about such, and more with current realities. The effect of eschatological expectations (transcendental divine intervention) is to help fulfill this larger purpose of exposing the true, transient nature of current empires—such powers are ultimately subject to God who will eventually bring about a transition to a new situation in which they are no longer in control. The actions of the prophets discussed in this chapter and the rebellions of 66–73 CE and 132–35 CE suggest that such an eschatological mood was strong in the first and early second centuries.[49]

If Wright is correct, apocalyptic eschatology is constituted by hope for certain historical ends in which Israel (or whoever) is able to live freely, without domination, in a new age of history. The intense eschatological mood of the first century CE spilled over into numerous attempts to be free of imperial domination, to forge a new historical reality. Even the doctrine of resurrection, so otherworldly in much contemporary thought, functioned partly, in the belief of some Jews, to mark such a historical shift:

> Resurrection functioned . . . not as an abstract doctrine about what happens to God's people (or to anybody) after death, but as a statement about the great turn-around within Israel's fortunes that would shortly take place, and about the fact that when this event happened those who had been loyal to Torah, but had died ahead of time would be raised to share in the blessings of the Age to Come.[50]

47. See Portier-Young, *Apocalypse Against Empire*, esp. 383.

48. Portier-Young, *Apocalypse Against Empire*, 45.

49. It is here also worth mentioning the Qumranic War Scroll. This text is so often said to represent the otherworldly eschatology of Qumran, however I find this conclusion problematic. There is no indication in the War Scroll that the final battle occurs anywhere else but in the midst of history. The War Scroll may have God helping the people to defeat the *Kittim*, but this is not too different from stories in, say, Joshua or the Kings narratives. In the War Scroll, following the depiction of the final victory, the people are told to take their captives and plunder, crush the nations and let their swords devour flesh. The land (Zion) is to be filled with glory, as well as cattle, gold, silver—the wealth of the nations. Those who once oppressed will bow down before the victors (and lick the dust from their feet). All of this leads to an eternal dominion. (1QM 19.2b–8).

50. Wright, "Christian Origins and the Resurrection of Jesus," 107–23. Wright goes on: "The resurrection of the dead was thus both a symbol for the coming of the new

This type of historical expectation also fits broadly into "non-apocalyptic" and pre-apocalyptic forms of eschatology.[51] Certainly early prophetic expectations of the future in Israel did not depict the "new age to come" as a perfected utopian bliss, much less the end of history. According to Bauckham:

> The Old Testament's classic picture of utopian existence: 'everyone under his vine and his fig tree' (e.g. 1 Kgs. 4:25; Mic 4:4). This is simply the life of the ordinary peasant family at its best: owning their own modest smallholding, producing enough to live and with leisure enough to enjoy it, and with no threat from the rapacious rich or foreign invasion. Even when imagining the idyllic future, Israelite peasants wanted no more than this in material terms.[52]

If Bauckham is correct, then the eschatological vision of Israel's prophets looked forward to a time when people could live in peace *within history*. There was no expectation that divine intervention would bring about an ontologically different existence.

What is difficult to determine accurately is the nature of the later eschatological expectation of prophetic figures in first-century Palestine. It is questionable whether first-century prophets should be directly connected to the early prophets of Israel, given the time separating them.[53] Certainly, apocalyptic texts were highly influential in first-century Palestine, and we can expect that the widespread apocalyptic mood of the time was a

---

ages, and itself, taken literally, one central element in the package: when YHWH restored the fortunes of his people, then of course Abraham, Isaac, and Jacob, together with all God's people down to and including the martyrs who had died in the cause, would be reembodied, raised to new life in God's new world."

51. The distinction between "apocalyptic" and "non-apocalyptic" is of course imprecise since there is no clear-cut division, but at best a spectrum. Such language does, however, help as a general descriptor.

52. Bauckham, *James*, 201.

53. Although, Aernie, having outlined the prophetic tradition in Second Temple Judaism, is persuasive: "It appears that the continued prophetic activity of the Second Temple period correlates with the Old Testament prophetic material in two ways. First, there is a tendency to relate, either implicitly or explicitly, leaders or other prominent figures within the Second Temple period with earlier prophetic figures in order to establish the authority of the former. Secondly, the prophetic material of the Old Testament itself is used as source material for new prophetic activity, either through literary re-presentations or exegetical practices. Thus, while the material from the Second Temple period witnesses in some ways to distinctions between its own prophetic activity and that described in the Old Testament, it seems that the organic prophetic tradition continued to exist in its own right and was applied in a variety of ways to the social and religious circumstances of the Second Temple period." Aernie, *Is Paul Also Among the Prophets?*, 51.

dominant influence on any prophet. Indeed, as stated earlier, apocalyptic is what prophecy looks like "under certain historical and theological circumstances."[54] There is an indissoluble connection between prophecy and apocalyptic and the distinction often drawn between the two is far too wide. Given the actions of the prophets we will soon discuss, it would appear that the eschatological expectations of first-century prophetic figures align broadly with apocalyptic eschatology. That is to say, the prophets of the first century CE did not look forward to the end of history or space-time, but rather to a radical, world-shattering vision or program, divinely sanctioned, manufacturing a transition from the corrupt present world order in the midst of ongoing history.

It should be noted that, following Dodd's thought in *The Parables of the Kingdom*, it is highly likely that within this sweep there was a range of eschatological expectation regarding the nature of the expected divine action and the scope of its effects. Among the subtle differences and unique details, some perhaps even looked forward to the end of history, though this was far from a dominant view. Broadly speaking, though, what has been described above covers the general nature of first-century eschatological expectation. Obviously this understanding of prophetic eschatology makes sense only in light of what we can ascertain about the beliefs of first-century Jewish prophets from their words and deeds. As we will see, the connection is consistent.

Though its lack of comprehensiveness does not do proper service to the complexity of the topic, this analysis should serve to clarify what I mean by "eschatology" in the remainder of this study. Though a more detailed exploration would be ideal, this is simply not the context in which to undertake it. Strictly speaking, the use of the term "eschatology" in this context is a misnomer in terms of the corresponding systematic field of study. In biblical studies, however, it is a redefinition of what has been called "eschatological."

Moving forward, the question arises as to why eschatological currents would run so strongly in the first century CE. Why were so many people so desperate for an end to the present order? The answer may well lie in the socio-political conditions of the time.

2.2   A Survey of Socio-Political and Economic Conditions Leading Up To and During the First Century CE

It would be to miss the point of popular prophetic movements simply to describe their different historical expressions without reference to the

---

54. Wright, *Paul: Fresh Perspectives*, 50.

socio-historical conditions that gave rise to them. A description of such conditions is no easy task, for as T. F. Carney has aptly stated: "The voices that speak to us from antiquity are overwhelmingly those of the cultured few; the elites."[55] For the remainder of the population, those whom popular prophetic movements represented, such vocalization is largely absent.[56] It is with caution, then, that Josephus is here adopted as the primary source material for such movements.

It should be admitted at this point that Richard Horsley's assessments, particularly in *Bandits, Prophets and Messiahs*, are a major influence on the content of this chapter. This is not without a critical awareness of potential problems with Horsley's readings. Horsley's work in *Bandits* is shaped by a concern for the role of the masses in first-century Palestine. Socio-economic forces occupy a central place in Horsley's analysis, to the point that it could be said to be functionally Marxist in nature. This is not a criticism as much as an acknowledgement—certainly, a historical materialist and dialectical reading of the primary sources could reap significant rewards in studying prophetic movements. That he is given to relying too heavily on Josephus as a primary source (an issue shared by the present chapter) is admitted by Horsley himself. The reality is that, apart from archaeological findings and sections of the New Testament, there is little in the way of primary sources regarding first-century Palestinian life.

The difficulty of presenting a socio-economic history of Palestine leading up to the first century CE cannot be overstated. What is presented here is necessarily generalized. Moreover, in the case of many episodes in the history of Israel described below there is no historical evidence apart from the OT, a set of texts unlikely to have been intended as a rigorous historical source. What we are bound to end up with in this section is an account that is less about "what actually happened" and more about what first-century CE residents of Palestine may have perceived to have happened, though the lines are often blurred.

The entirety of the first century CE in Palestine was dominated by the phenomenon of Roman imperialism. Subsequent to the dynasty of the Hasmoneans, which had begun following the Maccabean revolt of 167–142 BCE, Rome began to occupy Palestine in 63 BCE. For the Jewish people, this was another foreign empire in a succession that had ruled over them throughout their history, beginning with Egypt at the time of Moses.[57]

55. Carney, *Shape of the Past*, xiv.

56. Perhaps the most notable exceptions are the Gospels themselves.

57. Here I am assuming, as would have most first-century Jews, that the Exodus story is broadly a historical one, though it is not clear that this is the case. An alternative view—one of many to which I could point—is that of Howard-Brook, "*Come Out, My*

The event of liberation from Egyptian rule under the leadership of Moses provided the definitive narrative and experience for Israel inasmuch as it identified "their God as the one 'who brought you out of the land of Egypt, out of the house of bondage' (Ex 20:2)."[58] The foundation for Israel's identity was one of liberation from foreign rule by the hand of God, with whom they would come into covenant as a free peasantry.[59] Indeed, God was Israel's king, and there was, according to the narrative, to be no human king or state in the early period of the nation. This, of course, changed with the foreign and domestic military pressures that eventually led Israel to form a more centralized government, resulting eventually in the Davidic monarchy under which military concentration could occur. This monarchy did not, however, find the peasantry to be submissive; two revolts occurred against David (2 Sam 13–20) and, in the aftermath of Solomon's rule, the Israelite tribes were split into the northern and southern kingdoms.

It was in this period that court prophets appeared in both kingdoms, proclaiming God's judgement on the rulers, the elites, and the temple institution for their oppression and unjust treatment of the people, as well as criticizing the institution of the monarchy itself.[60] This was, in a sense, a call to return to what was deemed the original covenantal existence of early Israel. Whatever the historical reality undergirding the prophets' call may have been, the many warnings of the prophets were apparently confirmed when both kingdoms were eventually conquered and exiled, effectively collapsing the monarchies. The gathering of prophetic writings of the time seems to demonstrate that prophetic protest was vindicated in popular tradition. It is to this time of exile that the origins of apocalyptic literature can be traced in Second Isaiah, Ezekiel, and Zechariah, with the apocalyptic genre developing out of the prophetic tradition[61] and functioning to communicate eschatological salvation to those on the margins of Babylonian power.[62]

People!" Howard-Brook argues that the story of Moses was written as a response to the monarchical narrative ("Zion theology") presented in Samuel–Kings, and especially the Solomonic propaganda of Kings. According to Howard-Brook, the Moses narrative is not demonstrably historical—though there may have been a real Moses—but rather it is a myth (in the most positive sense), as is the existence of a pre-monarchical tribal confederacy. These claims, if true, do not have a significant bearing on this study, but they ought to be raised.

58. Horsley with Hanson, *Bandits, Prophets and Messiahs*, 5.

59. The phrase "free peasantry in covenant with God" belongs to Horsley, *Bandits, Prophets and Messiahs*, 5.

60. Horsley with Hanson, *Bandits, Prophets and Messiahs*, 7.

61. Following the conclusion of Hanson, *Dawn of Apocalyptic*.

62. Witherington, *Jesus the Seer*, 165–66. Witherington argues that apocalyptic does not necessarily deal with eschatology, though I contend his concept of eschatology

The eventual return of the southern kingdom was overshadowed by Persian and then Greek rule. Under this rule, vast projects of rebuilding were begun by the aristocracy, resulting in increased labor for the peasantry, much like that which occurred under David and Solomon. As Horsley points out, even by the time of Nehemiah there was a reestablishment of the old hierarchical social structure and thus a sharp divide in socio-economic conditions as the gentry took advantage of the poor (Neh 5:1–5).[63] The new temple, owing to the lack of a monarchy, became the seat of control for politico-economic power, which was now directed by the priesthood. The temple system in the Second Temple period was predictably criticized by some marginalized groups as represented in prophetic texts like Third Isaiah[64] and Second Zechariah.[65]

The eventual conquest of Palestine by Alexander the Great in the fourth century BCE and the ensuing cultural domination of the Seleucids often benefited the Jewish elite. They were generally comfortable with the religious, political, and cultural compromises with Hellenism that took place since conformity to Seleucid domination resulted in political and economic advantages for them.[66] Such compromise once again weighed on the rest of the population of Judea as the priesthood collected taxes, a practice that was viewed by the people as collusion with foreign empire (by none other

---

is too narrow. See the discussion of eschatology above.

63. Horsley with Hanson, *Bandits, Prophets and Messiahs*, 9.

64. Smith, *Isaiah 40–66*, 516. This theory of a third Isaianic author was proposed by Duhm, *Das Buch Jesaia*, 390–95. It is worth mentioning that John Oswalt, on the composition of Isaiah, notes that "at the present time, the idea of several independent books of Isaiah is in eclipse"; Oswalt, *Book of Isaiah: Chapters 40–66*, 4. This is not to deny the varied authorship and dating present in the final composition—chapters 40–66 were clearly written in a different historical situation than 1–39—but rather to assert the theological unity of the book. In other words, Isa 56–66 represents a section distinct from the rest of the book, deriving from a distinct historical situation, but nonetheless it must be understood in the context of Isaiah as a whole.

65. Though different sources criticize the temple for varying reasons, in particular ritual impurity and economic injustice, e.g., Zech 14:21; Mal 1:10; Ps of Sol 1:8; 8:11–13; Damascus Document (CD) 6:13–17; 1QS 8:1–10; 4Q174 3:3–7; 1QpHab 8:8–13; 12:9; Matt 24; Mark 13.

66. Portier-Young, *Apocalypse Against Empire*, 112. Portier-Young makes the important point that the Hellenization of the Near East was not a matter of cultural evangelism on the part of the Hellenistic kings, nor was there a conflict between "Judaism" and "Hellenism" as has often been suggested. Such conclusions would imply static cultures doing battle against one another, but this is simply not the case—cultures are always hybrid. Portier-Young suggests that Hellenization was actually a tool for domination since it asserted certain symbols of power embedded in Hellenistic culture and identity. Resistance against such symbols amounted to resistance against domination and the related threats against identity and practice.

than the supposed mediators between the people and their god). During the Seleucid period, there appeared texts such as Daniel and sections of 1 Enoch that formed the first full-blown apocalyptic literature. Such literature formed an expression of prophetic resistance:

> The historical apocalypses . . . oriented a terrorized people through these traumas to a vision of a future ordered by divine justice. Prophetic visions of past, present and future asserted a transience and finitude to temporal powers. These earliest extant historical apocalypses articulated a resistant counterdiscourse to the discourse and project of empire.[67]

Successive high priests, supported by the Seleucid regime, undertook projects of Hellenization, particularly in Jerusalem. There is no evidence of any meaningful challenge to such Hellenization so long as the population was left to live their lives under Torah.[68] This changed, however, under Antiochus IV's well-known religio-cultural persecution of the Jews. Moreover, the High Priest Menalaus—whose high bid for his position had landed him in financial trouble—raised taxes in order to cover the tribute to Antiochus IV since he and his predecessors had exhausted the temple funds.[69] As the civic powers of the aristocracy grew—comfortably colluding with the Seleucids, as most were—that of the rest of the population decreased. These and other factors inevitably led to acts of resistance and violence, and eventually a widespread revolt that had the effect of removing the Seleucid occupation of Judea and installing what would become the Hasmonean dynasty.[70]

For the Jews, the period of the Hasmoneans was the first time they had been free from foreign rule since the time before the exile. Even so, the Hasmonean period was fraught with problems of its own, both internal and external. Ultimately, Hasmonean rule was not to last as the Romans subjugated Palestine in 63 BCE. It should come as no surprise that, with

---

67. Portier-Young, *Apocalypse Against Empire*, 383.

68. Mørkholm, "Antiochus IV," 281.

69. Mørkholm, "Antiochus IV," 281. For another account of this period, see VanderKam, *Introduction to Early Judaism*, 18–24.

70. Josephus suggests the reason for the revolt was due to Antiochus' religious persecution in which, "Antiochus, carried away by his ungovernable passions and with the rankling memory of what he had suffered in the siege, put pressure upon the Jews to violate the code of their country by leaving their infants uncircumcised and sacrificing swine upon the altar" (*J.W.* 1.34). Josephus also gives a hint of a concern not only for the religious integrity of the nation but also the well-being of the people: "Mattathias lamented to his sons over the state of things, the plundering of the city and the spoiling of the Temple, and the misfortunes of the people, and said it was better for them to die for their country's laws than to live so ingloriously" (*Ant.* 12.267).

another foreign empire ruling them, the Jewish populace once again produced a concentration of prophets as had occurred under previous periods of imperial oppression.

Economically, the Jewish peasantry[71] of Palestine experienced regular domination by Roman authorities by way of taxation and tribute. While Rome and its puppet king in Palestine, Herod the Great (from 37 BCE), did not directly regulate agricultural production, it did control the trade of goods through the centralized system of the Jerusalem temple and through increasing concentration of land ownership in the hands of local elites and royals, who acted as imperial clients.[72] Family-based smallholdings were common, though the economic pressures imposed by Rome often led to land alienation amongst the poor who had no means of expanding trade.[73]

The traditional socio-economic arrangement in Palestine was epitomized by land smallholdings that made up a simple, agrarian way of life in which produce was consumed locally.[74] Larger, more developed landholdings were also common, however, particularly royal estates and those former Hasmonean properties that were in the hands of officials.[75] Emilio Gabba notes that the juxtaposition of small and large landholdings could not coexist without difficulty, particularly given the tendency for large holdings to expand.[76] Given restrictions, it would have been common for such

---

71. The meaning of the term "peasant" has often suffered from a lack of precision, and this charge has been labeled against Horsley in Borg, Review of *Bandits, Prophets and Messiahs*, 137. Borg suggests the category of "peasant" includes a broad range of people in an agrarian society like Palestine: "landless peasants, marginal landholders, reasonably secure small farmers and some with larger holdings." Borg insists on a reasonable degree of difference between a landless peasant and a more prosperous farmer. This is an important warning against over-schematizing the Jewish population into clear-cut divisions. The word itself is of far more recent derivation (possibly the Old French *païsan* or Late Middle English *paissaunt*) and is basically anachronistic when applied to first century BCE/CE Palestine. The Old French *païs* meaning "country" is likely derived from the Latin *pagus*, which also means countryside, that is, the area outside of a city. Thus a *païsan* is simply one who lives in the countryside. With this identification comes a set of basic characteristics—a peasant is generally a lower-class person who toils the land in subsistence agriculture relying on the most recent harvest. While acknowledging the important warnings of Borg and others, there is no reason to reject the use of "peasant" as a label describing a wide array of people in agrarian Palestine who were mostly rural subsistence agriculturalists, disconnected from the power structure of the Jerusalem temple.

72. Myers, *Binding the Strong Man*, 48–49.

73. Due to lack of and cost of transport and lack of technological means for preservation of goods; Myers, *Binding the Strong Man*, 49.

74. Gabba, "Social, Economic and Political History," 107.

75. Gabba, "Social, Economic and Political History," 108.

76. Gabba, "Social, Economic and Political History," 108.

expansion to come by way of the seizing of the lands of smallholders[77] who, having been driven off their land by famine or debt, would then likely have needed to offer their services as laborers to the larger property owners.[78] Later, under Herod Antipas, the region of Galilee became a food basket for the wealthy: 97 percent of the arable land was being cultivated and the focus was on feeding those living in the ever-growing cities.[79] Crossan, using Gerhard Lenski's modeling, has estimated that in an advanced agrarian society like Palestine 1 to 2 percent of the population may have consumed from 50 to 65 percent of the agricultural produce.[80] What was not consumed was stored, only to be sold back to the tenant farmer that had grown it, particularly during food shortages or when crops failed.[81] As it turns out, rural peasants were not impressed by imperial storehouses (Josephus, *Life* 70–73; 118–19). Understandably, the relationship between rich and poor was often characterized by discord.

Herod the Great's building projects exacted not only significant labor from the peasantry, but also taxes. Increases in population led to subdivision of peasant land as younger brothers were left landless because of inheritance laws.[82] As Carney summarizes, the basic hallmarks of the peasantry were "political powerlessness and straitened economic circumstances."[83] This was no doubt largely sustained by Herod the Great's centralized bureaucracy, which was probably a remnant of the ethnarchy of Hyrcanus during the Hasmonean era that Herod managed to strengthen and expand into districts containing primarily Jewish populations.[84] This administrative system divided the country into "sections" ruled by divisional commanders ("meridarchs") which were then subdivided into toparchies, and then again into villages, with the entire bureaucratic hierarchy being appointed by the crown.[85] Such an organized system would have allowed Herod to exercise

77. Strabo, *Geogr.* 16.2.37.

78. Gabba, "Social, Economic and Political History," 108.

79. Reed, *Archaeology and the Galilean Jesus*, 84, 88. Korb likens such activity to modern-day industrial farming and agribusiness; Korb, *Life in Year One*, 37, 87.

80. Crossan, *Birth of Christianity*, 154.

81. Reed, *Archaeology and the Galilean Jesus*, 89.

82. Horsley, "Ancient Jewish Banditry," 416–17.

83. Carney, *Shape of the Past*, 198. Myers, *Binding the Strong Man*, 51 describes three obligations of peasants in production; 1) to grow enough food to feed themselves and their animals; 2) to have enough to sow the following year, and; 3) to have surplus because of the social demands of reciprocity and redistributive systems (reflected in the law of Moses).

84. Jones, *Herods of Judaea*, 85.

85. Jones, *Herods of Judaea*, 85.

considerable control over Palestine and its population, particularly the Jews, who so distrusted him for his supplanting of the apparently legitimate Hasmonean dynasty and for his acquiescence with Rome.

Any possible outcry was dulled by the military presence of both Rome and mercenaries loyal to Herod.[86] Herod himself, being as unpopular with his subjects as he was, grounded his authority in force, with fortresses dominating the countryside.[87] Of Herod, Josephus reports:

> [The people] resented his carrying out of such arrangements as seemed to them to mean the dissolution of their religion and the disappearance of their customs. And these matters were discussed by all of them, for they were always being provoked and disturbed. Herod, however, gave the most careful attention to this situation, taking away any opportunities they might have (for agitation) and instructing them to apply themselves at all times to their work. No meeting of citizens was permitted, nor were walking together or being together permitted, and all their movements were observed. Those who were caught were punished severely, and many were taken, either openly or secretly, to the fortress of Hyrcania and there put to death. Both in the city and on the open roads there were men who spied upon those who met together. . . . Those who obstinately refused to go along with his (new) practices he persecuted in all kinds of ways. As for the rest of the populace, he demanded that they submit to taking an oath of loyalty, and he compelled them to make a sworn declaration that they would maintain a friendly attitude to his rule. Now most of the people yielded to his demand out of complaisance or fear, but those who showed some spirit and objected to compulsion he got rid of by every possible means.[88]

It is no surprise, then, that when Herod died in 4 BCE the disgruntled Galilean population complained determinedly to Jerusalem and Rome[89] and erupted in a series of popular revolts. According to Josephus, these revolts were led by the brigands Judas son of Ezekias (whose father had been executed by Herod the Great),[90] Simon (servant of Herod),[91] and Anthronges,[92] and the appearance and actions of these men seem to have been reminiscent

---

86. Horsley with Hanson, *Bandits, Prophets and Messiahs*, 31–33.

87. Jones, *Herods of Judaea*, 75.

88. Josephus, *Ant.* 15.365–69.

89. Josephus, *Ant.* 17.204–5; *J.W.* 2.84–87.

90. Josephus, *Ant.* 17.271–72; *J.W.* 2.56.

91. Josephus, *Ant.* 17.273–76.

92. Josephus, *Ant.* 17.278–85.

of the Davidic narratives and kingship tradition (non-gentry families, strong physical stature, formation of armed bands, guerrilla-style tactics, set up as "king" [messianic][93]). Whatever the result, the aim of these revolts was to overthrow Roman and Herodian power in order to return to the covenantal freedom and equity of early Israel:

> They stormed the royal palaces at Sepphoris and Jericho not simply as symbols of hated Herodian rule or to obtain weapons, but to recover property that had been seized by Herodian officials and stored in the palaces. Besides attacking both Roman and royalist forces, they also raided and destroyed the mansions of the gentry along with the royal residences. We can reasonably infer a certain resentment at prolonged social-economic inequity and exploitation.[94]

The eventual Roman suppression of the revolts resulted in around two thousand rebels being crucified (*J. W.* 2.75) and the destruction of Sepphoris (the center of Judas' movement) and Emmaus, with the former having its inhabitants enslaved. These events would no doubt have affected the worldview of Jesus, who was born around this time and raised in Nazareth, a mere three to four miles from Sepphoris.[95] Indeed, Herod Antipas quickly had Sepphoris rebuilt, and this would have required the labor of many a τέκτων,[96] probably including some from Nazareth. The rebuilding of Sepphoris as a Hellenistic city would have been a constant reminder of both Roman military power that had destroyed it in 4 BCE and the continual domination of the Empire. Antipas' eventual construction of the city of Tiberias (c. 18 CE) in honor of the emperor Tiberius was a further reminder to the Galilean population of Roman imperial power. Josephus writes:

> The tetrarch Herod, inasmuch as he had gained a high place among the friends of Tiberias, had built a city, named after him Tiberias, which he established in the best region of Galilee on Lake Gennesaritis. There is a hot spring not far from it in a village called Ammathus. The new settlers were a promiscuous rabble, no small contingent being Galilaean, with such as

---

93. As Horsley points out, Josephus refers to the fact that these men were set up as kings, though Josephus makes sure to avoid strictly Jewish messianic language such as "branch" and "son of David" to refer to them; *Bandits, Prophets and Messiahs*, 114–15.

94. Horsley with Hanson, *Bandits, Prophets and Messiahs*, 116.

95. Reed has shown that small villages like Nazareth were oriented toward larger cities. In the case of Nazareth its orientation would have been to Sepphoris, just three miles to the north. Reed, *Archaeology and the Galilean Jesus*, 115.

96. Brown, "Techniques of Imperial Control," 362.

were drafted from territory subject to him and brought forcibly to the new foundation. Some of these were magistrates. Herod accepted as participants even poor men who were brought in to join the others from any and all places of origin. It was a question whether some were even free beyond cavil. These latter he often and in large bodies liberated and benefited (imposing the condition that they should not quit the city), by equipping houses at his own expense and adding new gifts of land. For he knew that this settlement was contrary to the law and tradition of the Jews because Tiberias was built on the site of tombs that had been obliterated, of which there were many there. And our law declares that such settlers are unclean for seven days.[97]

In other words, Antipas forced many Galileans to populate his new capital of Tiberias, which was built on the site of Jewish tombs that had been destroyed to make room for the city, a violation of Jewish law. Whether or not Galilean Jews who settled on the site were fazed by this uncleanness is unknown. It is possible that such concerns are simply those of the Jerusalemite Josephus. It may have been that the peasant majority were simply unable to concern themselves with many purity laws due to more pressing economic burdens that such laws might exacerbate.[98] If the peasantry was concerned with such laws, it may have been that the economic windfall of Antipas providing housing was too advantageous to ignore.[99] A third possibility is simply that the force used by Antipas to populate the city could not be easily resisted. Whatever the case, it appears that economic pressures and/or the threat of violence forced many Jews to compromise their commitment to Torah and to deviate from the ideal of a covenant community like early Israel.

In 6 CE Herod's son and successor in Judea, Archelaus, was removed from power after the Jews appealed to Rome against him. At this time, Rome attempted to institute a census that, for the Jews, was not simply an economic problem; it was also a theological problem inasmuch as "enrolling in Rome's system meant admitting that the land and people were not

---

97. Josephus, *Ant.* 18.36–38.

98. "The major obstacles to rigorous conformity to the demands of the symbolic system [i.e. the purity system] for ordinary persons were economic. The daily circumstances of their lives and trades, especially for the peasantry, continually exposed them to contagion, and they simply could not afford the outlay of either time or money/goods involved in ritual cleansing processes." Myers, *Binding the Strong Man*, 75–76. Matthew's narrative depicts Jesus challenging this aspect of the Jewish purity system, such as his challenge to the interpretation of Sabbath rules (Matt 12).

99. Reed suggests that land dispossession was perhaps a common reason to migrate. Reed, *Archaeology and the Galilean Jesus*, 84.

after all sacred to Israel's god."[100] This theological and nationalistic impetus, combined with the economic pressure of Roman taxation,[101] occasioned resistance in Judea led by Judas the Galilean. Josephus' account of Judas is predictably hostile, though it does go some way toward implying the peasantry's desire for politico-economic liberation:

> Although the Jews were at first shocked to hear of the registration of property, they gradually condescended, yielding to the argument of the high priest Joazar, the son of Boethus, to go no further in opposition. So those who were convinced by him declared, without shilly-shallying, the value of their property. But a certain Judas, a Gaulanite from a city named Gamala, who had enlisted the aid of Saddok, a Pharisee, threw himself into the cause of rebellion. They said that the assessment carried with it a status accounting to downright slavery, no less, and appealed to the nation to make a bid for independence. They urged that in case of success the Jews would have laid the foundation of prosperity, while if they failed to obtain any such boon, they would win honour and renown for their lofty aim; and that Heaven would be their zealous helper to no lesser end than the furthering of their enterprise until it succeeded—all the more if with high devotion in their hearts they stood firm and did not shrink from the bloodshed that might be necessary. . . . In this case certainly, Judas and Saddok started among us an intrusive fourth school of philosophy; and when they had won an abundance of devotees, they filled the body politic immediately with tumult, also planting the seeds of those troubles which subsequently overtook it.[102]
>
> As for the fourth of the philosophies, Judas the Galilaean set himself up as leader of it. This school agrees in all other respects with the opinions of the Pharisees, except that they have a passion for liberty that is almost unconquerable, since they are convinced that God alone is their leader and master. They think little of submitting to death in unusual forms and permitting vengeance to fall on kinsmen and friends if only they may avoid calling any man master.[103]

---

100. Wright, *New Testament*, 173.

101. Horsley claims that the outbreak of revolt was "tax resistance." This is both economic and theological inasmuch as paying taxes to Caesar was, in some way, to acknowledge his lordship. Horsley, *Galilee*, 64.

102. Josephus, *Ant.* 18.3–5, 9.

103. Josephus, *Ant.* 18.23.

Horsley argues ardently that this "Fourth Philosophy" abstained from violence—Josephus himself makes no reference to the Fourth Philosophy engaging in violent acts.[104] This, however, is questionable. Though the Fourth Philosophy has tended to be wrongly associated with "the Zealots," Josephus' statement that this group sowed the seeds of the later troubles that overtook the nation does not inspire confidence in an image of non-violence.[105] Still, Horsley's assessment of the Fourth Philosophy is helpful in its acknowledgement of the group's eschatological focus. They were seeking to bring about the kingdom of God and, indeed, martyrdom featured in this philosophy, patterned on Dan 11:32–35; 12:1–3.[106] Part of the group's aim would appear to have been a return to the free peasantry in covenant with God, and this is particularly reflected in the allusions within Josephus' account to an apparent commitment to the Decalogue—"You shall have no other gods besides me." What emerges is a picture of at least part of the peasantry in early first-century Palestine who were suffering under the weight of socio-economic pressures, and who desperately anticipated the promised eschatological kingdom of God in which they would be free to live as a sovereign nation and as God's people, liberated from the socio-political oppression of the Roman Empire and its clients.

With the onset of direct Roman rule in Judea in 6 CE following the deposition of Archelaus came repeated Jewish revolts. This was, in part, due to the "crass and heavy-handed style" of successive Roman procurators.[107] Wright lists seven incidents that occurred under the procuratorship of Pontius Pilate (26–36 CE):[108]

1. Pilate tried to bring Roman standards into Jerusalem, but he backed down after a mass protest.

---

104. Horsley with Hanson, *Bandits, Prophets and Messiahs*, 196–99. Horsley argues that the Fourth Philosophy has been largely confused with an inaccurate picture of "the Zealots," who did not in fact exist prior to the war starting in 66 CE. Moreover, he points out that the adherents of the Fourth Philosophy were not concerned to engage in acts of violence, though they were prepared to *suffer* violence if necessary. See also Smith, "Troublemakers," 3:501–68 (esp. 542).

105. For an overview of the relation of Zealots and Sicarii, including discussion of their relationships to the Fourth Philosophy, see Smith, "Zealots and Sicarii," 1–19 (esp. 5, 18). See also Smith, "Troublemakers," 515–16.

106. Horsley with Hanson, *Bandits, Prophets and Messiahs*, 194.

107. Wright, *New Testament*, 174.

108. Wright, *New Testament*, 174. Wright relies on Josephus, Philo, Matthew, and Luke for these accounts.

2. He used money from the temple treasury to build an aqueduct, and crushed the resistance that this action provoked.[109]

3. He sent troops to kill some Galileans while they were offering sacrifices in the temple, presumably because he feared a riot.

4. He captured and condemned to death the leader of an uprising that had taken place in Jerusalem, involving murder; he then released the man as a gesture of goodwill during the Passover feast.

5. At the same Passover, he faced a quasi-messianic movement, having some association with resistance movements; he crucified its leader along with two ordinary revolutionaries.

6. He provoked public opinion by placing Roman votive shields, albeit without images, in the palace at Jerusalem, which according to Philo annoyed Tiberius almost as much as it did the Jews.

7. Finally, he suppressed with particular brutality a popular prophetic movement in Samaria. For this he was accused before the Roman legate in Syria, who had him sent back to Rome.

In Josephus' account of the protest resulting from Pilate's action in the first point above (*J. W.* 2.169–74), he records that the Jews were fervent enough to fall to the ground before sword-wielding soldiers, extending their necks and proclaiming their preparedness to die before transgressing their law. Such is not an isolated incident, for under the emperorship of Caligula (37–41 CE) a strikingly similar episode occurred:

> [Caligula] sent Petronius with an army to Jerusalem to install in the sanctuary statues of himself; in the event of the Jews refusing to admit them, his orders were to put the recalcitrants to death and to reduce the whole nation to slavery.[110]

The Jews, however, came out to meet Petronius, first at Ptolemais and then at Tiberias, in order to petition him to cease his mission. Their commitment to die rather than be forced to transgress their law persuaded Petronius to disobey his orders rather than overcome the Jews.[111] Horsley argues that this sequence of events was influenced by economic concerns, namely,

---

109. Horsley states that members of the Herodian family led this resistance. *Bandits, Prophets and Messiahs*, 39.

110. Josephus, *J. W.* 2.185.

111. Petronius was then ordered by Caligula to commit suicide, but fortunately for him this order came to Petronius subsequent to news of Caligula's death.

the strike instituted by the peasantry in their refusal to sow their fields.[112] No sowing meant no harvest, and thus no tribute.

An episode during the reign of the procurator Cumanus (48–52 CE) echoes similar tensions between the Roman occupiers and the Jewish populace:

> The usual crowd had assembled at Jerusalem for the feast of unleavened bread, and the Roman cohort had taken up its position on the roof of the portico of the temple; for a body of men in arms invariably mounts guard at the feasts, to prevent disorders arising from such a concourse of people. Thereupon one of the soldiers, raising his robe, stooped in an indecent attitude, so as to turn his backside to the Jews, and made a noise in keeping with his posture. Enraged at this insult, the whole multitude with loud cries called upon Cumanus to punish the soldier; some of the more hot-headed young men and seditious persons in the crowd started a fight, and, picking up stones, hurled them at the troops. Cumanus, fearing a general attack upon himself, sent for reinforcements. These troops pouring into the porticoes, the Jews were seized with irresistible panic and turned to fly from the temple and make their escape into the town. But such violence was used as they pressed round the exits that they were trodden under foot and crushed to death by one another; upwards of thirty thousand perished, and the feast was turned into mourning for the whole nation and for every household into lamentation.[113]

From each of these incidents involving Roman authorities, the impression is of mighty imperial power in conflict with impassioned local movements, not merely physically, but in a war of symbols and ideology. Roman standards and shields, for example, form more than mere articles of military or royal significance; they form symbols that embody the hegemonic ideology of Rome and reinforce a particular narrative of Roman domination and power. For Rome, acts of brutality functioned to bring stability and to sustain a notion of determinism, but so also did ideological symbols, or what we could call propaganda. Standards, shields, coins, statues, and theology all had the effect of signifying the narrative of Roman dominion and its inherent goodness, eternality, and immutability. As one Marxist critical theorist says concerning hegemonic ideology:

---

112. Horsley with Hanson, *Bandits, Prophets and Messiahs*, 40.

113. Josephus, *J. W.* 2.224–27.

> It is widely accepted as describing "the way things are," inducing people to consent to their society and its way of life as natural, good and just. In this way, hegemonic ideology is translated into everyday consciousness and serves as a means of "indirect rule" that is a powerful force for social cohesion and stability. . . . They provide theories about the economy, state, or education that legitimate certain dominant institutions and ideas, and prescribe conformist acceptance.[114]

Such would seem to be an adequate critique of Roman ideology and its attempts to legitimate Roman domination from what we have seen from events in and around the first century. This is not to say that such authority did not provoke powerful expressions of defiance and revolt (as has been shown). Nor does conformity necessarily imply contentment with "the way things are." Indeed, the ideology and economic pressure imposed by Rome conflicted deeply with the Jewish peasantry and their responses were varied, as we have seen. One of the ways it seems that members of the Palestinian peasantry confronted the ideology of Rome was with its own distinct ideology, or in the language of Myers, they confronted the *legitimizing* ideology of Rome with their own *subversive* ideology.[115] This is perhaps nowhere more evident in first-century Palestine than in the social phenomenon of prophetic figures.

2.3 Popular Jewish Prophetic Figures and Movements in the First Century CE

As we have seen, for some figures in Palestine in and around the first century CE the combination of occupation by Roman forces, nationalistic zeal, and covenantal tradition led to a commitment to brigandry and, in some cases, messianic movements. For others, resistance took another form in which covenantal tradition remained central. Such resistance was often nonviolent and supported by a kind of eschatological hope. It came in the form of popular prophetic movements.

Josephus is well known to have been critical of these movements, though his works remain a helpful source to determine their basic character. These characterizations, coupled with their antecedents in biblical tradition, provide a basis (at least, in the absence of more or better data) on which to build a picture of first-century prophetic movements in Palestine.

---

114. Kellner, "Ideology, Marxism, and Advanced Capitalism," 50.
115. Myers, *Binding the Strong Man*, 18.

There were two distinct types of Jewish popular prophet in the first century. Horsley writes:

> The principal function of the one, the oracular prophet, was to pronounce the impending judgment or redemption by God. The characteristic feature of the other, the action prophet, was to inspire and lead a popular movement to vigorous participation in an anticipated redemptive action by God.[116]

Horsley says elsewhere:

> There were two basic types of prophets contemporary with Jesus, the one being an oracular type of prophet basically similar to the classical oracular prophets in Jewish biblical traditions and the other type being patterned after the great "liberators" of early Israel.[117]

Webb criticizes Horsley's labels of "action" and "oracular" prophets, arguing that these labels are too narrow because action prophets may well have pronounced oracles, not least to call people to action, in addition to their group leadership.[118] Webb alternative typology categorizes popular prophets as either the "solitary prophet" (in place of oracular prophet) and the "leadership prophet" (in place of action prophet).[119] But Webb's criticism misinterprets Horsley's labels since, according to Horsley, "action prophets" is simply shorthand for "prophets who led movements."[120] "Action" refers not to a general concentration on physical actions, but more specifically to an orientation toward actions of deliverance, with oracles playing a possible supporting role.[121] Horsley's typology focuses on vocation rather than association. In any case, Webb's approach is too neat an attempt to place prophets in one or another category, though this is simply not possible. There is no reason to think that a prophet could not act as leader and solitary figure at different stages, leaving Webb's typology no less open to confusion than Horsley's. Paul Barnett has preferred the term "sign prophets" to Horsley's "action prophets" because he discerns a common pattern among such figures, including the fact that they all attempted a "sign."[122] Although no label will adequately describe all the nuances of any phenomenon, I find

---

116. Horsley with Hanson, *Bandits, Prophets and Messiahs*, 135.

117. Horsley, "Two Types of Popular Prophets," 436–37.

118. Webb, *John the Baptizer and Prophet*, 315.

119. Webb, *John the Baptizer and Prophet*, 316.

120. Horsley, "Two Types of Popular Prophets," 446, 460.

121. Horsley, "Two Types of Popular Prophets," 460.

122. Barnett, "Jewish Sign Prophets—A.D. 40–70," 679–97.

Barnett's label narrow enough to be avoided because it overemphasizes one aspect of the broader role of the action prophet. Likewise, Webb's replacement of Horsley's "oracular prophet" fares similarly. The use of the label "oracular prophets" in Horsley's typology refers simply to those who did not lead movements and who operated *primarily* in the realm of oracular prophecy. As with his label, "leadership prophets," Webb's "solitary prophet" is no more helpful a category, representing only a difference in emphasis (association) than Horsley (vocation). Horsley's typology of popular prophets is preferable for its vocational focus, which lies closer to the heart of the prophet's role than does their association.

Horsley's labels look backward to the Old Testament prophets. As we will see, those prophets contemporaneous with Jesus embodied models based on traditional Israelite figures. This was not merely a "religious" affinity, as could be mistaken when viewing the prophets through modern eyes. Rather, in the spirit of the OT prophets, both oracular and action, the vocation of these first-century figures was inseparably coupled with social and economic factors, particularly exploitation, injustice, and the sought-after liberation from these conditions. This is perhaps best demonstrated by the fact that such first-century prophets appear to have been largely antagonistic to aristocratic and literate groups. Literate groups seem to have been far more constrained by Scripture, seeing the covenant law of Moses as God's inspired will; among the Jewish peasantry, on the other hand, being as they were unable to engage easily with such texts in written form, the Spirit took a more spontaneous form.[123] This is not to say the peasantry was unaware of tradition and narratives of the past—popular prophecy often emulated the form of liberation movements such as those of Moses and Joshua in crucial ways. For the peasantry, though, prophetic movements were not confined to the past. The divide between peasants and elites,[124] though only a rough sketch of the more complex sociological phenomenon, can be traced back at least as far as the beginning of the post-Exilic period to the struggle between what Paul Hanson terms the "hierocracy" and "prophetic-visionaries."[125]

Beginning with "action" prophets, we now turn to look at some specific examples recorded by Josephus. Josephus is, for a number of reasons, critical of these figures, thinking them "charlatans" who led many people to their deaths. This, however, does not detract from the fact that they self-identified as prophets and/or were recognized as such by others. The legitimacy of

123. Horsley with Hanson, *Bandits, Prophets and Messiahs*, 160.

124. Aside from being sketched out in this chapter we also considered the tension between elites and peasants in the previous chapter in light of the social structure of a post-agrarian society such as Palestine.

125. Hanson, *Dawn of Apocalyptic*, esp. 9–10.

their prophetic identity may be disputed but the character of their perceived vocation is nonetheless prophetic since popular opinion judged it to be so. Indeed, we would do well to distinguish, as Horsley does, between the aims of the prophets (as far as we can discern) and their actions.[126]

Action Prophets

Action prophets tended to be those who led active movements in which there was an expectation of divine deliverance from the current evil order and often the eschatological transformation of this order into a just society ruled by God (the kingdom of God). Josephus reflects critically:

> Deceivers and imposters, under the pretence of divine inspiration fostering revolutionary changes, they persuaded the multitude to act like madmen, and led them out into the desert under the belief that God would there give them tokens of deliverance.[127]

Despite Josephus' obvious disdain for such figures and its effect on his reports, there is a relatively clear sense of these prophets' expectation of divine deliverance. The Romans fiercely suppressed these movements because they took on a subversive character that was construed as a threat. In other words, the hope of these movements was worked out in political symbolism and character. The power of such expectation led many to leave their homes, work, and villages in order to follow a prophet into the wilderness, the traditional place of revelation, providence, and liberation. It was here that people seem to have believed the plan of God would be revealed, just as it had been with Moses, and this would lead to a salvation event like the Exodus.

According to Josephus, there were numerous imposters in the period before the 66 CE revolt who led masses out into the wilderness and promised signs and imminent salvation (*J. W.* 2.259, 264; *Ant.* 20.160). Whether this included numerous prophetic figures is not entirely clear, but it is likely there is crossover between these imposters and the "pseudoprophets" given Josephus' repetitious contempt for both. Those explored below are only a sample of the prophetic figures around the time of Jesus,[128] though they are representative of a general pattern. The first of these movements from

126. Horsley, "Popular Prophetic Movements at the Time of Jesus," 5.

127. Josephus, *J. W.* 2.259.

128. Gray provides numerous more examples from Josephus than can be explored in this chapter. Gray, *Prophetic Figures*, 118–23.

around the time of Jesus of Nazareth requiring our attention did not in fact
begin with the Jews, but with the Samaritans.

The Samaritan Prophet

> The Samaritan nation too was not exempt from disturbance.
> For a man who made light of mendacity and in all his designs
> catered to the mob, rallied them, bidding them go in a body
> with him to Mount Gerizim, which in their belief is the most
> sacred of mountains. He assured them that on their arrival he
> would show them the sacred vessels which were buried there,
> where Moses had deposited them. His hearers, viewing this
> tale as plausible, appeared in arms. They posted themselves in
> a village named Tirathana, and, as they planned to climb the
> mountain in a great multitude, they welcomed to their ranks
> the new arrivals who kept coming. But before they could as-
> cend, Pilate blocked their projected route up the mountains
> with a detachment of cavalry and heavily-armed infantry, who
> in the encounter with the firstcomers in the village slew some
> in a pitched battle and put the others to flight. Many prisoners
> were taken, of whom Pilate put to death the principal leaders
> and those who were most influential among the fugitives.[129]

Although there is no number given to the followers of the nameless Samaritan prophet, Josephus gives the sense that it was sizable (πλῆθος[130]). Horsley
assumes word would have spread quickly of the impending deliverance,[131]
though there is no clear reason why; for all we know this prophetic figure
may have been active amongst Samaritan villages for some time before calling the people to follow him to Gerizim during the time of Pilate (c. 36
CE[132]). This conclusion is shown to be more likely by Josephus' claim that
there were ringleaders ("the principal leaders"), possibly a reflection of a
reasonable level of organization. That the Samaritan prophetic figure was
to regain the sacred vessels deposited by Moses perhaps suggests that his
self-understanding was that of an eschatological Mosaic figure.

---

129. Josephus, *Ant.* 18.85–87.

130. Frequently used in the Gospels of the multitudes who followed Jesus, for
example.

131. Horsley with Hanson, *Bandits, Prophets and Messiahs*, 163.

132. It is fairly likely that this event occurred in 36 CE, the final year of Pilate's
decade-long period as governor of Judea. Josephus records that Vitellius, governor of
Syria, sent Pilate back to Rome to face the emperor for his severity toward the Samaritans (*Ant.* 18.88–89). Fortunately for Pilate, Tiberius died before he arrived.

In Josephus' comments there are glimpses of the movement's anti-Roman sentiment and militant, perhaps even violent, opposition. Indeed, it seems that the Samaritan prophet's followers met together in Tirathana with arms (ὅπλον) ready for what Horsley describes as a potential eschatological holy war from Mount Gerizim.[133] Perhaps, if the prophet was seen as Mosaic in nature, his followers' actions reflect a desperation for eschatological liberation. Such liberation would entail freedom from occupying Roman forces and the economic and social pressure that accompanied it. It may also imply, as per Myers, "a symbolic articulation of Samaritan secession from the Jerusalem temple-based order, into which Samaria had been unwillingly incorporated since the time of the Maccabees."[134] Perhaps Pilate understood both, though whatever the case may be, he recognized in the movement a revolutionary quality and ordered troops not only to dispel it, but also to slaughter many of its members. Thus, Pilate embodied the violent Roman domination that may well have driven these villagers to embark on their course of revolt in the first place.

This particular episode reveals some important characteristics of the prophet from this period. Prophets were certainly no ahistorical phenomenon. The yearning for liberation in light of socio-political, economic, and perhaps theological oppression was central to this example prophetic activity. Moreover, prophetic expectation in this case seems to have included a belief that God would suddenly act in some way to rescue his people. This led the Samaritan prophetic movement to take otherwise unreasonable measures by facing off against Roman forces despite their inevitable and brutal defeat. The prophet and his followers believed God's action would be confirmed by a sign, in this case the uncovering of sacred vessels. It seems that the prophet and his followers, in taking their cues from past figures such as Moses and Joshua who led Israel to victory despite impossible odds, sought to subvert established power (represented by the Jerusalem temple) and conceived of a historical event in which they would finally be liberated, possibly as a Samaritan "nation."

Theudas

Appearing around 45 CE[135] was another prophetic figure, a Jew named Theudas. Josephus reports:

133. Horsley with Hanson, *Bandits, Prophets and Messiahs*, 164.

134. Myers, *Binding the Strong Man*, 61.

135. Josephus claims Theudas was active while Fadus was procurator of Judea, from 44–46 CE.

During the period when Fadus was procurator of Judaea, a certain imposter named Theudas persuaded the majority of the masses to take up their possessions and to follow him to the Jordan River. He stated that he was a prophet and that at his command the river would be parted and would provide them an easy passage. With this talk he deceived many. Fadus, however, did not permit them to reap the fruit of their folly, but sent against them a squadron of cavalry. These fell upon them unexpectedly, slew many of them and took many prisoners. Theudas himself was captured, whereupon they cut off his head and brought it to Jerusalem.[136]

In Acts 5, it is reported that the Pharisee Gamaliel speaks to the Sanhedrin about their anxiety over the movement of followers of Jesus. Gamaliel reminds them of two analogies of movements that, because they were the undertakings of men and not God, had failed, resulting in their destruction and that of their lead figures.[137] One of these movements is that of Judas the Galilean, and the other that of Theudas.[138] Horsley construes this as proof that, by the end of the first century CE, Theudas' movement was remembered alongside that of Judas of Galilee and Jesus of Nazareth, meaning that it must have been significant.[139] Smith, on the other hand, suggests that Luke's sparse details of the episode imply that the Theudas story had receded far into legend.[140] Smith is probably correct, although the lingering "legend" of Theudas, accurate or not, suggests he was well-known.

136. Josephus, *Ant.* 20.97–98.

137. Probably written within a decade of Josephus' *Antiquities.*

138. There are well-attested problems with Luke's account. The Theudas who is mentioned, assuming that it is the same Theudas as in Josephus, did not lead a rebellion until well after the implied time period of Gamaliel's reported address to the Sanhedrin in Acts 5 (prior to the conversion of Paul). In fact, Acts speaks of Theudas as a figure of the past, not merely in relation to the Acts 5 episode, but before Judas the Galilean (6 CE), a clear historical error. Mason, pointing out some significant similarities between the accounts of Josephus and Luke, argues that Luke was probably familiar with Josephus' account of Theudas and utilized it in his own narrative; Mason, *Josephus and the New Testament,* 208–14. If true, this fact could be construed in such a way as to undermine the significance of the Theudas story in Luke's account, i.e., it was not important or well-known, just adapted from Josephus. I am inclined to think, however, that Acts pre-dates Josephus' *Antiquities.* In any case, the historical problems associated with Luke's inclusion of this episode could be seen to highlight its importance if Luke was willing to include it despite its anachronism. Alternatively, the issue could simply be a modern construction given the different standards of accuracy expected in modern and ancient Greek historiography.

139. Horsley with Hanson, *Bandits, Prophets and Messiahs,* 165. Cf. Wright, *New Testament,* 175.

140. Smith, "Troublemakers," 3:514.

Josephus' detail that Fadus was procurator reflects more than a simple historical date. Prior to Fadus' proconsulate, Caligula had attempted to set up a statue of himself in the Jerusalem temple,[141] which led to nationwide resistance and a peasant strike.[142] War was only averted by Caligula's death in 41 CE (described above, where economic concerns were identified as part of the ordeal). Caligula's reign, which was exercised directly over Palestine rather than through a local client-king, was brutal for Palestinian Jews. Subsequent to Caligula's emperorship, Agrippa I, grandson of Herod the Great, was made king over Jewish Palestine. His dedication to Jewish traditions[143] would have seemed favorable when compared with Caligula's direct Roman reign, especially if Tacitus' report about lingering Jewish fear of another emperor repeating Caligula's commands is to be trusted.[144] Josephus' account of Agrippa, however, indicates he continued the economically burdensome building projects and financial appeasement of the Roman world that his grandfather had embarked upon.[145] Though Agrippa's comparably auspicious reign managed to avoid the resistance experienced under Caligula, his actions were unlikely to have garnered the pleasure of those who continued to be economically exploited.

The return to direct Roman rule under Fadus following Agrippa's death in 44 CE must have played heavily on the symbolic stage for the Jews. After three years without direct Roman rule, it now returned in the form of Fadus' tyrannical administration. As Josephus records:

> Fadus, on his arrival in Judaea as procurator, found that the Jewish inhabitants of Peraea had fallen out with the people of Philadelphia over the boundaries of a village called Zia, which was infested with warlike men. Moreover, the Peraeans, who had taken up arms without the sanction of their leaders, inflicted much loss of life on the Philadelphians. Fadus, on being informed of this, was greatly incensed that the Peraeans, granted that they thought themselves wronged by the Philadelphians, had not waited for him to give judgement but had instead resorted to arms. He therefore seized three of their leaders, who were in fact responsible for the revolt and ordered them to be held prisoner. Next he put one of them, named Annibus, to death, and imposed exile on the other two, Amaramus and Eleazar. Not long afterwards Tholomaeus the arch-brigand,

141. Josephus, *Ant.* 18.261; Philo, *Embassy*, XXX.203; Tacitus, *Hist.*, 5.9
142. Josephus, *Ant.* 18.263, 270, 272.
143. Josephus, *Ant.* 19.293–96, 300–11, 331.
144. Tacitus, *Ann.* 12.54.
145. Josephus, *Ant.* 19.326, 335–37, 343–52.

who had inflicted very severe mischief upon Idumaea and upon the Arabs, was brought before him in chains and put to death. From then on the whole of Judaea was purged of robber-bands [ληστής], thanks to the prudent concern displayed by Fadus.[146]

Josephus' account of Fadus is rather kind; Fadus' action against the Perean Jews was hasty and severe. The detail that he cleared Judea of brigands (ληστής[147]) might appear a positive development. However, as has already been suggested, the rise of brigandry was fueled by a desire to return to an idealized existence characterized by socio-economic liberation. It was, in part, a nationalistic warring with the dominant myths of Roman imperialism. Hobsbawm is enlightening in his cross-cultural study, *Bandits*:

> Social banditry is universally found wherever societies are based on agriculture . . . and consist largely of peasants and landless laborers ruled, oppressed and exploited by someone else—lords, towns, governments.[148]

Roman rule in Palestine no doubt conforms to this description. But more than this, Roman dominion was supported by a perceived divine sanction:

> Jupiter says, "For these I set no bounds in space or time; but have given empire without end." (Virgil, *Aen.* 1.257–96)

> But you, Roman, must remember that you have to guide the nations by your authority, for this is to be your skill, to graft tradition onto peace, to spare those who submit, but to crush those who resist. (Virgil, *Aen.* 6.808–53)

> All men had to bow to the commands of their betters; it had ben decreed by those gods whom they implored that with the Roman people should rest the decisions what to give and what to take away. (Tacitus, *Ann.* 13.51)

Further, regarding the Jews:

> Jews and Syrians were born for servitude. (Cicero, *Prov. cons.* 10)

Though Josephus claims Fadus kept the nation at peace,[149] such peace was achieved through violence and the threat thereof. Roman control was also retained by way of symbolic gestures. A prime example is Fadus' confiscation of the Jewish high priestly vestments in an attempt to restore

146. Josephus, *Ant.* 20.2–5.

147. Meaning not "thief" but "brigand" or "insurrectionist." Cf. *J.W.* 4.238–42.

148. Hobsbawm, *Bandits*, 19–20.

149. Josephus, *J.W.* 2.220

them to Roman control.[150] That the emperor Claudius, having been petitioned by the Jews, overturned the decision reveals that Fadus was harsh even by Roman standards.[151]

Fadus' harshness is perhaps most vividly recorded in Josephus' record of the movement led by the supposed prophet Theudas. It is unlikely to be coincidence that Theudas' movement began during the short imposition of Fadus. The movement seems to have been large, though we can only speculate as to its approximate size. Theudas' followers seem to have understood this event as implying an extended journey, eschatological in nature, indicated by the fact that they took "their belongings with them" (*Ant.* 20.97).[152]

According to Josephus' account, Theudas "told them he was a prophet, and that he would, by his own command, divide the river, and afford them an easy passage through it" (*Ant.* 20.97). Implied here is a predictive element to Theudas' activity. Certainly, there was an expectation of a divine sign to confirm God's action. There are a number of possible biblical episodes that could be the inspiration for Theudas' claim that he would separate the waters to create easy passage, though which one in particular is unclear. It could be that Theudas' actions were an allusion to Joshua and the crossing of the Jordan into a new promised land—a "reverse conquest" as Horsley suggests—constituting a journey into the wilderness to be purified, to "prepare the way of the Lord" (Isa 40:3; Mal 3:1) and perhaps even to commence a new "conquest."[153] Alternatively, or perhaps synchronously, Theudas could have been alluding to Moses and the leading of a new Exodus. Both suggestions would imply liberation from foreign domination, even in their own land.[154] A combination of the two experiences is not out of the question, and is likely given their apparent juxtaposition in biblical tradition (2 Kgs 2:6–8; Isa 51:9–11). Myers connects the episode to "the action of Elijah in the context of building a subversive prophetic movement" in 2 Kings 2,[155] a perceptive suggestion, though it is likely that Elijah's subversion is itself derivative of the Moses/Joshua tradition.[156] That

150. Josephus, *Ant.* 20.6; Gabba, "Social, Economic and Political History," 143.

151. Josephus, *Ant.* 20.7–14.

152. Dale C. Allison Jr. suggests that "the followers of Theudas forsook their possessions." *Jesus of Nazareth*, 89. I do not see how Allison arrives at this reading given the Greek text suggests the crowd took up (ἀναλαμβάνω) their possessions rather than forsook them.

153. Horsley, "Two Types of Popular Prophets," 457. Schwartz, *Studies in the Jewish Background*, 29–30, states matter-of-factly that Theudas was a latter-day Joshua.

154. Horsley with Hanson, *Bandits, Prophets and Messiahs*, 166.

155. Myers, *Binding the Strong Man*, 61.

156. It is not impossible that the episode alludes to Noah's or Jonah's experiences

Theudas' movement probably went unarmed[157] demonstrates that they believed God would intervene to defeat any Roman suppression that may result, as with the Egyptians at the Red Sea.

Though it is impossible to determine exactly what Theudas' self-perception and intention may have been, the background of Fadus' harsh reign, the Exodus tradition, and the conquest tradition suggest socio-political liberation was central. That this movement was seen as subversive, despite its nonviolence (in contrast to the Perean Jews mentioned by Josephus), is confirmed by Fadus' efficient action against it. Having killed many of the people "unexpectedly" (i.e., in a surprise attack), the troop of cavalry (ἴλα ἱππέων; 500–1000 men[158]) took Theudas alive, decapitated him, and carried his head into Jerusalem, presumably as an admonition against any who would attempt a similar act of subversion.[159]

Theudas' movement and actions demonstrate the continued existence of the subversive Mosaic prophetic tradition. As action prophet, Theudas led a movement of liberation like Moses from within imperial dominion. Unlike that of Moses, this liberation movement was probably nonviolent,[160] and was swiftly and militarily set upon by imperial forces. It would appear that Theudas' movement, despite it not posing a proactive threat against the occupiers, was perceived as necessitating such a violent reaction from them. Such betrays the movement's subversive nature and threat to the imperial order. The movement was not merely an escape from imperial power; it was a declaration of its independence and (nationalistic?) commitment to a tradition—indeed, a deity—contrary to the ideology of Rome. From Rome's perspective, the allowance of movements to gain independence would only lead to the slow sinking of the imperial ship as others inevitably

---

with water, or even the separation of the waters at creation itself, though I find these possibilities less likely than the suggestions above.

157. Hengel claims that the movement was armed; Hengel, *Zealots*, 230n5. Gray considers this claim and rightly argues that though we cannot be certain, the passage in *Ant.* suggests the opposite—"Josephus does not explicitly state that the group were armed, and they appear to have been overcome with ease by a relatively small military force." Gray, *Prophetic Figures*, 115–16.

158. Gray, *Prophetic Figures*, 200n12.

159. Schwartz asks, "How did Theudas threaten public order or any other legitimate concern of the Roman governor of Judaea? Of course we could easily fill in the story. Fadus might have feared the growth of a movement of enthusiasts of a latter-day Joshua; whether or not Theudas succeeded, such people might plan the conquest of the Holy Land, and it was best to nip the movement in the bud." *Studies in the Jewish Background of Christianity*, 29–30.

160. Cf. Josephus, *Ant.* 2.321, 326; 3.18 where he describes, contrary to the biblical account (Exod 13:18b), the Israelites being unarmed at the time of the Exodus, only being providentially provided with weapons subsequent to the sea crossing.

sought to follow. Thus, even seemingly innocuous attempts at liberation would have posed a threat, if only symbolically.

This episode provides further clarity regarding the nature of the prophetic vocation around the time of Jesus. From it we learn that prediction was an element of Theudas' alleged claims, though such prediction was not an isolated function. Prediction and promises of signs operated within the broader narrative universe of Palestinian Judaism, seeking to open the eyes of the people to the perception that God would soon act to bring liberation to them. This was the case with the Samaritan prophet, as it was with Theudas. Theudas' prophetic action symbolically called Rome to account for its injustices by declaring that God would subvert Roman claims to power and divine-appointment through the deliverance of an otherwise powerless people group. In following the model of Moses and Joshua, Theudas was declaring YHWH's covenant faithfulness hungered for by his followers.

The Egyptian Prophet

A still worse blow was dealt at the Jews by the Egyptian false prophet. A charlatan, who had gained for himself the reputation of a prophet, this man appeared in the country, collected a following of about thirty thousand dupes, and led them by a circuitous route from the desert to the mount called the mount of Olives. From there he proposed to force an entrance into Jerusalem and, after overpowering the Roman garrison, to set himself up as tyrant of the people, employing those who poured in with him as his bodyguard. His attack was anticipated by Felix, who went to meet him with the Roman heavy infantry, the whole population joining him in the defence. The outcome of the ensuing engagement was that the Egyptian escaped with a few of his followers; most of his force were killed or taken prisoners; the remainder dispersed and stealthily escaped to their several homes.[161]

At this time there came to Jerusalem from Egypt a man who declared that he was a prophet and advised the masses of the common people to go out with him to the mountain called the Mount of Olives, which lies opposite the city at a distance of five furlongs. For he asserted that he wished to demonstrate from there that at his command Jerusalem's walls would fall down, through which he promised to provide them an entrance into the city. When Felix heard of this he ordered his

---

161. Josephus, *J.W.* 2.261–63.

soldiers to take up their arms. Setting out from Jerusalem with a large force of cavalry and infantry, he fell upon the Egyptian and his followers, slaying four hundred of them and taking two hundred prisoners. The Egyptian himself escaped from the battle and disappeared.[162]

Josephus tells us that this event occurred under the procuratorship of Felix, spanning 52–58 CE. Felix succeeded two periods that would have intensified already fierce tensions between the Roman government in Judea and the Jews:

1. A period of famine in the late forties (*Ant.* 20.101)

2. The period of the proconsul Cumanus (49–52 CE), whose heavy hand against relatively minor incidents served to increase tensions and violence in Palestine (see *J. W.* 2.224–46; *Ant.* 20.105–36).

Felix persisted in Cumanus' style of rule, extending the same despotic methods of order against brigands (Tacitus, *Ann.* 12.54). As Horsley points out, this probably exacerbated rather than pacified the problems.[163]

The Egyptian declared himself to be a prophet (προφήτης εἶναι λέγων; *Ant.* 20.169) and had gained a reputation as such (προφήτου πίστιν ἐπιθεὶς ἑαυτῷ; *J. W.* 2.261).[164] Josephus' report in *Jewish War* of the number of people involved in the Egyptian's movement (thirty thousand) is likely an exaggeration,[165] though it is impossible to say for sure what the real number was. Horsley posits that, regardless of Josephus' accuracy, the number was probably in the thousands, not the hundreds.[166] There is a discrepancy about where the Egyptians' followers came from—*Jewish War* states that they came from the countryside (εἰς τὴν χώραν; *J. W.* 2.261[167]) but *Antiquities* implies they came from Jerusalem. There is no

---

162. Josephus, *Ant.* 20.169–72.

163. Horsley with Hanson, *Bandits, Prophets and Messiahs*, 169.

164. Gray, *Prophetic Figures*, 116.

165. In 44 CE, the population of Jerusalem, a city of around 450 acres, would have been no more than 80,000–90,000. Rocca, *Herod's Judaea*, 333.

166. Horsley with Hanson, *Bandits, Prophets and Messiahs*, 169.

167. Gray acknowledges that χώρα can mean country both in the sense of the opposite of the city or in the sense of a land or territory. In this sense the word could mean that the Egyptian simply came from Egypt (one territory) to Judea (another). Gray argues that the alternative is more likely, that the Egyptian came into the wilderness, "since Josephus, after saying in *War* 2.261 that the Egyptian appeared εἰς τὴν χώραν, states that he then led his followers ἐκ τῆς ἐρημίας (2.262), without suggesting that he had previously led them into the wilderness from somewhere else." Gray, *Prophetic Figures*, 200n14.

simple way to determine which account is the more accurate. Whatever the case may be, both accounts agree that the people were peasants or folk (rural-dwellers in *J. W.*; δημοτικός[168] in *Ant.* 20.169).

That this movement was patterned on the battle of Jericho led by Joshua is unambiguous. Like Theudas, the Egyptian looked forward to a new conquest in which God would defeat the land's occupiers. In this particular case, such a series of events would include the walls of Jerusalem (rather than Jericho[169]) crumbling, at least in the *Antiquities* account.[170] What is uncertain is if there is any meaning to be read into the prophet's Egyptian origin. Was he simply a Jew from Egypt, or was his identity somehow symbolic of the Exodus tradition?

We should also note the importance of the Mount of Olives in apocalyptic thought by the time of the first century CE, as demonstrated in early or proto-apocalyptic literature (e.g., Ezek 11:23; Zech 14:4). The Zechariah passage depicts God doing battle from the Mount of Olives against Jerusalem and the nations that have occupied it. This tradition is likely to have influenced the eschatological thought of those who joined the Egyptian in his would-be prophetic pronouncement of judgement against the city. This may imply an opposition not simply to Roman rule, but also to the Jerusalem power base, even the temple institution itself.

The Egyptian, like Theudas, adapted symbols from prophetic tradition giving them life in a new situation. He expected a sign, and its prediction functioned in the Jewish narrative world to legitimate the declared judgement by God against oppressors. The receptivity of the peasantry (in the three cases we have examined so far) would seem to demonstrate that prophets were most naturally welcomed by those who were excluded from the world of the powerful elite minority. Such episodes suggest that the marginalized were the most welcoming of the possibility of God's action, eschatological or not, of liberating the oppressed and judging the oppressors. That Felix, upon uncovering the Egyptian's plan, ordered the movement crushed again reflects that this aspiration to liberation was clear, even to foreign occupiers.

168. See also Josephus *J. W.* 1.648; *Ant.* 5.136 for similar uses of δημοτικός.

169. Horsley notes that, "The typology of Jericho-Jerusalem is also attested in 4QTestim from Qumran, in which Joshua's curse against whoever rebuilds Jericho (Josh 6 26) is apparently applied to those who have rebuilt Jerusalem." Horsley, "Two Types of Popular Prophets," 458n49.

170. The *Jewish War* account simply states the Egyptian "proposed to force an entrance into Jerusalem." This need not contradict the *Antiquities* account; although no explicit hope of a Jericho-like miracle is mentioned, the route taken by the movement is "circuitous," and the two accounts can easily complement one another in regard to this detail.

Other Action Prophets

In Josephus' writings there are other prophetic figures mentioned, though to a lesser extent than those discussed above:

1. Unnamed prophets active under the procuratorship of Felix who led people into the desert to witness signs of liberty (*J.W.* 2.259; *Ant.* 20.167–68);

2. Unnamed prophet under Festus who promised deliverance if people would follow him into the wilderness (*Ant.* 20.188);

3. Unnamed prophet who proclaimed God's command to go to the temple to witness signs of deliverance.

We need not discuss these figures in detail. As with the Samaritan, Theudas and the Egyptian, Josephus is clearly biased against them, labeling them imposters, deceivers, and false prophets. Moreover, like those other prophets, these figures led people to the wilderness or the temple in order to witness signs of deliverance. As with the other prophetic movements in first-century Palestine, these prophets are implied to have gained the support of the disenfranchised peasantry and looked forwarded to a liberating act of God, almost certainly to overthrow their oppressors.

All of these prophetic movements seem to reflect a perception of a traditional Israelite way of life, which ran deep in social memory, as the aspiration for those involved (regardless of whether such a way of life was ever a historical reality). Indeed, the "distinctively Israelite form taken by these prophetic movements indicates that resistance to Roman imperial rule was strongly rooted in Israelite popular tradition."[171] The unmistakable echoes of Exodus and Conquest themes symbolize not merely an adherence to Jewish religious loyalties, but to the longing for a renewed liberation in light of the Roman world order.

Each of the prophets described above, and indeed other action prophets mentioned by Josephus, are said to have led ample-sized groups. In some cases the numbers are vague, even contradictory across multiple accounts, but in most cases the indication is that the groups were sizable. Each of the figures identified themselves as prophets and were viewed as such by their followers. The movements were typically led to particular places of strong symbolic significance in light of Israelite history and literature. This includes the wilderness and the Mount of Olives, places variously associated with liberation, conquest, provision, and divine judgement.

171. Horsley, *Jesus and Empire*, 52.

"The 'content' of the prophetic movements indicates that they were movements of the discontented among the common people, certainly not of the comfortable."[172] It seems that the majority of these movements drew people from rural places, though there is some evidence that the excluded within urban areas also participated.[173] The movements above were able to gain the sizable support they did precisely because they evoked a powerful reaction among the peasantry. Such people, under the weight of various powers, sought the liberation described above, which implicitly suggests an "indictment of the established order of things and its replacement by a more equitable and just (liberated) social order."[174] Though the movements did not take the initiative for political "revolution," and indeed expected God to act imminently, they were nonetheless prepared to play an active role in their perceived hope.[175] Indeed some movements took up arms, but only in anticipation of divine action; there was no plan to engage in a violent overthrow of Roman rule. That the destruction of the dominant way of life was a requirement for liberation seems to be a given, and this should lead us to consider such movements as broadly apocalyptic. It is for this reason that those in the relevant positions of power, having discerned the nature of these movements, perceived them to be a threat against the established order and responded so brutally.

Scot McKnight notes about these first-century figures that they differ from the prophets of the Old Testament in at least one major way. While the actions of Israel's prophets were overwhelmingly focused on *judgement* (especially against Israel), the actions of these first-century prophets were primarily concerned with *redemption, political liberation,*

172. Horsley, "Popular Prophetic Movements," 13.

173. Josephus gives an account of an action prophet named Jonathan, a Sicarius whose movement occurred in Cyrene, North Africa in the 70s CE (*J.W.* 7.437–50; *Life* 424–25). Josephus explicitly states that Jonathan's followers consisted of "many of the poor" (οὐκ ὀλίγοι τῶν ἀπόρων; *J.W.* 7.438).

174. Horsley, "Popular Prophetic Movements," 13.

175. "The sign prophets were not political revolutionaries or insurrectionists in the ordinary sense. This is not to say that the movements they led were in no sense political. On the contrary, it is likely that these movements arose at least partly in response to the experience of foreign domination and that all of them, in one way or another, expected and looked forward to the end of Roman rule. In this sense, they were most definitely political movements. By saying that the sign prophets were not political revolutionaries in the ordinary sense, I mean that they did not have a practical plan for ousting the Romans by force; they were 'apolitical' in the sense in which Sanders has defined the term to mean 'not involving a plan to liberate and restore Israel by defeating the Romans and establishing an autonomous government.' To the extent that their vision of the future included an end to Roman rule, they expected that God himself would bring this about." Gray, *Prophetic Figures*, 138.

or restoration.[176] For McKnight, such actions would evoke the memory not of Isaiah, Jeremiah, or Ezekiel, but of Moses and Joshua. We can nuance McKnight's conclusion somewhat since, for these prophetic figures in this first-century milieu, Israel's political liberation implied God's judgement. Such hoped-for judgement, however, was to be directed against Israel's oppressors, rather than being focused on Israel itself, as it had been for most Old Testament prophets. If these first-century prophets were influenced by apocalyptic thought, they were influenced by the common apocalyptic theme of judgement against oppressive empires and rulers. The embodiment of eschatological deliverance in their actions was a coin with two sides: anticipated redemption and judgement.

Oracular Prophets

Whereas action prophets modeled their activity on archetypes such as Moses, Joshua and Elijah, a different kind of first-century Jewish prophet resembled prophets like Isaiah, Jeremiah, and Ezekiel.[177] Unfortunately, there are not many detailed examples of these oracular prophets from this period. Perhaps the most well-known example of an oracular prophet in the first century is John the Baptist. For now, however, our focus falls on another figure, our only other known major example.

Jesus Son of Ananias

At one point in *Jewish War,* Josephus describes a series of portents foreshadowing the downfall of the Jews, Jerusalem, and the temple (*J. W.* 6.288–315). The zenith of these signs is said to be Jesus, son of Ananias.

> But a further portent was even more alarming. The four years before the war, when the city was enjoying profound peace and prosperity, there came to the feast at which it is the custom of all Jews to erect tabernacles to God, one Jesus, son of Ananias, a rude peasant, who, standing in the temple, suddenly began to cry out,
>
>> A voice from the east,
>> a voice from the west,
>> a voice from the four winds;

---

176. McKnight, "Jesus and Prophetic Actions," 216.

177. Though it should be noted these two "categories" are not mutually exclusive, as the example of John the Baptist demonstrates.

> a voice against Jerusalem and the sanctuary,
> a voice against the bridegroom and the bride,
> a voice against all the people.[178]

Day and night he went about all the alleys with this cry on his lips. Some of the leading citizens, incensed at these ill-omened words, arrested the fellow and severely chastised him. But he, without a word on his own behalf or for the private ear of those who smote him, only continued his cries as before. Thereupon, the magistrates, supposing, as was indeed the case, that the man was under some supernatural impulse, brought him before the Roman governor; there, although flayed to the bone with scourges, he neither sued for mercy nor shed a tear, but, merely introducing the most mournful of variations into his ejaculation, responded to each stroke with "Woe to Jerusalem!" When Albinus, the governor, asked him who and whence he was and why he uttered these cries, he answered him never a word, but unceasingly reiterated his dirge over the city, until Albinus pronounced him a maniac and let him go. During the whole period up to the outbreak of war he neither approached nor was seen talking to any of the citizens, but daily, like a prayer that he had conned, repeated his lament, "Woe to Jerusalem!" He neither cursed any of those who beat him from day to day, nor blessed those who offered him food: to all men that melancholy presage was his one reply. His cries were loudest at the festivals. So for seven years and five months he continued his wail, his voice never flagging nor his strength exhausted, until in the siege, having seen his presage verified, he found his rest. For, while going his round and shouting in piercing tones from the wall, "Woe once more to the city and to the people and to the temple," as he added a last word, "and woe to me also," a stone hurled from the *ballista* struck and killed him on the spot. So with those ominous words still upon his lips he passed away.[179]

Jesus son of Ananias is contrasted with other figures, those Josephus calls ψευδοπροφῆται (*J.W.* 6.283–87). Following his account of Jesus, Josephus writes of God's providential care for human beings in attempting to show them "the way to salvation" through signs and warnings (*J.W.* 6.310). Jesus is clearly considered to be one of these signs. Appearing four

---

178. This way of presenting Jesus' first reported utterance is to diverge from the prose form of the Loeb edition of *J.W.* Setting the oracle in such a poetic form helps to draw out Jesus' use of classical forms of prophecy, as we will see below.

179. Josephus, *J.W.* 6.300–309.

years before the war (c. 62 CE[180]), he is reported to have declared woe upon Jerusalem for seven years and five months in the manner of the classical prophets. Horsley offers the following comparisons:[181]

1. Jesus, like Amos, prophesied judgement initially in a socio-political situation that seemed peaceful and prosperous to the ruling classes. The prophet, however, "knew better";

2. Like Amos and Jeremiah, Jesus went straight to the temple with a message of judgement;

3. His behavior of continuing his dirge on the doomed city is similar to Isaiah, who uttered his warnings naked and barefoot, or to Jeremiah, who had a yoke around his neck before the Babylonian siege began;

4. Jesus' message is reminiscent of the judgement and lament pronounced on Jerusalem by the classical prophets, especially Jeremiah (e.g., 7:34; 19; 22:1–9; 26);

5. Like Jeremiah, Jesus was arrested and mistreated.

In regard to this last point, Jesus son of Ananias seems to have garnered the opposition of "some of the leading citizens" who, apparently unlike the Roman Albinus, were angry about his predictions. It is possible that they comprehended the endangerment that the prophet and his judgements posed to the established social order. Among the common people the verdict was mixed: some apparently beat him while others fed him. It may be that Jesus, as a rural peasant, gained credibility amongst some of the common people precisely because he was an unlikely candidate for a prophet.[182] Moreover, his predictions about the temple may have impressed those who felt exploited by its economic reach.[183] To Albinus, Jesus seemed afflicted

180. According to Josephus, Jesus appeared during the procuratorship of Albinus who held office during 62–64 CE

181. Horsley with Hanson, *Bandits, Prophets and Messiahs*, 174–75.

182. Aune, *Prophecy in Early Christianity*, 136.

183. Gray critiques Horsley's suggestion that Jesus was a champion of the cause of the ordinary people because "the temple was not—or at least was not only—the symbol of the power of the ruling classes; it was the center and symbol of Jewish religious life" (*Prophetic Figures*, 162). She claims that an oracle of the destruction of the temple would have been resented by most Jews and not merely the aristocracy. This is debatable. Both Horsley and Gray are probably off the mark here—Gray is correct in arguing that Horsley's case goes too far since there is no evidence that Jesus divided people along class lines. Indeed, the oracle was leveled against *everyone* in Jerusalem. However, that Jesus was loudest at the festivals suggests that those from outside Jerusalem also heard him. It is not clear that non-Jerusalemites would have supported him, but given the anti-temple sentiment present amongst some at the time this is not unlikely.

by madness (μανία) so he released him. The magistrates (οἱ ἄρχοντες), on the other hand, believed him to be spirit-possessed (δαιμονιώτερον τὸ κίνημα).[184] Gray notes similarities (and also differences) between Jesus and the prophet Jeremiah: Jeremiah was also not deterred by punishment or imprisonment; he too was considered insane.[185] Where Jesus may possibly have been different from Jeremiah is that his perceived "spirit possession" might have been an indicator of a trance-like state, although not necessarily (cf. Mark 3:22). It is not clear whether this would lend him credibility and, if so, among which sections of society. In any event, Jesus' conscious commitment to his prophetic task, even to the point of suffering physical assault, may have been sufficient to earn him the label of maniac. Whatever the case, like Jeremiah and other OT prophets, Jesus uttered polemic against the temple and Jerusalem, predicting its downfall.

The first reported oracle of Jesus (*J.W.* 6.301) is one of doom.[186] It is also poetic, being composed of two strophes of three lines each.[187] The third line of each strophe summarizes the previous two lines, "a feature usually described as Semitic parallelism."[188] The strophes describe, respectively, the origin of the voice and its content. Jesus' references to a φωνή imply his own conviction of divine revelation; the voice is God's voice.[189] The content of the oracle indicates the targets of judgement, including "the bridegroom and the bride." This evokes Jer 7:34; 16:9; 25:10; and 33:11, which speak separately of judgement and also, in the case of 33:11, future restoration. Unlike Jeremiah, Jesus hints at no restoration, and it is impossible to know whether he thought such would occur. Though Aune argues that Jesus' oracle does not conform to the standard woe oracles of the OT

---

184. The Loeb edition of *J.W.* translates Jesus' perceived state as being "under some supernatural impulse" though the Greek is probably better translated "demon possessed." I am aware of the breadth of debate regarding the meaning of demon possession. It may be that Jesus' perceived demon possession is another way of talking about his being considered a "maniac" (μανία), that is, mentally ill. This is not the place to stage this discussion, and it is in no way crucial to this study.

185. Gray, *Prophetic Figures*, 160.

186. Aune, *Prophecy in Early Christianity*, 135–36.

187. Aune, *Prophecy in Early Christianity*, 136.

188. Gray, *Prophetic Figures*, 160.

189. Gray notes that some have identified this voice with the rabbinic understanding of *bat qol* (described in the previous chapter); *Prophetic Figures*, 160. Aune notes however that "Early Judaism tended to use the term 'voice' for 'voice of God,' or as a surrogate in order to avoid explicitly connecting God with the act of speaking. . . . When Joshua ben Ananiah repeatedly refers to the 'voice' coming from all directions (cf. Ps. 29) with negative implications, he is using a well-known, recognizable idiom which refers to the voice of God pronouncing judgment." *Prophecy in Early Christianity*, 136–37.

(on the basis that it does not specify the nature of the threat),[190] this obviously only applies to the form of the oracle as we have it—it is impossible to know what Jesus originally said and whether this oracle was more extensive than what has been recorded by Josephus. Indeed, it would not have been in Josephus' interests to report extensively on Jewish hopes for restoration. In all other features the oracle resembles OT woe oracles.

That Jesus' cry was loudest at the festivals indicates that his choice of time and place for proclamation was not accidental.[191] Like the classical prophets, Jesus must have understood that content alone was insufficient for having one's proclamation enter the national consciousness. The judgement needed to confront national myths of guaranteed liberation, prosperity, and security. Such myths were empowered not least by the temple institution, and the Feast of Tabernacles ("the feast at which it is the custom of all Jews to erect tabernacles to God") was a crucial event for legitimating the temple in the Jewish calendar. This feast, "considered especially sacred and important by the Hebrews" (*Ant.* 8.100), celebrated God's faithfulness to and harvest provision for the Israelites when they lived in booths in the wilderness. It was also the occasion on which Solomon dedicated the temple (*Ant.* 8.99–100) and the first occasion celebrated following the return from Babylonian exile. It is unclear whether the two latter events played a prominent role at the feast for first-century Jews. In any case, Jesus' prophetic judgement served to subvert the feast, as well as its participants' remembrance of God's providence and faithfulness; such characteristics would no longer be shown to Israel, but rather destruction would come to its capital and its "sanctuary."

Festivals were, around this time, particularly unstable occasions. Above we have already considered some hostilities that broke out during festivals, such as that under the procuratorship of Cumanus (48–52 CE) described in *J.W.* 2.224–27. According to other episodes in Josephus' accounts, tensions between Jews and Romans were high, as were those between pro- and anti-Roman factions among the Jews. The Gospels also provide a major account of a young prophet executed during a festival. Such unpredictability during festivals may explain why the elites of the city would be so opposed to a prophet of doom, even one who urged no violence.

Whatever may have been the case with Jesus son of Ananias, we know that there was no oracle of deliverance, only one of judgement. His oracle is an echo of the tradition of prophetic laments, particularly Jeremiah, and

---

190. Aune, *Prophecy in Early Christianity*, 136.

191. I understand "loudest" as a superlative compared not to other voices at the festivals, but to other proclamations of Jesus himself.

is reminiscent of other echoes heard several decades earlier from a Galilean prophet also named Jesus.

Other Oracular Prophets

It is of no surprise that Jesus bar-Ananias' oracles were not unique leading up to the time of the Roman siege of Jerusalem. Indeed, there appears to have been a number of other, less vividly remembered oracular prophets who proclaimed oracles or performed portents that were understood to communicate God's support of or opposition to the Jewish war effort:

> Numerous prophets, indeed, were at this period suborned by the tyrants to delude the people, by bidding them await help from God, in order that desertions might be checked and that those who were above fear and precaution might be encouraged by hope. In adversity man is quickly persuaded; but when the deceiver actually pictures release from prevailing horrors, then the sufferer wholly abandons himself to expectation.
>
> Thus it was that the wretched people were deluded at that time by charlatans and pretended messengers of the deity; while they neither heeded nor believed in the manifest portents that foretold the coming desolation, but, as if thunderstruck and bereft of eyes and mind, disregarded the plain warnings of God. So it was when a star, resembling a sword, stood over the city, and a comet which continued for a year. So again when, before the revolt and the commotion that led to war, at the time when the people were assembling for the feast of unleavened bread, on the eighth of the month Xanthicus, at the ninth hour of the night, so brilliant a light shone round the altar and the sanctuary that it seemed to be broad daylight; and this continued for half an hour. By the inexperienced this was regarded as a good omen, but by the sacred scribes it was at once interpreted in accordance with after events. At that same feast a cow that had been brought by some one for sacrifice gave birth to a lamb in the midst of the court of the temple; moreover, the eastern gate of the inner court—it was of brass and very massive, and, when closed toward evening, could scarcely be moved by twenty men; fastened with iron-bound bars, it had bolts which were sunk to a great depth into a threshold consisting of a solid block of stone—this gate was observed at the sixth hour of the night to have opened of its own accord. The watchmen of the temple ran and reported the matter to the captain, and he came up and with difficulty succeeded in shutting it. This again to the

uninitiated seemed the best of omens, as they supposed that
God had opened to them the gate of blessings; but the learned
understood that the security of the temple was dissolving of its
own accord and that the opening of the gate meant a present
to the enemy, interpreting the portent in their own minds as
indicative of coming desolation.[192]

It would appear from Josephus' accounts that apparent portents were often
accompanied by figures claiming to be prophets who would dare to interpret
the signs. While Jesus son of Ananias pronounced doom, these examples
seem to have announced coming deliverance. While Josephus, with the advantage of hindsight, is able to refer to them as charlatans and pretenders,
the point here is not their accuracy or truthfulness, but the fact that they
led many astray. In other words, some people perceived that they were true
prophets announcing divine revelation of coming deliverance.

These and other examples of portents recorded by Josephus (esp. *J. W.*
6.283–85, 297–300) demonstrate an intensely apocalyptic mood permeat-
ing much of the Jewish populace at the time. The only reported group who
took exception is the "learned" (though it is unclear whether Josephus' report of their understanding is *ex eventu*). This apocalyptic mood is perhaps
best demonstrated in *J. W.* 6.297–99 in which a vision in the sky, apparently
witnessed by a number of people, depicted heavenly armies surrounding
the cities. To some it must have seemed that such portents signaled God's
intervention against the Romans. The view that heavenly armies fought
on behalf of the people was of course derived from a long prophetic tradition (e.g., Zechariah 9–14). Such encouragement was balanced by portents
seemingly indicating coming destruction (*J. W.* 6.299–300) or false prophecies leading to disaster (6.283–85).

Given the evidence of the popularity of apocalyptic in the first
century, it is not surprising that it should be so concentrated around the
moment of Jerusalem's destruction. In light of the subversive character
of apocalyptic literature, it is understandable that the lower classes and
rural dwellers should embrace prophetic proclamations of hope and victory from oppression. That it was the educated who took most notice of
predictions of devastation, and who interpreted portents to mean the
same, may well demonstrate the difference in outlook between classes,
their perception of the future, and whether they were sympathetic toward
the aspirations of the common people for liberation and a return to the
covenantal way of life of early Israel.

192. Josephus, *J. W.* 6.286–96.

2.4 Glimpses of Jesus in Jewish Popular Prophets of the First Century CE

In this study of Jewish prophets and prophecy around the time of Jesus of Nazareth, we have examined two distinct but related types of popular prophets: action prophets and oracular prophets. These prophets existed in distinction to clerical prophets and sapiential prophets.

Such classifications require some tentativeness since there is no evidence that Jews and Christians in the first century felt it necessary to categorize prophetic figures. Indeed, the only distinction made by Josephus is between a προφήτης and a ψευδοπροφήτης. Modern attempts at further categorization are necessarily imposed on first-century prophetic figures in a way that is almost certainly foreign to how first-century Jews and Christians would have viewed them. The typology of prophetism in early Judaism suggested by Becker,[193] for example, is questionable for a number of reasons, not least because the rigid lines of distinction between his "types" are not derived from the primary sources so much as being imposed on them. Again, it is unlikely that Matthew and his contemporaries would have recognized such a division.

The dilemma of the classification of prophecy raises the larger question, deferred earlier in this chapter, of how to define prophecy. One aspect of this problem is the level of specificity to which such a definition should aspire. A number of definitions of prophecy have focused solely on the oral aspect of the phenomenon, such as those of Hill and Grudem.[194] This, however, is problematic since, as we have seen in a number of cases, there is no record of any speech as evidence of claims to prophethood, but rather only actions.

At this point we need to draw together some of the common threads that exist between the popular prophetic figures that have been presented. The first and perhaps most potent commonality is that each figure's activities are reminiscent of OT prophetic figures, whether that be Moses, Joshua, Elijah, Amos, Jeremiah, or another. Their words and deeds often embody

---

193. As summarized by Aune, *Prophecy in Early Christianity*, 107.

194. Both Hill and Grudem differentiate rather sharply between Old and New Testament forms of prophecy, though in all cases they define prophecy as an oral activity. Grudem says of Old Testament prophets that their "*very words* were words which God had given them to deliver," and of New Testament prophets that they speak "merely human words to report something God brings to mind." Grudem, *Gift of Prophecy*, 22, 51. Hill says of the Christian (New Testament) prophet that he/she is "a divinely called and divinely inspired speaker who receives intelligible and authoritative revelations or messages which he is impelled to deliver publicly, in oral or written form, to Christian individuals and/or the Christian community." Hill, *New Testament Prophecy*, 8–9.

the imagery of or directly echo such ancient Israelite traditions. It would be fair to assume that these traditions were vigorously present in the minds of Theudas, the Egyptian, and the other first-century Jewish prophets and that they were intentional in how they embodied their communication. We ought to point especially to Moses, the greatest prophet in Israelite tradition (Deut 34:10) and, according to Willem VanGemeren, "the fountainhead of the prophets" in whom the prophetic message was rooted.[195] Moses was ostensibly the first to receive, write, and teach the revelation of God.[196] His pattern provided the blueprint for the development of prophecy in subsequent centuries, including that of the Second Temple period, as reflected in the ongoing emulation of his example.

If Moses is indeed the model for later prophetic activity in Israel, then perhaps the *raison d'etre* of his prophetic role would enlighten any study into the vocation of later prophets. In a brief analysis of Moses' prophetic call and role, Dumbrell asserts that Moses was "the divine messenger whose function was to proclaim God's will to Israel and to keep them within the covenant."[197] That such a definition is applicable to later prophets is not difficult to substantiate—even in Second Temple Judaism the later prophets such as Elijah and Jeremiah are considered guardians and zealots for Torah (1 Macc 2:58; 2 Macc 2:1–9).[198] Moreover, eschatological prophets were regarded as "specially gifted for the interpretation of Torah (1 Macc 4:46)," and in later rabbinic Judaism prophecy was subordinate to Torah.[199] Such beliefs betray the situatedness of Jewish prophecy within the locus of covenantal fidelity, however such fidelity was understood amid the diversity of Second Temple Judaism. Bowman states that OT prophecy had two functions—prediction and rebuke.[200] I would suggest that such aspects of the prophetic role are not strictly functions as much as they are means to the more basic function of proclaiming God's will and actions, and enforcing the covenant as divinely-sanctioned messenger. Josephus seems to confirm this understanding when, recounting Jewish history, he states that:

> And so, as night had now fallen, the Syrian army retired to its camp and, when the herald announced that Achab was dead, they returned to their own country, first carrying the body of Achab to Samaria and burying it there. And when they

195. VanGemeren, *Interpreting the Prophetic Word*, 28.

196. VanGemeren, *Interpreting the Prophetic Word*, 28–34.

197. Dumbrell, *Faith of Israel*, 34.

198. Aune, *Prophecy in Early Christianity*, 124.

199. Aune, *Prophecy in Early Christianity*, 124.

200. Bowman, "Prophets and Prophecy in Talmud and Midrash," 107.

washed his chariot, which was stained with the king's blood, in the spring of Jezarel, they acknowledged the truth of Elijah's prophecy, for the dogs licked up his blood; and thereafter the harlots used to bathe in the pool in this blood. But he died in Aramathe, as Michaias had foretold. Now, since there befell Achab the fate spoken of by the two prophets, we ought to acknowledge the greatness of the Deity and everywhere honour and reverence Him, nor should we think the things which are said to flatter us or please us more worthy of belief than the truth, but should realize that nothing is more beneficial than prophecy and the foreknowledge which it gives, *for in this way God enables us to know what to guard against.*[201]

Though Josephus may well avoid covenantal and eschatological language because of his Roman audience, he seems to articulate that prophetic foretelling worked to warn against impending judgement, typically eschatological in nature, and to command the appropriate changes required to avoid such judgement. This indicates that prophets functioned as messengers who, like Moses, declared God's will and called people to covenantal fidelity. One Qumran text, 4Q375, appears to share this understanding of prophets, stating that they delivered the commands of God in order that people may "keep all these precepts" and that God may "repent of the fury of his great wrath in order to save you from your trials."[202] It is not surprising, then, that the prophets studied in this chapter fall broadly within this pattern.

The covenantal fidelity advocated by the prophets was not merely a desire for religious or legal faithfulness; rather the movements led by these prophets could be described as *revitalization movements.*[203] Such movements are, according to anthropologist Anthony Wallace, "usually conceived in a prophet's revelatory visions, which provide for him a satisfying relationship to the supernatural and outline a new way of life under divine sanction."[204]

---

201. Josephus, *Ant.* 8.416–18 (emphasis added).

202. 4Q375 1.2–4. Trans. Martínez and Tigchelaar, *Dead Sea Scrolls Study Edition,* 2:741.

203. Wallace, "Revitalization Movements," 264–65. Wallace suggests that attempted innovations within a cultural system have been labeled commonly as "'nativistic movement,' 'reform movement,' 'cargo cult,' 'religious revival,' 'messianic movement,' 'utopian community,' 'sect formation,' 'mass movement,' 'social movement,' 'revolution,' 'charismatic movement,'" though he brings all of these phenomena under his term "revitalization movement." He says, "A revitalization movement is defined as a deliberate, organized, conscious effort by members of a society to construct a more satisfying culture." This description seems apt for our purposes in describing the aim of the prophets in light of Josephus' accounts.

204. Wallace, "Revitalization Movements," 279.

It is unclear whether all first-century Jewish prophets experienced perceived revelatory visions, though this is not improbable given the potency of their conviction. What is clear is that they, by their words and actions, sought a new way of life that implied a return to a covenantal way of life that had ostensibly existed in early Israel (Wallace's "new way of life under divine sanction"). Indeed, this was the hope that the classical prophets themselves declared and petitioned for. Even Jesus son of Ananias, who proclaimed doom on Jerusalem with no explicit message of redemption, echoes judgements precisely because Israel had failed to embody its covenant obligations.

Directly related to a return to a covenantal existence is another Mosaic characteristic that is shared by the action prophets, namely a commitment to divine liberation amid dire circumstances. As discussed, this liberation implied the destruction of the dominant oppressive order and utilized the Moses and Joshua liberation traditions—unsurprising given their prominence in Israelite history. It would appear that a central aspect of the prophetic vocation, at least as demonstrated by the Palestinian examples studied here, is that of mediating the overturning of the current order for a new order typified by freedom from forms of oppression (deliverance/judgement) and/or announcing impending divine activity to do so. Even Jesus son of Ananias' woe oracles functioned to endanger the established order, as signaled by his torture at the hands of the guardians of that order. That woe oracles and other oracular forms of prophecy often had embedded in them an implicit petition and even declaration of a new order seems congruent with the social setting of the oracular prophets and with the reactions of opposing groups. Oracular prophets of the time were, like the action prophets, eschatologically oriented. For both types of prophet, their words and actions do one of two things described by Morna Hooker: they "mediate manifestations of divine power in events that bring with them either salvation or judgment [and] point to a divine activity which cannot otherwise be observed at present."[205] McKnight says that both can be summarized as the "embodiment" of God's will by the prophet.[206] That is, prophetic oracles are the spoken equivalent of the drama of prophetic actions and vice versa; both embody the will of God.

Class and status seemed to have played a central role in whether or not a person or group was sympathetic to the message of the popular prophet. This seems to reflect that the content was generally favorable toward the poor rural classes and critical of (some) elites. It is unclear whether criticism of elites is an essential characteristic of the prophetic

---

205. Hooker, *Signs of a Prophet*, 3.
206. McKnight, "Jesus and Prophetic Actions," esp. 222.

vocation demonstrated by the Palestinian prophets, though it is not difficult to imagine so: elites typically opposed prophetic movements, and the words and actions of the prophets typically critiqued political authority and envisaged a more equitable social reality.

Based on this analysis, a popular prophet in the first-century Palestinian context could be said to be *a divinely inspired*[207] *person who, operating primarily within the social milieu of the common populace, through intentional action or spoken oracle, influenced by apocalyptic eschatology, and displaying characteristics found in a biblical prophetic tradition, mediates or announces God's covenantal will—including God's deliverance and/or judgement—in order to call the recipients back to covenantal fidelity and/or point to a divine act of judgement and/or liberation.* While such a definition may appear broad, the condition of displaying characteristics found in a biblical prophetic tradition (particularly the Mosaic tradition)[208] and the notion of covenantal fidelity are quite specific and necessarily exclude, for example, strictly Graeco-Roman prophets and forms of prophecy.

If we were to broaden this definition to include clerical and sapiential prophets, then we could say a prophet, at least in Second Temple Judaism, is *a divinely inspired person who, in congruency with a biblical prophetic tradition, intentionally delivers revelation from God, either in the form of action or spoken oracle, which most often calls for the covenantal fidelity of the recipients and/or predicts important future events.*[209] This definition is in some ways more precise than those of Friedrich,[210] Boring,[211] Hill,[212] and

---

207. Such inspiration being understood as God's choice to communicate with and influence human beings by any elected means, especially dreams and visions.

208. See VanGemeren, *Interpreting the Prophetic Word*; Aernie, *Is Paul Also Among the Prophets?*, 10–28.

209. Webb, *John the Baptizer and Prophet*, 307–48 shows that the nature of clerical and sapiential prophecy tended to be prediction and the subject often events surrounding political figures (ascension, death). This is in contrast to popular prophecy.

210. "The prophet is essentially a proclaimer of God's Word." Friedrich, "προφήτης κτλ," *TDNT* 6:829.

211. "A prophet is an immediately-inspired spokesman for the (or a) deity of a particular community, who receives revelations which he is impelled to deliver to the community." Boring, "Apocalypse as Christian Prophecy," 2:44.

212. "A Christian prophet is a Christian who functions within the Church, occasionally or regularly, as a divinely called and divinely inspired speaker who receives intelligible and authoritative revelations or messages which he is impelled to deliver publicly, in oral or written form, to Christian individuals and/or the Christian community." Hill, *New Testament Prophecy*, 8–9.

Grudem.[213] It is also more specific than the more general term προφήτης,[214] which may include a myriad of other kinds of prophecy outside the bounds of first-century Palestinian Judaism. Like most studies on the topic of ancient prophecy,[215] the definition presented here is limited to a particular time (first century CE), place (Syro-Palestine) and culture (early forms of Judaism, including Christianity). It is, unlike some definitions, focused on *function* as well as form and this should be expected given this study's focus on social history.[216] Such a function can be summarized in a less technical fashion by repeating Brueggemann's concept of the prophetic imagination: the prophet functions to "nurture, nourish, and evoke a consciousness and perception alternative to the consciousness and perception of the dominant culture around us."[217] While we must be cautious since Brueggemann's concept could easily be applied outside of first-century Judaism, such alternative consciousness is the very essence of covenant fidelity.

The crucial question, indeed one that is central to this chapter, is what bearing, if any, the cited popular prophets have on studying the prophetic vocation of Matthew's portrayal of Jesus of Nazareth. Certainly, there are superficial similarities when comparing these prophets with a cursory reading of Jesus' ministry in the Gospel of Matthew—the support of members of the peasantry, the opposition of elites, Mosaic allusions, oracles of grief, judgements against the established order, the influence of apocalyptic, and so forth. Such similarities do not of course guarantee Jesus is one of the popular prophets, though there are reasons to assume that the Palestinian popular

213. "The main function of Old Testament prophets was to be *messengers from God*, sent to speak to men and women with words from God." *Gift of Prophecy*, 21. Such a proposition is remarkably broad, apart from the form of delivery (words only). There is no notion of any time-, place- or culture-specific considerations. In this way Grudem's definition, while basically true, could be used of any prophetic utterance.

214. This is not to say that the term προφήτης is unimportant, for indeed this is the word used of Jesus' prophetic identity in Matthew's Gospel. It is simply to say that προφήτης has a wider usage than what is being here defined. As Hill has said, "the semantic value of a word is not determined by its derivation, but by its usage in contexts." Indeed, we are here referring to only one such context(s)—first century Palestinian Judaism.

215. For example, Aune's *Prophecy in Early Christianity* is limited to the Mediterranean world in early Judaism and early Christianity (up until the second century CE). Witherington's *Jesus the Seer* is limited to, "the eastern end of the Mediterranean crescent and the nearby Middle Eastern regions . . . [from] about 1600 BC to approximately AD 300," with a major focus on biblical prophecy (1–2).

216. This is particularly potent in light of the notion of covenantal fidelity, which as outlined above is inextricably linked to divine liberation and a "new way of life under divine sanction." Wallace, "Revitalization Movements," 279.

217. Brueggemann, *Prophetic Imagination*, 3.

prophets provide a helpful comparison to Jesus that will serve to elucidate Matthew's presentation of his prophetic vocation. At the very least it can be said that Matthew's Jesus looks remarkably like other Jewish popular prophets of the first century CE. The similarity between the social setting of these prophets and Matthew's community (and indeed Jesus himself) further demonstrates the reasonableness of this assumption.

The Syro-Palestinian geography of the first century CE, with its common languages, history, and culture, forms a further basis for my claim that the Samaritan prophet, Theudas, the Egyptian, Jesus son of Ananias, and others share, in many ways, a worldview and understanding of prophecy with Matthew's community, and indeed with Jesus himself. There is clearly a divide between Matthew's early Christian community and the larger Palestinian Jewish community within which it lives in terms of their understanding of the identity of Jesus of Nazareth. This has significant ramifications for their understanding of God, the law, and social relationships. Nonetheless, that the Hebrew Scriptures and Jewish history form the center of a cultural world common to both groups should not be understated, for cultures create human conceptions and thus patterns of meaningfulness which are "assimilated and learned in the enculturation process."[218] The implication is that these co-habiting Jews and (primarily) Jewish Christians, having been enculturated within a specific history and understanding of the prophetic vocation, will hold a roughly parallel understanding of that vocation. This hypothesis stands whether Matthew's community was located in Galilee or in a nearby location such as Antioch; whatever the case, the Jewishness of the First Gospel assumes an equally high level of enculturation within Syro-Palestinian Judaism and its history.

It appears that those prophetic figures that operated in Palestine during the first century CE were firmly embedded in the broad cultural milieu of Palestinian Judaism and thus held a distinctly Jewish worldview, one which would undoubtedly have shaped their understanding of prophecy and the prophetic vocation. This is reflected foremost in their pattern of echoing past biblical prophetic figures. The traditions of liberation and hope for a return to a covenantally faithful existence which permeate prophetic history at every stage would have saturated the self-understandings of prophetic figures like the Samaritan prophet, Theudas, the Egyptian prophet, and Jesus son of Ananias. The recipients of Matthew's Gospel, a community equally embedded in Jewish culture, would have had the same traditions of prophecy and liberation permeate their community life, as it would have done for all marginalized Jewish groups in Palestine. The

218. Malina, *New Testament World*, 8–9, 24.

resulting practices may have varied somewhat but, overall, this understanding would have influenced the author of Matthew and his portrayal of Jesus' prophetic vocation. To make use of study of the prophetic vocations of contemporaneous Jewish prophets—with their self-understandings, symbolism, prophetic forms, methods, and popular appraisals—in order to understand Matthew's portrayal of Jesus as prophet would appear to be a fruitful venture. The aims, actions, and words of these prophets, regardless of how failed or delusional they might have been, provide us with a basis for defining prophecy and its characteristics, and a canvas on which to paint a Matthean picture of a Jewish prophet from Nazareth.

Chapter 3

Which of Jesus' Words and Actions
Are "Prophetic"?

As we turn our attention to Jesus' prophetic vocation in Matthew's Gospel, we must answer a crucial question: in light of OT prophetic traditions, and also the popular prophets of the first century CE, what actions or words of Jesus should be considered "prophetic"? This is a question that has spawned a variety of answers. In terms of actions, C. H. Dodd listed four as prophetic, David Aune only two, and Morna Hooker fifteen.[1] Do, for example, the healings of Jesus, which in at least some cases echo the actions of Elijah and Elisha, merit the label "prophetic"? What about his nature miracles, such as walking on water? Or his choosing of twelve disciples? Moreover, does an action of Jesus that is reminiscent of an OT prophet's action necessarily make it "prophetic"? All these questions are quite apart from how, exactly, to ascertain which of Jesus' words are prophetic in nature.

Having already said that, at the very least, Jesus looks remarkably like a Jewish popular prophet, and having defined such a figure, we have a starting point from which to consider such questions. In the last chapter we concluded that a popular prophet in the first century CE was one recognized as *a divinely inspired person who, operating primarily within the social milieu of the common populace, through intentional action or spoken oracle, influenced by apocalyptic eschatology, and displaying characteristics found in a biblical prophetic tradition, mediates or announces God's covenantal will—including God's deliverance and/or judgement—in order to call the recipients back to covenantal fidelity and/or point to a divine act of judgement and/or liberation.*

It was made clear that this definition does not encompass all varieties of prophets, but only one specific type that shares similarities with Jesus in

---

1. Dodd, "Jesus as Teacher and Prophet," 53–66; Aune, *Prophecy in Early Christianity*, 161–63; Hooker, *Signs of a Prophet*. These are discussed in McKnight, "Jesus and Prophetic Actions," 203.

terms of actions and words. This definition, with its reference to apocalypticism, may not apply to the ancient Hebrew prophets, but it does represent a later phenomenon that was clearly influenced by such prophets.

In order to determine the defining characteristics of Jesus' prophetic words and deeds, it will be helpful to distinguish between those characteristics of the popular prophet and the characteristics of their prophetic words and deeds themselves. This is complicated by the fact that some elements cross over. The following elements relate to the prophet:

- Divinely inspired

- Operating amongst common populace

- Acting intentionally

- Influenced by apocalyptic eschatology

- Displaying characteristics found in a biblical prophetic tradition

- Mediates or announces God's will

The following elements relate to the popular prophet's actions and/or words:

- Intentional

- Apocalyptic (inasmuch as it is looks toward a new eschatological state of affairs)

- Displaying characteristics found in a biblical prophetic tradition

- Mediates or announces God's will (calls recipients back to covenantal fidelity and/or points to a divine act of judgement and/or liberation)

There is much crossover since the distinction between the prophet and his/her activities is understandably blurred. Nonetheless, the above list gives us a basis for discussing which actions or words of Jesus classify as prophetic.

I am inclined to see more prophetic actions than the two named by David Aune (the purification of the temple and the cursing of the fig tree).[2] Aune's reason for limiting the number of actions that are deemed "prophetic" is that these two actions are "either a surrogate for or a dramatization of oracular speech."[3] Symbolic actions that are not substitutes for or dramatizations of oracular speech should, according to Aune, simply be deemed "symbolic" and not "prophetic." However, where Aune's approach sees prophetic actions as a replacement for the apparently more fundamental prophetic activity of oracular speech, I agree with Hooker that prophetic

2. Aune, *Prophecy in Early Christianity*, 161–63. It is not clear whether Aune thinks that there are additional prophetic actions of Jesus in the Gospels.

3. Aune, *Prophecy in Early Christianity*, 163.

actions are the dramatic *equivalents* of oracular speech.[4] The difference is subtle yet significant—the function of prophetic actions is not to stand in for prophetic speech, but, like oracular speech, such actions are intended to announce the will of God in and of themselves. That is to say, prophetic speech serves a particular purpose, and prophetic actions may fulfill the same purpose without being required to act as a proxy for such speech. This seems to be the case with the first-century action prophets, whose actions were deemed prophetic even without accompanying speech. Such a view widens the scope of what actions could be considered prophetic. Examples from within Matthew's Gospel include:

- Healings (e.g., 8:5–13; 9:27–31; 20:29–34)
- Feedings (14:13–21; 15:32–39)
- Exorcisms (e.g., 8:28–34; 9:32–34; 17:14–21)
- Nature Miracles (8:23–27; 14:22–33)
- Choosing the Twelve (10:1–4)
- Renaming Peter (16:18)
- Eating with tax collectors and sinners (e.g., 9:9–13)
- Scandalous behavior (e.g., 9:14–17; 12:1–8, 9–14)
- Riding into Jerusalem (21:1–11)
- The temple action (21:12–17)
- Cursing of the fig tree (21:18–22)
- The Last Supper (26:26–29)

Each of these acts conforms to patterns set by OT prophets or to elements of the action prophets' activities during the first century CE. Moreover, each of these acts qualifies as prophetic according to the criteria set out above. They are all intentional acts that resonate with some aspect of a biblical prophetic tradition. Each reflects some aspect of apocalyptic eschatology, even if not conforming to the conventions of apocalyptic qua literary genre. Perhaps most importantly, each act announces or mediates the will of God, either by calling people to covenantal fidelity or pointing to an act of divine liberation or judgement. In this way, they can each be described by Brueggemann's concept of the prophetic imagination—the task of nurturing, nourishing, and evoking an alternative consciousness to that of the dominant culture.[5]

---

4. Hooker, *Signs of a Prophet*, 38–39.
5. Brueggemann, *Prophetic Imagination*, 3.

Take, for example, the feeding stories: these acts arise from a need, and so are not premeditated as such, but they are nonetheless intentional once the need arises. The acts are reminiscent of the Mosaic stories of feeding in the wilderness. They are also eschatological since they point to what is hidden but is being revealed, God's power to save God's people, the creation of a new community, and the coming of the messianic banquet. Ultimately these acts both embody and point to God's will, in this case to provide for the people and liberate them from the crushing conditions under which they live and their effect of leaving the people without adequate nourishment. The same scheme can be applied to a harsher story, such as Jesus' temple action, though themes of liberation are less obvious than announcements of divine judgement that recall Jeremiah's actions and serve to warn of eschatological calamity. Both acts evoke an alternative consciousness to that of the dominant culture.

The same criteria as those applied to prophetic actions apply also to oracular speech. Some examples include:

- Calls to repent (esp. 4:17)
- Beatitudes (5:2–12)
- Law and "Antitheses" (5:17–48)
- Foretelling death and resurrection (17:22–23; 20:17–19)
- Woes against community leaders (23:1–36)
- Mourning over Jerusalem (23:37–39)
- Foretelling the temple's destruction (24:1–2)
- Testimony to the Sanhedrin (26:64)

Jesus' "woes" against community leaders in Matt 23 provide a paradigmatic episode of oracular prophecy in his ministry and, in some ways, they are strikingly similar to the oracles of Jesus son of Ananias performed decades later (though prior to the writing of Matthew's Gospel). These "woes" are intentional and resonate with declarations of judgement from the OT prophets, perhaps most notably Jeremiah. These announcements certainly represent an apocalyptic worldview, comparable to that reflected in 1 En 94:6–11; 97:7–10; 98:9–16; 99:1–2, 11–16; 100:7–9. Most obviously, Jesus' words against the community leaders are announcements of impending divine judgement and simultaneously warnings against covenantal infidelity.

Matthew's depiction of Jesus as prophet is varied and includes wide-ranging elements. Jesus is not merely a new Moses or Elijah, he is not simply another action prophet, nor is he simply an oracular prophet—Jesus is all of the above. This no doubt ties into Matthew's Christology: Jesus is Ἐμμανουήλ, and that theme is expounded, in part, by Matthew's presentation of Jesus in a range of roles. Indeed, God is not present with his people in only one way, but in many ways. For Matthew, one cannot simply talk about Jesus in one way because the Evangelist does not want his representation to resonate with only one ancient figure or tradition, but with many. In this way, Jesus can be portrayed as embodying a wide range of prophetic (and non-prophetic) styles.

The challenge for the remainder of this study is to explore this wide gamut of prophetic resonances whilst retaining a narrowness befitting meaningful exegesis of relevant passages. For this latter reason, only a representative selection of texts in Matthew's Gospel can be explored. But such a selection process raises a methodological issue. On the one hand, the aim is to comprehend Matthew's perspective on Jesus' prophetic vocation as distinct from the other Gospels (particularly the other Synoptics). On the other hand, we must avoid a situation in which we so emphasize the distinctives of the Matthean narrative that we ignore important similarities with other Gospels and thus distort Matthew's overall perspective.

One methodological approach to this issue, the one taken in this study, will be to turn our attention to texts depicting episodes that Matthew shares with other Gospels but which also display distinctive Matthean elements. Given the limited space available, this seems like one way to work toward holding Matthew's unique contribution in tension with his overall perspective that will, in numerous ways, share similarities with the other Gospels. To ensure that a range of prophetic themes are given attention, the exegetical portion of this study will be divided into four chapters, two that address a particular prophetic action of Jesus and two that address a particular occurrence of prophetic speech. These chapters will discuss, in narrative order, the Beatitudes (5:3–12), Jesus eating with tax collectors and sinners (9:9–13), Jesus' temple action (21:12–17) and Jesus' proclamations against the community leaders (23:1–39).

These episodes should provide an initial representative base for the way in which Matthew portrays Jesus as a prophet. By selecting these episodes, I am in no way claiming they are *the* paradigmatic prophetic episodes in Jesus' ministry. For example, his healings and miracles would have been seen as a major prophetic characteristic at the time. Such is reflected in the narrative detail that, up until the disciples relay popular opinion that he is a prophet in 16:14, Jesus' primary actions comprise healings and miracles. This would suggest that such actions inspired this popular belief. While an important element in this picture, Jesus' healings and miracles— together as a type of action—are neither unique to Matthew nor neglected by scholars. The same could be said of Matthew's temple action episode, though I am inclined to include it because it contains a section added onto Mark's account that conveniently recounts Jesus' compassionate healing of marginalized people. It is my view that this addition reflects a unique focus on Matthew's part, and lends a distinctive shape to his rendering of the story and to Jesus' prophetic vocation. The other episodes chosen contain material shared with other Gospels, but are either distinctive to Matthew as a unit (chapter 23[6]), edited significantly differently from other Gospels (the Beatitudes), or rarely discussed in relation to Jesus' prophetic vocation (eating with sinners). Each will help to provide a provisional picture of Matthew's portrayal of Jesus' prophetic vocation.

---

6. Matthew shares some of his proclamations with Luke 11, though Luke uses them in a different context. The result is that Matthew's proclamations are distinctive to him as a unit.

Chapter 4

The Beatitudes as Prophetic Speech

4.1 The Beatitudes and Narrative Criticism

THE BEATITUDES COMPRISE ONE of the most well-known passages in the Christian Scriptures. Though there have been a wide range of interpretive approaches to the Beatitudes, narrative criticism has, somewhat predictably, not been a popular method for interpreting them, or indeed other speech sections of the NT. For some, narrative criticism may prove insufficient for the task of exegeting Matt 5:3–12, particularly when that text is viewed in isolation.[1] There are a number of reasons for this, though in part such an attitude reflects a tendency to equate narrative criticism with New Criticism and its insistence on a solely text-immanent approach—what can narrative say about the Beatitudes if they are viewed self-referentially? I would suggest, however, that the equation of narrative criticism with New Criticism is unnecessary.

That narrative critics have shied away from detailed exegesis of the Beatitudes is a shame, since the tools of narrative criticism have the potential to reveal much about Matthew's message and, of particular relevance in this study, his thought regarding Jesus' prophetic vocation. Considerations of intertextuality, rhetorical devices, use of language, characterization, setting, and plot position—all narrative-critical tools—play a crucial part in exegesis of a speech event such as the Sermon on the Mount (SM) and the Beatitudes therein. Such tools, mixed with socio-historical research describing the context of the narrative, are a promising combination.

---

1. See Poland, *Literary Criticism and Biblical Hermeneutics*, 4. Poland argues that "the critical assumptions of modern formalist literary criticism are in many respects at odds with, or at least insufficient for, the full task of interpretation."

4.2 The Story So Far

Matthew's Gospel opens by stating that it is the Βίβλος γενέσεως Ἰησοῦ Χριστοῦ υἱοῦ Δαυὶδ υἱοῦ Ἀβραάμ. The use of γενέσεως is possibly an allusion to the creation account and indeed, by the time of Matthew, to the Greek title for what we now know as the first book of the OT.[2] Davies and Allison suggest the sentence may be read as "Book of the New Genesis wrought by Jesus Christ, son of David, son of Abraham," and that it is used to introduce the Gospel as a whole, not merely the subsequent genealogy (1:2–16).[3] They also suggest that the three names in 1:1 form the first half of a chiasm that is completed in the genealogy:[4]

   a Jesus Christ (1:1b)

      b David (1:1c)

         c Abraham (1:1d)

         c Abraham (1:2)

      b David (1:6)

   a Jesus (1:16)

That the central element in the chiasm is Abraham implies the centrality of the Patriarch to the meaning of the story about to be told.[5] In other words, the story of Jesus is embedded in the story of God's redemptive purposes being enacted in the world, a story that finds its origin in Abraham. This is confirmed by the emphasis given to Abraham and God's promises to him in Matthew's genealogy, which extends back to the Patriarch. As Carter notes, the purpose of a genealogy is not merely to pass on historical-biological information, but to associate the hero of a story with prestigious ancestors, thereby establishing the hero's status and nobility.[6] Matthew's genealogy, however, is odd in that wealth or power do not form the basis of Jesus' status. On the contrary, Jesus is placed squarely in the biblical story of Israel, in the

---

2. Davies and Allison provide more detail on the connection between Matt 1:1 and the notion of new creation and the first book of the OT. Davies and Allison, *Matthew 1–7*, 150–53.

3. Davies and Allison, *Matthew 1–7*, 153.

4. Davies and Allison, *Matthew 1–7*, 153.

5. Cf. Matt 28:19–20, in which the reference to making disciples of "all nations" alludes to the call of Abram in Gen 12:1–3. The character of Abraham frames Matthew's story.

6. Carter, *Matthew and the Margins*, 53. Carter gives as examples Tacitus, *Agr.* 4, and Josephus, *Life* 1–6.

promises to Abraham including blessing for the families of the earth (Gen
12:1–3), apparently including gentiles and outsiders (Matt 1:3, 5, 16[7]).

Up until this point, there is no mention of Moses or the prophets.
In terms of a study of the prophetic in Matthew this is worth observing.
Allusions to Moses and other prophetic figures are of course important
for Matthew as his story goes on. However, judging by their absence from
Matthew's introduction we ought to view them as narratively subservient
to the larger theme of Jesus as the one who will instigate a New Genesis. In
other words, the notion of a prophetic vocation in Matthew has a purpose
within the larger story of God's redemptive purposes and should not be
viewed independently of it.

Jesus is conceived through an act of the Holy Spirit (1:18), a possible
allusion to Gen 1:2 and the presence of the Spirit over the waters at creation.
Indeed, though the story may be about the New Genesis wrought through
Jesus Christ, this section is also the story of the γένεσις of Jesus himself
(1:18).[8] He is to be named Ἰησοῦς, from Yēšûaʾ ("rescue"), for he "will save
his people from their sins" (Matt 1:21). This notion of Jesus saving people
from their sins is important because it forms a programmatic statement
early in the narrative that describes the mission of Jesus as pronounced
by the angel of the Lord. This salvation from sins has typically been taken
as a reference to either religious or moral deliverance as distinct from political liberation.[9] Carter, however, calls such a contrast anachronistic in
that it fails to recognize the connection between sin and political bondage,
particularly in sinful socio-political and economic structures.[10] The narrative context of this saying supports Carter's assertion. Matthew's genealogy
brings to mind the story of God's people in the OT. That story represents
not primarily the movement toward a better personal morality (although

7. For an in-depth discussion of whether Tamar should be considered a gentile and
problems associated with Rahab's inclusion in the genealogy, see Bauckham, "Tamar's
Ancestry and Rahab's Marriage," 313–29.

8. It is also worth noting here the forty-two generations in Matthew's genealogy.
While there have been a range of interpretations of this number, Howard Clarke's assertion that forty-two should be read as "six 'sevens' or weeks, which again recalls the days
of Creation" is helpful in reiterating the Genesis theme in Matthew 1. Clarke, *Gospel of
Matthew and Its Readers*, 4.

9. See, for example, Davies and Allison, *Matthew 1–7*, 210: "Jesus saves his people
'from their sins'. This underlies the religious and moral—as opposed to political—character of the messianic deliverance. Liberation removes the wall of sin between God and
the human race; nothing is said about freedom from the oppression of the governing
powers (contrast Ps.Sol. 17)." See also Gundry, *Matthew*, 23–24, in which he implies
that the "typical messianic expectation among Jews" of deliverance from political oppression as primary is not met by Jesus.

10. Carter, *Matthew and Empire*, 76.

that may be an aspect of covenantal fidelity) but rather toward the holistic covenantal existence of a people under God as distinct from surrounding people groups. Such existence was to be a light to the nations (cf. Isa 42:6; 49:6; 60:3). The sins of figures such as Abraham and David were largely social—"deception, xenophobia, abuse of power, adultery, and murder."[11] That Matthew's genealogy makes note of the Babylonian exile further suggests social sins are in mind since prophetic criticisms of the kings in the OT revolve largely around idolatry and failure to rule justly, practices that led Israel into exile. For Jesus to save his people from their sins is, for Matthew, the liberation of God's people in order to live a life freed from forms of sin that oppress, exploit, and represent idolatry. In other words, Jesus will save his people from patterns of life that breed destruction precisely because they are not rooted in the will of God.

That the liberation spoken of is from "social sins" is a reading supported by the connection many commentators make between Matt 1:21 and Ps 130:8.[12] The Psalm as a whole draws a connection between sins (ἀνομία) and trouble from which Israel needs to be redeemed (λυτρόω). Indeed, the impact of sin seems to be the cause of the trouble Israel finds itself steeped in, and this trouble is national in nature, not only individualistic. Whilst the Psalm does not specify the nature of the trouble, other references to λυτρόω ("redeem/liberate" in Psalm 130) in the OT and Apocryphal writings would suggest it is political, if not imperial, in nature.[13] Matthew himself brings to mind the connection between sin and imperial domination when he evokes Manasseh and the exile (Matt 1:10–12), the latter of which was viewed by at least some as punishment for sin (2 Kgs 21:1–18). It would signal that Jesus saving his people from their sins implied a socio-political form of deliverance. *How* Jesus will save his people from their sins, however, is not yet clear in the narrative.

---

11. Carter, *Matthew and Empire*, 79. Carter's use of the term and concept "xenophobia" is unhelpful, however, given its anachronism.

12. This connection is not without its problems. While the LXX version of Ps 130:8 (LXX 129:8) uses λυτρόω to speak of deliverance, Matthew opts for σώζω. Moreover, while the Psalm speaks of being delivered from ἀνομία, Matthew opts for the more general ἁμαρτία. Matthew also broadens the Psalm's reference to "Israel" out to "his people" (λαός), from a singular (αὐτοῦ) to a plural (αὐτῶν).

13. See, for example, Exod 6:6; 13:15; 15:13; Deut 7:8; 9:26; 13:5; 24:18; 2 Sam 7:23; 1 Chr 17:21; Mic 4:10; 6:4. Each of these speaks of liberation in terms of redemption from Egypt or Babylon. Carter claims that about one-third of the approximately one hundred uses of λυτρόω in the LXX refer to redemption from Egypt or Babylon; Carter, *Matthew and Empire*, 195n52. λυτρόω is also used in speaking of deliverance from Assyria (Sir 48:20) and the Seleucids (1 Macc 4:11).

Already it is clear to the implied audience that Jesus is central to Matthew's story, that his role in God's purposes is significant. The nature of this significance is revealed in part by Matthew's quotation of Isa 7:14 in Matt 1:23, a citation which functions metonymically.[14] In its original context this passage reports the words of the prophet addressing King Ahaz of Judah who is under threat from imperial powers of the north (Isa 7:1–2). The message delivered is one of comfort. The imperial ambitions of Judah's enemies will not come to pass (7:3–9). Though Ahaz lacks the trust to ask for a sign of confirmation (7:10–13), God will give a sign anyway, the conception of a child named Immanuel (7:14). He will be a sign of God's presence and rescue from imperial power (7:16). However, God will also bring Assyria to punish Judah for its lack of trust (7:17–25). This prediction is reiterated in Isa 8:1–15 where the prophet reports the coming demise of Israel and Syria, and also the punishment of Judah at the hands of Assyria. The presence of Isaiah's son Shear-jashub in 7:3 adds a further dimension to the story: his name, which means "a remnant shall return," anticipates a future, a hope of new life, even beyond punishment at the hands of Assyria.[15]

Matthew's choice of this text implies its significance for his audience: Immanuel has come to rescue people from their sins and from imperial power, but the reality of destruction also looms for those who reject God's saving action. We can see how this message would have been important for a marginalized group such as Matthew's actual audience. They were, after all, living with both the threat of antagonistic local powers and of imperial Rome. Rome had already destroyed Jerusalem and its temple in recent memory, and so the question of how to live as God's people in the midst of imperial power was a pertinent one. Already, at this stage in his narrative, Matthew is beginning to hint at his answers to the formational questions, "who are we?" and "whose world is this?"

Another important consideration stemming from Matthew's use of Isaiah is that he chooses here to orient Jesus' mission with the words of a prophet. Throughout Matthew, the author makes frequent connections of this kind. Carter, assuming the metonymic function of orally delivered texts, suggests that Matthew sees the identity and agency of the prophet as

---

14. That phrases function metonymically in texts deriving from oral cultures in order to evoke not merely isolated sayings but larger narratives is a concept derived from Foley, *Immanent Art*. Richard Hays puts it another way: "Matthew is not merely looking for random Old Testament proof texts that Jesus might somehow fulfill; rather he is thinking about the *shape* of Israel's story and linking Jesus' life with key passages that promise God's unbreakable redemptive love for his people." Hays, "Gospel of Matthew," 176.

15. Carter, "Evoking Isaiah," 509.

important, and that his use of Isa 7 "specifies a particular prophet and set of circumstances."[16] That is to say, the prophet is not an incidental detail but an evocation of a concrete figure in a concrete historical situation. The historical situation of the prophet is assumed by Matthew to be analogous to Palestine at the time of Jesus. Both wear the shadow of the threat of imperial violence and rampant abuse of power. In choosing this text, Matthew seems to place himself, and indeed his depiction of Jesus, on the side of the prophets of Israel and the prophetic tradition over against those hierocratic traditions.[17]

It is not until Matt 2:1 that Matthew introduces a geographical reference point—Jesus is born in Bethlehem. In the same sentence Matthew also introduces an important character in the early scenes of his story: Herod. The designation of Bethlehem as the location, as well as the genitive absolute,[18] marks a shift to a new scene. This scene, unlike the previous one, marks a return not only to an identifiable place (Bethlehem), but also an identifiable time ("in the days of Herod"). For Matthew, Jesus' birth in Bethlehem fulfils the prophecy of Mic 5:2 and presumably associates him with David who was brought up and anointed in the same city (1 Sam 16:1–13). The juxtaposition of Bethlehem and "Herod the king" is striking, since it conjures up both a comparison of David with Herod, and of Bethlehem with Jerusalem. The first comparison is concerned mostly with kingship, and so falls out of the scope of this study. It does, however, elicit an alternative politics from that of Rome and its clients like Herod, a politics that Jesus is presumably meant to embody by being the "Son of David." The conflicting nature of such forms of politics is further demonstrated in the implied contrast between Jerusalem and Bethlehem (the "city of David"). It was of course Jerusalem where Herod had the temple rebuilt.[19] Matthew contrasts the grandeur of Herod's city and temple with the humility of Jesus' birthplace. Prophetic criticism of Jerusalem is abundant in the OT (e.g., 1 Kgs 9:6–9; Isa 64:10–11; Jer 2:1–3:5; 12:7; 22:5) and it was apparently seen as the place in which prophets were killed, a point later emphasized by Matthew himself (Matt 23:31, 34, 37; cf.

---

16. Carter, "Evoking Isaiah," 508–9.

17. The division between "prophetic Yahwism" and "the royal cult" of Jerusalem is addressed at length in Hanson, *Dawn of Apocalyptic*. Hanson's work is premised on the idea that there arose two opposing parties/traditions in Israel, a visionary-prophetic tradition and a hierocratic tradition. Such traditions are represented in different OT texts. More recently Wes Howard-Brook has expressed a similar dualism, albeit with a different approach and different conclusions to Hanson on a range of issues. Howard-Brook, "*Come Out, My People!*"

18. Τοῦ δὲ Ἰησοῦ γεννηθέντος ἐν Βηθλέεμ. Cf. Matt 1:18, where the genitive absolute marks the beginning of the first scene.

19. Josephus, *Ant.* 15.380–425.

Jer 2:30). That "Jerusalem" will react negatively to the birth of this prophet and alternative king is to be expected.

Whereas the reaction of Herod will be negative, there come μάγοι from the east seeking "he who has been born king of the Jews." It is debatable from what exact location the magi have come,[20] though Horsley notes they were "originally a caste of highest ranking politico-religious advisers or officers of the Median emperor, then in the Persian imperial court."[21] They may be intended to represent the peoples of the Parthian Empire, who lived in opposition to the Roman Empire. Their disobedience to Herod evokes the image of the Hebrew midwives in the Exodus story. Whatever their precise origin, the magi represent outsiders, gentiles. The coming of the gentiles is, of course, a prophetic theme in chronologically later parts of the OT (especially Isa 56–66). These outsiders form a collective character in Matthew that contrasts with the insiders, namely, Herod and all Jerusalem. Among these insiders are the chief priests and scribes, who make their first appearance here in the story (2:4–6) and who know where the Messiah is to be born. Mic 5:2 is quoted in Matt 2:6, emphasizing the prophetic theme of Christ's humble beginnings and his mission to Israel. Still, the insiders reject the child while the outsiders, the magi, worship him, a statement by Matthew reinforcing the place of gentiles in the community and the unfaithfulness of his Jewish opponents to the revealed will of God.

What follows, in which Joseph takes the mother and child to Egypt and Herod is tricked by the magi and responds by way of infanticide, is an obvious allusion to the story of Moses. While Jesus is compared to the child Moses who finds safety in Egypt, Herod is caricatured as Pharaoh. The implications are not minor: Herod represents the same death-dealing imperial reality as Pharaoh and other imperial figures. This is emphasized in the quotation of Jer 31:15 in Matt 2:18, a passage originally referring to the experience of exile at the hands of foreign powers and to hope for God's saving action and a return to the land. Further, in Matt 2:15, Matthew quotes the prophetic text Hos 11:1 which references God's love for Israel as the reason for calling them out of Egypt. The passage is applied to Jesus, thus identifying him with Israel, specifically its story of redemption from slavery in Egypt, and reinforcing the allusion to Moses. The prophetic character of Jesus, albeit as a child, is exposited in an initial and fractional fashion by this comparison to Moses. The nature of Jesus' prophetic mission is set out by way of the exodus theme—the audience is led to think that perhaps Jesus, like Moses, will be

---

20. Hagner provides a brief-yet-helpful discussion, arguing that of the most probable candidates, Babylon is the most likely. Hagner, *Matthew 1–13*, 27.

21. Horsley, *Liberation of Christmas*, 53–57.

a great prophet who will lead a new exodus.[22] If this is the case, the nature of this "new exodus" is not yet clear. Matthew then briefly explains Joseph's decision to relocate to Galilee owing to the continuing threat of a Herodian ruler. He concludes with a quotation whose source is unclear (Matt 2:23),[23] but which implies the importance of another otherwise insignificant place (Nazareth) and the "set apart" nature of Jesus.

John the Baptist is introduced suddenly in Matt 3:1. He requires some attention because he is immediately depicted in prophetic terms:

1. John is found in the wilderness (3:1), what Horsley calls "a symbolic place of purification and renewal."[24] It was a place of both marginalization and prophetic critique of Israel, particularly its leaders (1 Kgs 17–19; also Theudas and the Egyptian prophet). The wilderness was also a place of hope for God's redemption—a new exodus. Israel had experienced the wilderness following the exodus, and the prophets had subsequently spoken of the wilderness as a place of new beginnings (Jer 2:2–3; Hos 2:14–15),[25] judgement (Ezek 20:35–38), and restoration (Isa 41:18–19; 43:19–21; 44:3–4). Theudas and the Egyptian shared this hope.

22. The logic of this claim is based in part on the way in which Matthew utilizes his more overt Scriptural fulfillment passages. Of these passages in the opening chapters of Matthew, Richard Hays says, "This cluster of fulfilment quotations near the beginning of the Gospel conditions readers to expect that nearly everything in the story of Jesus will turn out to be the fulfillment of something pre-scripted by the prophets. Israel's sacred history is presented by Matthew as an elaborate figurative tapestry designed to point forward to Jesus and his activity." Hays, "Gospel of Matthew," 168. It is telling that soon after in Matt 3:3 we find a new exodus quotation from Isaiah (40:3). See Allison, *New Moses*, 194–99, for a more in-depth exploration of the new exodus theme in Matthew's early chapters.

23. Maarten Menken provides an extensive discussion in which he concludes that the quotation refers to Judg 13:5, 7. This, he says, explains why Matthew says it is a quotation from "the prophets" (plural)—"the prophets" indicates the corpus of the former prophets. Menken, "Sources of the Old Testament Quotation," 451–68. The implication is that the child, as with Samson, is "set apart." Hagner also provides a helpful overview, arguing for a range of possibilities. Hagner, *Matthew 1–13*, 40–42.

24. Horsley with Hanson, *Bandits, Prophets and Messiahs*, 177. Perhaps an indication that Horsley is correct is that "the wilderness of Judea" would not have been far from where Qumran would have been located (northwest corner of the Dead Sea).

Hutchison, "Was John the Baptist an Essene from Qumran?," 187–200, helpfully and astutely compares John with the Essenes and finds similarities but also crucial differences. This may suggest some relationship, or at least some common beliefs, values and practices, but not necessarily that John was himself an Essene.

25. France, *Gospel of Matthew*, 100.

2. John is wearing clothes made of camel's hair with a leather belt (Matt 3:4), suggesting he is like the prophets of old, particularly Elijah. The return of Elijah had been promised by Malachi (Matt 4:5–6), and this promise was developed in Jewish thought up until the time of Jesus and beyond, with many Jews believing that Elijah would return as a precursor and messenger before the end. Like Elijah, John is marginalized and will confront the dominant structures of society in the ensuing verses. John's garment would also have been the garment of the poor.[26] This is important, because while prophets of the past were able to function within society during the reign of a godly king, they were generally forced onto the margins of society during the reign of an evil king.

3. John eats locusts and wild honey, a sign of cutting oneself off from the dominant culture.[27]

Though John is called ὁ βαπτιστής, it is not his baptism with which we are first acquainted, but rather his preaching—Μετανοεῖτε, ἤγγικεν γὰρ ἡ βασιλεία τῶν οὐρανῶν.[28] Such a proclamation confronts the claims of the

26. Keener, *Gospel of Matthew*, 118.

27. James Kelhoffer points out that Lev 11 allowed for the eating of locusts, though it forbade the consumption of most other insects (against Deut 14:19 which forbade eating all winged insects). See Kelhoffer, "Did John the Baptist Eat," 293–314. Kelhoffer goes on to demonstrate that locusts have been eaten in the Near East for millennia, and citing Assyrian sources shows that they were eaten in times of hardship *but also* that they were desired by the wealthy. What this means is that John the Baptist's consumption of locusts, contra Carter, does not "self-evidently constitute a critique of the rich or point to a wilderness dweller." Carter, *Matthew and the Margins*, 95. Given however that John is not portrayed as wealthy, but rather on the margins, we should prefer to see his diet as inferring chosen hardship. Moreover there are cases in analogous scenarios to that of John's whereby people survived on wilderness foods (though not necessarily locusts; 2 Macc 5:27; Mart. Isa. 2:11; Josephus, *Life*, 11). See Kelhoffer, "Early Christian Studies among the Academic Disciplines,'" 6. Such people ate only what grew naturally, and this is another form of cutting oneself off from dominant culture. Simple living, and particularly eating, was praised by some, such as Josephus, who praised the simple diet of the Pharisees (Josephus, *Ant.* 18.12); John's diet was presumably much simpler.

28. The phrase "kingdom of heaven" is surprisingly difficult to define. While I do not wish to go into a lengthy discussion of what this phrase might mean in the main body of the text, some description is necessary since Matthew's Gospel assumes this knowledge. Marcus Borg has suggested that kingdom language has, historically speaking, a number of "resonances or nuances of meaning": (1) The power (δύναμις) of God; (2) Presence of God; (3) Life under the kingship of God; (4) A reality one can be "in" or "out" of; (5) Theo-political (i.e., a political metaphor); (6) An ideal state. See Borg, *Jesus in Contemporary Scholarship*, 87–88. Dale Allison has attempted to show that each of Borg's first five categories should be subordinated to the sixth (an ideal state), with "eschatological nostalgia for perfection" being the dominant sense. Allison, *Jesus of Nazareth*, 122. In my view this conclusion is too general and simplistic. Though Allison may be correct in saying that the kingdom of God is an ideal state, this in no way

βασιλεία of Rome—there is another kingdom, one that does not originate from Rome but from heaven itself.[29] John's demand for repentance places him squarely in the realm of the OT prophets. His language is both political (βασιλεία) and eschatological, pointing to the coming judgement, restorative action, and rule of God. That the proclamation is eschatological reflects that John is an eschatological prophet.[30] This is implied by Matthew's use of Isa 40:3 in Matt 3:3 where John is identified as the voice in the wilderness. The original context of the Isaiah quotation is the exilic community in Babylon who are promised the reversal of the situation of Babylonian control. This is to be seen, as in the exodus tradition, as *salvation* from imperial power, a conviction strengthened by John's proclamation of the empire of God[31] soon after his quotation of Isaiah. In a sense, John, like Isaiah's voice in the wilderness, is crying out the good news: "Behold your God!" (Isa 40:9). In this Isaianic passage, God comes with both reward and recompense (40:10) to overthrow the rulers of the earth (40:23) and raise up the lowly (40:29). From Matthew's allusion to this context it follows that John, as a wilderness prophet, would announce such events. His baptism

---

describes the uniquely Jewish understanding(s) of the phrase. I suspect Allison's eagerness to liken Jesus to other non-Jewish millenarian figures may be an issue here. Norman Perrin has shown convincingly that the phrase "kingdom of God" was not static, but had evolved over time. It was initially adopted from Canaanite usage in which the god acted as king, and eventually became understood as referring to God acting as king on behalf of his people; Perrin, *Jesus and the Language of the Kingdom*, 29–34. Certainly the OT and later Jewish writings give us the sense that there was an expectation that God would become king over the earth and would act accordingly (e.g., Zech 14:9; As. Mos. 10; 1 En 45:4–5). Pennington, in his lengthy study on Matthew's use of βασιλεία τῶν οὐρανῶν, argues that Matthean usage of the phrase is Danielic. The kingdom of heaven is contrasted with all earthly kingdoms and this is meant to give consolation that "with the coming of God's kingdom all will be made right" (330). This suggests that Matthew's use of "kingdom of heaven" implies an analogy with earthly kingdoms, though the heavenly character of God's kingdom is radically *other*, and indeed the existence of God's kingdom is a critique of the Roman Empire and a promise that it will be overthrown by God's in-breaking. See Pennington, *Heaven and Earth*, 253–330. Finally, for a remarkably economical definition of the kingdom, see Marshall, *Kingdom Come*: "The hope for the kingdom was essentially the hope for a definitive and permanent theophany, the tangible appearance of God to abolish evil, establish righteousness in the world, and bring creation to its goal and fulfillment" (39).

29. Though here I am demonstrating strong sympathy with empire-critical approaches to NT interpretation, it is worth noting the cautions offered in Willitts, "Matthew," 82–100. I am cautious here of not allowing the theme of "empire"—so easily anachronistic—to inappropriately dominate my reading.

30. As opposed to *the* eschatological prophet, a phenomenon about which I am skeptical.

31. Βασιλεία could of course, though typically translated "kingdom," be just as easily translated "empire" or "reign."

was most probably a symbolic act of identifying with the history of Israel through re-enacting the exodus (and other water-related events) and thus implying "return" from exile and national renewal.[32]

The Pharisees and Sadducees, who enter the narrative for the first time in Matt 3:7, embody for Matthew the antithesis of what John represents. John himself calls them a "brood of vipers" (3:7).[33] Matthew applies this saying to the issue of ancestry, discussed in 3:9–10, in which he has John criticize the Pharisees and Sadducees for assuming they will escape the "wrath to come" because of their descent from Abraham. John makes clear that judgement is coming upon Israel imminently: "*Even now [ἤδη]* the axe is laid to the root of the trees," an OT image of judgement of powerful nations (cf. Isa 10:33–34; Ezekiel 31; Dan 4:4–27).[34] John asserts that the coming judgement on Israel will "cut down" even those whose ancestry is honorable, such as the Pharisees and Sadducees, since they have not been faithful to their traditions. This is no doubt a polemical claim aimed at Matthew's own time. In any case, the identity of Abraham's children is determined not by physical descent but by repentance (Matt 3:9). Matthew introduces for the first time the symbol of fruit and the need to bear [good] fruit in keeping with such repentance (3:8, 10; cf. Isa 5:2; Jer 2:21; 11:16–17). Finally, John warns of another who will come after him, one for whom he is not worthy to carry his sandals; this figure will baptize with spirit and with fire (Matt 3:11). John goes on to describe his successor's vocation in terms of winnowing, or separating grain from chaff. Implied

32. Brown's explanation is, I think, the best proposal: "What was John doing? I suggest that John's baptism did not purify in the manner of existing rites of purification. Nor was it, in my opinion, intended as a substitute for them. Rather, John was organizing a symbolic exodus from Jerusalem and Judea as a preliminary to recrossing the Jordan as a penitent, consecrated Israel in order to reclaim the land in a quasi-reenactment of the return from the Babylonian exile." See Brown, "What Was John the Baptist Doing?," 45.

33. In the fifth century BCE, Herodotus declared that the vipers and winged serpents of Arabia were not born the way serpents were born elsewhere. Instead, the newborn creatures chewed their way out of their mother's wombs, killing their mothers in the process. This, he asserted, was to avenge their fathers who were slain by the mothers during procreation (Herodotus, *Hist.* 3.109, on Arabia). See Keener, "'Brood of Vipers,'" 7.

34. Carter argues that the image of an axe would have also brought to mind Roman power since the axe was "a symbol of Roman authority and a means of Roman execution . . . [denoting] the Roman official's authority to maintain public order and exact punishment." Carter, *Matthew and the Margins*, 98–99. It may be that Matthew has in mind the destruction of Jerusalem at the hands of Rome in 70 CE as the form judgment takes.

in this image of cleansing is the burning of the chaff, that is to say, negative judgement for those who bear bad fruit/will not repent.

Jesus then comes to John to be baptized. John initially protests, but Jesus claims that his baptism must occur to fulfill all righteousness (3:15). The notion of righteousness (δικαιοσύνη) is of course a hotly debated topic in NT studies,[35] and it is not immediately obvious as to whether righteousness here refers to God's just action or God's expectation of humans. Both are, for Matthew, related to covenant—God's faithful action in light of his covenants, and the faithful actions of humans in light of Torah and/or their other covenant obligations. It is only upon Jesus' actual baptism (3:16–17) that we can discern that the righteousness spoken of by Jesus refers to both that of divine and human action. On the one hand, God's action reveals that Jesus is the anointed one who will enact God's liberation. On the other hand, Jesus faithfully submits to God's will, thus demonstrating his and God's own righteousness. Further, for Matthew "fulfilment" (πληρόω; 3:15) tends to refer to the fulfillment of Scripture. As we have said, such Matthean Scriptural fulfillment passages are not a form of prooftexting, but function metonymically. They link Matthew's story of Jesus with Israel's story and Scriptures. For Jesus' baptism to fulfill all righteousness is for it to identify Jesus with Israel's history of faithfully going through the waters—out of Egypt and into the promised land—and the realization of God's covenant faithfulness in such events.[36]

When Jesus is baptized by John he experiences a prophetic commissioning (3:16–17). The heavens are opened, an apocalyptic motif,[37] and the Spirit of God comes upon him as with the servant in Isa 42:1 and the herald in Isa 61:1. The scene is also reminiscent of Ezek 1:1 and the prophetic

35. This is of course the case within Pauline studies, but to a lesser extent also applies to Matthean studies. See Przybylski, *Righteousness in Matthew*, 1–3, 91–94.

36. Earlier I noted the work of J. M. Foley in inspiring the idea, presented here, that phrases function metonymically in texts deriving from oral cultures in order to evoke not merely isolated sayings but larger narratives. Foley, *Immanent Art*. Foley argues, drawing on Jauss and Iser, that a text is heard within a "horizon of expectation" (what Foley calls "traditional referentiality"). In other words, according to the hearer's *a priori* understanding. Traditional Referentiality, says Foley, summons "a context that is enormously larger and more echoic than the text or work itself" (7). For Foley, "metonymy" refers to "a mode of signification wherein the part stands for the whole," and a text "is enriched by an unspoken context that dwarfs the textual artifact" (40–41). I take Foley's concept of metonymy as applicable to Matthew's fulfillment quotations and OT allusions, such as the present case of Jesus' baptism. Here passing through waters—indeed the Jordan—is an echo of the Mosaic-Joshuan water crossing stories and, possibly, other stories involving water (e.g., Noah, Elisha, and even the Spirit hovering over the waters at creation).

37. Nolland, *Gospel of Matthew*, 155.

commissioning therein, a possible allusion to the exilic setting of the prophet and God's impending liberation from imperial rule. God then speaks (3:17), calling Jesus "my Son, the Beloved, with whom I am well pleased." This statement again has clear links to Isa 42:1 and the calling of the servant who will "bring forth justice to the nations."[38] Indeed, Jesus will have a servant-like prophetic role that will no doubt involve suffering. To be sure, Matt 3 is loaded with prophetic themes, both in relation to John and Jesus. The scene is important for understanding Jesus' prophetic vocation because it is here that his commissioning takes place. In addition, Matthew's scriptural allusions give us a sense of his understanding of the character of that vocation, not least as a type of suffering servant who will enact God's δικαιοσύνη.

The scene then changes to another wilderness setting (Matt 4:1). Jesus' commitment to God's liberating work is tested here in a fashion analogous to that of Israel in the wilderness. He, like Moses, fasts forty days and nights (Exod 34:28), though the number forty also evokes other biblical events, not least Israel's forty years in the wilderness (Exod 16:35).[39] It is natural that this wilderness testing occurs immediately after Jesus' baptism in the narrative—after coming through the waters of the Red Sea/baptism, Israel/Jesus enters the wilderness and is hungry. Unlike with Israel, however, it is the διάβολος that tests Jesus, evoking the story of Job. The question becomes *with whom will Jesus' allegiance fall?* This is no abstract theological matter for Matthew's implied audience, living as they were in the Roman Empire. That Satan will claim control over the kingdoms of the world (Matt 4:8–9) means the story represents a challenge to Roman power, which is by depicted as controlled by the devil and thus by nature opposed to the reign of God. The tempter tempts Jesus first to use God's power to satisfy his hunger (Matt 4:3), second to demonstrate God's promise and protection (4:5–6; using Psalm 91 as a prooftext), and third to accept rulership over the world's empires (4:8–9). Each temptation represents a worthy end—production of food in a world of food shortage,[40] a sign of God's faithfulness, and mes-

---

38. This is confirmed by the fact that in Matt 12:18, Matthew's rendering of Isa 42:1 has ὁ ἀγαπητός μου ("my beloved") and εὐδόκησεν ("to be well pleased"). See Nolland, *Matthew*, 157.

39. Carter also notes forty days as: the length of Noah's flood (Gen 7:4, 12, 17), the duration of Ezekiel's stint lying on his right side (Ezek 4:6) and the predicted time until Nineveh's destruction (Jonah 3:4). Carter, *Matthew and the Margins*, 108. To this I would add forty days as the duration of the spying of the land in Num 13–14. It was for their unfaithfulness in response to the report of the spies that Israel was made to "bear its iniquity," a year for each day (Num 14:34).

40. Carter notes that in the context of the Roman imperial system, "Food was about power. Its production (based in land), distribution, and consumption reflected elite control. . . . [Nonelites] struggled to acquire enough food as well as food of adequate

sianic reign over the nations—though to meet such ends at the behest of the tempter, in ways that misinterpret and fall short of Torah, would be contrary to the vocation of Jesus as one saving people from their sins and fulfilling all righteousness. That the temptations represent the failure to live according to Torah is demonstrated by Jesus' quotation of Deuteronomy in response to each.[41] Jesus exhibits his loyalty to God, not to the animating power of sin and idolatry, and also proves to succeed in remaining faithful to God where Israel in the wilderness had failed.

The wilderness temptation story contains some obvious prophetic echoes. The aforementioned echo of Moses' fasting (Exod 34:28) is one. Another is the strong resonance with the story of Elijah in the desert (1 Kgs 19:4–8). Elaine Wainwright suggests that in this story Jesus is characterized intertextually "through the lens of the prophet and mediator of a covenant with the divine, namely, Moses and Elijah."[42] Wainwright goes on to say that, for Jesus, the marginal space of the wilderness is not simply one imposed on him, but is a space he embraces and from which resistance will be possible.[43] Indeed, the "new exodus" theme in the passage suggests that the setting of the wilderness is not peripheral to the purpose of the pericope. However, the wilderness and other places of marginality will become, throughout Matthew's Gospel, an important setting which effects how the nature of Jesus' prophetic vocation is perceived. Jesus' prophetic character is being progressively shown to be one that will demand righteous faithfulness to God and covenant, and also one that will challenge centers of power— power ultimately animated by ὁ διάβολος.

The final scenes that occur prior to the Beatitudes are those that describe the beginnings of Jesus' ministry. Jesus hears of John's arrest and so withdraws into Galilee (Matt 4:12). John's prophetic message has apparently not been received well by those in positions of power. This is perhaps implied by the fact that Jesus' withdrawal (ἀναχωρέω) recalls the magi's withdrawal from Herod to their own country (2:12), Joseph's escape from Herod to Egypt

---

nutritional value." See Carter, *Roman Empire and the New Testament*, 109–10. Malina's classic social-scientific study of the NT world also suggests this, though in speaking about the notion of the "limited good" Malina does not specifically mention food. See Malina, *New Testament World*, 89–90.

41. The Tempter's quotation of Ps 91:11–12 (Matt 4:6) is shown by Matthew to be a (willful?) misinterpretation of that text. If the Tempter's reading suggests that the Psalm guarantees God's protection, then Jesus' counter-quote of Deut 6:16 implies that to require a demonstration of God's faithfulness is to forfeit one's own faithfulness to God through Torah observance. That God's protection and human faithfulness are intertwined is a prophetic theme, such as in Jeremiah 7.

42. Wainwright, "Reading the Gospel of Matthew," 263.

43. Wainwright, "Reading the Gospel of Matthew," 264.

(2:14), and Joseph's withdrawal to Galilee to avoid Archelaus (2:22).[44] Jesus moves from Nazareth to Capernaum by the sea, "in the territory of Zebulun and Naphtali." This anachronistic designation makes way for another fulfillment passage (4:15–16), this time a quotation of Isa 9:1–2 which speaks of a people dwelling in darkness and death who see a great light. In its original context, the Isaiah passage had described hope to come in light of the terrible situation of Assyrian destruction (depicted in Isa 8).

Following the quotation of this passage, Matthew tells us that Jesus began to preach, and it seems that he is the fulfillment of Isaiah's "great light" (4:16). The message that Jesus preaches is undeniably prophetic—"Repent, for the kingdom of heaven has come near" (Matt 4:17). This was, of course, the content of John's preaching (3:2); Jesus has taken up the mantle of the arrested prophet. Such a pronouncement signifies not a "religious" claim in the modern sense, but a socio-political claim, though the implications of this claim are not yet revealed. The command to repent, or a description of repentance or non-repentance, can be found at numerous places in the prophetic corpus (e.g., Isa 1:27;[45] Jer 5; 34:15–17;[46] Ezek 14:6–11;[47] 18:30–32). In each

---

44. All use ἀναχωρέω. Of this passage, Deirdre Good states that, "The hostility of Herod anticipates the hostility of political powers to Jesus and his followers (described in detail in [Matthew] ten). The mages' recognition of Jesus anticipates receptivity on the part of foreign peoples." See Good, "Verb ἀναχωρέω in Matthew's Gospel," 2.

45. "Zion shall be redeemed by justice, and those in her who repent, by righteousness."

46. "You recently repented and did what was right in my eyes by proclaiming liberty, each to his neighbor, and you made a covenant before me in the house that is called by my name, but then you turned around and profaned my name when each of you took back his male and female slaves, whom you had set free according to their desire, and you brought them into subjection to be your slaves. Therefore, thus says the Lord: You have not obeyed me by proclaiming liberty, every one to his brother and to his neighbor; behold, I proclaim to you liberty to the sword, to pestilence, and to famine, declares the Lord. I will make you a horror to all the kingdoms of the earth."

47. "'Therefore say to the house of Israel, Thus says the Lord God: Repent and turn away from your idols, and turn away your faces from all your abominations. For any one of the house of Israel, or of the strangers who sojourn in Israel, who separates himself from me, taking his idols into his heart and putting the stumbling block of his iniquity before his face, and yet comes to a prophet to consult me through him, I the Lord will answer him myself. And I will set my face against that man; I will make him a sign and a byword and cut him off from the midst of my people, and you shall know that I am the Lord. And if the prophet is deceived and speaks a word, I, the Lord, have deceived that prophet, and I will stretch out my hand against him and will destroy him from the midst of my people Israel. And they shall bear their punishment—the punishment of the prophet and the punishment of the inquirer shall be alike—that the house of Israel may no more go astray from me, nor defile themselves anymore with all their transgressions, but that they may be my people and I may be their God, declares the Lord God.'"

of these OT cases, the prophets speak of impending judgement for those who continue to live in "unrighteousness" and salvation for those who take up justice. The command, in light of impending judgement, is to "Repent!"—transform your mind—for the reign of God is near. In other words, hearers must turn from their previous unfaithfulness to God in light of the fact that the saving reign of God is imminent. The implied prophetic resonances suggest that there may also be a negative element in that a failure to transform one's thinking and action will result in calamity. Such a suggestion would mean Jesus' proclamation aligns in some way with that of John. This proclamation—Jesus' first—is programmatic for Jesus' ministry.

The implied reader might expect that an earth-shattering event would occur in the next scene, but instead we find Jesus walking by the sea and recruiting two pairs of brothers, all fisherman, for his mission.[48] Juvenal reports that fish were claimed as imperial property: "[E]very rare and beautiful thing in the wide ocean . . . belongs to the imperial treasury."[49] That is to say, it is possible these four men were under some kind of coerced imperial arrangement.[50] Jesus, however, calls them to follow him in order that he would make them "fishers of people"[51] (Matt 4:19). The prophetic image of fishing is not common in the OT, but when used it refers to judgement on those who had worshipped false gods, oppressed the poor, or who, through imperial power, had exploited others and done violence (Jer 16:16; Amos 4:1–2; Ezek 29:3–16). Myers suggests the saying on Jesus' lips is an invitation for "common folk to join him in his struggle to overturn the existing order of power and privilege."[52] This message is prophetic in nature and Jesus intends for others to follow in his prophetic ministry, just as he has followed that of John. The men immediately leave their nets/

---

48. In his commentary on the parallel Markan passage, Ched Myers suggests that "Mark is obviously aware of the risk involved in appeal to prophetic and apocalyptic traditions, for they also were being used to bolster the triumphalistic eschatological expectations of Jewish nationalism. For this reason, Mark pursues a narrative strategy that consistently frustrates the equation between epiphany and victorious holy war." See Myers, *Binding the Strong Man*, 131. It is not necessarily the case that Matthew's narrative strategy consistently reflects the same goal, but in this particular pericope I think Myers' point can apply, with some caveats, equally well to Matthew as to Mark.

49. Juvenal, *Sat* 4.51–55. Quoted in Carter, *Matthew and the Margins*, 121.

50. Carter, *Matthew and the Margins*, 121.

51. As opposed to the NRSV's "I will make you fish for people," which inserts the verb where the Greek has a noun (ἁλιεύς).

52. Myers, *Binding the Strong Man*, 132. Myers is of course speaking of the Markan version of the story.

boats and follow him (Matt 4:20, 22), with "follow" (ἀκολουθέω) a literary device in Matthew to refer to discipleship.[53]

From there Jesus goes throughout all Galilee (Matt 4:23). The setting is again important—Jesus does not conduct his ministry in Jerusalem or other major centers, but rather in the rural areas amongst the common people. He is, after all, a popular prophet. He teaches in synagogues, and proclaims the kingdom, as expected from his programmatic statement (4:17). Accompanying this preaching is his "curing every disease [νόσος] and every sickness [μαλακία] among the people" (4:23). Howard-Brook draws an important parallel between the use of νόσος and μαλακία here and LXX occurrences in Exod 15:26 and Deut 7:15 in which the words describe the illnesses that afflict the Egyptians.[54] He concludes that these words could be used to signify what he calls "Egypt disease," or more broadly "empire disease," those illnesses that result from the oppressive conditions of life under empire.[55] As a result of these amazing healings, Jesus' fame spreads even to Syria, a place of gentiles, and their sick and afflicted are also brought to him (Matt 4:24). In addition to healing sickness, Jesus also casts out demons. The subject of the demonic in the NT is immense, and there is no space for discussion here, except to say that a number of scholars now point to both theological and psychological reasons why demonic possession in the NT is symptomatic of political and economic exploitation, such as that experienced under Roman imperialism.[56] When God's saving presence comes to his people in Jesus they

53. It is important to say that not every occurrence of ἀκολουθέω carries this meaning. As J. D. Kingsbury notes, the crowds in Matthew are said to "follow" Jesus, but this is not tantamount to a messianic confession. See Kingsbury, "Verb *Akolouthein*," 56–73, esp. 61. G. Kittel notes that the distinctive statistical evidence of the use of what he terms the "special use of ἀκολουθεῖν" is "strictly limited to discipleship of Christ." By this he means those occurrences that carry "religious significance." See Gerhard Kittel, "ἀκολουθέω," *TDNT* 1:213. Kittel goes on to say that the disciple of Jesus does, in external form at least, the same as the pupil of a rabbi. This may be correct, except in one crucial way. Whereas in later rabbinic literature a disciple picks his own master (*m. 'Abot* 1:6), Jesus chooses and confronts his own disciples. Whether or not the rabbinic method was already in place at the time of Matthew is uncertain. In any case Matthew's rendering suggests Jesus' method is more akin to the passing of the prophetic mantle in the OT (Elijah/Elisha) than to possible rabbinic analogies.

54. Howard-Brook, *"Come Out, My People!"*, 410. Howard-Brook notes that νόσος is used only eleven times in the LXX (411n15).

55. Howard-Brook, *"Come Out, My People!"*, 411.

56. Hollenbach's socio-historical study of demoniacs and public authorities is most relevant here. "Mental illness caused, or at least was exacerbated by, social tensions: it seems commonly accepted that social tensions of various sorts are at the core of the phenomena of mental derangement. Situations of social tension such as the following are often indicated as the causal context of possession: class antagonisms rooted in economic exploitation, conflicts between traditions where revered traditions are

are healed of such diseases and afflictions of empire, not merely in an individualistic sense, but in a social sense. Finally, Matthew tells us great crowds
followed Jesus from a range of places, both Jew and gentile.

Throughout these initial four chapters of Matthew, Jesus' prophetic
character has begun to be revealed. When Matthew seeks to explain events
in Jesus' life, he does so by linking him to the story of Israel in prophetic
terms. This is most obviously demonstrated by his almost uniform use of
prophetic quotations, but also by his frequent use of Mosaic echoes. Matthew's concern for Jesus' prophetic vocation is also revealed by his use of the
John the Baptist character. John is clearly described in prophetic terms, and
he resembles both an oracular prophet and an action prophet. His prophetic
message of repentance in the face of the imminent kingdom of heaven
echoes prophetic pronouncements of the past and his action of baptism
points to a new exodus, implying a new social reality. That Jesus' programmatic pronouncement is taken verbatim from John is a narrative device that
parallels Jesus' prophetic vocation with that of John. However, the story also
makes clear that Jesus is greater than John (Matt 3:11).

Jesus' commissioning (Matt 3:16–17), similar to other OT prophetic
calls (Isa 42:1; 61:1; Ezek 1:1), is notably the beginning of Jesus' public career. In other words, Matthew depicts the initiation of Jesus' public career in
prophetic terms. This is also the case with his first public proclamation (Matt
4:17). Further, Jesus' ministry activity begins with his wilderness testing in
which he demonstrates his faithfulness where Israel had failed. Such Torah
fidelity is crucial for Matthew's depiction of what is "prophetic," for the call to
covenant faithfulness that Jesus will make throughout the Gospel is central to
his prophetic vocation. Thus far, such a mission leads not only to prophetic
calls for repentance, but also to prophetic actions of healings and exorcisms—
actions each in their own ways reminiscent of prophets in the OT.

4.3 The Beatitudes

Matthew brings us to a new scene in which Jesus sees the crowds and sits
down on a mountain (Matt 5:1). This is another allusion to Moses and the

---

eroded, colonial domination and revolution." Hollenbach goes on to: "While a number of
demoniacs appeared to be from the upper classes of society (e.g., Luke 8:1–3), the larger
number of them must have come from the lower classes in response to the horrendous
economic conditions of the time. These conditions were enough to drive anyone mad,
especially those most sensitive to their destitution. The social-scientific theories delineated above indicate that demon possession flourishes in its various dynamics precisely
in such conditions as we know prevailed in Jesus' day." Hollenbach, "Jesus, Demoniacs,
and Public Authorities," 573, 580–81.

giving of the law on Sinai (Exod 19:3), the covenant of God made with Israel in order that it might be a kingdom of priests and a holy nation (Exod 19:5). Jesus' so-called "Sermon on the Mount" (SM) would, given this intertextual allusion, function the same way, that is, to outline a way of life for an alternative society. The mountain imagery also continues the characterization of Jesus as a new Moses leading a new exodus, this time with him giving the authoritative interpretation of Torah, that is, the authoritative vision of life together under God.

Moses was the prototypical prophet in Israel: the classical prophets of Israel essentially followed in the covenantal principles and prophetic line of Moses.[57] A hypothesis among some biblical scholars in relation to this is that there was a tradition, originating from Deut 18:15–18, that God would raise up an eschatological prophet like Moses. This prophet would speak the words of God as Moses did, and there is evidence that some Jews and Christians at the time of Jesus were mindful of this tradition (such as in 4Q175).[58] There has been much discussion of this tradition in relation to Luke–Acts, less so in regard to Matthew.[59] Teeple's well-known but dated study, *The Mosaic Eschatological Prophet*, declares confidently that in Matthew, Jesus is the eschatological prophet like Moses.[60] Matthew's association of Jesus with Moses in this eschatological sense could be argued by way of the presence of God's voice at Jesus' baptism (Matt 3:17) and the transfiguration (Matt 17:5)—"This is my Son, the Beloved; with him I am well pleased; listen to him!"—echoes of Moses' words in Deut 18:15. But there is a difference between making a possible theological connection within biblical texts and the historical existence of a widely held expectation of a new Moses. Horsley is right to point out the lack of evidence for such a wide-ranging expectation of a Moses-like eschatological prophet:

57. See VanGemeren, *Interpreting the Prophetic Word*, 28. See also Horsley with Hanson, *Bandits, Prophets and Messiahs*, 7. An example of the emulation of the Mosaic model and message would be Isa 1:17; Jer 7:6; 22:3; Ezek 22:7; Zech 7:10; Mal 3:5. Here these prophets (and others) seem to take up Mosaic principles concerning justice as written in Exod 22:21–22; Deut 10:18; 14:29; 16:11, 14; 24:17, 19–21, 26:12–13; 27:19.

58. Wise et al., *Dead Sea Scrolls*, 230.

59. See for example Witherington, *Jesus the Seer*, 330–35 (esp. 332). Witherington's material is heavily weighted toward Luke–Acts. Witherington argues that in Luke Jesus is the eschatological prophet like Moses (332). Aune, however, disagrees: "While Luke nowhere in his gospel presents Jesus as an eschatological prophet, he does appear to confirm the general notion that Jesus was indeed a prophet." Aune, *Prophecy in Early Christianity*, 155. See also Caneday, "'Baptized in the Holy Spirit,'" 5; Croatto, "Jesus, Prophet like Elijah," 451–65. The notable exceptions to the lack of discussion of this topic in relation to Matthew are Allison, *New Moses*, and Turner, *Israel's Last Prophet*.

60. Teeple, *Mosaic Eschatological Prophet*, 120.

It is difficult to find textual references to an eschatological prophet like Moses in biblical or post-biblical Jewish literature whether before or after the time of Jesus, except in the Qumran scrolls. . . . Nevertheless, since there are so very few references in the extensive finds at Qumran that could be construed as referring to an anticipated prophet like Moses, we cannot really conclude that the Qumran community itself focused much hope on an expectation of such a prophet—let alone use this as evidence for Jewish society in general.[61]

Even allowing for the fact that Qumran may have expected an eschatological prophet figure,[62] the evidence from within Matthew is at best minimal (though I will leave Lukan scholars to debate the issue in the context of Luke–Acts).[63] If Matthew does not portray Jesus as a so-called eschatological prophet like Moses, what is his aim in portraying Jesus as a new Moses? In light of his particular socio-historical concerns, Matthew seeks to characterize Jesus as a new Moses to present him as one who speaks the words of God with the same authority as the prophet of old. That Jesus is likened to Moses reflects a rhetorical move by the author to portray Jesus as superior to any proto-rabbinic figures. The connection with Moses also serves as a narrative device to remind the audience that something like the exodus liberation under Moses is again happening with Jesus. In the SM, we will see Jesus offer the authoritative interpretation of God's will, expressed through Torah and continuing through Jesus. As an interpretation of Torah, it will be a way of life for a liberated people.

61. Horsley, "'Like One of the Prophets of Old,'" 441. In a footnote Horsley expands: "R. E. Brown . . . pointed out some time ago that '*de facto* we know very little of the contemporary Jewish interpretation of this text [Deut 18:18]. The early rabbis rarely commented on it, and even the apocalyptic literature did not greatly develop such a typology of Moses.' F. Hahn . . . repeatedly admits the lack or lateness of sources, but still insists on his synthetic 'conception of the eschatological prophet.'" See Horsley, "'Like One of the Prophets of Old,'" 441n13.

62. Poirier, "Endtime Return of Elijah and Moses," 221–42. Poirier concludes that, "The Qumran sectarians expected both a priestly messiah and an endtime Prophet, figures that were probably equated with an eschatological return of Elijah and Moses, respectively" (241).

63. Contra Allison, who argues that the expectation of a coming prophet-like-Moses was "very much in the air in first-century Palestine." Allison, *New Moses*, 83. His case is, however, partly based on the assumption that Theudas (Josephus, *Ant.* 20:97–99) and other prophets mentioned by Josephus were claiming to be prophets like Moses according to Deut 18:15–18. This assumption is, I think, lacking proper grounds. Certainly, there was a Samaritan belief in an eschatological prophet-like-Moses, as Allison posits, though with Horsley I would argue that, far from proving this idea was widespread, the Samaritan belief may explain the paucity of Jewish expectation—they would have wanted no part in it. Horsley, "'Like One of the Prophets of Old,'" 442.

Matthew identifies the hearers of Jesus' teaching, namely his disciples (5:1). The crowd is also present (Matt 5:1; 7:28–29), and they seem to represent a collective character open to the teaching of Jesus but not a disciple.[64] Jesus' first speech is programmatic for his entire ministry in Matthew, and the stylized form of the Beatitudes and their prominent place at the beginning of this major teaching block suggest they are programmatic in and of themselves. These are also Jesus' first words since his initial programmatic pronouncement of 4:17, suggesting what is said here in SM is an exposition of Jesus' pronouncement in 4:17. That is to say, SM teaches in more detail what repentance entails in light of the imminent arrival of the kingdom of heaven. Matthew 5:2 says that Jesus "opened his mouth" (ἀνοίξας τὸ στόμα αὐτοῦ), a phrase that Hagner identifies as "a Semitic idiom used at the beginning of a public address."[65] The phrase introduces speech elsewhere in Ps 78:2, Job 3:1, and Dan 10:16. The idiom probably also alludes to Deut 8:3, quoted previously in Matt 4:4, where it is stated that a person lives by every word that comes from the mouth of God. The implication is that what Jesus is about to say comes not from him, but from God. It is a prophetic interpretation of Torah, Jesus' vision of life in the kingdom of heaven.

The Literary Form of the Beatitudes

It is helpful for us to briefly outline the literary form of the Beatitudes since by such analysis implied authorial intention can be inferred.[66] Typically the Beatitudes are understood as a literary form within a larger genre, and rightly so. While different suggestions have been offered, such as programmatic speech (Gnilka) or instruction for itinerant teachers or catechetic speech (Klein),[67] they have tended to describe functions rather than specific genres. Most scholars seem happy to call SM a sermon and leave it at that.[68] Indeed the genre of the Beatitudes, and the SM as a whole, remains largely unexamined.

64. Carter, "Crowds in Matthew's Gospel," 59.

65. Hagner, *Matthew 1–13*, 86. Also Guelich, *Sermon on the Mount*, 54; Gundry, *Matthew*, 67; Keener, *Matthew*, 164; Nolland, *Matthew*, 193.

66. Howell, *Matthew's Inclusive Story*, 50. I have substituted the term "literary form" in place of "genre" since the former is more appropriate in speaking of the Beatitudes because they are one part of a larger literary whole. I have also used "implied authorial intent" in place of "authorial intent" in order to emphasize that any notion of authorial intent can, except where explicit, only reflect the intent of the implied author.

67. Zamfir, "Who Are (the) Blessed?," 76.

68. Carter, "Some Contemporary Scholarship," 192.

The most comprehensive work on this subject is by Betz who concludes that the genre of SM as a whole is that of an epitome. An epitome is a composition made up of the sayings of a person deemed to be of primary importance with the purpose of allowing the later followers to "theologize creatively along the lines of the theology of the master."[69] Matthew himself describes SM as λόγος and διδαχή (7:28), and such a description appears to cohere with Betz's suggestion. SM as epitome is thus, according to Betz, comparable to Epicurus' *Kyriai Doxai*. Betz's argument has not been without detractors, not least Stanton who offers a substantial critique.[70] Stanton is right to challenge Betz's insistence that SM represents a single pre-Matthean source and that it is an anti-gentile section embedded in an otherwise pro-gentile Gospel. More importantly for us, Stanton argues that whereas *Kyriai Doxai* presented an entire philosophical system, SM focuses only on Jesus' ethical teaching.[71] Betz has responded by arguing that SM contains more than ethical teaching, including Torah interpretation, cult instructions, theology, cosmology, and eschatology,[72] though this need not necessarily represent a philosophical system. Both Betz and Stanton make worthy points. Stanton is correct that SM, unlike *Kyriai Doxai*, does not present an entire philosophical system, and Betz is right to argue that SM is more than ethical teaching.

Nonetheless, ethical teaching is a key component of SM. Betz says as much in his later commentary when he gives examples of literary analogues demonstrating that "placing a beatitude at the head of a collection of ethical maxims was almost a literary convention."[73] We should not, however, think that Betz is claiming that SM is merely a set of ethical principles since, as we have already seen, he claims SM contains more than ethical teaching. According to Betz, the Beatitudes, at the head of SM, serve as didactic reminders of the things recipients had heard before as presuppositions for the entire SM.[74] The Beatitudes "circumscribe the way of life of the faithful disciple of Jesus."[75]

Though moving us closer, the above analysis still does not define the literary form of the Beatitudes. Fortunately, Betz offers further help when he

---

69. Betz, "Sermon on the Mount (Matt. 5:3–7:27): Its Literary Genre and Function," in *Essays on the Sermon on the Mount*, 1–16 (15).

70. Stanton, *Gospel for a New People*, 310–18.

71. Stanton, *Gospel for a New People*, 311.

72. Betz, *Sermon on the Mount*, 73–80.

73. Betz, *Sermon on the Mount*, 105.

74. Betz, *Sermon on the Mount*, 93.

75. Betz, *Sermon on the Mount*, 97.

argues that a series of makarisms, such as the Beatitudes, constitute a distinct literary form in themselves.[76] Betz compares Matt 5:3 with contemporaneous Graeco-Roman texts and also 4 Ezra.[77] He concludes that the makarism found in Matt 5:3 is a mixed form, with the first line ("Blessed are the poor in spirit") being an "anti-makarism," a subversion of conventional values ("Blessed are the rich"), an unmasking of naïve but religiously sanctioned materialism.[78] This Beatitude is unfolded and developed in those that follow (5:4–12), and constitutes the self-consciousness of the community which "expresses itself in the sayings 'You are the salt of the earth' . . . and 'You are the light of the world.'"[79] For Betz, the rest of SM is nothing but a concretization and elucidation of 5:3, a statement on the basis of which the interpretation of Torah is carried out. Though such an assertion is probably an overstatement, it is true that the narrative flow of the Gospel suggests that the Beatitudes, and by extension SM, will put forth Matthew's understanding of Jesus' authoritative interpretation of Torah and his teaching on the way of life in the kingdom of heaven. Such teaching will confront and subvert conventional values present in both competing religious groups and Roman imperial society. In short, Matthew's Beatitudes are "makarisms," subversive makarisms at that, standing at the head of a set of community shaping didactic materials (SM) for which they act as an introduction.

It is also important for us to appreciate the prophetic-apocalyptic character of the Beatitudes. Robert Guelich notes that beatitudes in wisdom settings never occurred in groups of more than two and were usually formulated in the third person. Such beatitudes praised certain conduct and set it as a condition for blessing.[80] Guelich goes on to show, following E. Schweizer, that Matthew's Beatitudes are much closer to those series found in the woes of the prophets (cf. Isa 5:8–23) and the beatitudes of 2 En 42:6–14.[81] This, he says, gives them a very different *Sitz im Leben* and focal point to

76. Betz, "The Beatitudes of the Sermon on the Mount (Matt. 5:3–12): Observations on Their Literary Form and Theological Significance," in *Essays on the Sermon on the Mount*, 17–36 (22–25).

77. Elsewhere Betz says that "the beatitudes in the SM . . . are not drawn from ancient Greek mystery cults, but they have developed out of a Jewish matrix." Betz, *Sermon on the Mount*, 93.

78. Betz, "The Beatitudes of the Sermon on the Mount (Matt. 5:3–12): Observations on Their Literary Form and Theological Significance," in *Essays on the Sermon on the Mount*, 17–36 (33–34).

79. Betz, "The Beatitudes of the Sermon on the Mount (Matt. 5:3–12): Observations on Their Literary Form and Theological Significance," in *Essays on the Sermon on the Mount*, 17–36 (35).

80. Guelich, "Matthean Beatitudes," 417.

81. Guelich, "Matthean Beatitudes," 417.

their wisdom counterparts.[82] John Meier also wants to view the Beatitudes as distinct from wisdom literature, though related to it, and emphasizes their apocalyptic character.[83] His argument is, in part, that wisdom literature was conservative in its thought and forms, often asserting that good conduct reaps just reward. But when "wisdom ran into apocalyptic . . . The basic connection between right conduct and just recompense was not broken but projected onto a cosmic screen, with room for a type of reward that was postponed from this life to the next."[84] As such, the "blessings" of the Beatitudes are, for Meier, pushed to the final consummation.[85]

Meier is right to see a distinction between Matthew's Beatitudes and wisdom literature, but his characterization of beatitudes *vis-à-vis* apocalyptic is problematic. For Meier, apocalyptic assurances, at least in relation to beatitudes, entail promises and visions that apply to the "next life."[86] Speaking of the beatitude at the end of Daniel, for example, Meier says:

> Happy is the one who waits with patience and so arrives" at the promised consummation (Dan. 12:12). Apocalyptic gave cagey wisdom a paradoxical twist: Happy are the unhappy, for God will make them happy—on the last day.[87]

As we have stated, however, apocalyptic refers to the hope that God will act decisively *within* history, not merely beyond it. As N. T. Wright has said, apocalyptic is what prophecy looks like "under certain historical and

---

82. Guelich, "Matthean Beatitudes," 417: "Beatitudes, however, do occur in another literary genre, viz., the prophetic-apocalyptic literature. These beatitudes offer a contrasting *Sitz im Leben* and a totally different focal point. Whereas the former were more concerned with 'worldly well-being' growing out of a life lived in conformity with the principles of God and the wise, the 'apocalyptic' beatitudes were addressed to those who because of their faithfulness would be saved from the last judgment and enter the new age. The tone of these beatitudes is more that of consolation and assurance than that of parenetic exhortation." While I agree with Guelich that Matthew's Beatitudes are more prophetic-apocalyptic in nature than a form of wisdom literature, I find this perspective problematic. I have already addressed some issues regarding apocalyptic in chapter 2. Hopefully my reasons for rejecting the view that these apocalyptic beatitudes refer to the "last judgement" are clear in what follows, even if they address the question only indirectly.

83. Meier, *Mentor, Message, and Miracle*, 324–25.

84. Meier, "Matthew 5:3–12," 282.

85. "Happiness in this life was redefined in terms of patient endurance amid the eschatological woes, an endurance to be crowned with a reversal of fates and vindication when God's kingdom finally came." Meier, "Matthew 5:3–12," 282.

86. Meier, "Matthew 5:3–12," 282.

87. Meier, "Matthew 5:3–12," 282.

theological circumstances."[88] Still, though I think Meier's understanding of apocalyptic is problematic, I agree that the Beatitudes are in some sense apocalyptic. I'm also inclined to agree with Meier's insistence that the Beatitudes in Matthew include not merely passive dimensions of Christian living, but also active dimensions.[89]

In short, Matthew's Beatitudes act as an introduction to a set of teachings that outline the way of life for a community (SM). They are also a set of values that are presuppositions for the rest of this teaching. They are apocalyptic in character, assuming the action of God in history as a pretext for their fulfillment. The technical name for the literary form of the Beatitudes is the makarism. What exactly constitutes a makarism is a separate question that requires attention.

What Is a Makarism?

Most English Bible translations render μακάριος as "blessed." There is, however, a range of interpretations regarding what makarisms actually are. These include eschatological blessing,[90] congratulations (for being in a good situation[91] or for divine approval[92]), happiness,[93] religious joy,[94] and divine enablement.[95] An important contribution of recent decades is that of K. C. Hanson, whose social-scientific study attempts to locate Matthew's makarisms in foundational Mediterranean values, namely honor and shame.[96] For my discussion of makarisms, Hanson's study will be relied

88. Wright, *Paul: Fresh Perspectives*, 50.

89. "Precisely because God's future promise impinges on and molds our present lives, we who hear and believe the message of Jesus in the beatitudes are energized, galvanized, empowered to reflect God's saving action in our own Christian action. Precisely because the spiritually poor see through the shoddy promises and props of this world's power and wealth, precisely because Jesus' disciples refuse to accept this world as the absolute goal or mainstay of their existence, they have the courage to show God's mercy, to make God's peace, to 'do the right thing' willed by God in the face of persecution." Meier, "Matthew 5:3–12," 284.

90. Strecker, *Sermon on the Mount*, 30–31; Harrington, *Gospel of Matthew*, 78.

91. France, *Gospel of Matthew*, 160–61; Garland, *Reading Matthew*, 53–54; Guelich, *Sermon on the Mount*, 66–67; Nolland, *Matthew*, 197. Keener argues specifically that the good fortune is in relation to an ultimate future reality; Keener, *Matthew*, 165–66.

92. Gundry, *Matthew*, 68.

93. Betz, *Sermon on the Mount*, 92; Hagner, *Matthew 1–13*, 91; Meier, "Matthew 5:3–12," 281–85.

94. Davies and Allison, *Matthew 1–7*, 434.

95. Talbert, *Reading the Sermon on the Mount*, 57.

96. Hanson, "How Honorable! How Shameful!," 81–111.

upon heavily since, in addition to its exhaustively thorough analysis of makarisms, it remains relatively alone in situating the proper interpretive key for makarisms in the honor/shame values of Matthew's world. Though Hanson's work on makarisms has not been widely discussed, it is worth attention for its multi-focal approach (i.e., blending social-scientific insights, literary and linguistic analysis, and exegesis).

Hanson begins by defining honor and shame. Honor is not self-esteem or pride, but a status-claim that is affirmed by one's community—it is social, not psychological.[97] Shame on the other hand can be construed positively or negatively:

> Positively, shame is sensitivity towards one's reputation; thus a "shameless person" is one who is not appropriately sensitive, who does not respect social boundaries. Negatively, shame refers to the loss of status: humiliation. The sense is captured in the English "to be ashamed," and "to shame someone," etc.[98]

Mediterranean societies are, according to Hanson, agonistic such that honor is viewed as a commodity over which to compete. It is within the locus of this system, and not within the concept of blessing, that Hanson positions Matthew's makarisms. He shows that:

> אַשְׁרֵי and μακάριος may be related to, but are not synonymous with, the terms for blessing [בְּרָכָה, בָּרַךְ, בָּרוּךְ; εὐλογία, εὐλογέω, εὐλογήμενες]. Blessings and curses are formal pronouncements by someone in authority; in the case of blessing, bestowing God's positive empowerment. This may be from God directly, or from an authorized mediator: usually a king, a priest, or a clan patriarch. Pedersen summarized the fundamental content of blessing as: numerous descendants; fertility of flocks, herds, and fields; and dominance over enemies.[99]

A blessing proper is not a promise, but a formal conferring of favor and empowerment that cannot be rescinded.[100] In contrast, makarisms and their negative counterpart, reproaches ("woes"), are part of the word-field of honor and shame, as shown in the exhaustive examples given by

---

97. Hanson, "How Honorable! How Shameful!," 83.
98. Hanson, "How Honorable! How Shameful!," 83.
99. Hanson, "How Honorable! How Shameful!," 85.
100. Hanson, "How Honorable! How Shameful!," 87.

Hanson.[101] Though makarisms may have much in common with blessings, they are, in fact, distinct.[102]

Hanson also shows convincingly that makarisms cannot be equated with happiness or any other form of human emotion:

> One does not feel good who fears Yahweh (Ps 112:1), or walks in Yahweh's law (Ps 119:1), or is reproved and chastened by Yahweh (Job 5:17)! Similarly, one does not feel good who mourns or is persecuted (Matt 5:4, 10). So "happy" is a profoundly misleading translation and interpretation of the makarism.[103]

So, as Hanson asks, "if makarisms are neither authoritative blessings nor joyous emotions, what are they?" Hanson's thorough list of examples of the use of forms of אַשְׁרֵי and μακάριος shows that though most uses are formulaic (e.g., Matt 5:3–12; 16:17; 24:46), there are non-formulaic forms in the NT and Jewish literature, whether as nouns (Gal 4:15; Rom 4:6, 9), adjectives (4 Macc 7:15; Acts 26:2; 1 Cor 7:40; Titus 2:13), divine epithets (1 Tim 1:11; 6:15), or verbs (Luke 1:48; Jas 5:11).[104] In each case, the makarism is an affirmation made by an individual or community about another person, whether real or ideal. In addition, says Hanson, is that in virtually every case of a formulaic use of either אַשְׁרֵי or μακάριος, one could translate "How honored" or "O how honorable."[105] In other words, the content of a makarism, both in the OT and NT, is a value judgement, "the social imputation of esteem to an individual or group for manifesting desirable behavior and commitments."[106] It may be that makarisms appear in different literary contexts, but wherever they appear they articulate the esteemed values of the group or individual, pronouncing the subjects as "honorable."[107]

---

101. Hanson, "How Honorable! How Shameful!," 87–89.

102. "What do makarisms have in common with blessings? (1) Both makarisms and blessings are affirmative (i.e., positive expressions). And (2) makarisms occasionally extol the same attributes of success as blessings: numerous descendants, fertility, and domination over enemies (e.g., Ps 144:12–15). On the other hand, makarisms are fundamentally different from blessings in a variety of ways: (1) Makarisms are not "words of power." (2) They are not limited to pronouncements by God or cultic mediators. (3) They only refer to humans, and never to God or non-human objects. (4) They do not have their setting in ritual. And (5) one does not pray for a makarism, or refer to oneself with a makarism." See Hanson, "How Honorable! How Shameful!," 89.

103. Hanson, "How Honorable! How Shameful!," 89.

104. Hanson, "How Honorable! How Shameful!," 89.

105. Hanson, "How Honorable! How Shameful!," 90.

106. Hanson, "How Honorable! How Shameful!," 91.

107. Hanson, "How Honorable! How Shameful!," 92.

Matthew's Use of Makarisms in the Beatitudes

Hanson's thesis about makarisms shifts the debate over the nature of the Beatitudes, especially the discussion over whether they are either eschatological blessings/reversals or entrance requirements.[108] Both of these views are problematic, for as Powell argues, "If mourning (Matt 5:4) does not appear to be a virtue to which all should aspire, neither do peacemakers (5:9) sound like an unfortunate class of people who need to have their situation reversed."[109] The inability for either position to achieve anything approaching consistency or consensus suggests a new approach may be needed. If Hanson is correct, then the social setting of Matthew's Beatitudes must be viewed in an entirely new light, that is, within the honor/shame system. Matthew's Jesus is not announcing eschatological promises or entrance-requirements, but rather is pronouncing as honorable a particular set of values.

It should be clear, at least from a narrative-critical viewpoint, that these values are in some way connected with the imminent coming of the kingdom of heaven. In Matthew's story, the new age of fulfillment is at hand in the current moment. The command, in light of this moment, is to repent (4:17). The Beatitudes, if they are to be read correctly, must be viewed in light of this. By repentance we refer not to sorrow or regret, but the notion of μετάνοια, which refers to a type of conversion,[110] a transformation of one's mind or understanding, a redirection of the will. In saying all of this, we ought not view the Beatitudes as expanded commentary on the content of repentance, that is, as practical ways in which a person should repent—become poor in spirit, become mourners, become meek and so forth. Such could be construed as entrance-requirements; do these and you will inherit the kingdom. In other words, we might be tempted to see the Beatitudes merely as a set of performances and rewards. However, in light of Betz's suggestion that the Beatitudes represent subversions of popular wisdom, and of Hanson's positioning of the Beatitudes within the Mediterranean honor/shame culture, I am unconvinced by an entrance-requirement reading. On the contrary, the repentance being expounded in Matt 5:3–12 does not involve a change in specific actions, but rather a

---

108. The view of the Beatitudes as entrance-requirements is perhaps exemplified by Strecker, *Sermon on the Mount*, 30–34, and Windisch, *Meaning of the Sermon on the Mount*. Davies and Allison, *Matthew 1–7*, 439–67, and Guelich, "Matthean Beatitudes," 415–34; Guelich, *Sermon on the Mount*, 63–118, are among the better examples of the view that the Beatitudes are announcements of eschatological blessings/reversals.

109. Powell, "Matthew's Beatitudes," 461.

110. J. Behm, "μετανοέω, μετάνοια," *TDNT* 4:999–1006.

change in relation to one's understanding of the nature of the kingdom of heaven, and what it means to be God's people.

Who Are the "Poor in Spirit"?

Matthew's first Beatitude is programmatic in this respect. There has, of course, been debate over the meaning of the phrase οἱ πτωχοὶ τῷ πνεύματι. Many have accepted the notion that "the poor in spirit" refers to the humble.[111] Some have pointed to Qumran usages of the word "poor" (see 1QM 11.8–15; 13.14; 14.7; 1QpHab 12.3, 6, 10; 1QH 5.16–22; 18.12–15; 1QS 4.3; CD 1.5, 8–9) as speaking of those who are faithful to YHWH, humbly dependent on God; Matthew is said to be in agreement with this usage.[112] David Garland argues that the word "poor" itself, which originally referred to the materially poor, came to take on "religious connotations," the "humble pious who were beloved by God."[113] The Matthean addition of "in spirit" is what has led many commentators to conclude that Matthew "spiritualized" Q's original text and that the economically poor are not in mind in Matt 5:3. This interpretation seems incongruous, however, with the fact that 5:3 is grouped with the following three makarisms in 5:4–6 by successive alliterations,[114] and these other makarisms describe not pious attitudes but positions of vulnerability and abandonment. Assuming Matthew is consistent, we should expect the makarism in 5:3 to fit thematically with those in 5:4–6.

---

111. For example, Betz, *Sermon on the Mount*, 115–19; France, *Matthew*, 165 ("It is a positive spiritual orientation, the converse of the arrogant self-confidence which . . . causes a person to treat God as irrelevant"); Garland, *Reading Matthew*, 56; Gundry, *Matthew*, 67 ("a sense of personal inadequacy"); Meier, *Matthew*, 39–40; Strecker, *Sermon on the Mount*, 31–32. Luz claims the early church fathers mostly held this view; Luz, *Matthew 1–7*, 234–35. Such is not unlike the position taken by Luther: "For it is said plainly and bluntly: Blessed are the poor; and yet there is another little word along with that, viz. spiritually poor, so that nothing is accomplished by any one's being bodily poor, and having no money and property. For, outwardly to have money, property and people, is not of itself wrong, but it is God's gift and arrangement. No one is blessed, therefore, because he is a beggar and has nowhere anything of his own; but the expression is, spiritually poor. For I said already in the beginning that Christ is here not at all treating of secular government and order, but is speaking only of what is spiritual—how one aside from and over and above that which is outward is to live before God." Luther, *Commentary on the Sermon on the Mount*, 23.

112. For example, France, *Matthew*, 164–65.

113. Garland, *Reading Matthew*, 55.

114. The four makarisms in 5:3–6 exhibit alliteration in Greek, with each of the identified groups beginning with the letter Π. This suggests an intentional literary device that joins the four verses into a subset within the larger whole of 5:3–12.

The implied dichotomy drawn between humility and economic poverty by most commentators is, in any case, a misunderstanding of the nature of poverty. Poverty is typically understood by biblical scholars to be merely a lack of sufficient material needs. The result is that poverty of *spirit* is defined as distinct from material poverty, as reflected in the frequent contrast between Matt 5:3 with Luke 6:20b amongst biblical scholars.[115] But any definition of poverty in uniformly economic or "spiritual" terms is to misunderstand its all-pervasive nature. Such understandings likely derive from a modern individualistic perspective. The reality is much more interconnected. Even contemporary studies of global poverty recognize, for example, the relationship between economic deprivation and mental illness.[116] However, this relationship is only one expression of the mental and behavioral patterns of the poor being shaped by situations in which the dominant social structure is unfavorably disposed toward the lower class.[117] In other words, those who are materially poor learn to accept their place of subjugation in the web of social relationships, affirming their lack of social capital and becoming dependent on the systems that sustain their destitution. These legitimating systems are social, economic, and religious/ theological. The result is a mindset in which the dominant judgements about oneself are accepted and the hope of emerging from poverty is extinguished—a social script is formed.[118] Thus the psychological, material, and social aspects of poverty reinforce each other. This understanding of poverty is cross-cultural inasmuch as it can be applied to a range of social constructions, including advanced agrarian societies, and across a range of geographical places and historical eras.

115. For example, Garland, *Reading Matthew*, 56; Gundry, *Matthew*, 67; Harrington, *Gospel of Matthew*, 78; Stanton, *Gospel for a New People*, 299.

116. Such recognition extends back, academically-speaking, at least to the 1950–1960s. See Hollingshead and Redlich, *Social Class and Mental Illness*, and Langner and Michael, *Life Stress and Mental Health*. These works showed a direct relationship between the experience of poverty and a high rate of emotional illness.

117. An idea explored in Waxman, *Stigma of Poverty*.

118. The Brazilian educator Paulo Freire might have described this as a form of "banking education" in which the dominant class seek to educate the "peasants" because "the interests of the oppressors lie in 'changing the consciousness of the oppressed, not the situation which oppresses them'; for the more the oppressed can be led to adapt to that situation, the more easily they can be dominated." Freire, *Pedagogy of the Oppressed*, 74. This leads the poor to internalize the world of their oppressors, their social construction of reality, leading to the justification of social relations, institutions, class relations, and the distribution of wealth, power and privilege. Herzog points out that Freire lives in what Lenski called an advanced agrarian society that was macrosociologically similar to that of Jesus, even across historical eras; Herzog, *Parables as Subversive Speech*, 25.

We must certainly be careful not to impose this understanding of poverty anachronistically onto ancient thought. Still, something like this understanding of poverty, namely, that which holistically affects the inner and outer dimensions of the human experience, is reflected in some of the Qumran uses of the word "poor." I mentioned previously that commentators have pointed to Qumran as proof that "poor in spirit" refers to "religious piety." But this is not at all clear. The Qumran Habakkuk commentary (1QpHab 12), for example, speaks of the "poor" as those exploited by the "Wicked Priest" (12.3), who plans to destroy them (12.6) and has stolen their assets (12.10). The War Scroll speaks of God overcoming his enemies by the hand of the poor/oppressed (1QM 11.9, 13; 13.14). In 1QM 14.7, where the phrase "poor in spirit" is used directly (*'nwy rwh*), it is basically unclear as to the phrase's meaning except that the reference appears to refer to those at Qumran whose hands are feeble and whose knees shake (14.6) and who have been smitten from the hips to the shoulder (14.7)—this seems like a description of those who have been previously dominated in some sense.[119] If these Qumran texts do indeed reflect an understanding of the poor as the humble pious, this is only the case because the poor have been dominated and have little choice but to turn to God; their humility is the symptom of a deeper cause.

Much recent scholarship has rejected the view that Matthew's "poor in spirit" refers to simple humility, preferring to identify the poor in spirit with the downtrodden and destitute.[120] Ernest Best describes such people as fainthearted or despondent.[121] These definitions better capture the holistic nature of poverty described above. Powell notes that many commentators identify the poor in spirit with the עֲנָוִי, that is, the dispossessed and abandoned, as found in passages such as Isa 11:4; 29:19; 32:7; 61:1; Amos 2:7; 8:4; Zeph 2:3.[122] The phrase οἱ πτωχοὶ τῷ πνεύματι does not appear in the LXX, though a similar phrase—οἱ ταπεινοὶ τῷ πνεύματι—can be found in Ps 33:19,[123] often translated as "the crushed in spirit,"[124] though "humiliated in spirit" is also appropriate. Such designations, denoting an

---

119. Hagner notes that 1QM 14.7 indicates how the literal poor are identified as the righteous. Hagner, *Matthew 1–13*, 92.

120. See for example Carter, *Matthew and the Margins*, 131; Davies and Allison, *Matthew 1–7*, 439–45; Hagner, *Matthew 1–13*, 91; Nolland, *Matthew*, 200–201.

121. Best, "Matthew V.3," 255–58. It should be noted that, for Best, this despondency is the result of hearing the demands of Jesus' sermon.

122. Powell, "Matthew's Beatitudes," 463.

123. Ps 34:18 in English translations.

124. As in the RSV, NASB, NRSV, NIV, ESV.

undesired and passive reception of the status, describe poverty in a holistic sense—inwardly and materially.

To the inward and material aspects of poverty we should add a social dimension. Malina provides social-scientific insight as to what poverty might mean in the context of a Mediterranean honor/shame society. He argues that being "poor" is not an expression of class or economic rank, but rather refers to persons who cannot maintain their inherited social status (whatever level in society it may be) due to circumstances that befall them and their families.[125] For Malina, poor and rich do not designate two poles of a spectrum, but rather two minority categories of people, the socially ill-fated and the shamelessly greedy. In this way, the poor are not the peasantry *per se*, but rather the imprisoned, blind, debt-ridden (as in Isa 61), as well as those who are hungry, thirsty, and mourning (as in Matt 5:3–12);[126] those who have been socially exiled. This is not too dissimilar from Luz's assertion that the word πτωχός, the term used to translate וַעֲנָוִי in the LXX (e.g., Isa 61:1) and used in Matt 5:3, refers to those who are reduced to begging, in contrast to the πένης who has only a little wealth, but who works and has "sufficiency" (working peasants, artisans).[127] The latter remain socially acceptable while the former do not. Malina's understanding suggests more relativity and impermanence than that of Luz, with "the poor" representing a revolving category of people.[128] It is, however, not clear how quickly Malina thinks this turnover of poverty actually occurred. After all, those who were hungry and debt-ridden, for example, would not easily have emerged from this situation. Whatever the problems in Malina's approach may be, it makes the point well that experiencing poverty in a first-century Mediterranean setting was necessarily social in nature. This would have necessitated the shameful position of having to seek charity without having the means to reciprocate.[129]

In essence, to be "poor" or "poor in spirit" is to experience insufficiency in a holistic sense—internally, materially, and socially. Each aspect reinforces the others, and so as a person experiences material deprivation

---

125. Malina, *New Testament World*, 99–100.

126. Malina notes that a mourner is one afflicted with evil who by mourning protests the presence of evil. Malina also lists the blind, the lame, lepers, the deaf and the dead as in Matt 11:4–5, and the hungry, the thirsty, the stranger, the naked and the imprisoned as in Matt 25:34–36. Malina, *New Testament World*, 99.

127. Luz, *Matthew 1–7*, 231. Indeed the cognate of πένης is πένομαι, "to work hard."

128. "The poor would not be a permanent social standing but a sort of revolving category of people who unfortunately cannot maintain their inherited status." Malina, *New Testament World*, 100.

129. Malina, *New Testament World*, 94–95.

they correspondingly experience social marginalization/shame and, as the dominant narrative about oneself is internalized, the person experiences a breakdown in one's internal or spiritual life. Such experience is characterized by a number of issues such as a lack of necessary material goods, malnutrition, loss/theft of land, physiological sickness, mental illness,[130] disability, social ostracism, loss of honor and social capital, death of self or family members, and so forth. Such experiences also lead people to dependence on God, and this can take a variety of forms. We do of course witness these experiences throughout the Gospels, including Matthew. Jesus confronts issues of material lack (6:1-4, 11, 25-34; 14:13-21; 15:32-39) and greed (6:19-24; 19:16-30); tells parables about land loss (20:1-16 [implied]); heals the sick (8:1-17; 14:34-36; 15:28-31), mentally ill (8:28-34; 17:14-21), and disabled (9:1-8); challenges social ostracism and exclusion (15:21-28; 18:15-20; 19:1-15; 21:12-17); reinstates people into community life (9:20-22) and raises dead family members (9:18-19, 23-26), among other things. These characters that are characterized as "poor" almost uniformly show openness to the God reflected in the ministry of Jesus.

The Mourners, Meek and Hungry

If Matt 5:3 is indeed programmatic with respect to the rest of the Beatitudes, and SM as a whole, we should expect that our reading of "poor in spirit" is consistent with the verses that follow. This is particularly true regarding the makarisms in Matt 5:4-6 since, together with 5:3, these verses form a subgrouping (also true for 5:7-10). Both 5:3-6 and 5:7-10 contain precisely thirty-six words each, each sentence in 5:3-6 participates in a fourfold alliteration,[131] and both 5:6 and 5:10 contain δικαιοσύνη, all of which together suggests distinct groupings. We would expect both brackets to highlight a particular theme. As we will see, our reading of "poor in spirit" is supported by the fact that it makes sense of the subsequent three Beatitudes:

> Poor in spirit
>
> Those who mourn
>
> The meek

130. Hollenbach has argued, drawing upon studies by Fanon and others, that demon possession in traditional societies is a form of mental illness reflecting "class antagonisms rooted in economic exploitation." It is a retreat to an inner world where the subject can resist domination, and thus a form of accommodation. Hollenbach, "Jesus, Demoniacs," 573.

131. Each of the identified groups (poor in spirit, those who mourn, the meek, and those who hunger and thirst for righteousness) begins with Π.

Those who hunger and thirst for justice (δικαιοσύνη)

The second, third, and fourth Beatitudes spell out different aspects of the poverty described in the first. The mourners being described in 5:4 mourn because they experience the weight of poverty and domination, such as with the death of family members. Mourning in the OT is often in response to forms of domination and their effects, or the death or loss of people (e.g., Num 14:39; 2 Sam 13:37; 19:1; 1 Chr 7:22; 2 Chr 35:24; Neh 1:4; Isa 3:26; 16:9; 19:8; 61:1–3; Jer 4:28; 14:2; Dan 10:2). This is also the case in Matt 9:15, in which Jesus talks about it not yet being time to mourn the bridegroom. To mourn is to protest one's affliction with injustice or evil,[132] to acknowledge one's suffering and "the seeming slowness of God's justice."[133]

The meek (5:5) are the lowly. Πραεῖς could conjure a number of meanings based on Greek usage.[134] But that Matthew seems to evoke, if not quote, Ps 37:11 suggests that in the context of the Beatitudes he takes his meaning from the psalm. The LXX version of Psalm 37[135] renders πραεῖς in place of the Hebrew עֲנָוִים, the same term that πτωχοὶ replaces in passages such as Isaiah 61. In this sense, the meek of Matt 5:5 should be identified closely with the poor in spirit of 5:3. Qumran literature identifies the meek in Ps 37 as "the company of the poor who endure the time of error but are delivered from all the snares of Belial" (4Q171 2.9–10a). In short, the meek are the powerless who live under the domination of, according to the Psalm, "the wicked."

If a pattern has already been set, then those who hunger and thirst for righteousness (Matt 5:6) should be identified as part of this downtrodden group. To hunger and thirst denotes the human requirement of sustenance. But why hunger and thirst for δικαιοσύνη? As we noted earlier, righteousness in Matthew, and in the NT, is far too large and controversial a topic to deal with comprehensively in this context.[136] It is, however, worth noting that

---

132. Malina, *Christian Origins and Cultural Anthropology*, 203.

133. Hagner, *Matthew 1–13*, 92.

134. Aristotle, for example, speaks of meekness as good-temperedness in *Nicomachean Ethics*. The "good-tempered man is not disposed to take vengeance but rather to pardon." Aristotle, *Eth. nic.*, 4.11. Accordingly, Luz defines meekness as "well-measured, regulated mastering of wrath." Luz, *Matthew 1–7*, 236n68.

135. Ps 36:11 (LXX).

136. Representative views, helpfully summarized in Przybylski, *Righteousness in Matthew*, 1–3, include: (1) Strecker, who views righteousness as *Rechtschaffenheit*, a demand upon humans. (2) Fiedler, who sees righteousness as both eschatological gift and demand, though the gift precedes the demand. (3) Ziesler, who attempts to mediate between the above views by arguing some passages refer to demand, others to God's gift, though greater significance is given to those passages in which gift is the

the dichotomy typically drawn between righteousness as God's gift/action and righteousness as human faithfulness is, in this instance, beside the point. Both should theoretically lead to a just state of affairs that is being hungered after by those being referenced. "Covenant justice" may be a more helpful way to render δικαιοσύνη given the context, in which the downtrodden are in view.[137] The justice they seek is both the gift of God and the vocation of God's people.[138] Whatever the process, the justice itself is the setting right of a world corrupted by sin (cf. Matt 1:21), corruption that has resulted in a situation where some are poor in spirit, mourners, and meek.

For each of these designations Jesus ascribes honor. That is to say, he ascribes social status that is to be affirmed by the Matthean communities. He does not mediate blessing, nor does he label as happy those who embody the designations: the purpose, which we will explore in more detail below, is to reframe the values of the Matthean community in light of God's will.

---

intended meaning. In this view Matt 5:6 refers to God's gift. (4) Schweitzer and Lohmeyer, who also argue that each passage should be taken on its own merit, but that neither meaning, gift or demand, should be subordinated to the other. Also worthy of mention is Thom, "Justice in the Sermon on the Mount," 314–38. The paper explores popular conceptions of justice through a survey of one of the ancient world's most influential analyses of justice, Book 5 of Aristotle's *Nicomachean Ethics*. By doing so Thom shows how SM fits with some popular notions of justice, but also overturns others, thus exceeding popular expectations.

137. It is debatable whether "Righteousness" is the best translation in any case. Stassen and Gushee note, "Because our culture is individualistic, we think of righteousness as the virtue of an individual person. And because our culture is possessive, we think of it as something an individual possesses. But righteousness that an individual possesses is self-righteousness. And that is exactly what the gospel says we cannot have." Stassen and Gushee go on, speaking of Matt 5:6: "The Greek word here, *dikaiosyne*, and its root, *dike*, have the connotation of justice. Furthermore, Jesus is alluding to Isaiah 61, which rejoices three times that God is bringing righteousness of justice (vv. 3, 10, 11). The word there is the Hebrew *tsedaqah*. . . . It means *delivering justice* (a justice that rescues and releases the oppressed) and *community-restoring justice* (a justice that restores the powerless and the outcasts to their rightful place in covenant community)." Stassen and Gushee, *Kingdom Ethics*, 42 (emphasis original).

138. This way of putting it is to begin to touch on the idea of righteousness as covenant faithfulness. For all the complexity of this topic, we can say that the idea of covenant faithfulness draws a relationship between the faithfulness of God to God's own promises and the faithfulness of his people to God. It was also true, however, as N. T. Wright points out, that "If Israel was called to be the means of the creator's undoing evil in this world, now that Israel has fallen victim to evil she herself needs restoration. The god of creation and covenant must act to redeem Israel." Wright, *New Testament*, 272. In this sense God's action is perhaps primary, though this should be expected in a covenantal framework since God must always initiate a covenant.

Honorable Behavior

While the first stanza of four Beatitudes declares in different ways that the poor and downtrodden are honorable, the second stanza shifts emphasis. This second stanza does not focus on destructive states of being that are forced upon people, but rather on states of being that can be chosen and exhibited as behavior.[139] The first group deemed honorable are the merciful (5:7). The tradition of mercy in the OT is strong. The LXX version of Prov 14:21 says ὁ ἀτιμάζων πένητας ἁμαρτάνει ἐλεῶν δὲ πτωχοὺς μακαριστός ("Whoever dishonors one who labors for a living is a sinner, but honorable is the one who has mercy on the poor"). The LXX also adds a clause to Prov 17:5—ὁ δὲ ἐπισπλαγχνιζόμενος ἐλεηθήσεται—which Hagner translates as "the one who has compassion will be shown mercy."[140] It is not obvious that Matthew has these Proverbs in mind, though they do bear witness to the tradition of showing mercy to the poor, particularly in the OT. Neyrey notes that in some ancient writings, mercy is seen as dishonorable since the honorable man takes revenge and shows no mercy (e.g., Aristotle, *Rhet.*, 1.9.24).[141] This would seem to confirm that we have already said of the Beatitudes, namely that they are subversions of popular honor ascriptions.

The pure in heart (Matt 5:8) are also deemed honorable. Both Hagner and Carter connect this statement with Ps 24:4 and its assertion that those with clean hands and a pure heart receive blessing[142] from the Lord.[143] Both connect purity of heart with integrity, the consistency of outer

139. Hagner draws a distinction between the two stanzas in that the first four Beatitudes focus on "a state of mind or an attitude (and imply conduct only secondarily)," the next four refer "to the happiness of those who act." Hagner, *Matthew 1–13*, 93. Hagner is correct that there is a distinction between the stanzas and that the second stanza is focused on behavior. I disagree, however, with his construal of the first stanza.

Powell also makes a distinction between the two stanzas: "Acceptance of a two-stanza structure allows for a compromise solution to the reversal-reward debate: the first stanza (5:3–6) speaks of reversals for the unfortunate, and the second stanza (5:7–10) describes rewards for the virtuous." Powell, "Matthew's Beatitudes," 462. I also disagree with Powell, except for the fact that the second stanza, in contrast to the first, focuses on behavior.

140. Hagner, *Matthew 1–13*, 93.

141. Neyrey, *Honor and Shame*, 182–83. The passage from *Rhetoric* says, "To take vengeance on one's enemies is nobler than to come to terms with them; for to retaliate is just, and that which is just is noble; and further, a courageous man ought not to allow himself to be beaten."

142. Note that the "blessing" here is εὐλογία in the LXX, not μακάριος as in Matthew 5.

143. Hagner, *Matthew 1–13*, 94; Carter, *Matthew and the Margins*, 135. See also Davies and Allison, *Matthew 1–7*, 456; Guelich, *Sermon on the Mount*, 90–91; Luz, *Matthew 1–7*, 238–39.

action with inner disposition, thoughts, and motivations. Matthew uses καρδία in a number of ways: as the source of speech (Matt 12:34; 15:18); as the source of outward actions (15:19); as the place of inner thought (9:4; 24:48[144]), both sinful (5:27–28) and virtuous (22:37); as the place of true understanding (13:15); as a place of true forgiveness (18:35). Powell summarizes these passages as reflecting that the heart "cannot be linked definitively with any one sphere of human activity such as cognition or volition," and that, "Here, and elsewhere in the Bible, *kardia* seems simply to represent 'the true self,' what one really is, apart from pretense."[145] Purity of heart, therefore, refers to being truly virtuous, as opposed to only appearing so. Integrity is thus as good a description as any. Judging by its surrounding material, Matt 5:8 seems to proclaim as honorable those who do merciful and peaceful deeds out of a truly pure motivation. Interestingly, in Psalm 24 such integrity is contrasted with idolatry and false testimony (24:4). It may be that, for Matthew, merciful and peaceful deeds done out of an "impure heart" constitute forms of idolatry and false witness. The implication may be that Matthew believes kind and just acts done in order to gain honor are themselves not honorable in the eyes of God.

Regarding peacemakers, a number of associations have been made, including with Rome's *Pax Romana* and Roman domination;[146] with the Zealots and violent revolution;[147] with personal reconciliation;[148] with peace in social terms;[149] with war, persecution, and injustice;[150] and with bringing others to peace with God.[151] There is no reason why any of these possibilities should be discounted. Indeed, the Hebrew word *shalōm* would no doubt have been in the background of any Matthean understanding of "peace."[152] *Shalōm* is, as Hendrickx argues, "very rich in content" and "hard

---

144. In Matt 24:48 the Greek reads ἐὰν δὲ εἴπῃ ὁ κακὸς δοῦλος ἐκεῖνος ἐν τῇ καρδίᾳ αὐτοῦ, which most translations render in a way similar to the ESV: "But if that wicked servant *says to himself* . . . " I'm not sure why the phrase "says in his heart" is avoided.

145. Powell, "Matthew's Beatitudes," 472.

146. Carter, *Matthew and the Margins*, 135–36.

147. Hagner, *Matthew 1–13*, 94.

148. France, *Matthew*, 169; Gundry, *Matthew*, 72 (Gundry states that this peace is one's own with another, not in regard to bringing peace between others).

149. Nolland, *Matthew*, 205; Neyrey, *Honor and Shame*, 183–85.

150. Betz, *Sermon on the Mount*, 137–42; Davies and Allison, *Matthew 1–7*, 458.

151. Powell, "Matthew's Beatitudes," 473. Powell mentions this only as a possible meaning.

152. Matthew of course uses the word εἰρηνοποιός to refer to peacemakers, and the LXX typically opts for its cognate εἰρήνη to translate the Hebrew *shalom*. There are, however, over twenty words used to translate it.

to translate," though he goes on to say it is derived from a root meaning "complete," "intact," or "to be or to be in the process of being fulfilled."[153] Thus *shalōm* is harmony with God, self, others, and creation. Betz agrees: "Its dimensions are cosmic and involved the order of the universe as intended by the creator."[154] Betz thus relates "peace" to justice, and the sense that ethics involves humanity conforming to the standards set by the divine order.[155] Peacemakers are then those who have a deep and active commitment to the work of God's justice.[156] They are "those who work for the wholeness and well-being that God wills for a broken world."[157] Such a perspective is reflected in what comes later in SM, not least in calls for personal reconciliation (Matt 5:21–26), active nonviolent resistance to unjust systems and powers (5:38–42), love of enemies (5:43–48), forgiveness (6:10), and in the so-called "Golden Rule" (7:12). It is also worth noting Neyrey's assertion that a peacemaker is one who forswears a riposte to an honor challenge, thus being shamed for stepping apart from the expected behavior—"Shamed by his neighbor, he is honored by Jesus."[158] If Neyrey is correct, Jesus' ascription of honor to peacemakers is all the more subversive.

The final Beatitude in the second stanza, found in Matt 5:10, is that regarding those "persecuted for righteousness' sake." This is an appropriate end to the sequence, since those who work with a pure heart for mercy and peace/justice will experience persecution. As we mentioned above in the comment on Matt 5:6,[159] righteousness (δικαιοσύνη) can be understood as covenant justice, a gift from God and the vocation of his people, the setting right of a world corrupted by sin. For Matthew's Jesus, a people pure in heart, who do acts of mercy and peace/justice out of a true desire to do God's will, will not shy away from the face of persecution, which is a sure sign of social shame. Such shamed people, says Matthew, are to be deemed honorable in the kingdom of heaven.

To those who act mercifully, those who work for peace and justice, and those who do so with integrity and an unswerving commitment, Matthew's Jesus ascribes honor, that is, a positive claim of social worth. This

153. Hendrickx, *Sermon on the Mount*, 31.

154. Betz, *Sermon on the Mount*, 139.

155. Betz, *Sermon on the Mount*, 139.

156. Joseph P. Healey, "Peace: OT," *ABD* 5:206.

157. Kingsbury, *Matthew as Story*, 133.

158. Neyrey, *Honor and Shame*, 183–85.

159. Powell thinks that δικαιοσύνη is used in different senses in 5:6 and 5:10. This is because he, along with other commentators, takes 5:6 to refer solely to God's righteousness, but concedes that 5:10 must refer to behavior in keeping with God's will. Powell, "Matthew's Beatitudes," 474, 474n48.

is in the face of such actions attracting social derision from others in the form of shame. Again, the values expressed by Matthew, values that should shape the community of Jesus' followers, are subversions of popular values. Rather than being shaped by revenge, outward appearances, and passive conformity to the current state of things, Jesus' followers are shaped by mercy, integrity, peace, and the willingness to suffer on account of covenant justice. To be shaped by these values, both individually and communally, is to have had one's mind transformed in light of the imminent kingdom of heaven—to have repented.

"For Theirs Is the Kingdom of Heaven"

In addition to these subversive statements regarding what is considered honorable in Matthew's communities, the Beatitudes also contain a set of motivations or rewards for those to whom these descriptions apply. But what does it mean to say of the poor in spirit that "theirs is the kingdom of heaven"? This has typically been taken as either an eschatological reversal/ blessing or a reward for having fulfilled an entrance requirement. But if the makarisms themselves do not uniformly fit the pattern of either entrance-requirements (e.g., mourning) or situations demanding eschatological reversal (e.g., peacemaking), then how can the ensuing rewards be framed in these ways? Indeed, if our argument (following Hanson) is correct—that the makarisms represent subversive value statements about what should be deemed honorable in light of the imminent kingdom of heaven—then should not the ensuing rewards reflect this meaning?

Hanson himself argues that, in light of his argument,

> the motivations obviously may be realized within the community, and in this life. The described behaviors cannot be sustained by a hope after death: belonging in the "kingdom," comfort, mercy, the epithet "sons of God," etc., do not obtain in the afterlife, but in the community of faith.[160]

To repeat an earlier claim, the Beatitudes must be viewed in light of Jesus' proclamation that his hearers must repent (4:17): the structure of the narrative leads us to suppose that this is so. The Beatitudes describe the values of those who experience transformed thinking and living. Such people have come to see that it is not in fact the honorable in the eyes of the world who are to be found in the kingdom of heaven, but rather the poor in spirit, those who mourn, and the meek. This kingdom, a subversion of the kingdoms of the

---

160. Hanson, "How Honorable! How Shameful!," 100.

world, is constituted by those who are otherwise seen as dishonorable, and by those who embody mercy, integrity, peace, and covenant justice.

Such transformation of thinking is commanded in light of the imminent kingdom of heaven. That the kingdom is at hand should lead us to suspicion regarding the notion that the rewards described in the Beatitudes are "eschatological."[161] Those who repent will find they are among those counted in the kingdom of heaven *imminently*. If this kingdom is indeed at hand, then the present-tense statement "theirs is the kingdom of heaven" makes sense; the kingdom has come near, and the poor in spirit are numbered among those within it. This reward is not a true reward, since it is not earned. As Yoder has said, "One cannot simply, by making up his mind, set out to 'mourn' or to 'be persecuted for righteousness' sake."[162] On the contrary, the statement that "theirs is the kingdom of heaven" is meant to qualify the statement that the poor are honorable: when the kingdom approaches, the poor will "find themselves among those who are 'at home,' who 'fit' there, who are not out of place."[163]

In the same way, the other "rewards" are declarations of positions the relevant parties will find themselves occupying when the kingdom is at hand. Mourners will be comforted, not eschatologically, but in the imminent kingdom of heaven. The meek will inherit the earth.[164] Those who hunger for covenant justice will be satisfied, and so on. This is possible because the kingdom of heaven, and indeed SM, calls into being a people who will embody God's good purposes for Israel and the world. In such a community, it ought to be the case that mourners are comforted, that the merciful are shown mercy, that the pure in heart see God,[165] and that peacemakers

161. I mean "eschatological" in the sense it is commonly used, as referring solely to an "end-time" event(s).

162. Yoder, "The Political Axioms of the Sermon on the Mount," in *The Original Revolution*, 34–51 (40).

163. Yoder, "The Political Axioms of the Sermon on the Mount," in *The Original Revolution*, 34–51 (40).

164. To inherit the earth was for some a reference to inheriting the land of Israel (see 4Q171 3:9–11). However, prophetic texts such as Isa 65–66 also looked forward to the renewal of the whole earth. It is not clear which interpretation Matthew might have had in mind, but in any case we should not take the reference as referring to the meek *controlling* the earth; to do so would contradict the meekness that made them honorable in the first place. The inheritance of the land of Israel in the OT was, of course, always relative, since it was in fact God who owned the land (Lev 25:23). To inherit the earth may, then, refer to the appropriate life lived on the land and under God.

165. There is a long history of "theophanic" experiences in the OT, meaning simply that God was revealed in a special way to people. In the OT it relates to close relationship with the divine; it does not require a futuristic interpretation (see, e.g., Exod 24:9–11; Num 12:8; 14:14; Isa 6:5; Jer 29:12–13; Pss 11:7; 17:15; 24:6; 27:4, 8; John 1:18;

are called "children of God." That such things reflect the nature of the kingdom of God, and may in fact be ways of speaking about certain aspects of
the kingdom, is a notion justified by the bookending of the Beatitudes with
the phrase "theirs is the kingdom of heaven" (5:3, 10). Such bookending by
this present-tense phrase also helps us make sense of the fact that the other
six "reward" phrases (5:4–9) are future tense. Such occurrences need not
be read as future punctiliar events, but rather can be seen as anticipated
iterative results that occur when the kingdom of heaven has come.[166] The
use of the future tense in these cases is to be regulated by the overarching
theme of the imminent kingdom of heaven and the place within it for the
downtrodden, merciful, pure, and peaceable.

4.4 Jesus' Prophetic Vocation and the Beatitudes

We have already explored some of the ways in which the beginning of
Matthew's narrative depicts Jesus as a prophet. Indeed, Jesus is pictured
as a new Moses and, to a lesser extent, Elijah, as well as one echoing the
prophetic message of John ("Repent! . . . "), and as having experienced a
prophetic commissioning following his baptism. Further, Matthew's use
of prophetic quotations, as we have noted, is not merely an incidental
supplement but rather an evocation of concrete figures in concrete historical situations. Such historical situations are, for Matthew, analogous to
Palestine in the first century CE. As such, the current situation requires the
presence of a prophet, and this is reflected in the popularity of prophetic

---

Rev 22:4). See Malina, "Patron and Client," 10.

166. Wallace, in making the point that the future tense generally has an external
aspect, notes that, "The future is often listed by grammatarians as having an internal
portrayal at times. Thus its aspect is listed as occasionally internal, occasionally external. This tense is something of an enigma. . . . although its forms were no doubt derived
from the aorist . . . there are occasions in which an internal idea seems to take place
(thus it appears to share some similarities with the present). However, it is probably best
to see the future as the temporal counterpart to the aorist: Both are summary tenses
that can be used to describe an iterative or progressive action, but only in collocation
with other linguistic features." See Wallace, *Greek Grammar Beyond the Basics*, 501n16.
Another view is that of Porter who argues that the future tense "grammaticalizes expectation" rather than making direct assertions about the future. It serves in "speaking
of events in a different way." It should be noted, however, that Porter's view remains
contested, even if it is increasingly influential. See Porter, *Verbal Aspect in the Greek*,
439. R. Picirilli has helpfully stated that, "Though many of us may not be able to weigh
the linguistics theory involved, we can test application of the theory [of Porter et al.] to
the NT and evaluate how well it fits." See Picirilli, "Meaning of the Tenses," 554. See also
Campbell, *Verbal Aspect*, 127–61.

claimants during this period. For Matthew, Jesus no doubt fills this role. But how is this reflected in the Beatitudes?

The Shape of Jesus' Prophetic Vocation as Reflected in the Beatitudes

While some scholars, for example Hagner,[167] assert that the Beatitudes should be seen as being within the wisdom tradition rather than within the prophetic-apocalyptic tradition, there are reasons to counter this claim. Guelich points out that beatitudes of the wisdom tradition never occur in groupings of more than two.[168] Moreover, the themes of Jesus' makarisms are those found not primarily in wisdom settings but in prophetic settings—as we noted above, for example, Matthew's reference to the "poor in spirit" is most naturally influenced by the frequent references to the וַעֲנָוִי and YHWH's liberation for them in the OT prophets.[169] Further, Jesus' beatitudes are not to be viewed as freestanding ethical exhortations, but rather as an implied ethics rooted in the proclamation of the kingdom of God and the description of a people who are at home in it. Such proclamation of the kingdom is, generally speaking, a prophetic rather than a wisdom theme. This is not to draw too great a contrast between the prophetic and wisdom traditions, since they do cross over at points. It is, however, to say that the Beatitudes are more congruent with the distinctive shape of the prophetic traditions.

Jesus' commissioning in Matt 3:16–17 is, as I have contended, comparable with the anointing of the prophet with the Spirit in Isa 61:1. This comparison is carried on in the Beatitudes. Matthew 5:3 ought to be associated with Isa 61:1 and the bringing of good news (εὐαγγέλιον) to the poor since, in Matthew, the εὐαγγέλιον has already been identified with the proclamation of the kingdom (Matt 4:23), and the announcement that this kingdom belongs to the poor (5:3) is a surely an expression of Isaiah's good news. This association is further demonstrated in the way that Matthew echoes the message of comfort for those who mourn (5:4; cf. Isa 61:2b–3a, παρακαλέσαι πάντας τοὺς πενθοῦντας), the notion of the inheritance of the earth (κληρονομήσουσιν τὴν γῆν; 5:5; cf. Isa 61:7

---

167. Hagner, *Matthew 1–13*, 91.

168. Guelich, "Matthean Beatitudes," 417.

169. "The divine intervention which provides for the hungry (Isa 49,10; 65,13–14 [!], cf. Ps 107,5–6.9[!], 146,7), wipes off the tears of the crying (Isa 25,8), and offers consolation to the mourning (Isa 49,13; 51,3; 52,9; 57,18; 61,2; 65,18–19; 66,13; cf. Isa 30,19; Jer 31,13.16) is a widespread theme of the exilic and postexilic prophetic literature." Zamfir, "Who Are (the) Blessed?," 81.

[LXX]),[170] and the theme of righteousness (δικαιοσύνη; Matt 5:6; cf. Isa 61:3). Such verbal agreement can hardly be coincidental and suggests that Third Isaiah is at least a major aspect of the literary context for Jesus' proclamations in the Beatitudes. Matthew later alludes to Isa 61 in Matt 11:5, using the prophet's imagery as a description of Jesus' own ministry (this is then connected to a beatitude in Matt 11:6). In these passages, Jesus is both preaching and fulfilling the message of Third Isaiah; Jesus is a prophet like the Isaianic prophet. While Davies and Allison rightly interpret Matthew's allusion to Isa 61:1–3 as an expression of Jesus' messianic identity,[171] we can also discern a prophetic connection since the Third Isaiah text describes a prophetic figure announcing good news for the downtrodden. Moreover, given its lexical and thematic similarities to Isaiah 61, it is right to view the Beatitudes as a form of prophetic speech.

Narratively speaking, it is difficult to overstate the fact that in Matthew Jesus delivers the Beatitudes, and the whole of SM, on a mountain, an allusion to Moses. Jesus' prophetic ministry is, in part, shaped by the memory of Moses and the task of interpreting the law (as sections in the remainder of SM confirm). This suggests that the shape of Jesus' prophetic ministry in Matthew is oriented toward covenantal renewal within the Sinai tradition.[172]

Jesus' pronouncements in the Beatitudes also exhibit similarities with the seven beatitudes and reproaches of 2 En 52:1–14. This apocalyptic text makes for a problematic comparison since the date of its composition is unknown, though leading scholars argue it was written some time in the late first century CE.[173] Whether or not we can draw a meaningful comparison

170. David Flusser long ago pointed out that "the first three beatitudes as a whole depend on Isa. lxi, 1–2." Flusser, "Blessed Are the Poor in Spirit," 9.

171. Davies and Allison, *Matthew 1–7*, 466. Isaiah's use of מָשַׁח (*mashach*; "anointed") is ripe for messianic interpretation.

172. Stephen Cook makes the claim that this tradition, Israel's ancient covenantal beliefs revealed at Mount Sinai, are "an early, minority perspective from outside of Israel's and Judah's central state culture." Cook, *Social Roots of Biblical Yahwism*, 1. Such a tradition is reflected not only in Jesus, but also in other OT prophets. William Dever writes that "Eighth-century prophetic protest against social injustice was not a new reform movement, but was deeply rooted in the egalitarian traditions of early Israel and its ideal of agrarian reform." Dever, *Who Were the Early Israelites*, 199. Dever is talking about, in other words, the Sinai tradition.

173. The earliest manuscripts of 2 Enoch are quite late: "there is only a late translation (11th/12th century) or an originally Greek (Byzantine) text . . . the oldest of the Slavonic manuscripts did not appear before the 14th century." Bottrich, "'Book of the Secrets of Enoch' (2 En)," 38. See also Hagen, "No Longer 'Slavonic' Only," 7–34, for a discussion of the discovery of a Coptic version of 2 Enoch dating from the somewhere in the eighth–tenth centuries. Andrei Orlov, a leading 2 Enoch scholar, argues that the

between the social setting of Matthew and 2 Enoch is not really the point.[174] What is important is whether they share features of content, and what that might mean for Jesus' prophetic vocation in Matthew.

Second Enoch seems to demonstrate a compatibility between apocalyptic and makarisms, even if makarisms need not necessarily always be apocalyptic. Not all scholars, however, believe 2 Enoch should be deemed apocalyptic, at least in terms of its makarisms. Aune argues that the beatitudes found in 2 Enoch (52:1–14, as well as 42:6–14) attribute happiness to those who fulfill certain ethical injunctions and that none of these beatitudes reflect an apocalyptic worldview.[175] Aune goes on to say that Matt 5:3–12 (and Luke 6:20–23) has a clear eschatological significance unlike 2 Enoch; in doing so he seemingly equates the adjective "apocalyptic" with "eschatological."[176] Earlier we briefly explored the relationship between eschatology and apocalyptic, and I need not return to that substantial issue. For now, it will suffice to note that the perspective on apocalyptic that has emerged more recently emphasizes, according to Fletcher-Louis, two conceptual foci. The first is visions/revelations of secrets in order that humans might fulfill their created purpose of having divine identity by seeing the world as God sees it: "an epistemology grounded in the divine life."[177] Second, in apocalypses the Jewish temple cult defines the structure of the cosmos and access to its inner secrets; the temple is a microcosm of the cosmos that defines its nature.[178] Fletcher-Louis summarizes this by saying that such revelation, grounded in Torah- and temple-centered parameters, is sought for the social, economic, political, and ecological benefit of the world God has created.[179] Second Enoch exhibits such characteristics, particularly in its emphasis on Adam and on the true worship of God. Moreover, its

---

book should be dated prior to the destruction of the Second Temple owing to the sacerdotal elements of the narrative regarding Melchizedek. Orlov, "Sacerdotal Traditions of 2 Enoch," 103–14. Suter takes a more cautious approach, acknowledging the good work done by Orlov, but being hesitant to date anything but the Melchizedek section of 2 Enoch to pre-70 CE until the literary and philosophical unity of the book can be established. Suter, "Excavating 2 Enoch," 123.

174. Andersen argues that "2En comes closer in language and ideas to Mt than to any other part of the NT; but it does not resemble Rev, as might have been expected. It is more likely than Mt and 2En have a similar milieu than that a later Christian author of 2En was influenced by only one book of the NT." Andersen, "2 (Slavonic Apocalypse of) Enoch," 95n13.

175. Aune, "Beatitudes," 78.

176. Aune, "Beatitudes," 78.

177. Fletcher-Louis, "2 Enoch and the New Perspective," 127.

178. Fletcher-Louis, "2 Enoch and the New Perspective," 128.

179. Fletcher-Louis, "2 Enoch and the New Perspective," 128.

makarisms provide a revelation to its audience as to what God's perspective is in terms of ethics; in this sense, they could be deemed "apocalyptic." Moreover, 2 Enoch's makarisms are grounded in an eschatological framework: having listed what is honorable and shameful in 52:1–14, 2 En 52:15 says, "For all these things will be laid bare in the weighing-scales and in the books, on the day of the great judgment." Such is not so much a promise of eschatological reversal, but rather an exhortation to practice in the present what will be revealed in the future.

Why is any of this important? Because Matthew's makarisms display a number of characteristics that are similar to those in 2 Enoch. Indeed, Matthew's Beatitudes could be considered apocalyptic, at least according to the framework provided by Fletcher-Louis. Jesus' proclamation in Matt 5:3–10, like 2 En 52:1–14, does indeed reveal a kind of divine identity, an "epistemology grounded in divine life," by way of announcing what God deems to be worthy of honor. Such a divine identity is depicted in Matthew through the description of a people who, either through experiencing oppression or acting faithfully according to Torah, find themselves at home in the kingdom of God. The corollary of this is that those whose mind has been transformed to see what God sees (repentance) have accessed the revelation of God in Jesus. The difference, of course, is that for Matthew the vision of life reflected in the Beatitudes is not bound by temple-parameters, no doubt because by the time Matthew was written the temple had been destroyed. Indeed, Matthew is critical of the temple in later chapters, and this may reflect a marked difference between Matthew and apocalyptic texts. In saying this, the cosmic vision for which the temple acts as a microcosm is probably, for Matthew, symbolized not by the temple but rather by the Church (cf. Matt 16:17–19), or Jesus himself (e.g., the Last Supper, his death and resurrection). Moreover, like 2 Enoch's makarisms, those found in Matthew 5 are eschatological inasmuch as they are a call to repent and act in such a way as to practice in the present what will be revealed in the future[180]—God's New Genesis (Matt 1:1).

In this sense, Jesus is indeed an apocalyptic prophet. This phrase, however, tends to mean in scholarship something different from what I intend and thus is quite unhelpful. What I mean to say is that Jesus, as prophet, reveals the will of God in terms of what it means to be truly human. Such humanity is shaped by the prophetic call to repent, that is, to embrace an epistemology grounded in divine life, a form of knowing that

---

180. So Yoder: "This is what we mean by eschatology: a hope which, defying present frustration, defines a present position in terms of the yet unseen goal which gives it meaning." Yoder, "If Christ Is Truly Lord," in *The Original Revolution*, 52–84 (56).

is eschatological. As such, this kind of thinking subverts the dominant modes of thinking in the world.

Another question regarding the shape of Jesus' prophetic vocation reflected in the Beatitudes is whether or not he can be compared to other popular prophets in the first century CE. Obviously Jesus' prophetic activity in the Beatitudes is oracular in nature. The problem for us is that there is no record of an oracular prophet proclaiming makarisms in the first century. There are, however, reports in Josephus of prophetic claimants who announced divine liberation on the basis of portents (e.g., *J. W.* 6.286–96). It is difficult to draw a comparison with Jesus, however, since the kind of revolutionary liberation these prophets sought directly conflicted with Jesus' own assertion that God sees peacemakers as honorable. The only comparison that can really be drawn is that Jesus, like these prophets who announced oracles on the basis of portents, began his prophetic ministry on the basis of a sign given to him by God, namely, his prophetic commissioning in Matthew 3. This, for Jesus, was a sign of the coming kingdom, and it was only the imminence of the kingdom that could make possible a community capable of sustaining a life described by the Beatitudes.

The figure of the period most obviously comparable with Matthew's Jesus is Jesus son of Ananias (Josephus, *J. W.* 6.288–315). Though the latter spoke only in woe oracles (a subject to be picked up later in our discussion of Matt 23), the prophetic proclamation of shame is nonetheless the opposite side of the coin to the prophetic makarism. I will refrain from making too many comments here since a comparison with the son of Ananias is best left until the discussion of Jesus' own woe oracles. For now, it suffices to say that the use of honor/shame categories in prophetic speech was not unheard of in the first century CE, indeed it appears in one of our clearest accounts of a Jewish prophet of the time.

In short, the shape of Jesus' prophetic vocation, at least as reflected in the Beatitudes, represents an intersection of a number of variegated traditions. Jesus' makarisms resemble elements of OT prophetic proclamations, apocalyptic literature, the oracles of popular prophets of the first century CE and, to a much lesser extent, wisdom traditions. This makes the shape of Jesus' prophetic vocation difficult to bind to one prophetic category, though this may become clearer with the examination of other texts. It may also be the case that the author of the First Gospel sought to portray Jesus in such a way as to highlight his transcendence of stock prophetic categories. In this way, Jesus would represent the crescendo of Israel's prophetic history.

The Function of Jesus' Prophetic Vocation
in the Beatitudes

There are two perspectives from which to view the function of Jesus' prophetic vocation in Matthew. The first perspective is internal to the narrative, the second external to it. These perspectives are, in a sense, symbolized by the two hearers of the Beatitudes/SM—the crowds and the disciples.

In the Beatitudes Jesus, like Isaiah, proclaims good news for the poor. But whereas Isaiah describes a future scenario in which God will act decisively for his people, Jesus proclaims this as a present reality in light of the coming kingdom. By way of a transformation of the mind—repentance—the values found in the Beatitudes come to shape a community about whom these descriptions are a present reality. In this way, Jesus' prophetic speech is intended both to critique the dominant conception of reality, with its notions of who is honorable, and to inspire a renewed imagination that is able to comprehend life in the present, in which Isaiah's vision of mourners being comforted becomes reality *now*.

Within the story the intended recipient of this message is, in one sense, Israel, represented by the crowds. We will come to see later in Matthew that, for Israel, such a prophetic call to repentance has an added element: if Israel will not repent and embody its call as the light to the nations then such a choice will lead to destruction. By not heeding the word of the prophet and obeying God's will at the historical point of κρίσις, Israel experiences, as it has in its past, the expected consequence of its obstinacy. For Matthew, Jesus as prophet, like the prophets of old, had come to warn Israel of such impending disaster, and by the time of the writing of the Gospel this, of course, has already occurred in the form of the Roman defeat of the Jews in Palestine and the devastation of Jerusalem. The prophet is, in a sense, the "interpreter of the events of [their] time in the light of the divine word."[181] The content of God's will is described in the Beatitudes in the form of a call to transformed values and community life.

At a very basic level, the function of the prophet is truth-telling. Such truth is derived from some form of revelation from God that discloses God's will. This kind of revelation is, for Matthew, consistent with the faithful interpretation of Torah and the future that God is bringing forth in the world. Such truth-telling is well reflected in the Beatitudes, a prophetic upending of dominant assumptions that contradict God's will. What requires Jesus' confrontation of these dominant values is that a people formed by such values will not be capable of embodying the way of life God desires. Such life is set

---

181. Zamfir, "Who Are (the) Blessed?," 82.

out not only in the prophets of old but also in the remainder of SM. Prophetic truth-telling functions to critique harmful moral, ritual, economic, and political systems and ill forms of existence, but also to point to an alternative way of life that conforms itself to the pattern that God has set forth from the beginning, a pattern God will bring to fullness in the end.

To this we must add that such truth-telling is not an expression of the prophet's moral, ritual, economic, or political rationalizations or preferences. Indeed, the prophecy is the result of divine revelation. It is true that Matthew's account gives us no account of Jesus' words here reflecting an experience of direct divine revelation. However, in narrative-critical perspective what we do see in Matthew's story is that Jesus delivers SM on a mountain, an obvious allusion to Moses and the receiving of the law. If Matthew is comparing Jesus to Moses, we could infer that, like the law given to Israel, Jesus' speech to his disciples is derived from divine revelation.

External to the narrative, we see that the intended recipients of the Beatitudes are Matthew's communities, or, more broadly, the church, represented in the story by the disciples. For Matthew, as reflected in the Beatitudes, the starting point of a community that embodies God's coming kingdom in the present is a transformation of the mind. Thus, repentance is a crucial theme in the First Gospel. Hanson says:

> Matt 5:3–10 provides the introduction to Jesus' public ministry and Matt 23:13–31 its conclusion. Consequently they form an honor/shame inclusio around Jesus' public teaching. Furthermore, the evangelist has not only employed them as formal and semantic antitheses, but has paralleled keywords throughout their formulations.[182]

Given that Matt 5:3–10 and 23:13–31 both call for repentance, it should be said that, by way of this inclusio, Matthew intended to emphasize the centrality of repentance in redeemed communities. The challenge to dominant values found in the Beatitudes (and also in the "woes" of Matt 23) is the basis of an alternative vision and practice of life. The proclamation of such alternate values demands repentance from its hearers. Such a call to repentance was central to the message of the OT prophets. All through the prophets, repentance was conceived as a return to YHWH that resulted in restoration (e.g., Isa 44:22; 45:22; Jer 3:10–22; 18:8; Ezek 14:6; 18:30; Hos 3:5; 6:1; 14:1; Joel 2:12; Zech 1:3–6).[183] The prophetic message is thus fundamentally the call to return to the foundational values of Israel, not least in care for the vulnerable and marginalized. Such a return is predicated on a turning of one's whole

---

182. Hanson, "How Honorable! How Shameful!," 104.

183. Wright, *Jesus and the Victory of God*, 248.

being toward YHWH since it is only by way of such transformation that a restored community can exist. For Matthew, the Beatitudes represent such a call in that they seek, amid a world of contrary values, to conform the mind of their hearers to the mind of God. It is a call to a renewed imagination that can perceive the presence of God's reign.

Matthew uses the theme of Jesus as prophet to address issues facing his communities. The first is the pressure faced because of Jewish opponents. It is not clear whether Matthew directly blames these opponents for the disaster of Jerusalem's destruction. However, as we saw in chapter 1, Matthew does seem to view these opponents as social and theological descendants of those past figures he does deem responsible. For Matthew, the destruction of Jerusalem was a sign that his opponents' interpretation of Torah was unfaithful. It is important to use a descriptor like "unfaithful" since Torah interpretation in the first century cannot be said to have been a matter of "right" and "wrong," not in abstract terms at least. As we discussed earlier, Torah interpretation was an expression of community life, not merely "theology." Different teachers made different legal rulings, or *halakhah*, but they were always expressions of how God's people ought to live (*halakhah* literally meaning "behavior" or "walking"). If Matthew describes the Torah interpretation of his opponents as being based on something other than justice, mercy, and faithfulness (Matt 23:23) then this is an expression of the belief that such interpretation was unfaithful to the Law and the Prophets, which were expressions of God's will for the life of God's people.

That Matthew's opponents were, in his view, unfaithful to Torah and thus to God is strongly implied in the Beatitudes. Here Jesus' subversion of popular values is an implicit call for repentance, for a turn toward faithfulness to God's will. Any competing interpretation of Torah and the prophets is, for Matthew, an expression of unfaithfulness. This is further reflected in Matt 5:12 whereby Matthew claims that "they" who persecuted the prophets also persecute those who follow Jesus. To mention that this is a reference to Matthew's opponents hardly seems necessary. The meaning of the comparison between those hostile community leaders of the first century with those who persecuted the prophets of old[184] is implied.

In light of this, we can say that a central aspect of Jesus' prophetic vocation in Matthew is faithful interpretation of Torah. Such interpretation is not simply a matter of "religious" ritual, but about the shape of the covenantal community. The Beatitudes reflect this vocational characteristic in that they outline the contours of truthful interpretation of God's law and call the

---

184. I think it is the case that Matt 5:12 refers to prophets of the past and not to Christian prophets.

audience to repent, to turn and become faithful in the present to the eschato-logical reality—the New Genesis—God is bringing about in Jesus.

If Matthew critiques his Jewish opponents in the Beatitudes, so too does he critique Roman imperial power. As Carter has said, "The first four Beatitudes critique the political, economic, social, religious and personal distress that results from the powerful elite who enrich their own position at the expense of the rest. They delineate the terrible consequences of Roman power."[185] The remaining four Beatitudes, which esteem just actions, also form a critique of Roman power since they constitute descriptions of those who are at home in an alternative kingdom. The expression of God's will and the nature of God's alternative reign—divine mercy and justice—form a prophetic critique of any system of rule or pattern of social and personal life that does not conform to God's life-giving will as reflected in God's past con-cern for the poor and future restoration. In the Beatitudes, Jesus as prophet is describing the experience of God's reign in the present, an experience that will come to its fullness at a later time. Such a description is also a proclama-tion of God's deliverance of his people from their sins, since a community shaped by the Beatitudes has been liberated from those values that prop up the oppressive infrastructure of the dominant way of life.

The Matthean Community as "Prophetic"

Matthew's depiction of Jesus also functions in the identity formation of his communities in that the churches are to emulate the attitude and example of Jesus, a prophet greater than their enemies. Most pertinently for this study, Matthew directly compares the community to whom he speaks with the prophets ("Blessed are you when people revile you and persecute you . . . for in the same way they persecuted the prophets who were before you"; 5:12). It is not clear whether Jesus intended to raise up prophets to follow after him. It is clear, though, that Matthew believes the persecution suffered by the prophets of old is like that suffered by his communities. The prophets are not explicitly identified. They are either the literary prophets or, more broadly, any past spokespersons for God whom we cannot exhaustively identify. The reason for persecution is given in Matt 5:10—it is because of "righteousness," that is, because of the proclamation and enacting of cov-enant justice, the setting right of a world disturbed by sin. By naming the incongruity between God's design and human suffering, prophets inevitably experience such suffering. Such an irony is necessary since in proclaiming God's will that violence and oppression should cease the prophet must

185. Carter, *Matthew and the Margins*, 131.

absorb violence rather than retaliate against it, or else perpetuate a cycle of injustice contrary to the implications of the very message being announced. Being a prophet is not merely a matter of being a messenger of God's will; it is also about manifesting God's will, even in suffering. Though the prophets and the Matthean community suffer because of their righteousness, like Jesus, they are also rewarded (5:12).

The parallel between the prophets and the Matthean community should not be construed merely in terms of prophetic suffering. A vocational comparison is also implied. The community, which is integrated into the tradition of the prophets, find one of their primary tasks is to proclaim God's covenant justice, even in the face of opposition. Just as Jesus has taken on the vocational role of the prophets in proclaiming the gospel for the poor, mourning, and meek, so too must the community of those that follow him take on this role, even if it will lead them to persecution on his account. This is why Matthew warns his community to be on the lookout for ψευδοπροφήτης (7:15): their presence in the community means the sabotage of the true prophetic message expressed in the Beatitudes and SM, and this leads to "bad fruit," or injustice.

This reading is, I believe, supported by the placement of the succeeding pericopes. Jesus, as prophet, calls the community to embody Israel's vocation as light to the nations in Matt 5:14–16 (cf. Isa 10:17; 42:6–7; 49:6; 60:1–3). He then declares his intention not to abolish but to fulfill the Law and Prophets (Matt 5:17–20). There is an intimate connection between the Law and Prophets, with the latter functioning as proclaimers or "enforcers" of the former.[186] Jesus implies his prophetic role—and, by extension, that of the Matthean community—is to be understood as covenant enforcement with a view to his hearers fulfilling Israel's call. Indeed, to fulfill all righteousness is, according to Matthew, to place oneself faithfully within the story of Israel, which is framed by God's covenant with Israel and the way of life set forth within it. This raises the question, "what position regarding the Law does Matthew ascribe to Jesus?" I concur with Snodgrass who says,

> To Matthew's way of thinking, Jesus *neither* set aside any of the
> law *nor* interpreted it the way many of his contemporaries did
> . . . the proper understanding of the law is attained through a

---

186. Luz notes the connection between the Law and Prophets here saying, "One can either think of the prophetic/predictive significance of the law and prophets—indeed, in Judaism Moses is also a great prophet (cf. Deut 18:15), or one can think of their function of giving directions or instructions—for Matthew in particular the prophets were also important witnesses for the love commandment (cf. Hos 6:6 = Matt 9:13; 12:7)." Luz, *Matthew 1–7*, 213–14.

"prophetic" reading of it that sees love and mercy as its real focus.[187]

It is no wonder, then, that Jesus is depicted as Moses at the outset of the Beatitudes. Jesus, as the new Moses who ascends the mount to deliver this proclamation, is the prophet *par excellence* who calls for covenantal fidelity.

4.5 Conclusion

In this chapter, we have explored a range of implications deriving from Matthew's Beatitudes regarding Jesus' prophetic vocation. As I have stated, these are not to be taken as primarily historical claims, but rather claims regarding the perspective we can construct from Matthew's narrative.

Matthew certainly believed that Jesus was a prophet. Indeed, the beginning of his narrative goes to some lengths to portray Jesus in prophetic terms, especially as a new Moses leading a new exodus. This characterization continues through the introduction of John the Baptist and the beginning of Jesus' public ministry. We have seen that Jesus' programmatic statement regarding his own ministry, "Repent, for the kingdom of heaven has come near" (4:17), is itself prophetic in nature, and thus his ministry is initiated in prophetic terms.

This theme continues in the Beatitudes. The nature of Jesus' prophetic vocation as reflected in this passage is multi-faceted, with Matthew portraying Jesus in such a way that he embodies elements of a number of prophetic traditions, including the OT prophets, apocalyptic, and first-century popular prophecy. His proclamation in the Beatitudes is particularly reminiscent of Isa 61, and the announcement of good news to the poor. Jesus as prophet announces a new set of values, framed in the honor/shame language of the Mediterranean world, that critique the dominant values of the world and offer a new way of life together according to God's will. Such a way of life is discerned and shaped by Jesus' authoritative reading of Torah.

The values espoused in the Beatitudes subvert normal expectations, and call hearers to repentance, a transformation of the mind leading to conformity with God's will. Such a change of mind should lead to a reframing of what is deemed honorable in the world, with the poor, marginalized, and powerless becoming the objects of social esteem. Such values form the basis of a community that embodies the social ethic described in the Sermon on the Mount. The announcement of these values is inherently prophetic because it calls people back to the foundational values of

187. Snodgrass, "Matthew's Understanding of the Law," 369 (emphasis original).

God's covenant with Israel (justice, mercy, faithfulness, etc.), and is also eschatological in that it calls people to enact in the present the reality that God will bring about in the future.

In other words, the prophetic truth-telling exhibited in the Beatitudes functions to critique harmful moral, ritual, economic, and political systems and ill forms of existence, but also to point to an alternative way of life that conforms itself to the pattern that God has set forth from the beginning, a pattern God will bring to fullness in the end. For Matthew, such truth-telling confronts both his Jewish opponents, with their competing interpretation of Torah and its consequential effects on community life, and also Roman power, with its values and structures contrary to the will of God.

For such prophetic truth-telling, Jesus, and also those who follow after him as prophets, will face persecution. Far from being an unfortunate situation, however, this is an unavoidable aspect of the prophetic vocation, to absorb violence in order to bring the cycle of violence to an end. Prophets, after all, do not merely proclaim God's will, they also must embody it in action. For Matthew, the prophet *par excellence* is Jesus, the new Moses calling his people to covenant fidelity and demonstrating it throughout the Gospel.

Chapter 5

Eating with Sinners as Prophetic Act

OUR NEXT SELECT PASSAGE is found in Matt 9:9–13—the story of Jesus calling Matthew and dining with tax collectors and sinners in "the house." This passage is not as distinguished as the Beatitudes and its history of interpretation is basically uncontested.[1] The only major point of interpretive discussion regarding this passage has been the identity of Matthew and his relationship to Levi (cf. Mark 2:13–17; Luke 5:27–32). Why, then, is this pericope meaningful in the study of Jesus' prophetic vocation? As we will see, the act of eating often embodies a powerful form of prophetic drama, not only in connecting to prophetic traditions from Israel's past, but also in connecting to eschatological themes. Moreover, this act, in the context of Matthew's social and narrative world, makes a potent prophetic statement about the present since the prophet's action reveals an aspect of God's will.[2] Before we enter into further discussion of such issues related to the text, however, it will be helpful to identify the place of the pericope in Matthew's wider narrative.

5.1 The Literary Context of Matt 9:9–13

Matthew 9 follows soon after the Sermon on the Mount (Matthew 5–7), in which Jesus proclaims the central convictions and ethical standards that describe communities that have repented in light of the coming kingdom of heaven. Matthew 9 appears in an identifiable subsection—Matt 8–9— that narrates episodes in which Jesus demonstrates in deed the substance

---

1. As an indication, Luz's commentary does not include an otherwise characteristic "History of Interpretation" section for this passage. Luz, *Matthew 8–20*, 31–35.

2. McKnight labels as "prophetic actions" those actions that are "personal embodiments of what the prophet perceived to be his calling to reveal to Israel and Judah." McKnight, "Jesus and Prophetic Actions," 205.

of the message he has preached in Matt 5–7 and the healing power spoken of in 4:23–25 (cf. 9:35).[3]

In Matt 8:1, Jesus descends from the mountain and great crowds follow him. In 8:2–4 Jesus heals an unclean man,[4] the first of ten healings[5] in Matt 8–9 (8:2–4; 5–13; 14–15; 16–17; 28–34; 9:1–8, 18–19, 23–26; 20–22; 27–31; 32–34). Both the descent from the mountain and the total of ten healings may point to Jesus as a new Moses,[6] though this is debatable.[7] The miracle stories themselves demonstrate Jesus' authority over sickness and other physical ailments, nature, and demons. The stories are straightforward, with very little secondary detail.[8] It is not obvious why this might be the case, though Garland's suggestion, following Hull, that Matthew "does not want the reader to be distracted by the technique [of the miracles] and miss the significance of the person of Jesus," is a possibility.[9] Equally compelling is Luz's suggestion that Matt 8–9 offers a narrative thread, containing the healing stories, in quick succession, without a break in time or place,

---

3. It is questionable whether Matt 8:1 is part of this section. It is probably a transitional sentence. For the sake of ease of reference, I will include 8:1.

4. English translations tend to render λεπρός as "leprosy," though this is misleading since leprosy in contemporary parlance refers to Hansen's disease. In ancient usage, however, λεπρός referred to a variety of skin diseases, as well as diseases in houses (see Lev 13–14). The disease itself may not have been as serious a concern as the social isolation it caused by way of making the subject impure. Garland notes that Lev 13 is concerned not with the spread of the disease so much as the spread of the impurity. Garland, *Reading Matthew*, 93. Such impurity caused someone to lack wholeness and to be not in their correct place since they were profane and might defile others. Hence, they would be unable to take their place in the covenant community under God. See Malina, *New Testament World*, 161–97.

5. On the number ten in Israelite thought, see Lang, "Number Ten," 218–38 (esp. 224).

6. Garland might be correct that the ten miracles demonstrate that Jesus' "words and deeds are clothed with the authority of God," though there is nothing in the text itself that would lead us to draw this conclusion, except in a general sense. Garland, *Reading Matthew*, 91.

7. See Keener, *Gospel of Matthew*, 258. Those in agreement include Teeple, *Mosaic Eschatological Prophet*, 82; Sanders, *Historical Figure of Jesus*, 146. Arguments include that Matthew was not counting the miracles (Gundry, *Matthew*, 138); that there were only nine miracles (Meier, *Matthew*, 79); and that "the interpolation of non-miraculous materials breaks the alleged string of ten" (Kingsbury, "Observations on the 'Miracle Chapters,'" 561).

8. This is apparent even without comparing Matthew's redaction to Mark's versions of the pericopes.

9. Garland, *Reading Matthew*, 91.

that culminates in the responses of the people, including the scribes and Pharisees (9:33–34).[10]

The healings of Jesus are of course not unprecedented since healings are reported in the OT. Perhaps the most well-known story of a miraculous healing in the OT is that of Elisha's healing of Naaman in 2 Kgs 5. The story makes clear that the healing is attributable to God, not the prophet; when asked by the Syrian king to heal Naaman, the king of Israel replies, "Am I God, to kill and to make alive . . . ?" (2 Kgs 5:7), and when healed Naaman says, "Behold, I know that there is no God in all the earth but in Israel" (5:15).[11] Though the act is attributed to God, Elisha's self-understanding is such that the prophet is a critical part of the healing—"Let him come now to me, that he may know that there is a prophet in Israel" (5:8). Though Naaman's anticipation of a more dramatic performance is mistaken (5:10–12),[12] such expectation also reflects a belief in the crucial role of the prophet. Another episode of healing occurs in Isa 38, with King Hezekiah being told by the prophet that he is going to die and to put his affairs in order (Isa 38:1). Hezekiah prays to God to grant his recovery (38:2–3), which God announces through the prophet (38:4–5). Again, God is credited with the healing but the prophet is an indispensable part of the process, a channel through whom God declares the divine will. Such is not dissimilar to the healings in Num 12 and 21. In the first case, Miriam is caused to become infected with a skin disease and Aaron turns to Moses for help. Moses cries out for God to heal Miriam and God has her sent out of the camp for seven days and she is healed. In Num 21:4–9 the Israelites complain and YHWH sends serpents among the people which proceed to bite them. They turn to Moses for help, asking him to pray to YHWH. His prayer results in God commanding the fashioning of the bronze serpent. In both these stories involving Moses the healing is seen to be the act of God, but the prophet is seen as the mediator of the healing in speaking on behalf of the people.

It is not clear that identical attitudes to healing existed in the time of Jesus, but there are indications that they were at least similar. That people come to Jesus for healing suggests they saw the need for a recognized mediator. Still, the people praise God when they are healed (Matt 9:8) because God had given such authority to people (in and through Jesus), a sign that the healing was not simply attributed to Jesus himself. Jesus' prophetic vocation is—like Elisha, Isaiah, and especially Moses before him—expressed in

---

10. Luz, *Theology of the Gospel of Matthew*, 63–64.

11. Westermann, "Salvation and Healing," 12.

12. Westermann, "Salvation and Healing," 12.

the act of healing. This act constitutes a mediation of the power and authority of God. For Matthew, such acts are a fulfillment of Isa 53:4—"He took our illnesses and bore our diseases" (Matt 8:17). Whatever the meaning of this much-debated OT verse, it is clear that Jesus' healings are, for Matthew, connected to his fulfilling the words of the prophets.

In addition to the healings is Jesus' calming of a storm (8:23–27). The story is probably christological in function,[13] serving to identify Jesus as God's Messiah and, possibly in some sense, equal to God.[14] The sea was seen as a chaotic force that God orders, or with which God battles (e.g., Gen 1:6–10; 6–10; Job 38:8–11; Pss 74:13–14; 77:16; 89:8–11; 104:7; 107:23–30; Jonah 1:4–16). Jesus seems to take on this role in this pericope. But another dimension is that of the story's allusion to the biblical account of the parting of the Red Sea (Exod 14; 15:10). This imagery is echoed in Isa 43:1–2 where it refers to YHWH's coming salvation of Israel from exile. This prophetic dimension is present alongside the messianic theme Matthew seeks to display in this periscope.

Following the crowd's comparison of Jesus with "their scribes" in Matt 7:29, chapters 8–9 begin the extended theme of the escalating conflict between Jesus and the community leaders (9:3, 11, 34). This, in part, sets up the sending out of the Twelve in Matthew 10 since the opposition of the leaders necessitates the mission to Israel. The conflict also provides a narrative opportunity to feature Jesus' teachings about persecution, fear, conflict, and rewards (10:16–42), a relevant message for Matthew's embattled audience. More pertinent to our study is Jesus' statement, following the healing of the centurion's servant, that "many will come from east and west and will eat with Abraham and Isaac and Jacob in the kingdom of heaven, while the heirs of the kingdom will be thrown into the outer darkness" (8:11–12a). This reference to the eschatological banquet, and who will be present at it, is striking in that it subverts Israel's notions of divine election and continues the Matthean Jesus' redefinition of the nature of the kingdom of heaven (cf. 5:3–12).

It is in the midst of all of this material that Jesus' calling of Matthew and eating with sinners takes place in Matthew's Gospel. That Jesus fulfills the words of the prophets and acts according to the prophetic tradition in

---

13. Though this is not to say that it does not serve discipleship and soteriological-ecclesiological functions as well. See Bornkamm, "Stilling of the Storm in Matthew," in *Tradition and Interpretation in Matthew*, ed. Bornkamm, Barth, and Held, 52–57; Luz, *Matthew 8–20*, 21.

14. The disciples' cry, "Save us, Lord," suggests this is a possibility. Keener notes that σῴζω was "sometimes addressed to deities at sea—cf. [Matt] 14:30; Acts 27:20, 31; Diod. Sic. 4.43.1; Ach. Tat. 3.5." Keener, *Gospel of Matthew*, 280.

the surrounding episodes suggests that Matt 9:9–13 is likely also to include a prophetic dimension. If healings were indeed viewed as prophetic actions, then Jesus' prophetic role is reflected in Matt 9:9–13 since disease and sin were thought to be linked, as reflected in Jesus' statement that, "Those who are well have no need of a physician, but those who are sick" (9:12; cf. 4:24; 8:16).[15] Sin was seen as a form of disease,[16] as well as a cause of it, and Jesus dines with sinners, a sign of their healing. This brings 9:9–13 into thematic unity with its surrounding pericopes.

On a further literary note, the structure of Matt 9:9–13 suggests its form is that of a *chreia*, a literary or rhetorical form identifiable by its formula: a provocation addressed to a sage/hero followed by their (clever) response.[17] The second half of Matt 9:9–13 seems to follow this form with a provocation (9:11) and a response (9:12–13), which follow on from an event involving the sage/hero which sets the scene for the challenge (9:9–10). The purpose of the *chreia* was to characterize a famous person or hero, and they were used extensively to characterize philosophers.[18] That the pericope takes the form of a *chreia* gives us a partial clue as to its purpose and reveals it to be congruent with Matthew's implied aim, discussed earlier—to characterize Jesus as the authoritative teacher of Torah and God's will and as superior to the Pharisees.

5.2 The Significance of Eating Together

In her essay entitled "Deciphering a Meal," Mary Douglas makes the point that

> A code affords a general set of possibilities for sending particular messages. If food is treated as a code, the messages it encodes will be found in the pattern of social relations being expressed. The message is about different degrees of hierarchy, inclusion and exclusion, boundaries and transactions across the boundaries. Like sex, the taking of food has a social component, as well as a biological one.[19]

---

15. The saying seems to reflect common belief in the ancient world, with versions also found in Plutarch, *Mor.* 230F; Diogenes Laertius, *Lives* 2.70.

16. Pilch, "Health Care System in Matthew," 103.

17. Neyrey, *Honor and Shame*, 118.

18. Smith, *From Symposium to Eucharist*, 228.

19. Douglas, "Deciphering a Meal," 61.

Rouwhorst follows Douglas, arguing on the subject of table community in early Christianity that,

> Meals and meal customs are important indicators of the identity of groups and communities. From social and cultural anthropologists we may learn that every meal—especially when taken together by more than one person—encodes significant messages about social and hierarchical patterns prevailing in the group. The message is especially about social boundaries. While eating together people are wittingly or unwittingly drawing a boundary between those who are participating in the meal and those who are not, whether the latter have been excluded deliberately or because simply they have not been invited or do not belong to the group of people used to eating together. Moreover, the behavior of those participating may entail messages about the social and hierarchical relations existing between those partaking of the meal themselves.[20]

Both authors highlight a critical aspect of the practice of eating together for this portion of our study, namely the social codification inherent in table fellowship.

Such anthropological insights should not be deemed anachronistic when applied to the world(s) of Matthew's Gospel. Indeed, many ancient texts lay bare the social aspects of meals. In the pseudepigraphic work Joseph and Aseneth,[21] food is a powerful symbol that defines social boundaries. Aseneth, an Egyptian, is said to be as beautiful as "the daughters of the Hebrews," but because she eats unclean food, she herself is unclean.[22] The difference between Jews and gentiles is represented in the story by their acts of eating.[23] Indeed, Aseneth is converted in the context of a meal with a heavenly *anthropos*, who shares with her a honeycomb.[24] In sharing food with the *anthropos*, Aseneth is transformed, sharing in his angelic qualities:

> And her father and mother and his whole family came from the field which was their inheritance. And they saw Aseneth like the appearance of light, and her beauty was like heavenly beauty.

20. Rouwhorst, "Table Community in Early Christianity," 69.

21. The dating of Joseph and Aseneth is debated, with suggestions as late as the fifth century CE. As Humphrey notes, however, "scholars now generally place the piece in an era much earlier than the fifth century, many looking toward the late first century CE as the most likely time of composition." Humphrey, *Joseph and Aseneth*, 30.

22. See *Jos. Asen.* 8.5–7.

23. Lieber, "I Set a Table," 64–65.

24. Lieber, "I Set a Table," 67–68.

> And they saw her sitting with Joseph and dressed in a wedding garment. And they were amazed at her beauty and rejoiced and gave glory to God who gives life to the dead. And after this they ate and drank and celebrated.[25] (*Jos. Asen.* 20.6–8)[26]

It is noteworthy that the family celebrates with a meal, "perhaps re-establishing their own boundaries of kinship."[27] The meals in Joseph and Aseneth clearly signify social boundaries, either through being transformational spaces that lead to a crossing of boundaries, or as expressions of inclusion (which are always, simultaneously, acts of exclusion).

Meals also signify the inner dynamics of a group, including hierarchical structure. The Community Rule of the *Yahad* is a good example of this:

> [The *Yahad*] shall eat together, together they shall bless and together they shall take counsel. In every place where there are ten men of the Community council, there should not be missing a priest amongst them. And every one shall sit according to his rank, before him, and in this way they shall be asked for their counsel in every matter. And when they prepare the table to dine of the new wine for drinking, the priest shall stretch out his hand as the first to bless the first fruits of the bread and the new wine.[28] (1QS 6:2–5)

There has been some debate regarding the relevance of this passage for the meaning of the meal practices of the *Yahad* in relation to the wider Graeco-Roman world, namely, whether the meals are "anti-Hellenistic,"[29] but such discussion is unlikely to yield many conclusions at this point. In any case, this discussion is less important to us than the social dynamics *within* the *Yahad* community that are signaled by the meal. The meals of the *Yahad*, according to 1QS 6, appear to have reflected group identity (they "shall eat, pray, and deliberate communally," thus marking off the limits of their community) and group hierarchies (they sit according to rank, with the priest occupying the principal place). The meal thus reflects the broader shape of the community. To eat with the community was to be among the community and, though the text is not explicit, it appears that

---

25. Translation by Burchard, "Joseph and Aseneth," 234.

26. There are different numbering systems for Joseph and Aseneth; I have opted for Reissler's system, as used by Burchard, "Joseph and Aseneth," 177–247.

27. Lieber, "I Set a Table," 77.

28. Translation from Martínez and Tigchelaar, *Dead Sea Scrolls Study Edition*, 1:521. A similar account is found in Josephus, *J.W.* 2.131.

29. For an analysis of a variety of claims see Eckhardt, "Meals and Politics," 180–209.

outsiders are not welcome. Moreover, the meal also encoded the values of the community, including order, purity, and authority.

The *Yahad* meal did not only signify the inner dynamics of the community as it was. Eckhardt draws a comparison between the community meal in 1QS6 and the "eschatological banquet" in 1QSa 2:17–22. These meals are strikingly similar and reveal that the hierarchical order in the community meal also applies to the eschatological era.[30] In other words, the *Yahad* believed that the order they enacted in their meals was eschatologically patterned. Their meals were a reflection of the coming age. So too were the community dynamics and social values with which the meal was encoded. It would be logically problematic to simply presume that such eschatological assumptions are mirrored by Jesus in the meals he attends/initiates, but this is a point to which we will return; this Qumran text simply represents a precedent for such ideas.

That meals often reflected social hierarchy is demonstrated in Paul's first letter to the Corinthians. In 1 Cor 11:17–34, Paul corrects the Corinthian church for the way it practices the Lord's Supper. It is debatable whether the practice of the Corinthians reflects economic or social patterns,[31] but in any case, there is some hierarchical structure and a form of boundary-setting that Paul challenges. In seeking to reform the eating practices of the Corinthians, Paul is seeking to "create a new Christian social identity."[32] Moreover, the banquet was "an important vehicle for distributing honor. . . . An association's private banquet was the chief venue for announcing, awarding, and parading honorific deeds."[33] Such honoring often took the form of being given the privilege of reclining on a couch of honor, being crowned with a wreath, public announcement of the person's benefaction, and other similar acts.[34] According to Rachel McRae, it is this use of the honor and shame code that Paul deplores and overturns in light of Jesus' teachings about equality, humility, and mutuality.[35] It is not that Paul is trying to strip the meal of social significance altogether, but rather that he is seeking to alter its social significance in the minds of the Corinthians in light of the gospel—not *de-encoding* but *re-encoding*.

It is also worth mentioning the meals that occur in Matthew's Gospel outside of chapter 9. One of the most relevant episodes is perhaps that of

---

30. Eckhardt, "Meals and Politics," 202.

31. McRae, "Eating with Honor," 166.

32. McRae, "Eating with Honor," 166.

33. McRae, "Eating with Honor," 169, 170–71.

34. McRae, "Eating with Honor," 171.

35. McRae, "Eating with Honor," 181.

Jesus' feeding of over four thousand people (15:32–39). This story of course comes soon after Jesus' feeding of over five thousand (14:13–21) in which those fed are, ostensibly, all Jews—twelve baskets remain after the meal, an allusion to the tribes of Israel. Between the two stories is the pericope about the Canaanite woman (15:21–28) in which the scope of Jesus' mission is expanded to include gentiles.[36] From here, Jesus heals the crowds who, in response to his healings, glorify "the God of Israel" (15:31). The phrase "the God of Israel" is used only here in Matthew and probably suggests the crowd is not comprised of Jews. This is the same crowd defined as the four thousand in 15:32–39.[37] Following the feeding, there are seven baskets remaining, another numeric reference like, but perhaps subtler than, the twelve baskets before it. The seven baskets, as pointed out by Grant LeMarquand, are a reference to gentiles.[38] What is important for us is that the second meal story expands upon the first with regard to whom is included. The feedings redefine the scope of those who are welcome in the kingdom, having been recipients of the generosity of God, like the Hebrews in the wilderness. That is to say, the meals define the limits of inclusion, or in this case, expunge them. God's generous provision is undoubtedly a theme as well, especially when these stories are viewed against the backdrop of the story of the manna in the wilderness in Exod 16.

36. For an explanation of the reasoning behind such a statement, see LeMarquand, "Canaanite Conquest," 237–47.

37. Commentators are split on whether this crowd is in fact gentile. Cousland notes that Boring, Davies and Allison, Garland, Gnilka, Hagner, Hare, Luz, and Sand claim the crowd is Jewish, whereas Blomberg, Bruner, Carson, Davies, France, Morris, and Mounce argue they are gentile. Cousland himself argues the former on the basis that the phrase "God of Israel" was not a typical expression in non-Jewish usage, and that the phrase has covenantal nuances and possibly liturgical overtones. Cousland, "Feeding of the Four Thousand," 1–23. Though Cousland notes that these stories follow that of the Canaanite woman, I would contend he does not take sufficient stock of the significance of the narrative sequence of these passages. It is also, in my view, completely tenable that Matthew, a Torah-observant Jew seeking in part to bring harmony between Jews and gentiles in his Christian community, would portray gentiles as adopting covenantal speech. As noted above, this phrase is used only here in Matthew, and it seems an odd place to uniquely emphasize "Yahweh's covenantal care for [the Jews]" (19).

38. LeMarquand suggests the seven loaves allude to Deut 7:1: "When the Lord your God brings you into the land that you are entering to take possession of it, and clears away many nations before you, the Hittites, the Girgashites, the Amorites, the Canaanites, the Perizzites, the Hivites, and the Jebusites, *seven nations* more numerous and mightier than you." This connection is not randomly asserted by LeMarquand, but is an extension of the Canaanite woman's request for mercy (Matt 15:22), a reference to and reversal of Deut 7:2. LeMarquand, "Canaanite Conquest," 237–47.

Another meal in Matthew occurs in the parable about a wedding feast (22:1–14) in which the king initially invites only a select group. Upon their refusal to attend, the king tells his servants to go to the main roads and invite as many as they can find. The king eventually casts out a man who attends the banquet but who is not wearing the appropriate attire. The parable is about the kingdom of heaven and so should not be taken historically. However, the parable does imply that the function of banquets has to do with inclusion within some social circle and that there was an accepted social code of conduct for such occasions.

Though it should not be directly applied to Matthew's narrative, it is worth noting that Luke's version of the wedding feast parable (simply called a "great banquet") includes a preface in which Jesus clearly instructs his disciples not to use meals to reinforce hierarchy and expectations of reciprocity (Luke 14:12–14). In Matt 26:6–13, Jesus does not hold a feast for the socially outcast as he teaches in Luke 14, but he does attend the meal of Simon the leper. The pericope itself gives no explicit indication that this is controversial, though Matt 9:11 has already seen Jesus' opponents questioning his eating with outcasts. Indeed, it was expected that one would not partake in table fellowship with those who might affect their purity or that of their group. The woman coming to anoint Jesus would have caused shock since a woman should not have approached him without being accompanied by a male relative.[39] There is also some evidence within Graeco-Roman contexts that "women who were associated with banquet settings were seen in the popular imagination as prostitutes."[40] At the very least, says Kathleen Corley, "the presence of a woman at a meal scene alone would indeed have signaled sexual innuendo to ancient readers."[41] Such a meal scene embodies a subversion of popular expectations and challenges certain notions of inclusion and hierarchy.

Finally, there is the story of the Passover meal in Matt 26:17–25. Again, we see an instance where the meal defines a social circle. It is not clear with how many disciples in total Jesus eats, though he reclines at table with the Twelve—whether this is a special space, or whether there were only twelve in total, is unclear.[42]

39. Malina, *New Testament World*, 47–48.

40. Corley, *Private Women, Public Meals*, 63.

41. Corley, "Anointing of Jesus," 64. It is worth noting a possible alternative view—"our narrative describes a dinner in a private house rather than a formal banquet. It is possible that meal practices were less rigid in villages and among poorer people." Miller, "Woman Who Anoints Jesus (Mk 14.3–9)," 222. Miller herself questions this assertion.

42. The former is probably more likely, since Passover was an extended evening of celebration and the formal part of the meal marked only one section. Jesus was

Meals also influenced the relationship between the two parties sharing together. Hospitality, a broader concept than table fellowship but inclusive of it, was generally regarded as a virtue in antiquity.[43] S. C. Barton defines it as "a social process by means of which the status of someone who is an outsider is changed from a stranger to a guest."[44] He goes on to outline three stages of this process: *evaluation* (testing the stranger as to whether they threaten the purity lines of the group), *incorporation* (taking them as a guest under the patronage of a host in accordance with cultural-specific codes), and *departure* (the stranger is now transformed into a friend or enemy depending on whether honor has been satisfied or infringed).[45] Such hospitality was a public and sacred duty.[46] Table fellowship was of course only one form hospitality might have taken, but this outline is helpful in making sense of the sociological significance of meals in antiquity, in particular the potential for a change in the nature of the relationship between two parties.

There is obviously a wealth of ancient texts on this subject, particularly from a Graeco-Roman background, and whilst a broader discussion would be interesting, it would also be excessive for the purposes of the present chapter. These few examples are sufficient to impress upon us that meals encoded certain social realities. These include group boundaries and hierarchy, as well as group values. Meals also had the potential to transform the relationship between two parties, whether positively or negatively, depending on the honor/shame dynamics on display at the meal.

5.3 The Prophetic Drama of a Meal

We must begin this section with a brief comment about "prophetic drama," since it is by no means clear what this means. Probably the most developed thought on this topic is that of David Stacey:

> Prophets occasionally turn to dramatic action, as when Isaiah walked naked or Jeremiah smashed his pot. These actions are usually quite simple and mundane. . . . Occasionally these actions are not specially contrived, but everyday, oft-repeated actions, that are deliberately taken over and used as prophetic material. . . . The essence of the action is not its complexity but

probably also accompanied by women and the householder who hosted the group. Nolland, *Gospel of Matthew*, 1065.

43. G. Stählin, "ξένος," *TDNT* 5:1–36; Mittelstadt, "Eat, Drink, and Be Merry," 132.

44. Barton, "Hospitality," 501.

45. Barton, "Hospitality," 501.

46. Barton, "Hospitality," 501–2.

the deliberation and purposefulness with which, in its simplic-
ity, it was carried out.[47]

Stacey adds that the act is carried out under divine compulsion.[48] It is for
this reason, he says, that to stress a distinction between oracle, action, and
fulfillment is an error, since all three are part of one divine reality.[49] When
prophetic drama occurs, it brings a person, action, or object into "relationship with some unseen event or reality, usually something on a much larger
scale than the drama itself."[50] What matters is not the form the drama takes,
but the divine purpose it embodies, the greater reality to which it points.
The prophet mediates the divine will by revealing it in the form of a dramatic action.[51] This was what the OT prophets were doing when they enacted
such drama, whether it be simple (e.g., Jeremiah's smashed pot representing
the smashed city; Jer 19) or more complex (e.g., Ezekiel's actions related to
his hair; Ezek 5). We also see such drama enacted in the ministry of Jesus
throughout the Gospels, for example, his miracles, his calling of the Twelve,
his entry into Jerusalem, his disruptive action in the temple, and the Last
Supper.[52] To these examples we ought to add Jesus' meals with sinners, given
the way these events embody God's purposes.

Regarding Jesus' action in Matt 9:9–13, there is little if any precedent
for such prophetic drama in the OT. Not that food and drink do not appear in the prophetic literature. On the contrary, the prophets frequently
utilize images of food and drink. In fact, there are so many such references,
stretching from Isaiah (Isa 1:11, 19–20, 22) through to Malachi (Mal 3:10–
11), that Robert Carroll claims they amount to "a virtual metaphysics of
food and drink."[53] Certainly the prophets are replete with images of food
and drink, either plenty or lacking, in raw or manufactured form, as well

47. Stacey, "Lord's Supper as Prophetic Drama," 65–74.

48. Stacey, "Lord's Supper as Prophetic Drama," 87.

49. Stacey, "Lord's Supper as Prophetic Drama," 87.

50. Stacey, *Prophetic Drama in the Old Testament*, 260. Here Stacey refers to F. W.
Dillistone's suggestion that prophetic drama is a "metaphorical conjunction between
present situations and future events." Such a suggestion is not without difficulty, since
there is a sense in which all prophetic actions, dramatic or otherwise, point in some
way to God's future action as a reference point for action in the present. On the other
hand, however, is the possibility that particular prophetic actions or speech may not
point to the future except in an eschatological-ethical sense more general than what
Dillistone intends.

51. So Hooker's assertion that prophetic signs or dramas are "the dramatic *embodiment* of the divine purpose, which otherwise may well be at present hidden" (emphasis
original). Hooker, *Signs of a Prophet*, 38–39.

52. For these and other examples, see Hooker, *Signs of a Prophet*, 35–54.

53. Carroll, "YHWH's Sour Grapes," 115.

as meals and feasts. They are signs of YHWH's favor or lack thereof, often with reference to the future (e.g., Isa 7:21–22). Scarcity of food and drink can be a symbol of environmental disaster (e.g., Jer 14:2–6), foreign invasion (e.g., Jer 5:17; Joel 3:11–14), exile (e.g., Isa 5:13–14), or other forms of divine punishment (e.g., Mic 6:14–15). Indeed, there are even images in the prophets picturing YHWH actively providing food and drink that poisons the people (Jer 8:14; 9:15). Such an "inhospitable banquet"[54] is described by William McKane in this way:

> the gruesome reversal of the benevolent host and wholesome hospitality. . . . The nations are gathered for a banquet, but the wine which is supplied will not gladden their hearts; instead of reaching a climax of good cheer it will end in sickness, madness and destruction.[55]

While the prophets do not set a direct precedent for eating with sinners, they often use the images of food and drink, or a lack thereof, to symbolize God's punishment.

Food is also used as a positive symbol in OT prophetic writings and in writings referring to prophets. In 1 Sam 9, Samuel eats with Saul before the prophet anoints him to be king of Israel. In 1 Kgs 18, following the contest between YHWH and the prophets of Baal, "in celebration of Yahweh's victory and kingship, the earthly king is sent back up the mountain by the prophet of Yahweh to eat and to drink. It is Yahweh who provides the victory banquet."[56] This event, an echo of Exod 24:3–11, marks the renewal of Israel's covenant with YHWH as mediated through the king.[57] In 2 Kgs 4:42–44, in the midst of a famine, Elisha commands that twenty loaves of barley and ears of grain be given to the sons of the prophets, even though this food is in no way sufficient to feed one hundred of them. The narrative reports that they all ate, with some food left over, "according to the word of YHWH" (4:44). In Jer 22, the prophet associates eating and drinking with obeying covenant commands and thus with all being well (22:15), and in Isa 25:6–9 YHWH's salvation is pictured as a feast of rich food and well-aged wine set out on a mountain. Similar uses of images of food and eating occur in non-prophetic texts, for example, in Ps 111:5 where YHWH is said to provide food for those who fear him, and this is connected to YHWH's

---

54. Carroll's phrase. Carroll, "YHWH's Sour Grapes," 123.

55. McKane, *Critical and Exegetical Commentary on Jeremiah*, 636.

56. Roberts, "God, Prophet, and King," 640.

57. Roberts, "God, Prophet, and King," 632–44.

remembering the covenant.[58] Another passage worthy of mention is Isa 58:6–12, in which wayward Israel is promised renewal if it shares its food with the hungry, in addition to sheltering the poor, clothing the naked, and satisfying the needs of the oppressed.[59] The food mentioned in this command is not a positive symbol in the same way as in the other passages, though the act of eating with the marginalized is associated with positive realities: faithfulness to God and renewal of the nation.

In most of the cases above, food is associated with Israel's covenant with YHWH. Such references probably find their theological source in Exod 24. Here the people of Israel commit themselves to all the words of YHWH, after which Moses, Aaron, Nadab, Abihu, and seventy of the elders of Israel experience a theophany and, beholding God, they eat and drink (24:1–11). This event confirms the covenant that YHWH has established with Israel. It is also worth pointing out that, as Stacey notes, "the central feature of Jewish worship in the Old Testament was a meal, the *zebah selamim*, traditionally rendered 'peace offering.'"[60] In other words, at the very core of Jewish covenantal life was a meal that symbolized peace between YHWH and Israel (Lev 3; 7:11–34).

If Moses is indeed the paradigmatic prophet of Israel, it is no surprise that prophets in Israel's subsequent story, whether in the former or latter prophets, utilize the image of food in connection with covenant renewal and enforcement. Does then Jesus, himself a prophet, do the same in Matthew? This is not to say that Matthew had any of the above texts specifically in mind when he wrote his telling of the story of Jesus' meal with outcasts. It is to say, however, that this tradition of food being associated with covenant was present in Matthew's symbolic universe, so he could not avoid the implications of using such symbols. In other words, the use of these symbols would stimulate certain associations, many of them rooted in the OT prophets, within the imaginations of Matthew's audience, even if they were unconscious of such a process or the source of the symbols.[61]

---

58. In addition, Gen 26:30–31; 31:54; Exod 18:12 all depict meals that serve to ratify covenants between people.

59. Blomberg, "Jesus, Sinners, and Table Fellowship," 40–41.

60. Stacey, "Lord's Supper as Prophetic Drama," 85.

61. I mention a potential lack of awareness of the sources of such symbols because the majority of Matthew's audience would have been either illiterate or only very basically literate. Torah education may have been common amongst boys (though it is difficult to know exactly how common), but it was extremely rare amongst girls since it was designed to produce Torah readers in synagogues; women could not be synagogue readers. See Hezser, *Jewish Literacy in Roman Palestine*, 496–504. This is not to mention the gentiles present among Matthew's audience. It is not clear how familiar different sections of Matthew's audience may have been with Torah, at least

What are the implications of such nutrimental symbols? According to the prophets, that depends on the nature of the meal. If the meal were one of scarcity or inhospitality, then the implication would be that YHWH's judgement has come upon the sinners and tax collectors. But, of course, this is not the case. The meal is sufficient to feed "many tax collectors and sinners" (9:10), even to the point that soon afterwards Jesus can refer to the reputation he has developed—"Look, a glutton and a drunkard, a friend of tax collectors and sinners!" (11:19). It is fair to say the meal in Matt 9 is hospitable. Here it seems we have Jesus renewing covenant, but not with those in positions of power (such as kings in the past), but with outcasts.[62] As discussed above, the act of eating together opens the way for a change in the relationship between two parties; in this case, a change is made possible between God (by way of God's prophet) and Israel's outcasts.

This shift is not without significance. If there were to be prophetic renewal of covenant with Israel, the expectation would have been that it be enacted in conjunction with the authorities as it had in the past. Jesus' subversion of this expectation may in fact be the initial impetus for the opposition of the Pharisees to Jesus' ministry, the beginning of their conflict, at least according to Matthew's narrative. While the scribes have already denounced Jesus (9:3), the Pharisees' critical question in 9:11 is the first of many that will come from them. Their apparent concern is that Jesus eats with sinners or, in other words, unclean people.[63] This would not have been a problem had Jesus been an "ordinary person," since it is hard to imagine the Pharisees monitoring and objecting to regular folk associating with sinners in such a way. But Jesus was not "ordinary"; he was someone announcing the kingdom of God,[64] and this was validated by his authoritative teaching and miracles. As was outlined above, to eat with such outcasts in a hospitable fashion would be to extend group boundaries to include them and to imply that the group values inclusion of outsiders more than purity concerns. The Pharisees were scrupulous about purity and ritual laws. What becomes apparent in this pericope is that there is a distinct difference

---

in terms of a direct familiarity.

62. "Outcasts" here does not refer to the poor, but to those who are outsiders on the basis of their failure, for whatever reason, to uphold the Mosaic covenant. Blomberg makes an interesting observation about a passage in Tobit that is relevant: "Tobit proves exemplary in commending almsgiving to the poor and needy, but 4:17 shows that, even in a context of enjoining charitable giving, feeding the hungry, and clothing the naked, one can read, 'but give none [of your bread] to sinners.'" Blomberg, "Jesus, Sinners, and Table Fellowship," 42.

63. According to *m. Hag.* 3:6, a tax collector rendered a house unclean by entering it.

64. Wright, *Jesus and the Victory of God*, 274.

between Jesus' and the Pharisees' perception of community boundaries.[65] This itself stems from a fundamental disagreement over interpretation of the Mosaic law. This disagreement will come to a crescendo in Matt 23–25 (esp. 23:23), where we learn that Jesus prioritizes justice, mercy, and faithfulness over strict adherence to purity laws.[66] Earlier in Matthew, we have already been given glimpses of this disagreement, such as in 3:7–10 and 5:20. We are given a further glimpse in Jesus' quotation of Hos 6:6 (Matt 9:13), a quotation to which we will soon attend. The Pharisees' question about why Jesus eats with sinners implies that they understand the potential social repercussions of Jesus' act of hospitality—at stake is the definition of group boundaries and, by extension, the identity of faithful Israel and the current social order itself. For Jesus to eat with outcasts is for him to dramatize God's hospitality to those considered sinners. Crossan calls this "open commensality," saying it was "a strategy for building or rebuilding peasant community on radically different principles."[67] This was, for Crossan, an expression of the heart of Jesus' program of a "shared egalitarianism of spiritual and material resources."[68] Such may have been the case—though the label "egalitarian" should be used with caution[69]—however it would be to truncate Jesus' "open commensality" to imagine it was simply a program of social reconstruction. Jesus' eating with outcasts was also a sign of God's covenant renewal with those considered impure and unacceptable, enacted by one at whose authoritative teaching the people were amazed (7:28–29). Moreover, in addition to Crossan's insistence upon the social reconstructive aspects of the meal, Jesus' action pointed to an eschatological reality that conceptually went beyond mere historical materialism, a point to which we will soon return.

Covenantal renewal, inclusive of outcasts as it is, would be a threat to Pharisaic influence, as well as that of other elites. The Pharisees would have perceived this to be an implication of Jesus' act of sharing a meal with sinners, or if not, then certainly of Jesus' words. Jesus' statement, "For I came not to call the righteous, but sinners," is here thick with meaning. It should not be misread as implying the Pharisees are righteous and are in no need of attention. Hagner notes that this makes no sense in the context of Matthew

---

65. "Jesus and the Pharisees are in conflict [in Matt 9:6–13] over the community boundaries and the criteria of acceptance." Saldarini, *Pharisees, Scribes, and Sadducees in Palestinian Society*, 168.

66. For one account of Jesus' alternative to the holiness paradigm of the Pharisees, see Borg, *Conflict, Holiness, and Politics*, 135–55.

67. Crossan, *Historical Jesus*, 344.

68. Crossan, *Historical Jesus*, 341.

69. Elliott, "Jesus Was Not an Egalitarian," 75–91.

as a whole (esp. 21:31), since the Pharisees *are* in need of righteousness.[70] Matthew's notion of Jesus calling sinners is perhaps better understood as Jesus *inviting* sinners.[71] This translation better captures the connection between the act of "inviting" and the context of a meal to which people have been invited. One explanation for the meal's threat to Pharisaic dominance is explained by Morna Hooker: "When Jesus outrages the religious authorities by dining with outsiders, the meal is a foretaste of the messianic banquet, and a symbol of those who will be invited to the feast—and of those who will be excluded."[72] In other words, the Pharisees have *not* been invited. I am inclined to modify such a suggestion, however, since in the parable of the wedding feast in Matt 22:1–14 the antagonistic characters are invited to the wedding but refuse to attend. If this same dynamic is present in Matt 9, which I think makes narrative sense, we have the Pharisees refusing an invitation to Jesus' meal, thus bringing on their own exclusion, because it contravened their table practices and relativized their social standing. They, like the "sinners," are invited to covenant renewal. But because of their refusal, Jesus' action is not simply a sign of covenant renewal with Israel's outcasts, it is also a sign of judgement against those leaders who, by their interpretation of the law, would cause Jesus' table companions to be outcasts. It is not that the Pharisees are excluded outright—they too are in need of a physician—but rather that they experience the consequence of their own deluded self-image, which prevents them from perceiving what is before them. As a result, the leaders have experienced scarcity of food in respect to the banquet that Jesus hosts, both in the present and in an eschatological sense, and this is the prophetic symbol of their judgement. Jesus subverts Pharisaic expectations that they will be rewarded for their purity and ancestry (cf. 3:9) while continuing the prophetic tradition of pronouncing judgement against Israel's leaders. In addition, Jesus' action is a foretaste of the future eschatological banquet, a theme to be explored below. All of this is encoded in the prophetic drama of the meal.

5.4 Matthew's Use of Hosea 6:6

That the emerging conflict between Jesus and the Pharisees over the interpretation of the law is a central theme in Matt 9:9–13 is confirmed by Jesus' quotation of Hos 6:6. This use of Hosea highlights the contrasting nature

---

70. Hagner, *Matthew 1–13*, 240.

71. As suggested by Hooker regarding the verb καλέω. Hooker, *Signs of a Prophet*, 114n16.

72. Hooker, *Signs of a Prophet*, 40.

of Jesus' understanding of Torah with that of his opponents, specifically his insistence on the primacy of mercy over purity concerns.[73] This confirms our analysis above regarding the nature of the disagreement between Jesus and the Pharisees.

The tail end of Matt 9:9–13 is structured in three parts:[74]

1. A proverb: "Those who are well have no need of a physician, but those who are sick." (Matt 9:12)

2. A challenge: "Go and learn what this means," followed by a citation from Hos 6:6: "I desire mercy, not sacrifice." (Matt 9:13a)

3. The summary: "For I have come to call not the righteous but sinners." (Matt 9:13b)

The logical flow of this section is not immediately obvious. Parts a) and c) are congruent, but b), with its quotation of Hosea, does not seem to fit as easily. In a) and c) Jesus seems to be explaining his mission, while in b) he is criticizing the Pharisees. This difficulty is largely overcome if we see the Hosea quotation as an aspect of Jesus' explanation of his mission. The critique of the Pharisees[75] does not stand in solitude, but rather intertwines with Jesus' explanation of his mission since *his mission is also the mission of Israel* and the Pharisees have not been faithful to it, meaning that Jesus' mission must also be *to* Israel. Jesus uses the Hosea text to show both that he is faithful to God's call to Israel and that his opponents are not. He also uses the Hosea text to show that his interpretation of the law eclipses that of the Pharisees—he is fulfilling the Law and the Prophets, and thus Israel's covenant obligations, by his mercy to sinners. Again, we see that covenant faithfulness is in view, and that Jesus' quotation of Hosea serves to bolster a kind of covenant enforcement, both positively (describing the mission of Israel) and negatively (implying the failure of the Pharisees to keep covenant).

---

73. There has been debate over the meaning of Matthew's quotation of Hos 6:6, specifically over whether καὶ οὐ inἜλεος θέλω καὶ οὐ θυσίαν should be translated "and not" (implying that sacrifices were unnecessary) or "more than" (comparing the relative importance of mercy and sacrifice). Here I take the latter view, if this was not already clear.

74. Ottenheijm, "Shared Meal—a Therapeutic Device," 1.

75. Ottenheijm argues that, "It is not necessary to read Matthew's use of the term *go and learn* as criticism, as if his opponents had not read Hosea." In addition, he points out that the phrase appears in rabbinic literature. Ottenheijm, "Shared Meal," 14–15. Ottenheijm is in principle correct—the phrase need not necessarily be antagonistic—though Matthew's use appears to be critical since he is suggesting his interlocutors do not understand the meaning of the Scripture.

The original context of Hos 6:6 is that of an announcement of judgement. In the chapters leading up to 6:6, Hosea announces YHWH's accusation against Israel and its impending punishment in light of its transgression of the covenant and failure to repent. There is, however, the offer of reconciliation if Israel will acknowledge its guilt and seek the face of YHWH (5:15). YHWH's desire for steadfast love ("mercy" in the LXX) is paralleled with "the knowledge of God," and A. A. Macintosh suggests this is because the prophet believes "goodness, kindness in moral behavior . . . and the proper recognition of Yahweh's ethical nature" is to know God, and these are set in contrast to cultic activities.[76] Israel is apparently unable to repent on its own, however, and YHWH will act unilaterally to heal them so that they may repent and live faithfully (Hos 6:11–7:1).[77] Jesus' use of Hos 6:6 would presumably carry at least part of this broader meaning, in addition to the isolated meaning of 6:6 itself.[78] The implication for the Pharisees is not without weight—because they have prioritized sacrifice over mercy, they have embodied the attitude and actions of those who in the past had judgement announced against them by Hosea. In doing so, they show they do not know God and incur the judgement of YHWH, a reality symbolized by their lack of invitation to the meal. Jesus seems self-consciously to take on the role of the prophet announcing the meaning of God's will expressed through the covenant. Jesus' prophetic vocation is expressed in this episode by more than his mere quotation of a prophetic text; the scene, the characters, and the dialogue all coalesce in such a way as to suggest Jesus consciously uses the Hosea text in a fashion consistent with the original prophetic message. This is especially true regarding Hosea's insistence that Israel is unable to repent without YHWH's prior saving action that makes possible its return to God (6:11–7:1): just as Jesus calls Matthew without his prior explicit repentance, so too does he call sinners as a saving action prior to their repentance. They are, after all, in need of a physician. In this way, we might see Jesus' meal itself as the saving act leading to repentance.

---

76. Macintosh, *Critical and Exegetical Commentary on Hosea*, 234.

77. This theme—that Israel's repentance and faithfulness is predicated by divine initiative—is found throughout the prophets (e.g., Isa 46:12–13; 43:22–25; 44:22; Jer 3:6–4:2, esp. 3:15–16; 31:31–34; 50:19–20; Ezek 16:60–63). See Dempsey, "'Turn Back, O People,'" 52–55; Sprinkle, *Paul and Judaism Revisited*, 38–67.

78. As mentioned in a footnote in the previous chapter, phrases often function metonymically in texts deriving from oral cultures in order to evoke not merely isolated sayings but larger narratives. See Foley, *Immanent Art*. "Matthew is not merely looking for random Old Testament proof texts that Jesus might somehow fulfill; rather he is thinking about the shape of Israel's story and linking Jesus' life with key passages that promise God's unbreakable redemptive love for his people." Hays, "Gospel of Matthew," 176.

The prophetic message that Jesus both enacts and elucidates by his words in this episode is summed up by his quotation of Hos 6:6. In one sense, the theme being debated in this story is that of righteousness, and this may be indicated by the reference to righteousness in 9:13. The Pharisaic complaint about Jesus relates to righteousness; by eating with sinners he has broken their practices of table fellowship.[79] Such practices, while perhaps distinctive, were based on a tradition of "using priestly laws concerning purity, food and marriage in order to separate, protect and identify Judaism."[80] For the Pharisees, such practices were markers that determined who was righteous—who was faithful to God's covenant—and their question (9:11) probes at whether Jesus is in fact a righteous Jew. Matthew is of course concerned with righteousness throughout his Gospel and this is perhaps best indicated in 5:20 when his audience is told that, "unless your righteousness exceeds that of the scribes and Pharisees, you will never enter the kingdom of heaven."[81] Even though Matthew has Jesus call his audience to a greater righteousness in 5:20, it is not immediately clear at that point what such greater righteousness entails. What follows in the Sermon on the Mount describes the demands of righteousness according to Jesus, though it is not the entirety of Jesus' teaching on righteousness. The conflict in 9:9–13 is the setting for further teaching on righteousness, as is the conflict in 12:1–8 where Jesus also quotes Hos 6:6. Regarding these episodes, Mary Hinkle Edin says:

> Twice Jesus quotes Hos 6:6 to Pharisees who are questioning his or his disciples' carefulness with respect to righteous behavior. "I desire mercy and not sacrifice" is the response of Jesus to concerns that he is failing to practice the righteousness he preaches. Along with other material in the gospel that speaks of mercy and righteousness, these two conflicts suggest that, in Matthew's Gospel, to be righteous is to show mercy.[82]

Matthew's use of Hos 6:6 is not simply a matter of finding scriptural support for Jesus' actions. Rather, in the context of a burgeoning conflict

---

79. These are practices designed to separate the group from others who are deemed impure. For a short summary, see Saldarini, *Pharisees, Scribes, Sadducees*, 215–16.

80. Saldarini, *Pharisees, Scribes, Sadducees*, 216.

81. Nolland offers an alternative translation of this verse: "For, I say to you, unless your righteousness is abundant—more than [that of] the scribes and Pharisees—you will certainly not enter the kingdom of heaven." Nolland, *Gospel of Matthew*, 215, 223–24. The effect on meaning is slight, "but the central focus moves away from comparison with the scribes and Pharisees and onto a concern, in the first instance, for an abundant righteousness."

82. Edin, "Learning What Righteousness Means," 356.

over the meaning of Torah, the nature of righteousness, and the identity of the faithful community, Jesus' appeal to Hos 6:6 serves to set an interpretive marker for how God's will ought to be discerned and the law embodied by the covenant people. In other words, Jesus' use of Hos 6:6 is an expression of an alternative hermeneutical approach to Torah, one whose precedent is found in the hermeneutic of the prophets[83] and which means Jesus follows in the prophets' hermeneutical method. The prophetic tradition of Israel was constituted by individuals called by God to hold Israel and its leaders to account for their infidelity to YHWH's covenant, most often demonstrated by their idolatry and injustice. What the prophets proclaimed so forcefully was that Israel's life, if it were to be faithful to YHWH, could not simply be characterized by separation from what is unclean. Such would be a deficient response to YHWH's saving actions. The prophets continually insisted upon the need for the social dimensions of Israel's life to conform to the redemption they had experienced by the hand of YHWH at the Exodus. Hence mercy ("steadfast love" in the Hebrew of Hos 6:6) becomes a primary expression of Israel's covenantal fidelity.[84] Jesus has already intimated this as his hermeneutical approach to Israel's scriptures when he teaches, "In everything do to others as you would have them do to you; for this is the law and the prophets." (7:12). His use of Hosea builds upon this hermeneutical approach and reveals it to be distinctly prophetic in nature.

5.5 Eschatological Aspects of Jesus' Table Fellowship

In Isa 25:6–9, part of an apocalyptic section within Isa 24–28, YHWH's salvation is depicted as a feast of rich food and well-aged wine set out on a mountain.[85] Passages depicting eschatological banquets occur in other apocalyptic literature also, such as in 1 Enoch where we read that, following the judgement of the mighty, the exalted and the rulers, "the Lord of Spirits will abide over [the righteous and elect], and with that Son of Man shall they eat and lie down and rise up for ever and ever" (62:14). There are also references to an eschatological banquet in the rabbinic literature,

---

83. See Sprinkle, *Paul and Judaism Revisited*, 38–67 for an excellent summary of the OT prophetic program of restoration vis-à-vis the Deuteronomic program, which gives great insight into the contrasting hermeneutics at play.

84. "Describing Hosea's use of חֶסֶד, Katharine Doob Sakenfeld explains that the word is "used as a summary term for Israel's carrying through on covenant commitment both to exclusive worship of the Lord and to *communal justice;* that is, *hesed* represents the entire decalogue in a single word." Edin, "Learning What Righteousness Means," 359.

85. Sloyan, "Holy Eucharist as an Eschatological Meal," 447.

such as in *b. Pesah.* 119b: "The Holy One, blessed be he, will make a great banquet for the righteous on the day he manifests his love to the seed of Isaac. After they have eaten and drunk, the cup of blessing will be offered to our father Abraham." Whatever the variations between these and other similar passages, there was certainly around the time of Jesus a concept of an eschatological or messianic banquet that was present in the collective consciousness of a range of groups.

Interestingly, accompanying the Isaiah and 1 Enoch passages quoted above we see images of the judgement of God's enemies—foreign enemies (Isa 25) and the elite (1 Enoch). Indeed, the use of eschatological banquet imagery does not simply represent abstract descriptions of what may happen at some future point. Rather these images are, at least in part, polemics designed to challenge contemporary ideas about who is included among the faithful/righteous, and to offer a counter-narrative to competing accounts of God's inclusion/exclusion. They may also represent a counter-narrative to how things appear at a given time, for example, when Israel's enemies are dominant and YHWH seems absent (so Isa 25). As we noted above, Jesus' table language in Matt 8:11–12 functions in this eschatological and subversive fashion. I contend, then, that it would be narratively consistent for the function of such language to carry over to chapter 9 and the story of Jesus eating with outcasts. Indeed, it is widely thought that passages depicting the eschatological banquet likely form part of the tradition background for the Eucharistic passages in the Gospels;[86] there is no reason why such passages could not also form part of the religio-cultural matrix for the Gospels' portrayals of Jesus' other meals, including Matt 9:9–13. In other words, Jesus' eating with sinners can be seen, along with other meals in the Gospels, as a portrayal and sign of the eschatological feast described in Isa 25 and elsewhere.[87] In this way, Jesus' prophetic action of eating with sinners is focused not only on covenantal renewal; it also contains a forward-looking element inasmuch as it focuses on eschatological renewal and judgement. These elements, past and future, are related, since they both embody God's will, with the eschatological reality a fulfillment of covenantal promises.

In Jesus' action of eating with sinners we see a sign of the coming eschatological reality. Jesus' prophetic act here points toward what could be termed "the great reversal." This idea traverses the narrow edge between restoration of Israel on one hand and judgement of Israel on the other. Both will occur, but according to Jesus this will not be as had been

---

86. See for example Wright, *Jesus and the Victory of God*, 558–59; Theissen and Merz, *Historical Jesus*, 405; McKnight, *Jesus and His Death*, 328–34;

87. So Jeremias, *Jesus' Promise to the Nations*, 63.

commonly imagined. This concept, apart from being present in Matt 9:9–13, is also reiterated later in another meal, the parable of the wedding feast in Matt 22:1–14. Here we are told of the diversity of those being invited and the refusal of some of these invitees to attend. In other words, those who are present at the banquet are not those whom the Pharisees and other groups expect.

Further to the eschatological dimensions of Matthew's meal scene, and relating to the wedding feast parable, is the connection made between feasting and marriage by Matthew when he fuses the meal in 9:9–13 to Jesus' assertion, made in response to a question about his eating practices, that he is a bridegroom (9:14–17). The marriage metaphor is common in the OT as a description of God's relationship with Israel, most comprehensively in Hos 1–3.[88] If there has been some sort of break in the marriage between God and Israel, "the eschatological age will be a time when the marriage between God and Israel will be renewed,"[89] as in Isa 62. By juxtaposing these images of meal and wedding in two pericopes, it may be that Matthew was seeking to make clear a connection between the meal and OT marriage themes, such that the meal itself is a wedding banquet presaging the later parable in Matt 22. In this way, Matt 22 acts as a kind of commentary on 9:9–13. The new age in which right relationship with God will be restored has in a sense arrived because the bridegroom is present, even if it has yet to be ultimately fulfilled.[90] That the marriage material in the OT is connected to covenant relationships is clear and, by adopting this imagery, Matthew is adding another covenantal layer to the picture—all are invited, but some will be included and others excluded based on their response to the invitation. The result will apparently be surprising.

That the new age has both arrived and not arrived in Jesus' meal points to a problem that arises for us in regard to eschatology more generally: the divergence, discussed in chapter 2, between seeing it as relating only to final events or as including transitional, non-final events. In other words, does the eschatological banquet that Jesus anticipates in his meals with sinners occur at some ultimate end point of history, or at some other time? Moreover, is the banquet a literal event, or is it a metaphor describing "the joy of the coming age of salvation"?[91] This problem is not made easier by the plurality of Jewish views on the subject. Steffen identifies four categories

---

88. See Zvi, "Observations on the Marital Metaphor," 363–84.

89. Long, "Jesus the Bridegroom," 38.

90. The tension between fulfillment and non-fulfillment is probably behind Matt 9:15 (cf. Mark 2:20), in which Jesus speaks of the time when the bridegroom will be taken away. This is probably a warning against an over-realized eschatology.

91. Pitre, "Jesus, the Messianic Banquet," 135.

describing the range of beliefs among Jews in the first century concerning expectations of the eschatological banquet:[92]

1. *A metaphorical universal terrestrial banquet*: includes blessing of the righteous, including from all the nations, and judgement of God's enemies. Refers not to a single event, but describes an entire age which includes the restoration of the remnant to their homeland. This view appears in the OT, Jewish apocalyptic and rabbinic literature.

2. *A metaphorical restricted terrestrial banquet*: a view found mostly in the Qumranic literature. The Qumran community believed the Messiahs would reverse their fortunes, judge their enemies, and bless them greatly. Only the righteous remnant of Israel is included.

3. *The banquet as a single event at the inception of the messianic age*: the banquet does not describe the whole messianic age, but one exemplary event of judgement of evil and of the prosperity of the righteous. Sometimes includes the righteous from other nations, but not always. Sometimes terrestrial, sometimes heavenly.

4. *The banquet as metaphorical for heavenly bliss*: refers to future blessings of banqueting in the garden of eden, paradise or heaven. Found in early Jewish apocalyptic literature.

One problem with Steffen's typology is that it does not give sufficient attention to the referent of eschatological language more generally in the OT and elsewhere. In other words, it assumes that eschatological language must necessarily refer to a final event, even if that event is not momentary, but an extended messianic age.[93] George Caird's classic work on this topic is helpful at this point.[94] Caird acknowledged that the biblical authors believed the world would have an end in the future, just as it had had a beginning. However, Caird also recognized that the biblical authors "used end-of-the-world

92. Steffen, "Messianic Banquet."

93. Steffen is, of course, not alone in this. There are numerous examples of this assumption. One whose view is indicative is Dale Allison. See especially Allison, "Plea for Thoroughgoing Eschatology," esp. 664n7, "I shall ignore another objection to my thesis, namely, that a literal reading of eschatological language fails to understand its metaphorical functions." See also Allison, *End of the Ages Has Come*, 84–90: "When a document depicts the present or immediate past in apparently eschatological terms, talk of metaphor is appropriate only if the redemption remains distant; for as we shall see straightaway, if it is thought to be proximate, the present becomes the time immediately before the redemption and hence naturally draws to itself the language of eschatology. This has nothing to do with metaphor" (88). Also noteworthy is Allison, *Jesus of Nazareth*.

94. See Caird, "Language of Eschatology," 243–71.

language metaphorically to refer to that which they well knew was not the
end of the world."[95] Caird resolves this tension by positing that there can
exist in the biblical texts, without contradiction, long-range and short-range
aspects of eschatological expectation. He uses Daniel as a prime example,
since there is an imminence to some of its eschatological expectations, yet
there is also the presence of a final judgement in Dan 12:1–3.

Caird's approach to eschatology is enormously helpful in dealing
with the difficulty of Matthew's eschatological expectation. After all, on
one hand in Matthew's later chapters, particularly the latter part of chapter 23, we see Jesus' references to judgement becoming concretized in the
form of predictions regarding Jerusalem's coming destruction, historically
speaking a non-final event. Given that a crucial aspect in all Jewish accounts of the messianic banquet is the judgement of God's enemies, one
might suspect that, for Matthew, the banquet occurs in the regular flow
of history at a non-final "eschatological" moment of judgement, namely
Jerusalem's destruction. But any hastiness to accept this perspective is
moderated by another dimension of Jesus' eschatological expectation. We
must remember that in the aftermath of Jerusalem's destruction the notion
of a great banquet, including the judgement of unfaithful Israelites, has not
materialized in any complete sense. Indeed, the opponents of Matthew's
communities are those rabbinic groups, an increasingly significant socio-
religious group in Palestine, descended from the Pharisees on whom Jesus
had announced judgement. It might understandably have been difficult to
see how God's judgement had vindicated the righteous.

It is possible that the eschatological banquet is embodied in the life
of the faithful community of Jesus' disciples in Matthew's time, compris-
ing as it did faithful Israel and those gentiles who had been welcomed in
(cf. Isa 25:6–8; 56:6–7). However, it is difficult to imagine that the meals
and fellowship of the Christian community in the time of Matthew were
the ultimate fulfillment of the expectation of the eschatological banquet.
Scot McKnight's reflections on the work of Caird may be helpful in finding
a way through the dilemma:

> In his vision of human history, Jesus saw no further than A.D.
> 70, and to this date he attached visions of the final salvation, the
> final judgment, and consummation of the kingdom of God in all
> its glory. That history took another course does not at all mean
> that Jesus was in error; rather, like the Hebrew prophets before
> him, he saw the next event as the end event and predicted events
> accordingly. This perspective was typical of Jewish prophecy

95. Chenoweth, "Apocalyptic Eschatology," 5.

from of old; the next event was seen as the end event, but that next event resulted in a series of unfolding events. Prophecy carried with it an innate poetic ambiguity.[96]

Jesus' prophetic preview of the eschatological banquet is perhaps best thought to refer to both the life and table fellowship of the later covenantal community and to a time of final restoration. This is the nature of his prophetic role and announcements, as was the case with the Hebrew prophets. In one sense, the meals of Matthew's mixed communities were a kind of eschatological banquet, both an emulation and fulfillment of Jesus' meals with sinners. In another, the meals of the Matthean communities were, like Jesus' meals, signs of a future reality that had implications in the present. This is, incidentally, Matthew's understanding of "fulfillment" more generally: that it is multi-referential. His so-called "fulfillment passages"—quotations from the OT which find their fulfillment in events in Jesus' life—are a prime example. These passages may come to fulfillment in Jesus, but they also clearly had some original fulfillment that was unrelated to Jesus.[97] This is important because it means Matthew saw the original circumstance and object of the prophetic text as only constituting part of the fulfillment.[98] This was not based on an arbitrary choice to render a new meaning for an old text, but rather Matthew's conviction that in Jesus there was a new dimension to the divine purpose that places the original text in a wider context.[99] So Viljoen:

> Matthew's links between the Old Testament and the fulfilment in Jesus often are unexpected, but they emerge from the same God who acted in the history of Israel and spoke through the prophets and now brought his redemptive scheme to its end result. Matthew recognizes ongoing patterns in the work of God.[100]

If this is Matthew's understanding of fulfillment, then Jesus' own actions could be equally as multi-referential as the words of the prophets, pointing

---

96. McKnight, *New Vision for Israel*, 12.

97. For example, Matthew's first fulfillment passage in 1:23 is a quotation of Isa 7:14. While Matthew sees Jesus' conception as a fulfillment of the passage, in its Isaian context it referred to the coming birth of Hezekiah as a sign to King Ahaz of Judah that the Syro-Israelite coalition will not conquer his people. We could also point to Matt 2:15, and its quotation of Hos 11:1. In its original Hosean context the phrase "Out of Egypt I called my son" clearly referred to Israel, though Matthew has it refer to Jesus' return from Egypt as a child after Herod's death.

98. Contra Moule, who claims that Matthew ignored the original context of the passages and thereby did violence to their meaning. Moule, *Origin of Christology*, 128.

99. Indeed, this seems to be the logic of Patristic hermeneutics as well.

100. Viljoen, "Fulfilment in Matthew," 313.

both to the fellowship of the Matthean communities and the final eschatological banquet. Again, this is not arbitrary, but a linking of imminent
fulfillment with the wider context of the divine plan, in this case the perceived eschatological reality.

What were the implications of the eschatological reality? This brings
us back to the idea discussed above of an eschatological meal whose guests
are unexpected. For both the Pharisees and the Qumranites, "the pursuit
of purity was the means to realize the preconditions for eschatological
restoration."[101] Their eating practices separated them from gentiles and
impure Jews, despite the universalistic eschatological visions found in
Isaiah. For the Matthean community—those who followed the way of the
prophet Jesus—the future eschatological restoration, as revealed in Jesus'
example and teaching, required the radical reconfiguring of purity and
table fellowship in the present.[102] The eschatological reality reflected in
Isaiah had already been inaugurated, including its blessings and judgements, and this reality was being manifested in the world in a way that was
contrary to the expectations of Israel. This all begins with Jesus' action,
which foreshadows both the imminent and long-term eschatological realities. In his prophetic role, Jesus depicts who will be vindicated as the new
Israel when the kingdom has come in full.

In his table fellowship with sinners we see that Jesus reorients eschatological expectations. He does this by subverting the assumptions of his
enemies regarding who will be included in the eschatological banquet, the
symbol of ultimate restoration. In Wright's words, Jesus is redefining the
family, the new Israel, opening it to anyone "who wanted to be allied with
his kingdom-movement."[103] In order to do this, Jesus makes use of a daily
ritual which is also a powerful theological symbol—the act of eating—and
reconfigures its meaning so as to express the will of God. Such a dramatic
use of commonplace events and objects is not unlike the OT prophets. We
might think of Jeremiah's breaking of a clay vessel to symbolize YHWH's
judgement of Jerusalem (Jer 19), his purchasing of a field as a sign of God's
future restoration of Israel (32:1–15), Ezekiel's use of his own shaved hair as

101. Bird, *Jesus and the Origins*, 104.

102. There is no evidence that Jesus ate with gentiles (or that he did not), though
ἁμαρτωλός ("sinners") could refer to both impure Jews and gentiles. See Bird, *Jesus and
the Origins*, 106. In light of Jesus' teaching and actions toward gentiles, however, it is
natural that the Matthean communities would see table fellowship with gentiles as an
extension of Jesus' own meals with "sinners." It was, moreover, a common expectation
that gentiles would be included in the eschatological blessing of Israel (cf. Isa 2:1–4;
25:6–8; 60:3–4; Mic 4:1–2; Zech 8:20–23; Mal 1:11; also *Sib. Or.* 3), and Matthew's community may have viewed table fellowship with gentiles as a form of participation in this.

103. Wright, *Jesus and the Victory of God*, 430–31.

a sign of YHWH's judgement and coming exile (Ezek 5:1–4), Elisha's command for King Joash to shoot an arrow as a sign of the king's impending victory over Syria (2 Kgs 13:14–19), and so forth. The prophetic vocation includes the dramatization and transformation of the mundane so that it becomes a powerful symbol and sign of God's will revealed through the prophet. Jesus' prophetic vocation follows this pattern.

It is also the case that the prophets dissolve the barriers between the past, present, and future. We have already discussed the role of prophets as covenant enforcers. Such a role involves the dissolution of the distance between God's revealed will in the past and the present moment. But this also works in regard to the future. In the OT examples of prophetic actions listed above, to which we could add numerous other examples, we see instances of future realities—themselves somehow wrapped up with the will of YHWH—impinging on and demanding a response in the present. Jesus' action provides a glimpse of the future reality breaking into the present moment and demanding a response. The response required is itself dependent on the individual. For "sinners," what is required is an acceptance of the invitation to join the banquet. For the Pharisees, the demand is that they transform their minds that they might accept the perspective of Jesus, symbolized in his acceptance of outsiders and summarized in his teaching about righteousness and Hosea 6. The prophet calls the individual to a moment of crisis in which they must choose between, on the one hand, obedience to God's will expressed in covenant and future fulfillment or, on the other hand, rejection. As with the prophets of old, Jesus' invitation is rejected by the community leaders. Their place at the eschatological banquet is thus called into question, while that of the sinners who have accepted Jesus' invitation is affirmed.

5.6 Jesus' Action in Light of Old Testament Prophetic Actions

One of the problems in studying Jesus' prophetic vocation in Matt 9:9–13 is that Jesus' action in this pericope has few direct comparisons to OT prophets. As we have seen above, images of food and eating are present in the prophets, and the meaning of such images carries over to Matthew to a large extent. Moreover, Jesus' use of Hos 6 suggests a self-conscious connection with the OT prophetic tradition. OT prophetic figures do share meals as a symbol of some kind (e.g., Exod 24:3–11; 1 Sam 9; 1 Kgs 18; 2 Kgs 4:42–44), though they are rarely the focus of any particular story. Moreover, it would be nearly impossible to know if any of these or other passages was in the mind of the author of Matthew as he wrote his Gospel, or whether these and other passages are a direct influence on Jesus' action.

What then shall we make of this? Jesus' action in Matt 9:9–13 proves difficult since it utilizes a prophetic image (eating) and its accompanying saying associates it with the prophetic tradition, yet the action is not common among the OT prophets in terms of its form. In a sense, these need not concern us, since many of the actions of the OT prophets are idiosyncratic, and have no discernible precedent, for example, Isaiah's walking naked for three years (Isa 20:1–6), Jeremiah's purchasing of a field (Jer 32:1–15), and Ezekiel's building a mini-Jerusalem, lying on his sides for extended periods, and cooking over dung (Ezek 4). The form of Jesus' action need not be an echo of the action of any particular OT prophet. What is important, though, is that Jesus' action shares an underlying purpose with the actions of OT prophets. Our argument up to this point has been that Jesus' action in Matt 9:9–13 functions in part to announce God's inclusion of those deemed outsiders, to subvert the boundaries of groups like the Pharisees. This represents the purpose of this particular action in its particular context, but this is distinct from a more fundamental purpose that subsumes such particular prophetic actions. The more basic purpose of prophetic actions is to dramatize God's will, as expressed in Israel's covenant, and to call Israel to faithfulness to the covenant's demands. The prophetic actions of the OT prophets like Isaiah, Jeremiah, and Ezekiel fulfill this purpose. Moreover, since his action in Matt 9:9–13 also fulfills this purpose—as we have seen—Jesus' action conforms to the underlying *raison d'être* of the prophetic tradition; indeed, Jesus belongs in the prophetic tradition.

Jesus' act of eating with sinners may share an overarching purpose with the OT prophets, though this conclusion does not help us make sense of Jesus' action in light of OT prophetic traditions. At a broader level, we can see that Jesus' meal is consistent with prophets of the past in its implied message of judgement against Israel's leaders. However, the revelation of God's will undergoes a shift in the prophetic actions of Matthew's Jesus as compared with most of his prophetic predecessors. Judgement is still present, but it is accompanied to a much greater degree by the kind of mercy expounded by Hosea.[104] Jesus is more extreme than his prophetic forerunners in repudiating an excessive concern for purity at the expense of mercy, even for those deemed outside the covenant. Jesus' action in Matt 9:10–13 signifies judgement only as an extension of its primary message of hope, in this case for outcasts.

---

104. See McKnight, "Jesus and Prophetic Actions," 205–14, who notes that the actions of OT prophets are most often acts of judgement.

At a more specific level, Jesus' act of eating with sinners does resonate with certain OT prophetic stories. As we know, Matthew portrays Jesus as like Moses. The miracles of Matt 8–9 are most probably to be compared with those of Moses,[105] such that Jesus' miracles are an expression of his Moses-like prophetic vocation. But so too was the provision of food seen as a Mosaic characteristic, with Exod 16:1–36 as a focal point both in Moses' leadership[106] and in a later provision-of-food tradition. This tradition is carried through Elijah and Elisha, both of whom are confirmed as prophets in the tradition of Moses because of their own provision of food (cf. 1 Kgs 17:6–7; 8–16; 19:5–8; 2 Kgs 2:19–22; 4:1–7; 42–44). Moreover, there later came an expectation of a second exodus in which the blessings of the first would be repeated, including the provision of food (e.g., 2 Bar. 29:8; Mek. 5.63–65; Eccl. Rab. 1.9).[107]

It is well known that Matthew alludes throughout his narrative to the coming of a new exodus.[108] It may be that Jesus' act of eating was seen as part of this tradition, a sign among others that Jesus would lead a new exodus. One difficulty with this interpretation is that unlike the manna in the wilderness in Exod 16, Jesus' meal in Matt 9:9–13 was not miraculous; perhaps we are better off to see allusions to Exod 16 in the feeding stories in Matt 14–15, but not chapter 9. Still, this may be to posit too great a dichotomy between miraculous and non-miraculous feeding events, one that ancients would not have been concerned with. Each of the food provision stories from Exodus, 1 and 2 Kings, and other ancient texts that we have mentioned appear indifferent to the method of the provision itself; they are instead more concerned with the meaning of such events.[109] In the cases listed, the provision of food is either an act of mercy or an act of peace signaling the nature of YHWH's dealings with humanity.

Both themes—mercy and peace—are present in food traditions that are and are not "miraculous" in form. We occasionally see them without an expectation of reciprocating action (as in 1 Kgs 17:8–16). More often such

105. See Acts Pil. 5:1; Ps.-Clem. Rec. 1:57. See also Bacon, Studies in Matthew, 187–89. Allison, New Moses, 207–13, sees no Moses typology in these chapters, but his denial relates to the possible correlation of Matthew's ten [nine?] miracles in chapters 8–9 and the ten plagues in Exod 7–12; I agree with Allison on this matter, but do not see this as requiring the denial of a more general Mosaic comparison.

106. Gilmour, Juxtaposition and the Elisha Cycle, 142.

107. Lierman, New Testament Moses, 107.

108. See, for example, Allison, New Moses, 194–99; France, Gospel of Matthew, 63, 81; Garland, Reading Matthew, 29; Keener, Gospel of Matthew, esp. 108–9; Wright, New Testament, 384–90.

109. If the form of these events is important, it is only in relation to its bearing on the meaning.

provision implies or explicitly states an expected response. In the case of the manna in the wilderness story, the larger trajectory of the narrative suggests that the manna is an act of mercy in order that Israel may fulfill its task of establishing a covenant with YHWH and entering the land of Canaan. But it is also true that the feeding in the wilderness sets up an image, one that will later become common, of fellowship between YHWH and Israel. This is continued soon after in Exod 24:3–11 when we see the ratification of the Mosaic covenant. This confirmation includes a meal signifying covenant renewal (24:11). William Dumbrell notes that the short mention of this meal "is important incidental information, since it sets the goal to which the Bible looks in fellowship relationships. This meal on the mountain becomes the focus of later OT projection (cf. Isa 25:6–8; Rev 19:7–9), indicating final fellowship in the kingdom of God."[110] I would suggest the pattern for this fellowship has already been set, or at least previewed, in Exod 16.

We can also see the peace dimension of this food tradition strongly reflected in 2 Kgs 6:8–23. Here we find the story of the Syrians looking for Elisha in order to seize him. Having surrounded the city of Dothan in which Elisha is staying, they prepare to attack it. Elisha prays to YHWH to strike the Syrians with blindness. He then proceeds to lead the blinded army to Samaria where the king of Israel is encamped. The king asks Elisha whether he should strike down the Syrians, but Elisha responds in the negative, noting that the king would not strike down those he has taken as prisoners of war. Elisha instead counsels the king to set before the Syrians a meal prior to releasing them. The opponents feast together after which the Syrians return to their king. The conclusion to the story suggests the Syrians never again raided Israel. The meal as an act of reconciliation and sign of peace is striking and is no doubt an expression of the fellowship reflected in Exodus' meals, which in turn was a standard symbol in the ancient Near East.[111]

The point is that the provision-of-food tradition is not focused on "miraculous" acts of feeding *per se*, but on the fellowship embodied in such meal events. This brings episodes like Exodus 16 together with texts such as Isa 25:6–8 into the same tradition of YHWH's provision of food for Israel and/or the world. Jesus may not provide food miraculously in Matt 9:9–13 (he does so elsewhere), however he does embody the fundamental meaning of the fellowship meal tradition that began with Moses and continued

---

110. Dumbrell, *Faith of Israel*, 38–39.

111. Such an arrangement seems to have been present in other times and places in the ancient Near East. For example, see the Hittite text *KUB* XIV 3: ii 63–64: "The guarantee in the Hatti land is such: if we give bread and drink to somebody, then we do not harm him in any way." See Liverani, *Myth and Politics*, 14; Goldstein, "Provision of Food," 104.

through the actions and words of the prophets—making peace between those who were once separated and establishing fellowship between humans and YHWH. Though individual texts discussed here may not have been in the mind of Matthew at the time he composed his Gospel, they informed his symbolic universe by way of a common tradition stemming from Moses, and thus are manifested in the text itself. The same would be true of Jesus himself, both in a historical sense and a narrative sense. In other words, Jesus embodies the symbolism of his world—by sharing a meal with outcasts, he necessarily embodies the meaning of such an act in relation to them, in this case peace, reconciliation, and fellowship. In eating with sinners, Jesus is consistent with a strand of the Mosaic prophetic tradition, namely, the provision of food, one that is found in the stories of the former prophets and the eschatological imagery of the later prophets.

Finally, I must comment briefly on Jesus' call of Matthew in Matt 9:9 and its relation to the OT. The pericope begins with (1) Jesus walking along; (2) Jesus seeing a named individual; (3) the individual going about their daily tasks; (4) Jesus calling the individual to discipleship; (5) the individual following him.[112] The structure has already occurred in Matt 4:18–22, and this structure is itself arranged in the same way as in the story of Elijah's call of Elisha in 1 Kgs 19:19–21. This may suggest that the call to follow was itself seen as a prophetic act, not unlike Elijah's call. This is supported by the distinction of this model of calling disciples from rabbinic practice, where the disciple chose the rabbi.[113] Though our focus in this chapter is not specifically the calling of Matthew, the fact that this act introduces the meal scene, and that the meal scene is found within the larger context of a string of stories that paint Jesus as a prophet like Moses, suggests that this pericope may be read to further outline the nature of Jesus and his prophetic vocation. This vocation is both similar and dissimilar to the prophets who came before him. Jesus calls people to follow, it is true. But Jesus also calls people to a more demanding form of faithfulness—unlike Elisha, who is allowed to return to bid his family farewell, the disciples simply drop what they are doing and follow Jesus. Jesus' call is consistent with the elevated rigor of his interpretation of Torah in Matt 5–7. This willingness to embody the tradition whilst also subverting, challenging, or intensifying certain aspects of it occurs at two levels in the Gospel, intrinsically and extrinsically. At an intrinsic level, we see Jesus, a character internal to the narrative, prophetically reconfigure tradition in a way that conforms to his own hermeneutic

112. Davies and Allison, *Matthew 8–18*, 96. See also Davies and Allison, *Matthew 1–7*, 392–93.

113. Davies and Allison, *Matthew 1–7*, 396.

and special relationship to YHWH. At an extrinsic level, we see Matthew, as both real and implied author, doing the very same thing to traditional materials by way of his main character, the prophet Jesus.

5.7 Jesus' Action among Other First-Century Prophetic Actions

Jesus' action in Matt 9:9–13 does not seem to have any particular similarities with the actions of other known first-century prophetic figures. However, as with OT prophets, such is not necessary to draw comparisons, since disparate and idiosyncratic actions may share a common function.

We recall Horsley's typology of first-century popular prophets and his distinction between oracular prophets and action prophets. Horsley describes the principal function of the latter as being "to inspire and lead a popular movement to vigorous participation in an anticipated redemptive action by God."[114] As we have seen, prophetic figures in first-century Syro-Palestine such as the Samaritan Prophet, Theudas, and the Egyptian Prophet all led groups of people in actions that sought God's liberation of their followers from the domination of their oppressors. Their primary adopted symbolism was that of the exodus and conquest narratives, and their aim was to return to an idyllic covenantal existence, a reality they perceived to have existed in Israel's past. Though the primary function of their actions was redemptive, they also implied judgement against their oppressors, a companion of the hoped-for redemption.

It is important to notice that the immediate hoped for results of covenantal fidelity and divine action are, for the first-century prophets, distinct from that of the OT prophets. The OT prophets primarily announce judgement and call for repentance, while the first-century prophets dramatize their desired redemption and hope for deliverance in addition to calling for repentance. This is not to say that the OT prophets never look forward to deliverance; the most obvious example of anticipation of deliverance in the prophets is the hopeful material found throughout Deutero- and Trito-Isaiah. This is not surprising, since Israel's exilic and early post-exilic situations more closely resemble the imperial domination the nation experiences in the first century CE than does the pre-exilic situation of the majority of the OT prophets. In other words, the historical situation of the prophet and the nation has a major effect on the nature of the prophetic message being spoken or enacted. It makes sense that judgement is a key theme when Israel governs itself and that redemption is a more prominent theme during

114. Horsley with Hanson, *Bandits, Prophets and Messiahs*, 135.

exile or occupation. This also illuminates the first-century prophets' focus on Mosaic and conquest symbols.

With Jesus, we see elements of both the OT prophets and the first-century prophets, though he is not the first prophetic figure in Matthew's narrative for whom this is the case. In Matt 3, we see John the Baptist preaching and baptizing. He is clearly a prophet, demonstrable by his call for repentance and his clothing.[115] John's action of baptism embodies the repentance to which he is calling people. But the act is also an echo of Israel's experience of traversing through water in the exodus and conquest narratives. In John's case, however, God's judgement is not directed at other nations, but at those within Israel who have failed to embody covenant faithfulness—the very people who were assumed to be true Israelites. Themes of repentance and judgement suggest an OT prophetic influence, while John's dramatization of God's past deliverance of Israel, notably in the exodus, suggests a likeness to other first-century prophets, at least in function, if not form. John's ultimate concern, besides pointing to the Messiah who will follow him, is to call Israelites back to covenant faithfulness, the "bearing of fruit in keeping with repentance."[116] The implication of John's criticism of the Pharisees and Sadducees—that they should not presume to call Abraham their father (Matt 3:9)—is that those who respond to his call, whatever else they might be, are Abraham's children, members of God's faithful covenant community.[117]

At first glance, the deliverance that John announces in the speech that accompanies his act of baptizing appears quite distinct from that proclaimed by other first-century prophetic figures. While these figures proclaim a deliverance from oppression, John seems to proclaim deliverance through repentance from the imminent judgement carried out by the expected figure who will "baptize with fire" and "burn the chaff" (Matt 3:2, 11–12).[118] As Webb points out, however, the proclamation of the other first-century prophets almost certainly implied the judgement of their enemies, and this makes them similar to John in this respect.[119] Moreover, John's call to covenant faithfulness is not merely a call to personal moral uprightness; by calling his audience to

115. John wears a garment of camel's hair and a leather belt. It is generally agreed that this description is meant to liken John to Elijah (2 Kgs 1:8), though Becker refutes this, preferring instead to see John's costume as that of a prophet more generally. Becker, *Jesus of Nazareth*, 44.

116. Bearing fruit was a metaphor in the OT for doing God's will, in accordance with Israel's covenant. E.g., Ps 1:1–3; Isa 27:6; Jer 17:7–10; Hos 9:15–16.

117. Hooker, *Signs of a Prophet*, 9.

118. Webb, *John the Baptizer and Prophet*, 355.

119. Webb, *John the Baptizer and Prophet*, 355–56.

repentance and covenant faithfulness, John is calling his audience to fidelity to the story of Israel and its dealings with YHWH, a story including God's promises to deliver Israel from their enemies in return for their obedience. I would contend that this is symbolized in the echoes of the exodus/conquest found in John's act of baptizing—the journey through the water of those he baptized—and his location in the wilderness. John's act of baptizing seems to reflect his belief, like the other first-century prophets, that those who would join him in the required symbolic action would experience soon-coming deliverance and possession of the land, and probably that they would witness YHWH's defeat of their enemies.[120] The actions of the various prophets were different—baptism, ascending Mount Gerizim (Samaritan prophet), crossing the Jordan (Theudas), ascending the Mount of Olives (Egyptian prophet)— and they echo varying aspects of the OT Exodus-Conquest narrative, but the hoped for result was similar.

In Matthew, Jesus continues John's ministry (3:2; cf. 4:17; 10:7; see also 14:2; 16:14),[121] at least in part, and the similarities of their prophetic actions are evident, even in Jesus' eating with sinners. Again, this is not to say that the specific actions themselves are the same; this is clearly not the case. But the function of such actions can be shown to be at least similar, if not more. In Matthew, both John and Jesus are concerned with communicating God's will as expressed in Israel's covenant and calling Israel back to fidelity to it (repentance). Jesus' eating with outsiders communicates a shocking element of God's will, namely the scope of who is included in the covenant, and is a call for others to join the meal, and to enact such meals, whether actually or metaphorically. John's baptism and criticism of the community leaders function in much the same way. The actions of the Baptist and Jesus' meal with sinners both also announce conditional

120. Webb rightly notes the caution we must take in advocating the meaning of such symbols. Webb, *John the Baptizer and Prophet*, 360–66. There is, of course, no "proof" that the above interpretation is correct, particularly in terms of the historical John that Webb seeks to study. In the context of Matthew, however, John appears as a character, not as an historical figure in his entirety. In Matthew's story we see numerous Exodus references leading up to chapter 3, and all we know about John in this chapter is his act of baptizing, his wilderness location, and his preaching. I believe the first two aspects of John's presentation, viewed in continuity with the previous scenes in Matthew, point strongly to the interpretation I have given above.

121. From a more historical Jesus-oriented view, Webb agrees, and this assumption forms part of the logic for undertaking his study of John the Baptist. See Webb, *John the Baptizer and Prophet*, 22–23, 383. Webb follows Sanders in his assertion of a Jewish eschatological line between John the Baptist and Paul (and the other apostles) on which we should locate Jesus. See Sanders, *Jesus and Judaism*, 8 (see also pp. 3–18, 91–95). For a detailed study of the question of the relationship between John and Jesus, see Dapaah, *Relationship Between John the Baptist*.

judgement on those who are unwilling to submit to God's will. In addition, both actions embody an announcement of God's deliverance.

This last point requires attention, since it raises an aspect of Jesus' prophetic vocation that is distinct from John and the other first-century prophetic figures. The deliverance to which these latter figures looked forward seems to amount to, at least in the case of the Samaritan and Egyptian prophets, the dramatic action of God to defeat their enemies, not unlike in stories involving Moses and Joshua. Judgement would come swiftly and it would lead to deliverance by direct intervention, though the prophet and his followers would participate. John the Baptist's hope for deliverance is somewhat similar in that he proclaims the coming of one who will baptize in fire and who will clear the threshing floor, separating the wheat and burning the chaff. This second image is found in the OT (e.g., Prov 20:26; Isa 18:4–5; 27:12–13; Jer 51:33; Mic 4:12–13) and other apocalyptic literature (e.g., 4 Ezra 4; 2 Bar 70:1–2). John, if we interpret him against the background of these traditions, implies that the time of eschatological judgement has arrived, and the Coming One will carry out finally the judgement that was promised. John's later confusion about Jesus (Matt 11:3) probably derives at least in part from the fact that his expectation about the nature of the Coming One's vocation has gone unmet.

John expects the one who comes after him to clear the threshing floor. The threshing metaphor for judgement is difficult, since the OT and apocalyptic traditions that utilize it are diverse in their understanding about how such judgement will be carried out. For example, Isa 18:4–5 has YHWH actively cutting down the unnamed enemy, yet Jer 51 seems to suggest that God's destruction of Babylon will occur at the hands of Babylon's enemies, that is, indirectly. Mic 4 has Israel doing the threshing, breaking "many nations to pieces," while Isa 27:12–13 has YHWH doing it, resulting in Israel being regathered to worship in Jerusalem. These options are not necessarily mutually exclusive, but they do reflect some divergence about the range of meanings understood from the metaphor. It may be that the metaphor was simply understood in a range of ways.

Whatever the case may be, the metaphor points to judgement. The fact that John's expectation about Jesus' role as the baptizer-in-fire and thresher has gone unmet suggests that his concept of divine deliverance conflicts with what Jesus actually does in Matthew's story. Though it would be interesting to analyze all the ways in which Jesus disappoints John's expectations in Matthew, in this chapter we can attend only to the present eating pericope and related points of interest. That Jesus disappoints John's expectations is not to say he subverts them entirely at every point. Certainly, as we have said, Jesus' inclusion of outsiders in his meal functions as a judgement against those who have not been invited. It is not immediately clear what form the judgement will take if the community leaders will not repent, though Matthew's later narrative, particularly chapter 23, gives a hint as to the socio-political ramifications of Israel's continued disobedience. Though it is not clear whether Jesus' prediction about Jerusalem's impending destruction is what John had in mind in regard to the coming judgement, it is true that both shared the view that judgement was coming and the vocation to announce it.

If John is indeed similar to the other first-century action prophets in seeing the positive aspects of God's coming deliverance as including the possession of the land currently occupied by foreigners and corrupt Israelites—a new conquest—then we must say that in this respect Jesus departs from such expectations. Later, Matthew will warn faithful Israelites to flee when the time of judgement arrives (24:15–22), a sure sign that those faithful to the covenant will not possess the land, nor participate in God's judgement. In Matt 9:9–13 deliverance takes on a different tone altogether. Liberation first consists in God's presence with those outcasts who have accepted Jesus' invitation to hospitality. Though we should take care when imbuing Matthew's theology with a post-Nicene concept of Jesus' divinity, his description of Jesus as Ἐμμανουήλ (1:23) signals that he sees Jesus as at least the embodiment of the presence of God in some sense.[122] Whatever the case may be, Emmanuel chooses to identify through the act of table fellowship with those who are outcasts. In fact, Matthew goes further than this. Emmanuel self-identifies as a metaphorical "physician" (9:12). Luz alludes to the implication of such identification: "physicians were suspect because they were often unclean."[123] Whether this is true in this case or not, it is clear that in Jesus God's presence makes its way among those thought to be outside the covenant. In a sense, the act of eating with sinners embodies the prophetic speech of the Beatitudes; the outcasts who accept Jesus' merciful invitation are declared to be honorable according to the convictions of the kingdom of heaven, even despite their dishonorable status in the world. As such, they will experience the liberating promises of the Beatitudes now, in the present, in the community formed around Jesus and embodying the values of the kingdom. Indeed, unlike John's notion of liberation that comes to those who will first repent, Jesus' liberation, like that proclaimed by many of

122. See Hagner, *Matthew 1–13*, 20–21, who notes the original Isaianic context of Matthew's quotation. On Matthew's Ἐμμανουήλ theme, see Kupp, *Matthew's Emmanuel*, 109–37.

123. Luz, *Matthew 8–20*, 33.

the OT prophets, precedes and makes possible the required repentance.[124] Jesus may enforce the covenant, but he does so as a "physician."

It is difficult to overstate the subversive nature of Jesus' act of eating with sinners, particularly in regard to the interpretation of Torah, a point supported by Jesus' use of Hos 6:6. By enacting the latent social implications of Hosea's radical interpretation of Torah, Jesus relocates the presence of God from the temple structure to the fellowship of those who would heed his invitation to eat with him, particularly when merciful reconciliation occurs (cf. 18:20). In this sense, what Jesus enacts in the meal is a crucial aspect of his program stated by Matthew in 1:21—he will save his people from their sins. As we discussed previously, this salvation is not simply religious or moral in nature, but rather relates to the whole existence of the person—personal, social, political, and so forth. Though this story may not deal specifically with every dimension of the person, there is a wide scope of personal and social maladies, those we have discussed throughout this chapter, which this meal challenges.

While it would be exegetically problematic to use the single episode found in Matt 9:9–13 as a full representation of Jesus' prophetic program of deliverance, the picture that emerges from it is remarkably distinct from the other prophets of the first century CE, including John. While we cannot say for sure from this single pericope that Jesus did not share their particular socio-political hopes, we can suggest that his prophetic message of deliverance involved elements beyond the mere ousting of Roman forces and the repossession of the land. Jesus' prophetic actions point to the renewal of people at a range of levels in accordance with God's will expressed in covenant. Matt 9:9–13 would seem to focus largely on the personal and communal aspects of such an existence.

5.8 Conclusion

Jesus' act of eating with sinners and tax collectors represents a powerful but often overlooked episode in his prophetic ministry. In sharing table fellowship with outcasts, Jesus redefines the boundaries of Israel in light of the coming kingdom, the kingdom he is inaugurating. In fact, his opening of the boundaries is itself an expression of the kingdom. Just as meals functioned to repair relationships between two parties, Jesus seeks to repair and reinforce relationships within Israel by redefining the boundaries of "in"

---

124. See Dempsey, "'Turn Back, O People,'" 47–66; Sprinkle, *Paul and Judaism Revisited*, 38–67.

and "out." Moreover, Jesus seeks to repair the relationship between Israel and YHWH and invite Israelites to repentance.

There are, of course, those who will not heed the prophet's call. Jesus proclaims judgement on them by his action since they are not found at the table, but rather insist on retaining their exclusionary practices that stem from a reading of Torah that gives precedence to the purity code. In announcing judgement on the leaders, Jesus continues the prophetic tradition of critiquing power in light of God's covenant with Israel. This is a powerful challenge to the status quo, a threat to the established order, but not for the sake of some revolution—it is the effect of the kingdom of heaven breaking into Israel's (and the world's) reality.

Jesus' prophetic act, combined with his quotation of Hos 6:6, reveals a significant aspect of his prophetic hermeneutic—like the prophets, Jesus calls on Israel to embody the mercy, the steadfast love, that they had been shown by YHWH, particularly at the exodus. In doing so, Jesus defines what righteousness according to Torah entails, namely, to show mercy. Certainly, it is not the kind of righteousness imagined by the Pharisees, or at least the Pharisees as presented by Matthew. Jesus' hermeneutic marks a fundamental point of departure between himself and his opponents.

Jesus as a prophet of Israel not only looks back to God's covenant with Israel as the defining gauge of Israel's present life, but also looks forward to the expected eschatological moment. In particular, his action alludes to the expectation of an eschatological banquet, a theme already raised in Matt 8:5–13. Jesus redefines his opponents' expectations about who will be included in this eschatological meal, and in doing so brings together the past, present, and future since the God who has relationship with Israel through the covenant instituted in the past will bring all things to completion in the future; the present moment is the task of living faithfully in between these moments, and in light of them.

Jesus' prophetic act in Matt 9:9–13 takes a form that is consistent with the OT prophets, in particular the provision-of-food tradition embodied by Moses, Elijah, and Elisha. Jesus makes use of a well-known ritual, that of table fellowship, dramatizing it and infusing it with new meaning in his context. In turning a commonplace symbol into a powerful sign of God's covenantal will and of the coming eschatological reality, Jesus is like the OT prophets, announcing God's covenantal will and calling Israel back to faithfulness to it. In fact, Jesus' call of Matthew in 9:9 exhibits the way in which his call to faithfulness is even more demanding than that of the OT prophets—in this case Elijah—and demonstrates his willingness both to adopt and to subvert various aspects of the prophetic traditions he inherits.

Jesus also exhibits some similarities with other first-century prophets, especially in their desire for divine liberation and judgement. However, Jesus' understanding and embodiment of what such liberation entails extends beyond the socio-political liberation from Rome sought by many of his contemporaries. Jesus' call to covenant includes the renewal of all aspects of life, not only those national dimensions but also the personal and communal. As such, it embodies a much fuller notion of covenantal existence.

In short, what we see from this episode is that Jesus is firmly rooted in the Jewish prophetic tradition, but in a new situation that is distinct from that of the OT prophets. Like his predecessors, Jesus was

> a prophet like the prophets of old, coming to Israel with a word from her covenant god, warning her of the imminent and fearful consequences of the direction she was travelling, urging and summoning her to a new and different way.[125]

Jesus, through a dramatic and subversive use of an everyday act, revealed that he was among the prophets of Israel. But for Matthew, Jesus was also bringing the imagination of the prophets to life in a new situation of impending national disaster. Like the prophets, he called for renewed righteousness; in Matt 9:9–13 we see that this righteousness necessitates imitating God's mercy. Summoning Israel to such covenantal fidelity meant Jesus was thrust into conflict with the nation's leaders. There would come a time when embodying the will of YHWH would lead him into even more direct confrontation with them. To such a time we now turn.

---

125. Wright, *Jesus and the Victory of God*, 163. Wright is of course describing the historical Jesus rather than the Matthean Jesus, though based on what has been discussed in this part of the study, Wright's description applies *mutatis mutandis* to Matthew's portrayal.

Chapter 6

Jesus' Temple Action in Matthew as Prophetic Action

THE MEANING OF JESUS' temple action[1] in Matt 21:12–17 has, in recent decades, proven to be highly contested amongst biblical scholars. The precise problem that Jesus was confronting is disputed, as is Jesus' intention for his action. Indeed, the very historicity of the episode is debated, and no interpretive approach seems to enjoy clear majority support.

It is with some diffidence then—given the sheer volume of material that has been produced—that we turn to the temple episode. It is perhaps the most predictable story to which we will turn our attention in terms of studying Jesus' prophetic vocation in Matthew, though such predictability is most likely a sign of the degree to which Jesus' temple action is considered "prophetic." And rightly so: Matthew seems to make a point of transitioning to this pericope with a brief interlude in which the city of Jerusalem is asking of Jesus, "Who is this?" The answer received is concise: "This is the prophet Jesus, from Nazareth of Galilee" (Matt 21:10–11).

We begin this chapter by briefly surveying the competing approaches to this story. This will allow us to appreciate some of the key works on the subject, and also make some methodological remarks about how my own approach will proceed. From that point we will begin to consider in greater depth Matthew's narrative account of Jesus' dramatic temple action.

---

1. I have chosen to avoid the traditional phrase "cleansing of the Temple," opting instead for the more generic term "Temple action." In avoiding the traditional label, I am agreeing with Bauckham: "In the first place, [the term 'cleansing of the Temple'] may suggest that Jesus' concern was with the ritual purity of the Temple. . . . But, secondly, the term suggests that Jesus actually accomplished a purification of the Temple, whereas most recent treatments of the episode recognize that Jesus could have intended only a symbolic action, a kind of prophetic 'demonstration.'" Bauckham, "Jesus' Demonstration in the Temple," 72.

6.1 Interpretive Approaches to Jesus' Temple Action

Some scholars have helpfully attempted to set out a survey of approaches to Jesus' temple action. Thomas Yoder Neufeld lists six approaches,[2] while Klyne Snodgrass has seven.[3] Combined, they variously insist that the temple action represented:

1. A purification of the temple's profanation by corrupt commerce

2. A condemnation of the temple hierarchy for systemic economic oppression/violence

3. Divine judgment for the temple's role as symbol of violent resistance to Rome (Yoder Neufeld)

4. Anticipation of the temple's destruction as part of the imminent advent of God's reign

5. Divine destruction because the temple's mediating role conflicted with Jesus' view that people could enjoy unmediated access to God (Yoder Neufeld)

6. An act of violence contributing to the achievement of dominance

7. A symbolic objection to distinguish between holy and profane (Snodgrass)

8. An attack on the sacrificial system (Snodgrass)

9. A prophetic protest pointing to eschatological hope (Snodgrass)

Here we begin to see various spectra—whose poles are the various dichotomies in scholarly opinion—on which almost all of the above views fall. The first relates to the apparent intention of Jesus' action. Some approaches point to purification of some kind as the primary aim, others indicate that Jesus' act was a symbol of coming destruction.[4] This is the spectrum posited by Wright (the poles being "cleansing" and "acted parable of destruction").[5] The second and related spectrum relates to the problem being confronted by Jesus' action, between some kind of corruption on the one hand, and nationalism on the other.

---

2. Yoder Neufeld, *Killing Enmity*, 62–65.

3. Snodgrass, "Temple Incident," 429–80.

4. The notable exception is the view that Jesus' act was one of violence seeking some form of dominance. This is the view expressed by Glancy, "Violence as Sign in the Fourth Gospel," 100–117.

5. Wright, *Jesus and the Victory of God*, 413.

A third spectrum—eschatological/non-eschatological referents—is highlighted by Perrin's survey, which is organized in a way that brings eschatology to the fore as the dominant typological category.[6] Perrin notes that this spectrum is related to the one first mentioned above (purification/destruction), with non-eschatological approaches being related to purification of the temple, and eschatological approaches related to its impending destruction (or redundancy). Perrin's survey is as follows:

Non-eschatological approaches ("cleansing"/reform of abuse in the temple)

1. Protest against shady business practices occurring in the temple[7]

2. Protest against practices compromising the temple's cultic purity[8]

3. Confrontation against connection between holiness and Jewish militancy[9]

4. Precursor to Jesus starting a military revolution[10]

Eschatological Approaches (declaring salvation-historical crisis point, redundancy, or imminent destruction of the temple)

1. Signifying the removal of the present temple as preliminary to establishment of eschatological temple/kingdom of God[11]

2. Declaring the time for the gentiles to come to Zion had arrived[12]

---

6. Perrin, *Jesus the Temple*, 88–91. Perrin is adamant that, though his survey is organized by a dichotomy between eschatological and non-eschatological readings, this is only for convenience, and the dichotomy is false—"the pitting of an eschatological reading of the Temple event against a non-eschatological reading ceases to do full justice to either."

7. Hengel, *Was Jesus a Revolutionist?*, 15–16; Bauckham, "Jesus' Demonstration in the Temple"; Hooker, "Traditions About the Temple," 7–19.

8. Jeremias, *New Testament Theology*, 145, 219n92; Meyer, *Christus Faber*, 263–64; Richardson, "Why Turn the Tables?," 507–23; Betz, "Jesus and the Purity of the Temple," 455–72; Casey, "Culture and Historicity," 306–32.

9. Borg, *Conflict, Holiness, and Politics*, 181–89; Buchanan, "Symbolic Money-Changers in the Temple," 280–90.

10. Brandon, *Jesus and the Zealots*, 332–34; Horsley, *Jesus and the Spiral of Violence*, 297–300.

11. Sanders, *Jesus and Judaism*, 61–70; Fredriksen, "Jesus and the Temple," 293–310; Fredriksen, "Historical Jesus," 249–76; Meyer, *Christus Faber*, 262–63.

12. Jeremias, *Jesus' Promise to the Nations*, 65–66; Dunn, *Partings of the Ways*, 62–64.

3. Declaring the cessation and imminent transcendence of the temple cult[13]

4. Self-declaration of Jesus' messiahship, as fulfillment of Scripture, or by virtue of implying authority over the temple, or as self-designation as new sin offering[14]

Perrin's own view is that Jesus' temple action was a prophetic condemnation of the fiscal abuse that had come to characterize the temple administration, as well as a sign of his own role as (re)builder of the eschatological temple.[15] This is worth noting, since Perrin's view implies that it is possible for the view that Jesus was calling for reform to be reconciled with the view that he was proclaiming the temple's destruction, that is, for non-eschatological and eschatological views to complement one another.[16]

There are no doubt options available that fit neatly into neither the spectra nor the surveys mentioned here. However, our purpose here is not to give an exhaustive list of approaches, but to give an indication of the kinds of readings that tend to vie for our assent. Similarly, it is not our purpose here to offer our own typology of possible readings. Further, it is worth pointing out that many readings of this story are related to the study of the historical Jesus and this is not our area of concern.[17] We are focused on Matthew's presentation of the story and its meaning within his narrative, not with an objective notion of what might have *actually* happened, if they can even be neatly separated. Still, these approaches are relevant to our study since historical Jesus research still uses the Synoptics as source material and thus the approaches are rooted in the Gospels' accounts of the episode. They are, then, helpful for orienting us to the episode in light of historical scholarship. Which approach then, if any, is that of the implied author in Matthew? We must of course turn to the text to find out.

13. Neusner, "Money-Changers in the Temple," 287–90; Crossan, *Historical Jesus*, 357–58; Chilton, *Temple of Jesus*, 121–36.

14. Witherington, *Christology of Jesus*, 111–15; Wright, *Jesus and the Victory of God*, 490–93; Ådna, "Jesus' Symbolic Act in the Temple," 461–76; Ådna, *Jesu Stellung zum Tempel*, 335–76.

15. Perrin, *Jesus the Temple*, 92.

16. Keener agrees when he suggests that "prophecies of [the Temple's] destruction typically rested on the view that it had already been defiled (cf. 23:38; 24:15)." Keener, *Gospel of Matthew*, 499.

17. For example, Borg, Chilton, Crossan, Horsley, Perrin, Sanders, Wright. Glancy's work is focused on John's version of the story.

6.2 The Narrative Context of Jesus' Temple Action
in Matthew

Following Matt 9, we find Jesus' second teaching block (his so-called "Mission Discourse," 10:1—11:1) in which he calls his twelve disciples—whose number indicates his identification with and intention to restore Israel—and sends them out having taught them regarding his mission. This mission will inevitably bring persecution (10:16–25) and enmity (10:34–39), as well as danger, such that fear is apparently an expected response that requires addressing (10:26–33).

In Matt 11:2–30 the text shifts in tone from the preceding chapters. Previously the reception of Jesus' ministry had been overwhelmingly positive, with the exception of the criticism of the Pharisees in 9:34. But from Matt 11:2 onwards, and especially from 12:1, confusion and conflict begin to develop. In Matt 11:20–24, we are given the information that some cities have rejected Jesus and by 12:14 the Pharisees have already set out to conspire against him (ὅπως αὐτὸν ἀπολέσωσιν) after Jesus' critical response to their challenge regarding eating lawfully on the Sabbath. Such contests recur throughout Matthew until the time Jesus enters Jerusalem (e.g., 12:22–32; 15:1–9; 16:1–4; 19:3–9). Up until Matt 16:12, Jesus' ministry remains in Galilee and its surroundings as he reveals the kingdom in different ways in word and deed and continues to instruct his disciples. This section includes his third teaching block (13:1–52) in which Jesus explains the rejection of his ministry by some. This is followed by Jesus' rejection in his hometown (13:53–58).

Matthew 16:13–28 marks another major shift in the narrative, bridging the sections about Jesus' ministry in Galilee with those about his journey to Jerusalem. Matthew 16:13–28 itself is the well-known passage in which Jesus' messianic identity is proclaimed by Peter and Jesus reveals its true meaning and outcome, namely confrontation with the authorities in Jerusalem, death, and resurrection. Peter's rebuke provides the narrative opportunity to have Jesus explain the true nature of discipleship—taking up one's cross.

All of this paints the picture of what will occur during the remainder of Matthew's story. Within Matt 17:1–20:34, Jesus travels with his disciples toward Jerusalem, teaching them about life in the kingdom, particularly in his fourth teaching block (Matthew 18). On this journey, Jesus also faces ongoing challenges from the community leaders (19:1–12), as well as requests from others (19:16–30; 20:20–28, 29–34). He also continues to speak about his impending death and resurrection (17:22–23; 20:17–19).

When Jesus reaches Jerusalem, the stage has already been set for confrontation. Matthew 21:1–17 transitions the story from being set outside of

Jerusalem to inside the city and, according to Weren's structure for Matthew that we have adopted, this double pericope functions as a narrative hinge.[18] This hinge bridges the narrative sections detailing the increasingly tense aftermath of Jesus' cruciform explanation of his vocation (16:13—20:34) with Jesus' judgements against Jerusalem and the events leading to his death (21:18—25:46). We should expect that 21:1-17 would help us make sense of the combative events that surround it. Given the importance of Jerusalem throughout Scripture, especially for the prophets, it ought not surprise us that Jesus' dramatic entrance to the city is narratively significant. As Matthew depicts it, Jesus' final act prior to entering the city (21:1-9) is self-consciously prophetic. The story contains manifold layers of meaning and, though we cannot go into great depth, we can at least say that Jesus adopts elements of Graeco-Roman processions and subverts them in accordance with the prophetic hope, found especially in Zech 9-14, of God entering Jerusalem in victory over the nations.[19] That the story ought to be read in light of Zechariah is confirmed by Matthew's quotation of Zech 9:9 (21:5). Within Matthew's unfolding story it would appear that Jesus' procession on a donkey, rather than a war horse, expresses his coming peacefully to the city.[20] This provides a lens through which to interpret the meaning of his identity as the Son of David, which had been ascribed to him only a few verses earlier (20:31; cf. 1 Kgs 1:32-40). In short, Jesus' prophetic action subverts both pagan notions of kingship and Israel's expectations regarding God's victory over the nations.

A prophetic lens is, of course, not the only one through which this story could or should be read. This prophetic lens is merely our focus in this study. In light of the cues provided by Matthew, Jesus' procession ought to be understood also as a kingly act, symbolizing a royal claim. Such a messianic claim is a sign that the kingdom of heaven is imminent. We should note, too, that Jesus' kingship is characterized by symbols of peace. This is in contrast to the crowds who lay down branches on the road (21:8), a symbol probably alluding to the Maccabean period when palm branches were used in celebration of military victory (1 Macc 13:51; 2 Macc 10:7).[21] The crowds

18. Weren, "Macrostructure of Matthew's Gospel," 171-200 (esp. 200).

19. Carter, *Matthew and the Margins*, 414.

20. Hagner, *Matthew 14-28*, 594. See also Luz, *Matthew 21-28*, 7-8; "[T]he Messiah of Zech 9:9-10 does not mount a horse; instead, he will abolish war chariots and weapons and bring peace to the nations. . . . That Jesus rides on a donkey is to be understood as an expression of his kindness, peaceableness, and gentleness."

21. Regev, *Hasmoneans: Ideology, Archaeology, Identity*, 210. Beale and McDonough, speaking of Rev 7:9, note that palm branches alluded to the Feast of Tabernacles, where Israel thanked God for the fruitfulness of their crops (occurring at the

correctly recognize the meaning of Jesus' procession—he is king!—but are mistaken as to the nature of his kingship.

The implications of such an event are difficult to overstate. It is no surprise that, in response to the procession, the whole city is stirred up in a fashion similar to its earlier agitation in 2:3—they correctly recognize the political implications of Jesus' prophetic drama. Having entered the city, Jesus' first act is to enter the temple and this leads us to the episode in focus in the present chapter.

6.3 The Temple in the First Century CE

It is important in this study to give primacy to Matthew's narrative for interpreting the Matthean account of Jesus' temple action. This is for two reasons: (1) our knowledge of this episode is reliant on the Gospel narratives; and (2) I am interested in Matthew's account of this event, not a hypothetical historical reconstruction. Still, as I have maintained, historical data is vital for the interpretation of narrative, particularly narrative written or set in periods distant from that of the interpreter. To understand the significance of a narrative event, it is crucial to understand the historical phenomena that give meaning to that narrative. For this reason, it is important to turn our attention to the temple in the first century CE—to understand Jesus' action in the temple, we must understand the nature and meaning of the temple itself within the context of first-century Palestine. We cannot possibly hope to explore this topic in anything but a cursory fashion, but we must take time to outline some points relevant to this study.

N.T. Wright states straightforwardly, "The Temple was the focal point of every aspect of Jewish national life."[22] He notes three aspects of the temple and its significance that deserve special attention: "the presence of YHWH, the sacrificial system, and the Temple's political significance."[23] In terms of the first aspect, Carol Meyers describes YHWH's presence in the temple in this way:

> The Temple in conception was a dwelling place on earth for the deity of ancient Israel . . . The symbolic nature of the Jerusalem

---

end of the harvest) and, more relevantly for us, commemorated divine protection in the wilderness following the exodus. This latter dimension reminded the people of God's victory over the Egyptians. The authors note that in 1 Macc 13:51 and 2 Macc 10:7, as in Philo, *Alleg. Interp.* 3.74, palm branches signify victory over an enemy. Beale and McDonough, "Revelation," 1108.

22. Wright, *New Testament*, 224.

23. Wright, *Jesus and the Victory of God*, 406–7.

Temple . . . depended upon a series of features that, taken together, established the sacred precinct as being located at the
cosmic center of the universe, at the place where heaven and
earth converge and thus from where God's control over the universe is effected.[24]

The notion that the temple was the dwelling place of YHWH, indeed the
center of the cosmos, set Israel apart from other nations.

That the temple was also the place of sacrifice meant that it was the
focal point of the relationship between YHWH and humanity. Through sin
offerings, the sin of the people was dealt with that they might experience
purification and forgiveness. More than that, other regular sacrifices such
as the burnt offerings and peace offerings provided regular expressions of
celebrating YHWH's presence with the people. Such sacrifices went beyond
mere functional processes in the present—the existence of sacrifices was connected, at least for some, to the eschatological hope of Israel. Indeed, sacrifices would be present in the eschatological temple envisioned by Ezekiel
(Ezek 40–48, esp. 44:15–31). If this was an image of YHWH's glorious future
for Israel, nay for the world, then sacrifice in the present was an institution
ontologically connected to the *telos* of creation itself.[25] Again, Jesus' action has
consequences for this worldview that will be explored below.

Wright's third point—that the temple had political significance—has
extensive implications. To suggest the temple was Israel's religious center
is problematic because of the implications of "religion" in our contemporary age, particularly the way moderns define "religion" as separate from
"politics" ("sacred" and "secular").[26] But such a distinction would be foreign
to Matthew's world. The Jerusalem temple was indeed a "religious" center,
but it was also a center for governing and for commercial interests.[27] The
high priest was a governing figure as well as a "religious" figure, as the NT
(including Matthew, esp. 26:57–67) reflects with regard to Caiaphas. The
temple had also been rebuilt by Herod,[28] much to the dissatisfaction of
some groups since it was a reflection of Herod's control over the priestly

24. Carol Meyers, "Temple, Jersualem," *ABD* 6:351–59.

25. Even for groups like the Essenes who rejected the post-Maccabean temple as
corrupt, sacrifice was still connected to eschatological hope since they believed a new
temple would one day stand, unblemished and to the correct specifications (4QFlor
6–7). See Mathews, "John, Jesus and the Essenes," 111.

26. For an excellent overview of "religion" in the first-century Mediterranean world,
see Wright, *Paul and the Faithfulness of God*, 1:246–78.

27. Jeremias, *Jerusalem in the Time of Jesus*, 21–27, provides an overview of some of
the commercial life of the temple.

28. Josephus, *Ant.* 15.380–425.

bureaucracy.[29] Such an act and the fierce antagonism it produced further reflect the politicized nature of the temple.

The commercial nature of the temple should not be thought to be unique or shocking, as if Jesus' action stemmed from the disillusionment of having realized that trading occurred within it. After all, economic activity was a regular aspect of just about every cult in the first-century world,[30] probably including synagogues in Galilee.[31] In the context of the Jerusalem temple, commercial activity was an accepted practice as moneychangers and merchants provided important services,[32] including providing animals and firewood for sacrifice, washing priestly vestments, and currency exchange. The temple also functioned as a bank, as demonstrated by the fact that the Roman procurator of Judea, Florus, seized seventeen talents from the temple treasury (Josephus, J.W. 2.293). Moreover, as the NT makes clear, taxes were collected through the temple institution, and Josephus informs us that debt records were apparently kept there.[33] Commercial activity in the temple was such that Martin Goodman refers to it as an "industry."[34]

Though commercial activity in the temple was normal, this did not mean that all was well with such arrangements. Much of the peasantry apparently regarded the temple as somehow corrupt or oppressive,[35] as reflected in the fact that among the first acts to be committed when insurrectionists overtook the temple in 66 CE was the burning of the debt records.[36] This act probably resulted from the elites' use of the temple institution for their own

29. For other ways in which Herod ruled the high priesthood, see Schwartz, "One Temple and Many Synagogues," 389–91.

30. See Kraybill, *Imperial Cult and Commerce in John's Apocalypse*, 134, for a discussion of temple banks and the presence of temples in places of commerce.

31. See Saldarini, *Pharisees, Scribes, and Sadducees in Palestinian Society*, 52–53, who argues that "[in Palestinian villages] it is likely that the town assembly for business and celebration was coextensive with the assembly for prayer on Sabbath and feasts (the synagogue). It probably met in the town square, in the courtyard or room of a large house or in the town assembly building rather than in a building dedicated exclusively to public worship . . . The same prominent and (more or less) learned leaders who directed the community probably led the synagogue since political and religious society were one." For Saldarini, "This makes more understandable the opposition to Jesus, the outsider, by Jewish village leaders who saw him as a threat to their social position and disruptive of their traditional way of life."

32. See *t. Ketub.* 13:20; cf. Exod 30:11–16.

33. Josephus, J.W. 2.427.

34. Goodman, "First Jewish Revolt," 417–27.

35. See Evans, "Jesus' Action in the Temple," 319–44.

36. Josephus, J.W. 2.427. On the possibly symbolic and manipulative nature of this act, see Goodman, *Ruling Class of Judaea*, 154.

economic gain, especially through the *prosbul*.[37] Joachim Jeremias claims that the high-priestly family owned shops in the temple area[38] and Josephus referred to the high priest Ananias (47–c. 55 CE) as "a great procurer of money" (ἦν γὰρ χρημάτων ποριστικός).[39] Jeremias adds that, according to *t. Menah.* 13:22, "The Temple was said to be going to rack and ruin because of avarice and mutual hatred."[40] There is also evidence that the poor found the burden of taxation to be excessive.[41] It appears that the wealthy and their retainers had twisted the temple into an institution that served their own financial interests, such that Herzog can say:

> The temple was . . . at the very heart of the system of economic exploitation made possible by the monetizing of the economy and the concentration of wealth made possible by investing the temple and its leaders with the powers and rewards of a collaborating aristocracy.[42]

We can see how such a situation would lead to conflict. Indeed, popular outcry occurred at different times (e.g., Josephus, *J.W.* 1.524; 2.84–92; *Ant.* 17.304–10, 342–44). After all, what was at stake for many among the peasantry was not merely some capital lost to taxation, but their participation in the food economy—their very survival. Even apart from the corruption present within the temple system, the very fact of the temple itself was a symbol of economic oppression—Herod's rebuilding project required funding and much of it was found by way of land taxes.[43]

Outcry related to the temple was not limited to financial matters. Both the temple priesthood and the Herodian dynasty collaborated with Rome and many groups viewed this as a compromise, one that resulted in periodical

---

37. See Adams, *Social and Economic Life in Second Temple Judea*, 113, who describes the *prosbul* as an institutional body, arising during the Roman period, that "allowed creditors to seek repayment of debts, even during the Sabbatical Year, with the support of the judicial system." Such a system allowed the lender to sidestep the legislation in Deut 15:3.

38. Jeremias, *Jerusalem*, 49.

39. Josephus, *Ant.* 20.205.

40. Jeremias, *Jerusalem*, 49.

41. Josephus notes that under Herod the Great, taxation was significant: "As his expenses were beyond his abilities, he was compelled to be harsh to his subjects." Josephus, *Ant.* 16.154. Tacitus notes that in 17 CE the provinces of Syria and Judea begged for relief from overly burdensome taxation. Tacitus, *Ann.* 2.42. We could also point to the episode of the widow in Mark 12:41–44 as an illustration of the effect exploitative taxation occurring at the hands of the temple authorities.

42. Herzog, *Jesus, Justice, and the Reign of God*, 137.

43. Josephus, *Ant.* 15.109.

conflict. This is well illustrated by an episode in which Herod placed a golden eagle over the gate of the temple—a sign of Roman power—and it was cut down by a group of young men influenced by two teachers of the law, the pair of whom were burnt alive as punishment.[44] The temple had, for many, become a symbol of political and ideological compromise with the imperial occupiers, as well as being an economically oppressive institution.

It is also worth noting that access to the temple was hierarchical. This is described in some detail by Josephus (*Ag. Ap.* 2.102–9):

> All who ever saw our temple are aware of the general design of the building, and the inviolable barriers which preserved its sanctity. It had four surrounding courts, each with its special statutory restrictions. The outer court was open to all, foreigners included; women during their impurity were alone refused admission. To the second court all Jews were admitted and, when uncontaminated by any defilement, their wives; to the third male Jews, if clean and purified; to the fourth the priests robed in their priestly vestments. The sanctuary was entered only by the high-priests, clad in the raiment peculiar to themselves.[45]

This hierarchy of access was not simply a practical or professional exclusion, as if limited access to the sanctuary was the equivalent of a "Staff Only" sign. We must remember that the sanctuary was deemed the center of the cosmos, the place where heaven and earth met. A hierarchy of access was, in effect, a grading of identities and their relation to the divine. The stratification of value along class, gender, and ethnic lines no doubt had both theological and sociological implications, not least ideological support for ongoing nationalism and aristocratic dominance.

Such a cursory outline of the temple in and around the first century CE gives us a glimpse of some of the theological, liturgical, sociological, political, and economic aspects at play. The many problems inherent in the temple system led to conflict in the first century CE, but this was not an unprecedented reality. There was, of course, a tradition of temple critique, stretching back to the OT prophets.

6.4 Prophetic Critiques of the Temple

Critiques of the first temple are present throughout the prophetic corpus of the OT. Such critiques accompany a broader pattern of prophetic

44. Josephus, *Ant.* 17.148–67.
45. Josephus, *Ag. Ap.* 2.102–5a.

denunciation of socioeconomic sin. This is not to say that the prophetic treatment of the temple is uniformly negative. The prophets often speak positively of the temple, even if only implicitly, either in its contemporary form, in the abstract, or in an eschatological sense (e.g., Isa 18:7; 24:23; 44:28; 66:6; Jer 50:28; 51:11; Ezek 40–48; Mic 1:2; Hab 2:20; Hag 1:1–2:9; Zech 6:12–15; Mal 3:1).

But some prophets who at times speak positively of the temple, such as Jeremiah and Ezekiel, also dispense harsh criticism against it. Jeremiah's so-called "Temple sermon" (7:1–34) typifies this critique. Here the prophet is not concerned with any inherent problem with the temple. Rather, he rails against self-deception that is based on the presumption of YHWH's favor, which exists because of the guarantee provided by the presence of the temple.[46] Jeremiah seems to suggest his hearers took the temple as evidence for God's unqualified support: "Do not trust in these deceptive words: 'This is the temple of the Lord, the temple of the Lord, the temple of the Lord'" (7:4). The pretension of unconditional divine favor—a distorted doctrine of election—allows the people to waive their covenantal obligations and so they forego justice within Israel, as well as for refugees, orphans, and widows whilst shedding innocent blood and committing idolatry (7:5–7). The people's belief in unreserved deliverance also allows them to violate other covenantal laws (7:8–10). For Jeremiah, there is a connection between loyalty to the temple and the injustice he names.[47] It is in this context that Jeremiah accuses his hearers of making the temple a "den of robbers" (7:11), an accusation that Jesus will echo in his temple action[48] and that we will further discuss below. Because of the evil that has been named, Jeremiah proclaims impending judgement on the temple and the people. "Jeremiah insisted that the Temple did not ensure that Yahweh would bless the community";[49] on the contrary, obeying YHWH's voice and call is the prerequisite for the deuteronomistic blessing of living in the land (Jer 7:5–7, 13). Jeremiah does not outline concern for the purity of the temple system *per se*, but rather for the broader covenantal life of the community, especially in social and economic terms, as well as fidelity of worship.

---

46. "Israel could feel itself so sure of the immanent presence of Yahweh that it forgot his transcendent lordship. That this danger did in fact have a deep and harmful effect on the popular attitude of Israel is evidenced by the criticism of Israel's worship made by the prophets." Clements, *God and Temple*, 79.

47. Grimsrud, *Instead of Atonement*, 135.

48. For other citations and allusions to Jer 7:11 amongst Jews and Christians in subsequent centuries, see Ferda, "Jeremiah 7 and Flavius Josephus," 158–73 (esp. 158–59).

49. Grimsrud, *Instead of Atonement*, 135.

Ezekiel also, for reasons similar to Jeremiah, critiques Israel and its temple in Ezek 8–11. He refers to the "great abominations that the house of Israel are committing" in the temple (8:6). This is connected with Israel's idolatry (8:5–18), violence (8:17), and, more generally, the nation's failure to walk in YHWH's statutes, behaving instead as do the nations surrounding them (11:12). The worship of Tammuz (8:14), the Sumerian deity embraced by the Babylonians, is probably a symptom of Babylonian vassalage and thus of foreign domination, a situation somewhat comparable to that of Israel in the first century CE. Whatever the case, it appears that in Ezekiel's account, unlike in Jeremiah's, the people have assumed that "The Lord does not see us, the Lord has forsaken the land" (8:12b).[50] Surprisingly, it is the *prophet* who must announce that the glory of YHWH remains present in the temple (8:4). However, the judgement Ezekiel announces declares that YHWH will indeed leave the temple (10:18). Though Ezekiel's prophecy seems to assume different attitudes in the community with regard to Israel's election than does Jeremiah's, both posit that judgement is at hand because of Israel's covenant infidelity in the form of idolatry and social sin. For Ezekiel, the problem with the temple is not that it reinforces a false sense of divine favor, but that it has become an epicenter for Israel's idolatry and capitulation to Babylon, which according to the prophet has profound social implications. Like Jeremiah, Ezekiel does not think there is an inherent problem with the temple, nor is he concerned with the purity of the temple system for its own sake. Rather, like Jeremiah, Ezekiel is concerned with the broader covenantal faithfulness of the community.

For both Jeremiah and Ezekiel, criticism of the temple expresses their broader prophetic vocation in a context of crisis that is publicly denied or ignored. Brueggemann summarizes the task of the prophet in such "numbed" situations as having three parts:[51]

1. To offer symbols that are adequate to confront the horror and massiveness of the experience that evokes numbness and requires denial.

2. To bring to public expression those very fears and terrors that have been denied and suppressed.

---

50. According to Block, people in the ancient Near Eastern region had already established a motif of divine abandonment dating back at least to Sumerian times. In some cases, foreign invaders used this motif to portray that the god of the defenders had fled in submission to the superior god of the invaders. The god might also abandon the temple city because of social maladies or failure to meet worship obligations. Sometimes the god would turn against the city and become its enemy. See Block, *Book of Ezekiel*, 275–76; Block, *Gods of the Nations*, 113–47.

51. Brueggemann, *Prophetic Imagination*, 45–46.

3. To speak metaphorically but concretely about the "deathliness" that hovers over and gnaws within communities.

Brueggemann goes on to say of Jeremiah that the prophet is "frequently misunderstood as a doomsday spokesman or a pitiful man who had a grudge and sat around crying."[52] But, Brueggemann notes, Jeremiah's grief served another purpose, namely to embody an alternative consciousness, one that knows what others refuse to know and articulates what others refuse to acknowledge.[53] This is a helpful summary of the prophetic vocation generally, but also specifically in relation to prophetic criticism of the temple. What the prophets "know" is not primarily that the temple will come under judgement for Israel's sin—though that is true—but rather that YHWH was not known through or because of the temple but through YHWH's faithfulness to Israel and call to covenantal relationship. Hence Jeremiah's reiteration of the fact that YHWH brought Israel out of Egypt and commanded them not to make sacrifices but to obey "that it may be well with [them]" (Jer 7:22–23). Likewise, Ezekiel's declaration of YHWH's faithfulness to Israel, even in exile, and the promise to gather Israel, replacing their heart of stone with one of flesh that they may walk in YHWH's statutes (Ezek 11:16–20).

6.5 Other Critiques of the Temple

Though prophetic critiques of the Solomonic temple are of great importance to our study, it is also the case that criticism of the second temple, particularly its leaders, is also found among first- and second-century texts.

We begin with Josephus since he appears consciously to view the events of 66–73 CE through the lens of Jeremiah, including the temple sermon (Jer 7:1–34).[54] For example, Josephus quotes Jeremiah within his reporting of the words of the prophet Jesus ben Ananias:[55]

> A voice from the east, a voice from the west, a voice from the four winds; a voice against Jerusalem and the sanctuary, a voice against the bridegroom and the bride [φωνὴ ἐπὶ νυμφίους καὶ νύμφας], a voice against all the people.[56]

52. Brueggemann, *Prophetic Imagination*, 46–47.
53. Brueggemann, *Prophetic Imagination*, 47.
54. This is the convincing case made by Ferda, "Jeremiah 7," 158–73.
55. Ferda, "Jeremiah 7," 166–67.
56. Josephus, *J.W.* 6.301.

> And I will bring to an end the sound of mirth and gladness,
> the voice of the bride and bridegroom [LXX: φωνὴν νυμφίου
> καὶ φωνὴν νύμφης] in the cities of Judah and in the streets of
> Jerusalem; for the land shall become a waste. (Jer 7:34)

Both prophets are speaking about the impending destruction of Jerusalem, including the temple. Josephus writes approvingly of Jesus' prophecies and prophetic role, including his judgement against the temple, his antagonizing of its leaders, and his subversion of the Feast of the Tabernacles (*J. W.* 6.300). Jesus' apparent choice to begin his oracles during the feast was a challenge to Israel's trust in God's unconditional provision and protection—as was Jeremiah's temple sermon—since the feast celebrated God's provision and faithfulness in the harvest and divine protection and victory in Israel's history.[57]

Josephus believes Jeremiah had predicted not only the fall of the temple in the prophet's own day, but also in the first century CE as well (*Ant.* 10.79–80). Josephus also takes on a Jeremian persona, condemning his contemporaries in light of his deuteronomistic theology, one he has in common with Jeremiah. This persona is also exhibited when Josephus, addressing the rebels at the walls of Jerusalem (*J. W.* 5.348–419), appeals to Jeremiah's judgements regarding transgressions and compares them to the current situation (5.391–93). Like Jeremiah's temple sermon, Josephus' case against the rebels includes the shedding of innocent blood (*J. W.* 5.382; cf. Jer 7:6–7), theft, murder, and adultery (5.402; cf. Jer 7:9) such that the temple has "become the receptacle for all" (5.402; cf. Jer 7:11).[58] Indeed, according to Josephus, the rebels "transfer their brigands' exploits from the country[side] . . . to the Temple" (*J. W.* 4.261), such that it has become their "base and refuge, the magazine for their armament against us; and the spot which is revered by the world and honored by aliens from the ends of the earth who have heard its fame, is trampled on by these monsters engendered in this very

---

57. It is worth noting a possible connection here between Jesus son of Ananias and Matthew's Jesus: Jesus son of Ananias prophesies during the Feast of the Tabernacles, subverting its meaning, while Matthew's Jesus enters Jerusalem to a display of branches laid on the road (Matt 21:1–11). Beale and McDonough note that palm branches alluded to the Feast of Tabernacles and its commemoration of God's protection in the wilderness: Beale and McDonough, "Revelation," 1108. It is possible, though not certain, that both Jesuses are, in their own ways, subverting the notion of divine protection encapsulated in the Feast of the Tabernacles.

58. Ferda, "Jeremiah 7," 169. Ferda goes into greater depth about the formal and literary similarities between *J. W.* 5.381–414 and Jer 7 than we are able to manage here. That Josephus has Jeremiah 7 in mind when writing this passage is suggested by the fact that "The mention of 'adulteries' is conspicuous since he uses that term nowhere else in descriptions of revolutionary activity" (Ferda, "Jeremiah 7," 170).

place" (*J.W.* 4.262). The rebels, according to Josephus, believe they will be saved because they reside in the temple (*J.W.* 5.459, 564; 6.98–100), another allusion to Jeremiah's critique of Israel's temple ideology.[59]

Speaking more generally, Josephus notes that during the 50s and 60s of the first century CE, the high priests committed theft and violence (*Ant.* 20.181, 206–7).[60] This is similar to some post-70 CE pseudepigraphic texts that blame Israel's sin for the temple's demise (*Lad. Jac.* 5.8–9; *Apoc. Ab.* 17.7; *L.A.B.* 19.6–7; *4 Bar.* 1.1, 8; 4.4–5; *Sib. Or.* 4.115–18), in some cases even accusing the priesthood itself (in an interpolation following *L.A.E.* 29.3 in several manuscripts[61]; *2 Bar.* 10.18).[62] In one case, *T. Mos.* 7, likely written around 30 CE,[63] the author speaks of "destructive and godless men, who represent themselves as righteous," but who are deceitful, false, devouring, and gluttonous.[64] These men are said to consume the goods of the poor, though they claim their criminal deeds are according to justice, and they touch impure things though they publicly seek to avoid being polluted. Evans is surely correct when he claims *T. Mos.* 7 refers clearly to a "wealthy and powerful priestly aristocracy."[65] This text would appear, then, to be a criticism of the corruption of the temple priesthood contemporaneous with Jesus.

Rabbinic literature also records what appear to be first-century criticisms of the temple and its leadership. In *m. Ker.* 1:7, we are told that Simeon ben Gamaliel protested because the price of a pair of doves had been lifted to a gold denar, about twenty-five times the correct value.[66] The rabbis also criticize the high priestly family of Annas for refusing to tithe, an omission apparently justified by an exegesis of Deut 14:22–23, of which the rabbis disapproved (*Sifre Deut* 105 [on Deut 14:22]).[67] Evans points to numerous other episodes of rabbinic criticism of temple leaders (e.g., *Sifre Deut* 357 [on Deut 34:1, 3]; *t. Menah.* 13:18–19, 21; *t. Zebah.* 11:16–17; *b. Pesah.* 57a; *y. Ma'aś Š.* 5:15) for their greed, violence, and oppression. The rabbis were apparently also critical of the way in which high priests were appointed by "kings," that is, gentile rulers (*t. Yoma* 1:7), often by way of bribery (*Pesiq.*

---

59. Ferda, "Jeremiah 7," 170–71.

60. This episode, and those following, were brought to my attention by Evans, "Opposition to the Temple," 235–53.

61. Johnson, "Life of Adam and Eve," 2:268, 270n29b.

62. Evans, "Opposition," 237.

63. Priest, "Testament of Moses (First Century A.D.)," 1:920–21. See also Evans, "Opposition," 250–51n5–6.

64. Priest, "Testament of Moses," 930.

65. Evans, "Opposition," 238.

66. Evans, "Opposition," 238.

67. Evans, "Opposition," 239.

Rab. 47:4).[68] Indeed, the rabbis placed the blame for the destruction of the temple on the greed and hatred of the priestly families:

> As to Jerusalem's first building, on what account was it destroyed? Because of idolatry and licentiousness and bloodshed which was in it. But [as to] the latter building we know that they devoted themselves to Torah and were meticulous about tithes.[69] On what account did they go into exile? Because they love money and hate one another. (*t. Menah.* 13:22)[70]

The rabbis also, like Josephus, made use of Jeremiah's temple sermon as a way to explain the destruction of the second temple. Tucker Ferda lists *b. Naz.* 32b; *Sifre Deut* 342:1; *Pesiq. Rab Kah.* 14:2; *Lam. Rab.* 31:2; 56:1; *Zohar* 1:55b as examples of passages in the Talmud and midrashic literature in which Jer 7 is cited in speaking about the destruction of the second temple.[71]

There is, of course, also the example of the Qumran community whose criticisms of the temple and its leaders are plentiful. Apart from referring to the high priest as the "Wicked Priest" (1QpHab 1.3; 8.9; 9.9; 11.4), the Qumranites accuse him of robbing the poor (1QpHab 8.12; 9.5; 10.1; 12.10; CD 6.16) and accumulating wealth (1QpHab 8.8–12; 9.4–5; CD 6.15; 4QpNah 1.11).[72] They also took issue with the temple tax (4Q159 2.6–8) and the ritual purity of the priesthood (CD 6.11–7.6; 11.18–12.2).[73]

While there are more texts to which we could turn our attention, we have seen a sample of the way in which Jeremiah and Ezekiel, as well as authors of texts in and around the first century CE, critiqued the temple and its leaders. Similar themes carry across from the First to the Second Temple, though they are not identical. The OT prophets place much emphasis on idolatry and injustices—the covenantal unfaithfulness—that

---

68. Evans, "Opposition," 239, 240–41.

69. I note that this report of the high priests' meticulousness about tithes could possibly contradict the *Sifre to Deuteronomy*'s claim that Annas' high priestly family refused to tithe (*Sifre Deut* 105), though this Midrash's criticism does not seem to extend to other high priestly families. Still, I wish to acknowledge the contradiction, and note that ancient sources, like modern ones, may not be as consistent as we would often like.

70. Translation from Neusner, *Tosefta*, 162. Cited in Evans, "Opposition," 241.

71. Ferda, "Jeremiah 7," 159.

72. Evans, "Opposition," 242. Evans acknowledges that the Wicked Priest likely originally referred to a Hasmonean, and thus could be thought not to represent the thought of the Qumranites during the time of Jesus. Evans disagrees with such a premise, arguing that the critical views carried over to the time of Jesus and that every High priest in Jerusalem was referred to as the "Wicked Priest."

73. Evans, "Opposition," 243–46.

the temple system helps perpetuate. Some authors and groups from the Roman period share these concerns, especially as regards the violence, oppression, and greed of the temple leaders. While the prophets have an eye on the wider covenantal infidelity of Israel as a whole—with the leaders of the temple as an exemplification of this—texts from the Roman period place a much stronger emphasis on the corruption of the temple itself and its effects on the wider community.

6.6 The Matthean Jesus' Critique of the Temple

Having painted a picture of critiques of the Jerusalem temples in both the Babylonian and Roman periods, we now turn to the critique by the Matthean Jesus. Is the critique embodied in Jesus' temple action similar to OT prophets like Jeremiah and Ezekiel, and/or to other first-century figures?

Echoing Isaiah

Leaving aside for a moment Jesus' physical act of driving out traders and turning over furniture, we note that early in the temple episode Matthew has Jesus refer to two statements from within the OT prophetic writings— Isa 56:7 and Jer 7:11—stringing them together into a single statement. The first half of the statement, the allusion to Isa 56:7, forms part of a larger section of divine discourse in its original context:

> And the foreigners who join themselves to the Lord,
>   to minister to him, to love the name of the Lord,
>   and to be his servants,
> all who keep the sabbath, and do not profane it,
>   and hold fast my covenant—
> these I will bring to my holy mountain,
>   and make them joyful in my house of prayer;
> their burnt offerings and their sacrifices
>   will be accepted on my altar;
> *for my house shall be called a house of prayer*
>   for all peoples.
> Thus says the Lord God,
>   who gathers the outcasts of Israel,
> I will gather others to them
>   besides those already gathered. (Isa 56:6–8)

Isa 56 begins what most commentators still consider the final section of Isaiah (56–66; "Third Isaiah"). The section was probably written in the midst of the theological crisis during the period just after the return of the exiles to Jerusalem.[74] The themes early in the section prefigure debates that will characterize Judaism in later times, namely, the inclusion of outsiders and the nature of covenant faithfulness. The temple also figures prominently: "Yhwh's house (56:5) and holy mountain (56:7) make a prominent appearance at the very beginning of Trito-Isaiah."[75]

In Isa 56:1–8 the prophet seeks first to summarize the covenantal demands of YHWH: "Keep justice, and do righteousness, for soon my salvation will come, and my righteousness be revealed" (56:1). Isaiah 56:2–8 seeks to outline what obedience to such a command looks like in practice. Specifically, 56:3–8 defines justice and righteousness in terms of inclusion of outsiders, counteracting the kind of exclusivism represented by texts like Haggai and Zechariah,[76] and also Ezra-Nehemiah. Isaiah 56 suggests that foreigners and unclean people ("eunuchs") who are faithful to the Mosaic covenant have a place not only in the people of God (56:3–4), but also in the temple itself (56:5–7). The prophet makes the claim that God desires to include foreigners in Israel's chief acts of worship in a restored temple, namely, keeping the Sabbath (56:6) and offering sacrifices on the altar (56:7). This positivity toward outsiders is in contrast to the criticism the prophet holds for Israel's leaders (56:9–12) and Israel as a whole for its idolatry (57:1–13). Later in Isa 56–66, the prophet will further outline what the requisite covenantal fidelity looks like, both for outsiders and ethnic Jews. This is perhaps most notable in Isa 58 where the prophet defines true worship in terms of social and economic justice (58:6–8), claiming this takes precedence over formal and ritual forms of worship (58:3–5). The prophet continues in the deuteronomistic tradition of promising that faithfulness will be met with YHWH's restoration and peace (e.g., 58:6–12; 65:13–25), and iniquity with ruin (e.g., 65:1–12).

Like other OT prophets who critique the temple and its leaders, the author of Isa 56–66 is positive about the temple (e.g., 56:5, 7), even though it has probably not yet been rebuilt when he writes. Though the author is positive about the concept of a restored Jerusalem temple, he is critical of certain dimensions of Israel's ethical life that enable injustices to occur. Brueggemann names Torah obedience through the lens of "self-protective punctiliousness" as an example.[77] In other words, in Isa 56 the prophet critiques the national ethnocentrism and exclusiveness of the community.

74. Brueggemann, *Isaiah 40–66*, 164.

75. Niskanen, *Isaiah 56–66*, xx.

76. See Hanson, *Dawn of Apocalyptic*.

77. Brueggemann, *Isaiah 40–66*, 165.

We can infer that the prophet's declaration of the covenantal obligations of social and economic justice suggest such obligations were not being met by the community and its leaders at the time.

Here we can see how Jesus' echoing of Isa 56 makes sense in Matthew's story. Matthew has already weaved into his narrative numerous instances of gentiles and outsiders who demonstrate greater faithfulness than Jewish figures. Jesus' genealogy includes gentiles (Matt 1:3, 5), and the Magi are characterized positively (2:1–12), as are the Roman centurion (8:8:5–13) and the Canaanite woman (15:21–28). Narratively speaking, it is natural for Matthew to pick up on the internationalizing interpretation of Torah found in Isa 56. If we accept that Matthew uses Isa 56:7 metonymically (i.e., referring to part of Isa 56 in order to evoke the whole text), we can see how Jesus is recalling Isaiah's great vision of God's restoration of Israel, and the inclusion of the nations in the covenant people.

This inclusion of outsiders, and not cultic purity, is behind Matthew's use of Isaiah's notion that the temple ought to be a house of prayer. It is not that Matthew's Jesus is upset that God's house ought to be a house of prayer but is being used for some alternative purpose, such as trade.[78] The trading of animals, after all, was an accepted practice in the temple, one that was necessary for the functioning of the temple's cultic system since sacrifice required a supply of suitable animals.[79] In other words, the temple cult necessitated animal trade. If Jesus had been seeking to restore the temple's cultic purity, criticizing temple trade in and of itself would have been an incoherent tactic since Jesus could hardly have done so without calling into question the temple's cultic activities themselves. Whatever Jesus is criticizing, it is not the presence of trade qua trade in the temple.

If Matthew's Jesus is evoking Isaiah's inclusive vision, why then does Matthew omit the end of Isaiah's phrase, "for my house shall be called a house of prayer *for all peoples* [ἔθνος]"? A common response among commentators is to argue that Matthew's Jesus is merely making the point that the temple ought to be a house of prayer, and that the "for all nations" part of Isaiah's phrase is irrelevant to Jesus' action in the temple.[80] But this assumes that Matthew has no interest in the wider context of Isa 56, that he is simply pulling his quotation out of its literary context.[81] This conclusion is, to be fair,

78. So France, *Gospel of Matthew*, 600–601.

79. Sanders, *Jesus and Judaism*, 63.

80. See for example France, *Gospel of Matthew*, 786–87; Hagner, *Matthew 14–28*, 600–601; Nolland, *Gospel of Matthew*, 844; Stanton, *Gospel for a New People*, 355–56.

81. See Foley, *Immanent Art*, 1–60. Foley's notion of "metonymic intertextuality" is helpful. I suppose it is possible that Matthew is merely quoting Mark's version of the story, and leaves out a section he finds unhelpful, but it seems highly unlikely, given his

a possibility, and we ought not automatically impose a modern concern for literary context onto the Evangelist. The problem with this conclusion, however, is that in other parts of his story Matthew is interested in the context of OT texts he cites,[82] and we have seen this in our earlier discussions of Matt 1:23 (Isa 7:14), Matt 3:3 (Isa 40:3) and Matt 4:15–16 (Isa 9:1–2). The other difficulty with the view described is that it potentially contradicts Matthew's repeated concern for the place of gentiles in the people of God. In my view, Matthew has in mind Isaiah's great vision of the Lord gathering all peoples, and this figures into Jesus' critique.

Lastly, I note that Jesus' action of driving out temple traders and overturning furniture suggests he is less positive about the temple than Isaiah. Jesus' action would have disrupted the sacrificial cult, even if only symbolically, and this suggests Jesus was content to do so. This would not appear to be the actions of someone who wished to repair this system. Isaiah imagines a restored temple with the nations flocking toward it, while Jesus predicts the demise of the temple (21:18–22), and this marks a major departure from Isaiah's vision by Matthew's Jesus. This less positive view of the temple is not surprising, however; as we have seen, other prophetic figures in and around the first century CE were critical of the temple itself, seeing it as corrupt. This is a shift from the attitude taken by the prophets of the OT. Such may explain Jesus' omission of "for all nations" from his quotation of Isaiah; for Jesus, the temple is not a house of prayer "for all nations" because the temple will fall. Thus, it ought not be seen as a light of hope for the gentiles. In other words, Jesus' omission of the "for all nations" part of Isaiah's vision is an aspect of his prediction of the temple's demise, its judgement.

Reverberating Jeremiah

Earlier we discussed the context of Jer 7:11 and there is no need to cover this terrain again, except to summarize our earlier comments. In Jer 7, the prophet harshly critiques the self-deception of Israel in its belief that the presence of the temple will guarantee YHWH's favor, a belief that has led to the waiving of covenant obligations since unqualified deliverance was apparently assured. The result will be judgement, according to the words of the prophet.

---

penchant for quoting the OT, that Matthew would use an OT quote with whose source he was unfamiliar.

82. For a solid study in the context of quoted Scripture texts in Matthew (focusing on Matt 22:34–40), see Carter, "Love as Societal Vision," 2:30–44.

Jeremiah's rhetorical question, placed on the lips of YHWH—"Has this house, which is called by my name, become a den of robbers [bandits] in your sight?"—is not a critique of the temple itself. Rather, it is a critique of the fact the temple has become a place of refuge for those unfaithful to Torah,[83] which is consistent with Jeremiah's overall critique throughout the section. Jeremiah uses the image of a "den of bandits," a reference to one of the caves in the hills outside Jerusalem "where thieves fled after they committed a crime, a place of hiding and refuge from punishment."[84] The image implies that Israel uses the temple as a place of refuge in the wake of their covenantal infidelity; they deny justice to the vulnerable—refugees, orphans and widows—whilst shedding innocent blood, stealing, lying, and committing adultery and idolatry (Jer 7:5–9). They then come to the temple, with its ritual and liturgical practices, as if it would cover up their iniquities and guarantee YHWH's deliverance (7:10–11). In other words, the existence of the temple apparently emboldens Israel's leadership to wield its power in order to exploit the marginalized. In a sense, the temple legitimates their actions because the presumption of divine presence and protection within and through the temple system bestows on its mediators divine sanction so long as it stands, hence Jeremiah's assertion that the words "This is the temple of the Lord . . ." are deceptive (7:4). The temple, then, has for Jeremiah become an ideological instrument of oppression and of a corrupt political economy.

In the second half of Jesus' verbal critique of the temple in Matt 21:13, he makes an obvious allusion to Jer 7:11 ("but you are making it a den of robbers [bandits]"). However direct this reference might be, we are left with a number of probable choices as to what Jesus could mean:

1. Jesus could be criticizing the sellers and money-changers for their corrupt or inappropriate business in the temple, referring to them as robbers;

2. He could be critiquing in strong terms the "bandits," those who lead the nation and run the temple, for their economic exploitation and their mismanagement of the institution, such that it has become an object of judgement;

3. He could be criticizing literal bandits (λῃστής), revolutionaries who have violently rebelled against Rome, and their foolish nationalism that will lead to the ruin of Jerusalem and the temple.

83. Brueggemann, *Commentary on Jeremiah*, 79.
84. Bracke, *Jeremiah 1–29*, 77–78.

The first two options are, admittedly, somewhat related and not mutually exclusive, though they are distinct enough to require separation; a critique of the traders themselves is quite different from a critique of the temple leadership. Noting the range of interpretive approaches to this episode explored earlier in this chapter, we must preface any choice by remembering the narrative-critical dimensions of this study and our commitment to interpreting Matthew's pericopes in light of his larger story. In other words, in this study I am not strictly interested in a historical reconstruction of the episode.

The first option above—which amounts to seeing Jesus' critique as against shady business practices or a polluted temple cult—though popular amongst scholars, has little basis when read in the context of Matthew's story. Matthew is certainly concerned with Israel's covenantal obligations. Temple purity could theoretically constitute an aspect of this concern, though narratively there is very little foundation for such a conclusion within Matthew's interpretive scheme. Matthew's central hermeneutic for understanding covenant is love, mercy, justice, and faithfulness (5:44; 7:12; 22:37–39), which is expressed in a primary concern for the social and economic dimensions of the people of God (e.g., 5–7; 18:15–20; 23:23). The ritual purity of the temple system or other liturgical systems is not a major concern for Matthew. Indeed, it could be argued that he is critical of such concerns, particularly when they eclipse his own (e.g., 23:23–28). Equally important, a concern for the purity of the temple does not seem to be at the forefront of the words of the prophets whose words are summoned by Jesus in Matthew 21. In the case of Jeremiah, the prophet predicts the destruction of the temple not because of a corrupted cult, but because of broader covenantal unfaithfulness in socioeconomic terms. All of this suggests Jesus' concern is not the traders and money-changers. After all, as we have seen, trading and money-changing were a normal and accepted part of temple life. It will not do to make an assumption about the meaning of this episode based on the form of Jesus' action (overturning the traders' equipment) that flies in the face of the prophetic context of Jesus' words—it makes more sense to view Jesus' action through the lens of his explanatory declaration and the prophetic contexts from which it derives. Ritual purity of the temple may have been a concern for those at Qumran and other groups, but it is not at the forefront of Matthew's story.[85]

---

85. It is worth pointing out that the traders do not escape unscathed from the temple encounter, since, as Neyrey says, to be driven/thrown out of a building brought shame upon the one removed. Other examples in Matthew include 8:12, 31; 21:39; 22:13; 25:10. Despite this insight, I have chosen not to build too many conclusions on social-scientific perspectives since opening that methodological Pandora's box would be outside the scope of the current study.

This line of reasoning should also make us question whether Matthew has in mind literal "bandits" when Jesus cites Jer 7:11. Matthew never seems to make this a concern elsewhere in his story. The Jeremian source material speaks of bandits as a metaphor for Israel, with emphasis on the nation's leadership. *Targum to Jeremiah* confirms this judgement when it renders Jer 7:11 as "a house of an assembly of wicked men," almost certainly a reference to a synagogual context.[86] Given the targum treats Jeremiah's "bandits" as equivalent to wicked members of the synagogue, it is likely that the prophet's reference to bandits was not taken too literally, at least in the first century CE.[87]

We conclude, then, that Matthew's Jesus follows Jeremiah in directing his criticism at the national leaders who controlled the temple. Like Jeremiah (and Third Isaiah), Jesus sees covenantal unfaithfulness occurring in the form of exploitation and exclusion of the poor and the outcast and this is reflected in Jesus' subsequent action of healing them (Matt 21:14–15). Jesus' concern about the exploitation of marginalized people has already been reflected in Matthean pericopes, including his healings, his feedings, and his dispute with the Pharisees about the Sabbath (12:1–8). Such concern is also reflected in his temple action. It is, as we have seen, a concern regarding the temple that he shares with others among his contemporaries.

Why, then, does Jesus drive out the traders and overturn their furniture? After all, there was nothing inherently wrong with the practice of trading in the temple. The same, of course, could be said about the fig tree (21:18–22)—there was nothing inherently wrong with the tree! It would be a mistake to imagine that Jesus' prophetic action in the temple was simply the result of aggression toward temple services, just as it would be a mistake to view Jesus' cursing of the fig tree as a sign of his aggression toward the tree. The driving out of the traders and the overturning of their tables is, rather, a prophetic sign of the broader covenantal failure of the people, especially their leaders. The disruption of the temple is a sign that it has become Jeremiah's den of bandits and the action is meant to draw attention to the "bandits," their nationalistic zeal (as in Isaiah 56), and their oppression of the poor. Moreover, Jesus' action is a sign of the destruction that is to come to the temple, just as Jeremiah had proclaimed its destruction in his time (Jer 7:12–15). The presence of the temple had become, as Jeremiah had argued, a legitimating force allowing Israel's leadership to wield its ideological power in order to exploit

86. Ferda, "Jeremiah 7," 159.

87. It is worth noting that *Tg. Jer.* probably originated during or slightly before the first century CE. This places it "into a sphere of exegetical activity roughly contemporary with Matthew, encouraging us to make use of its traditions where such comparison seems warranted." Knowles, *Jeremiah in Matthew's Gospel*, 50–51n1.

the poor. In other words, the temple had become a mechanism of oppression in a corrupt political economy. Apparently, for Jesus, this made the temple a symbolic target for his own prophetic action.

That the people ought to repent and produce fruit is implied by the fig tree episode in 21:18–22 (cf. 7:15–20). The fig tree was a symbol used in the OT to depict an ideal state (e.g., 1 Kgs 4:25; 2 Kgs 18:31; Isa 36:16; Mic 4:4; Zech 3:10) and the image of a fig tree being destroyed a sign of this ideal state vanishing in the face of judgement (e.g., Ps 105:33; Isa 34:4; Jer 5:17; Hos 2:12; Hab 3:17). There are also instances where the fig tree is used as a symbol for Israel itself, such that there is no fruit and the tree must be cut down, or that its destruction removes the possibility of it bearing fruit (e.g., Jer 8:13; Hos 9:10, 16; Mic 7:1; Joel 1:7, 12). The eschatological vision of many of these passages is not subtle. William Telford describes the fig tree as,

> An emblem of peace, security, and prosperity and is prominent when descriptions of the Golden Age of Israel's history, past, present, and future, are given. . . . The blossoming of the fig-tree and its *giving of its fruits* is a descriptive element in passages which depict Yahweh's visiting his people with *blessing*, while the *withering of the fig-tree*, the destruction of withholding of its fruit, figures in imagery describing *Yahweh's judgement* upon his people or their enemies.[88]

Telford goes on to claim that the reason given for such judgement is a corrupt temple cult, although I would maintain that the broad contexts of the judgement passages themselves describe a wider sense of covenantal breach. Telford is helpful though when he points to the connection in the Jewish mind between the fruitfulness of the trees (Israel) and the maintenance of the temple service.[89] For the rabbis of the first and second century CE, "the fruits had lost their savour when the temple had been destroyed, a state of affairs that was, however, to be reversed in the Messianic Age."[90] Matthew reverses this, such that Israel's breaching of God's covenant, primarily by Israel's leaders and legitimated by the temple, would lead to a situation in which the temple would be destroyed—the lack of fruit would destroy the temple, not the lack of a temple destroy the fruit. In my view, this suggests Jer 8:13 is perhaps the primary text in view for Matthew in the fig tree pericope, especially since he has quoted Jer 7:11 only a few sentences earlier. For Jeremiah, the infidelity of Israel was greater than the mere failure of

88. Telford, *Barren Temple*, 161–62.
89. Telford, *Barren Temple*, 195.
90. Telford, *Barren Temple*, 195.

the temple cult—his focus was the failure of the nation's leaders, as we have seen. Matthew adds a new dimension in the temple/fig tree episode, since the nation's leaders have failed to recognize the One who comes to them, the One who calls the nation to repent and offers to heal it.

6.7 Jesus' Healings in the Temple

Unique to Matthew's version of the temple action pericope is the account of the blind and lame coming to Jesus in the temple and Jesus healing them (21:14). This detail is important for Matthew's characterization of Jesus and for understanding his vision of covenantal faithfulness.

That the blind and lame were in the temple at all is worthy of note. Some OT traditions demanded their exclusion from the temple (2 Sam 5:8), especially if they were priests (Lev 21:17–18).[91] Further, Deuteronomy 15:21 banned the sacrificing of blind and lame animals since they had a defect. Josephus notes that people with gonorrhea and leprosy were excluded from the city altogether (J.W. 5.227) which, though not illuminating anything about the status of the blind and lame in the temple, demonstrates that purity concerns did lead to the exclusion of some. Moreover, the Qumran community argued for the exclusion of the blind and lame (1QSa 2:8–9; CD 15:15–17). When viewed together, all of this suggests that some Judeans probably thought the blind and lame should have been excluded from the temple. Luz claims that 2 Sam 5:8 "had never been used in Judaism to regulate entrance into the temple,"[92] though he offers little in the way of support. Luz does point to m. Hag. 1:1 in support of his argument and the text commands the exclusion of the blind, lame, and others from appearing at the temple during the three chief feasts of Judaism; Luz says that this was a humane consideration since they are not able to travel.[93] The same consideration ought to also apply to others listed in m. Hag. 1:1, such as the deaf mute, the mentally disabled, children, the sick, and the immobile elderly, all of whom would have various reasons for begging merciful reprieve from their obligation to travel. It is not clear, however, why this humanitarian consideration would be necessary for androgynous persons, intersex persons, women, and slaves, all of whom are also mentioned in the list of m. Hag.'s exceptions and none of whom would have an inherent difficulty traveling. In my view, this casts doubt on the sustainability of Luz's appeal to m. Hag. 1:1. Ultimately, with the available evidence, it is impossible to know

91. Keener, *Gospel of Matthew*, 502.

92. Luz, *Matthew 21–28*, 12–13.

93. Luz, *Matthew 21–28*, 13n78.

for sure whether those in control of the temple institution in the early-mid first century enforced 2 Samuel's exclusion of the blind and lame, but there is evidence to suggest some exclusion was practiced.

Though we cannot be sure of the extent of the temple's exclusivity in Jesus' time, Matthew seems to have characterized the temple as having been exclusive, such that the presence of the blind and lame is notable. Rather than exclude the blind and the lame from the temple, as David would have done, Jesus heals them. As R. T. France points out, Matthew expects his audience to make this comparison when he has the "children" crying out in the temple, "Hosanna to the Son of David" (21:15). Jesus' act in the temple is in stark contrast to his ancestor—rather than uphold the purity of the temple, he opens it to the blind and lame, even disrupting the operation of the temple itself.

The narrative proximity of the blind and lame to Jesus' reference to Isa 56 suggests Matthew sees the blind and lame as included among the "outcasts of Israel" mentioned in Isa 56:8, a segment of those who are to be brought to God's holy mountain in the prophet's vision. Jesus has already used Isaianic imagery to assure John that his healing of the blind and lame are signs of his identity as "the one who is to come" (Matt 11:5; cf. Isa 29:18; 35:5–6; 61:1 [LXX]). Likewise, his healing in the temple functions to legitimate his identity and ministry by way of Isaianic resonances. The prophet flagrantly challenges the purity values of his opponents in order to reveal the true will of God, which has already been communicated to Israel through the prophets of old (e.g., Mic 4:6–7). We can recall Jesus' earlier use of Hosea's declaration that God desires mercy and not sacrifice (Matt 9:12; 12:7), a pithy expression of what covenantal faithfulness entails. Here Jesus is proclaiming judgement on the temple and its leaders since even at the very site of their liturgical life they have failed to embody the merciful love of God to which their liturgy points. The children's cry "Hosanna" is a kind of alternative liturgy that correctly names the salvation of God in their midst (21:16; cf. Ps 8:2).[94] Ὡσαννά finds its OT context mostly in the Psalms (12:1; 20:9; 28:9; 60:5; 108:6; 118:25), always as an address to YHWH, though it is occasionally addressed to the king, as in 2 Sam 14:4 and 2 Kgs 6:26. Though a kingly reference is possible, I think it more likely that the cry of the children in Matthew is to be associated with the Psalms so that the children cry out to Jesus and, in doing so, ascribe to him some kind of divine significance (cf. Matt

94. Lohse notes that Ps 118, with its use of Ὡσαννά, was sometimes interpreted messianically, "so that the Messianic hope was probably echoed in the hosanna which the Jewish community raised in the pre-christian period." Eduard Lohse, "ὡσαννά," *TDNT* 9:682–83.

1:23).[95] That Matthew goes on to quote from the Psalms (8:2 [LXX]) in Matt 21:16 supports this; indeed Matthew's quotation of Ps 8:2 explicitly attaches a liturgical meaning to the children's cry.

That Jesus is identified as representing God in some significant way is important (cf. Matt 1:23). No doubt there are messianic overtones to this episode, a sense that in Jesus the promise of Israel has been fulfilled and the blind and lame are being gathered with the faithful. But this should not preclude the importance of Jesus' prophetic identity and its bearing on the pericope: in calling Israel back to its covenantal obligations as God's people, and in calling Israel to look forward to its eschatological hope, Jesus is communicating to Israel the will of its God and acts as God's special representative at a time of great crisis. This crisis apparently escapes the notice of Israel's leaders and we are reminded that in Isaiah's prophecy it is the watchmen of Israel—and not the blind—who are unable to see (Isa 56:10). This contrast between the physiologically blind and spiritually blind is one that Matthew himself exploits (Matt 9:27–31; 12:22–24; 20:29–34; cf. 15:14; 23:16–26),[96] which suggests that healing of the blind in 21:14 and elsewhere connotes more than physical healing. Indeed, Jesus calls Israel to perceive the present in light of the past and future, but only the outcasts do so, as Third Isaiah had said.

At a conceptual level, and in relation to Jesus' comparison with David, Jesus' actions of disruption and healing suggest that he takes the theological side of the prophets against what might be seen as the ideological descendants of David and Israel's monarchy/hierocrats.[97] As a prophet, Jesus proclaims and enacts God's covenant with Israel, as we have recognized. But this covenant, expressed in Israel's history and Scriptures, was interpreted in numerous ways. Jesus' embrace of outcasts makes clear that his hermeneutic includes the rejection of the purity codes of his opponents, while his healing of outcasts is a sign of his acceptance of the call for social and economic justice found throughout the classical prophets.

Jesus' actions in the temple episode signal a wholly different understanding of what holiness entails and, by implication, what God—who is holy—is like.[98] After all, holiness throughout the OT is based on YHWH's

95. It may also be that both associations are being made simultaneously, a kingly ascription for Jesus by the crowd overlapping with a divine one. Still, I think the latter association is at least primary.

96. Luz, *Theology of the Gospel of Matthew*, 68.

97. Here I am borrowing the conceptual framework of Hanson, *Dawn of Apocalyptic*.

98. On Jesus' revision of holiness, see Borg, *Conflict, Holiness, and Politics*, esp. 135–55. Borg argues that Jesus, at different times, both substituted *and* modified the notion of holiness. More specifically, Jesus sometimes substituted holiness with compassion

character and actions. Jesus' embrace of the blind and lame in the temple implies his understanding of holiness is in tension with parts of the OT, including the Holiness Code itself (Lev 21:17–18).[99] Such revision of Israel's covenantal obligations in light of divine revelation was not, however, strange in Israel's history since the prophets occasionally engaged in it. One example is Third Isaiah's insistence on the inclusion of foreigners, eunuchs, and outcasts (56:1–8), even though the Torah is less enthusiastic about this (Deut 23:1–6). Such revision is included in the role of the prophet, not on the basis of preference or the changing of the times, but on the basis of divine revelation about the character of YHWH through YHWH's word and actions. Jesus engages in such revisionary activity in Matthew in both teaching (e.g., Matt 5:17–48) and action (e.g., eating with sinners). The temple episode appears to be another example of this, even if Jesus is largely reiterating Third Isaiah's earlier revision. That Isaiah's prophecy had not been embraced by Israel meant that it needed to be repeated, albeit in a different, more dramatic way. Such prophetic revision had implications for how Israel ought to perceive its own vocation; holiness was to be embodied in mercy rather than sacrifice and all the zealous segregation inherent in that system.[100]

It would be a mistake, however, to think that this might mean Jesus had come to purify the temple system. As E. P. Sanders suggests, Jesus could have symbolized the purification of the temple by the pouring out of water; the overturning of tables suggests something stronger: destruction.[101] I would add that if the Matthean Jesus had intended to purify the temple it would make little sense to heal outcasts within its precinct but outside the realm of its official authority since the reform would not continue following Jesus' departure. Ultimately, God's holiness could not be imitated by way of the temple because it was synonymous with a socio-religious ideology that was antithetical to what such holiness entailed. As Marcus Borg notes, Jesus revises the content of the *imitatio dei*, such that "'You shall be *holy* because I am *holy*' becomes 'Be *compassionate* as God is

---

(e.g., Matt 9:13; 12:7; 23:23), and other times modified holiness such that it—and not uncleanness—was contagious. I am not so sure that substitution and modification ought to be so cleanly bifurcated—substitution could just as easily be construed as redefinition—though I am in broad agreement with Borg's thesis.

99. Leviticus 21 deals specifically with the holiness of priests, and so the text cited does not restrict the blind and lame from the temple outright. Still, the restriction of the blind and lame from the priesthood suggests blindness and lameness were barriers to holiness (Lev 21:6).

100. "Both the healing stories as well as the accounts of his social intercourse portray [Jesus] as defying the rules of segregation fostered by the 'symbolic order of Judaism.'" Rajkumar, *Dalit Theology and Dalit Liberation*, 95.

101. Sanders, *Jesus and Judaism*, 70.

compassionate."[102] Or, as Hosea had said, the knowledge of God was merciful love (Hos 6:6). Jeremiah, in his own way, had criticized the temple along these lines, and now Jesus was doing the same.

Further, if Matthew has Jesus follow in the tradition and theology of the classical prophets, he also has Jesus follow in the tradition of Moses. As Allison points out, Jesus' acts of healing are described by Matthew as τὰ θαυμάσια ἃ ἐποίησεν, "the wonders he did," which is noticeably similar to the way the final sentence of the LXX Pentateuch describes Moses' deeds: τὰ θαυμάσια . . . ἃ ἐποίησεν Μωυσῆς.[103] Dale Allison's assertion of a New Moses theme in Matt 21 could be correct, but I am not yet persuaded of it. Certainly, however, Jesus' favorable comparison with Moses lends authority to what Jesus does. This in turn gives credence to Jesus' revision, in line with the prophets, of holiness and, more broadly, the interpretation of the law.

In light of all this, I would argue that the healings in Matthew's version of the temple episode are actually the crux of the pericope.[104] In it, Jesus' critique of the temple establishment, and Israel as a whole, is given tangible content and his channeling of the Isaian and Jeremian traditions is given material expression. It is also noteworthy that it is Jesus' act of healing—and not his overturning of tables—that causes the chief priests and scribes to become incensed. By including healings, Matthew does not want us to miss an important point—the temple has come under judgement because the institution has not fulfilled its purpose, though Jesus has fulfilled it and so Israel's outcasts are coming to him. This provides an unexpected fulfillment of Isaiah's vision. The prophet's action points toward the presence of God and, interestingly in this case, God's presence is not in the temple but is manifest in the prophet himself. It is difficult to overstate the enormity of this last point. The temple was thought to be the meeting place of YHWH and Israel, indeed, between heaven and earth. It was also thought to be a prefiguring of the eschatological temple (Ezek 40–48, esp. 44:15–31) and sacrifices were thus an expression of the *telos* of creation. For Jesus to embody God's presence—and to be implying that the temple did not—was to radically subvert Israel's view of the nature of creation and the substance of its future hope; the beginning, end, and purpose of history was not the temple, but Jesus and the kingdom he was inaugurating.

---

102. Borg, *Conflict, Holiness, and Politics*, 139. I disagree with Borg that this necessarily means that compassion *replaces* holiness—why can it not be that compassion replaces *purity* as the content of holiness?

103. Allison, *New Moses*, 251.

104. As distinct from the other Gospels' versions of the pericope, obviously, since they do not mention the healings.

Though in Jesus' action of disrupting the temple we see a powerful critique of the temple leadership and Israel, Matthew wants to go further. Jesus' healings are a prophetic sign of this kingdom that is coming in his person and ministry. We recall Brueggemann's pattern of the prophetic community,[105] that critique alone does not constitute the fullness of the prophetic task—there must also be the presence of an energizing hope.[106] In Matthew's temple story, I would contend that this element is especially present in Jesus' healing of the blind and lame. Throughout Matthew, Jesus has healed as a sign of the kingdom's arrival (see esp. 4:17; cf. 4:23). Jesus' healing may critique covenantal infidelity—manifest as violence, socio-economic injustice, and inhospitality to outsiders—but it is also a vision of what the kingdom of heaven is like. It is a tangible expression of Israel's failure, but it also gives tangible content to Israel's hope. This hope comes into special view because, though many in Israel believed the presence of God had yet to return to the temple,[107] the time of YHWH's return had finally arrived, and it was occurring in the deeds of this prophet Jesus. In Matthean language, the kingdom of heaven was near and its blessings were being poured out not on disobedient Israel, but on outcasts, as demonstrated in the healing actions of this prophet Jesus. Jesus' healing in the temple was not simply a sign of the kingdom's nearness, but also of its nature.

If Jesus' healings are a sign of the coming kingdom—and are a key narrative theme in this pericope—they are such in more than one sense. Jesus' healings, in and of themselves, point to God's presence in some special sense since healing, though certainly not unprecedented in first-century Palestine, was not common.[108] But it is also the case that the healings constitute judgement and hope because of *who* it is that is healed, namely, those implied in

105. See Brueggemann, *Prophetic Imagination*, esp. 59–60.

106. Of course, in saying this I am not implying that both aspects of the prophetic vocation must be explicitly present in every episode of the prophet's ministry.

107. There is debate about whether in Second Temple Judaism the presence of God was thought to be in the temple. Some, like Davies, "Presence of God in the Second Temple and Rabbinic Doctrine," 32–36, point to evidence that some perceived God had returned. Others, like Wright, *Jesus and the Victory of God*, 615–24, point to contrary evidence suggesting that some longed for God's return. I don't see why these sets of evidence should be thought to be contradictory. In my view they signal heterogeneity among schools of thought about the presence of God in the temple at the time.

108. Not common, at least, in the surviving Jewish texts of the period. Eve concludes that "Josephus records few miracles of healing; Philo records none. The *Genesis Apocryphon* narrates a healing/exorcism of sorts, as does the book of Tobit, and there are one or two other places in the Apocrypha and Pseudepigrapha where healing is mentioned or a biblical healing recalled. . . . This leaves Jesus as unique in the surviving Jewish literature of his time in being portrayed as performing a large number of healings and exorcisms." Eve, *Jewish Context of Jesus' Miracles*, 378.

the vision of Isa 56. In Matthew, Jesus' healings cannot be divorced from their prophetic context for this is what gives them their unique narrative meaning. Jesus' healing of the blind and lame was a clear sign of his connection to Isaiah's vision. In a time of both foreign oppression and corruption of Israel's leaders, Isaiah's vision was given new meaning in a new situation, and a new prophet was called on to speak God's will to the nation. But this prophet went further than Isaiah—God's presence dwelt in him in a special way, and as one empowered by the Spirit (Matt 3:16) he began to manifest the reign of God in the midst of Israel's corruption, in this case by healing Israel's outcasts. For this reason, the term "sign prophet" is inadequate when speaking of Jesus; his acts may indeed constitute a sign of the coming kingdom, but they are also expressions of its substance.

6.8 "Hosanna to the Son of David"

The result of Jesus' healing action is that the children cry out "Hosanna!" in the temple. Earlier I suggested that this constitutes an alternative liturgy to that of the temple that accurately recognizes God's salvation occurring before the children's eyes. This is in contrast to the chief priests and scribes, who apparently become outraged not because Jesus overturns the tables but because he heals the blind and lame.

It is not immediately obvious who the "children" are. They could be literal children or could be a metaphor for something else. If they were literal children, this would be an important detail since, according to *m. Hag.* 1:1 children were excluded from the temple (although as we mentioned above it is unclear whether this is for humanitarian reasons or not). Either way, Luz thinks that Matthew awkwardly places the "children" into the story so he can make use of (the LXX version of) Ps 8:2 in v. 16,[109] but I find this unconvincing. For Matthew to have inserted the "children" so that he could use the psalm as a rhetorical strategy to best the temple leaders would be odd since more devastating texts from the OT could be found without requiring the narrative presence of the children. It is more likely that the psalm is used by Matthew as an afterthought due to the presence of the children.[110]

This is not the first appearance of "children" in Matthew's story. In 11:25–27, the identity of Jesus and the meaning of his works are said to have been hidden from the wise and understanding and revealed to the νηπίοις. Whoever these infants are, they are not only literal children, though they

109. Luz, *Matthew 21–28*, 13.

110. And perhaps both Matthew's inclusion of the children and his use of the psalm reflect traditions about what actually happened.

may include them. The child metaphor can be found in other Greek language Jewish texts where νηπίοις refers to "simple" or "infantile" people (e.g., [LXX] Pss 19:7; 116:6; 119:130; Philo, *Migration* 29–30; *Good Person* 160). Matthew could have used one of a number of words alternative to νηπίοις to refer to literal children (παιδίον, παῖς/παιδός, τέκνον), as he does in Matt 18:3 and 19:13,[111] so his use of νηπίοις suggests literal children are probably not in view. If Matthew's use of νηπίοις is synonymous with the Jewish texts listed above he may be implying that the people who cry out to Jesus are the "simple," though we should point out that Matt 11:25 appears to refer more specifically to Israel's meek who have responded positively to Jesus' ministry, those who labor and are heavy laden.

That Matthew's "children" in 21:15 are not to be taken literally is further supported by the fact that the cry of the children is identical to the first part of the crowds' cry in response to Jesus' procession in 21:9 (Ὡσαννὰ τῷ υἱῷ Δαυίδ). The repeated hosannas, as well as their narrative proximity, suggests that the crowds and the children are related characters,[112] though to what extent is not clear. These children, like those mentioned in 11:25, have seen the amazing works of Jesus and correctly discerned their meaning whilst the chief priests and scribes—the wise and understanding—will come under judgement for their refusal to repent. In a sense Matt 21:14–16 is a "real life" example of Matt 11:20–30.

Despite the enthusiasm of the crowds and the children in 21:1–17, their acceptance of Jesus as Son of David will later create a narrative tension: the crowds respond positively to the prophet's message and action, but they will subsequently call for his crucifixion (27:22–23). The difficulty of understanding the narrative function of οἱ ὄχλοι in Matthew is well known, and no consensus exists as to their role.[113] In regard to Matt 21, Luz thinks that the crowds ought to be distinguished from the "unresponsive 'entire city'" on the basis of such an apparent distinction in 21:9–10.[114] Indeed, *all* (πᾶσα) the city being stirred up is reminiscent of *all* (πᾶσα) the city's reaction to the statement by the Magi (2:3).[115] Unfortunately, the power of this argument dissipates upon the presence of an armed ὄχλος at Jesus' arrest (26:47,

---

111. Note that his use of τέκνον in 9:2 refers to what appears to be an adult. It is possible that the story is about a child, but the absence of parents—who are present in other child healing stories—makes this doubtful.

112. "The two scenes [Matt 21:1–11, 12–17] are so closely connected that scholars since the 1960s have increasingly regarded the two as a single pericope." Campbell, *Of Heroes and Villains*, 96.

113. Carter, "Crowds in Matthew's Gospel," 54–67.

114. Luz, *Theology of Matthew*, 73.

115. Stanton, *Gospel for a New People*, 182.

55) and upon the cry of the ὄχλοι calling for Jesus' crucifixion (27:15–23). I am inclined to agree with Warren Carter's assessment, that the crowds' role is ambiguous and multilateral.[116] J. D. Kingsbury astutely describes this multifaceted characterization: the crowds show that they are well-disposed toward Jesus, especially in comparison with the leaders (e.g., 9:2–8; 21:9, 15; 22:23–34), and Jesus has compassion on them, but the crowds also obstruct Jesus (9:23–25a; 20:31) and participate in his arrest and execution (26:47, 55; 27:15–23) whilst Jesus is at times very critical of them (11:7, 16–19; 13:1–2, 10–13).[117] The crowds are often favorable to Jesus, but they are not his disciples, and they will eventually turn on him. This is apparently in contrast to the children, for whom Jesus gives thanks (11:25), who reinforce the acclamation of the crowds but who, unlike the crowds, never turn on Jesus. If I am correct and the crowds and the children are somehow related in Matthew 21, the relationship is contrastive—the children cry out praise to Jesus and never turn on him, while the crowds cry out the same praise but eventually cry out "crucify him!" Both groups identify him as the Son of David,[118] as some kind of savior ("Hosanna!"), and as somehow acting as an agent of God, and yet some will still turn on him.

Why is this important? This contrast of the crowds and the children provides an interesting window into Jesus' prophetic vocation in Matthew. Just as Peter in Matt 16:13–28 correctly identifies Jesus as Christ and Son of God but is mistaken in his assessment of the meaning of such titles, the crowd crying "Hosanna to the Son of David" appears to have mistaken the

116. Carter, "Crowds in Matthew's Gospel," 55, 67.

117. Kingsbury, *Matthew as Story*, 24–25. I disagree, however, with Kingsbury's assertion that the crowds' identification of Jesus as a prophet is in itself a sign of their lack of faith because "Jesus is in reality the Messiah Son of God." I do not see why these categories are mutually exclusive such that the crowds are to be deemed misguided for calling Jesus a prophet. If anything, given Matthew's own characterization of Jesus as prophet, we should conclude this identification to be incomplete, not incorrect. I am in agreement with Allison's critique of Kingsbury's position, that Matthew could well have regarded Jesus as a prophet *and* much else, and that given positive uses of "prophet" in Matthew, the assumed antithesis between that title and "Messiah Son of God" is questionable. See Allison, *New Moses*, 312–14.

118. Margaret Daly-Denton's work on the title "Son of David" is helpful in that she states that to be "a son of" was not, in Semitic thought, primarily a matter of genealogy, but of character. To say Jesus is the "Son of David" is to say he is a David-like figure. Daly-Denton, "David in the Gospels," 422. This may contribute to our understanding of why the crowd so misunderstood Jesus. It is also worth noting that Acts 2:30 refers to David as a prophet for having foreseen and spoken about the resurrection of Christ. It is not clear, however, whether the view that David was a prophet was widespread among first century Jews and Christians. See also Kingsbury, "Title 'Son of David' in Matthew's Gospel," 591–602, for a helpful study on Matthew's ambivalent use of the title "Son of David."

nature of Jesus' being the Son of David. The crowds are blind to the peaceful nature of the Son of David's vocation: as we discussed earlier, the presence of palm branches in 21:8–9 implies military victory is on the mind of the crowd when they cry "Hosanna." It is probably the case that such military revolution is implicit in the crowds' understanding of Jesus' prophethood (21:11).[119] This is supported by the depth of fear this designation of Jesus as prophet elicits in the chief priests and Pharisees, a fear so great that they refrain from arresting Jesus on account of this designation despite their desire to do so (21:45–46).[120] It is difficult to explain the nature of the threat that the crowd poses to the leadership apart from their implied readiness to undertake violence—they are prepared for a military campaign led by the Son of David, Israel's great warrior. It is probably also the case that the crowds' praise of Jesus scandalizes the leaders.[121] Should we attribute the crowd's fervency simply to their belief that Jesus was a prophet? After all, the Son of David title carries messianic and military undertones, and in Jewish memory God had promised David that one of his royal descendants would establish the throne of his kingdom forever (2 Sam 7:12–16). Still, the Son of David title seems to be connected closely with Jesus as prophet in addition to Messiah (21:9–11). Moreover, there were prophetic figures in the OT who had engaged in warfare for Israel, namely, Moses and Joshua, and the memory of such had been present in the first century CE, as demonstrated in the stories of the Samaritan prophet, Theudas, and the Egyptian prophet. The crowds' expectation that this Galilean prophetic-messianic figure would lead Israel to liberation is disturbed, however, by Jesus' subsequent words and actions. Though the crowds continue to be amazed by Jesus' verbal sparring with

119. Allison has suggested that the crowd is not simply referring to Jesus as *a* prophet, but as *the* prophet (ὁ προφήτης), alluding to Deut 18:15, 18 and the prophet-like-Moses tradition. From a narrative-critical perspective I simply do not think there is sufficient evidence to make a decision on this, though I admit that the crowd seeing Jesus as the prophet like Moses, ready to lead a new liberation from Roman occupation, would support my case here. However, the fact that the prophet-like-Moses is in Deut 18 known by his *words*, and that in Matt 21 Jesus is called a prophet on the basis of his *actions*, puts doubt on Allison's claim. Allison, *New Moses*, 78n183, 314.

120. It should be noted that, in a number of cases within Matthew, Jesus is called "Son of David" and this results in opposition from the community leaders (2:3–4; cf. 1:1; 9:27–34; 12:23–24). Whether or not this title was controversial at the time of Jesus, or perhaps just at the time of Matthew, is unclear. Either way, within the story world of Matthew the title connotes something that the leaders find seriously objectionable. Stanton, *Gospel for a New People*, 180–85.

121. Saldarini leaves open the question of whether it is the political danger of Jesus' acclamation or the crowds' praise that worries the leaders, though he deems the latter more probable. It is important to note that Saldarini is focused mostly on Luke's account. Saldarini, *Pharisees*, 178.

the community leaders (Matt 22:33), his address to them (and the disciples; 23:1) in Matt 23 ends in his prediction of Jerusalem's downfall, not its deliverance, and the destruction of the temple. It is not until they participate in Jesus' arrest that we see the crowds again.

The children, on the other hand, cry "Hosanna" not because of signs of impending military liberation, but because Jesus heals in the temple. They correctly discern the Isaianic nature of Jesus' prophethood (cf. Isa 29:18; 35:5–6; 61:1 [LXX]), the one who comes in word and deed to call Israel back to wholeness as understood through its covenant with YHWH. This is striking because it is the "simple" of the world who perceive the presence of the kingdom of heaven in Jesus' actions, whereas the leaders—the wise—respond indignantly. In other words, the children provide corrective commentary on the crowds' acclamation.

What does all this reflect about Jesus' prophetic vocation, then? We can point out the obvious: the prophet's words and actions are not fully comprehended by all, if most, let alone acceptable to all. Matthew's story demonstrates this quite plainly at points, and the triumphal entry/temple episode demonstrates this. Matthew's Jesus does not go out of his way to elucidate for his audience the meaning of his words and actions. On the contrary, his prophetic utterances and actions seem designed to coax the imagination of his hearers and to call forth faithfulness from those who have "ears to hear." This could be likened to the way some scholars have talked about Jesus' parables.[122] The pericope following the temple episode about the fig tree is another example of the obscured character of prophetic word and action, this time aimed at the disciples. In the case of the crowds in Jerusalem and the children in the temple, Jesus' actions and words receive a mixed response. At first all respond positively. However, having apparently understood Jesus' political critique of Roman power, we find later that the crowds have not grasped the nature of the kingdom that Jesus is inaugurating and that their Davidic nationalist fervor remains. In other words, the crowds had comprehended Jesus' critique, but not the hope he was offering Israel. Jesus' use of prophecy, like the prophets before him, left open such possibility of misunderstanding. In contrast, the children show signs of comprehending Jesus' critique of the temple and its leaders but also the prophetic hope he offered.

---

122. See, for example, Dodd: a parable is "a metaphor or simile drawn from nature or common life, arresting the hearer by its vividness or strangeness, and leaving the mind in sufficient doubt about its precise application to tease it into active thought." Dodd, *Parables of the Kingdom*, 5. The similarity I'm pointing out suggests that study on the connection between parables and the prophetic would be worthwhile.

The implication of all this is that Jesus' prophetic word and deed in Matthew requires a response, something it always manages to cajole from its hearers/witnesses. In some cases it is amazement, in others confoundment, in others comprehension, in others still glimmers of hope. Comprehension need not imply a positive response, since it might also yield hostility, as in the case of the community leaders. Prior to the temple episode in Matthew's story we have already experienced the demise of one prophet, John, and we will soon spectate the death of another; the Evangelist is under no illusions as to the effect of prophecy on the prophet—martyrdom—and we will explore this theme in our next chapter.

6.9 Conclusion

Jesus' temple action is obviously a complex, multidimensional episode. The temple itself, by the time of the first century CE, was perceived by many as being corrupt and oppressive. The economic, political, and religious pollution was thought to have stemmed from the corruption of the temple leadership. The temple had become an institution that represented stratification along lines based on social hierarchy, and this provided ideological support for nationalism and elite dominance. Such realities had come under the criticism of prophets in Israel's past, not least Isaiah and Jeremiah, and was the target of first-century critique from figures like Jesus ben Ananias, Josephus, and others whose stories are told in later rabbinic literature. The OT prophets' criticisms focused on national covenantal infidelity—idolatry and injustice—that the temple system had come to help perpetuate, while first-century figures tended to focus more narrowly on the corruption of the temple itself and the resulting social effects.

What we see in Matthew's account of Jesus' temple action is a critique consistent with, but also distinct from, both the OT prophets and some other first-century figures. Jesus' action and words are especially reminiscent of Isaiah and Jeremiah, which is hardly surprising given that he quotes them. These prophets had earlier proclaimed the centrality of covenantal faithfulness and the inclusion of foreigners within the people of God whilst fiercely condemning Israel's nationalism, exclusiveness, and skirting of its covenantal obligations, especially by the nation's leaders. Jesus' disruption of the corrupted temple and his embrace and healing of outcasts embodies such prophetic utterances, although unlike Isaiah Jesus does not envision a restored temple, but rather his actions symbolize its demise. Like the prophets before him, Jesus' concern is not with the ritual purity of the temple, nor with its cleansing. In fact, Jesus is unconcerned with the temple cult *per se*. He is concerned, however, to proclaim God's judgement on the temple leadership for its covenantal failure, to symbolize the coming demise of the temple itself, and to offer a glimpse of God's healing kingdom in order that Israel might repent.

Jesus' healing of the blind and lame—unique to Matthew's telling of this episode—challenges certain understandings of purity and holiness and offers a vision of God's will and covenantal faithfulness that is characterized by merciful love. In doing so, he engages in revision of Israel's covenantal obligations, a thoroughly prophetic practice. Such love, especially as displayed by the inclusion of outcasts, is prefigured in the vision of the prophets, and Jesus embodies it as an expression of the kingdom of heaven, as an outpouring of God's blessings on outcasts, although Israel's leaders remain blind to it. Moreover, Jesus' subversion of the Son of David identity, whereby he heals rather than conquers, ought to shatter Israel's perception of God's promises and its own vocation. Still, most do not comprehend the meaning of Jesus' prophetic words and deeds and, if they do, they are likely to wish violence against him.

Chapter 7

Matt 23 as Prophetic Speech

In this chapter we move forward to Matthew 23. It is here we find speech that in many ways resembles that found in Matt 5:3–12 and, since we have already discussed this latter text, we have an opportunity for comparison.

Matthew 23 is, of course, a lengthier text than 5:3–12 and so we must be careful to understand the parameters of this chapter. What follows is not a general study of Matthew 23, but rather a study of Jesus' prophetic vocation as reflected within that chapter. As has been our pattern, we first begin with a brief outline of Matthew's plot leading up to Matthew 23 in order to determine the narrative context of the passage.

7.1 The Narrative Context of Matt 23

Within the literary structure of Matthew outlined previously, chapter 23 falls within the narrative block that comprises 21:18—25:46. This section, which follows the hinge text in which Jesus enters Jerusalem and disrupts the temple (21:1–17), reports on Jesus' activity and teaching in Jerusalem. This section also leads onto Matt 26:1–16, the final hinge in Matthew which itself leads into the crescendo of Jesus' death, resurrection, and the mission to all nations.

This section of Matthew's story is characterized by increasing tension between Jesus and his opponents. This tension begins, in a general sense, much earlier in Matthew when Jesus' birth causes Herod and all Jerusalem to be "troubled" (ταράσσω; 2:3), a reaction similar to that of the inhabitants of Jerusalem at 21:10 after Jesus' procession (σείω; "agitated"). More specifically, tension with the community leaders begins indirectly when, following Jesus' first discourse, the people compare him favorably with the scribes (7:29). In Matt 9:11, the Pharisees directly address the activities of Jesus, asking his disciples why he eats with tax collectors and sinners. By

9:34, the Pharisees are openly denouncing Jesus and, by 12:1–14, after Jesus responds critically to a Pharisaic challenge, they conspire against him (ὅπως αὐτὸν ἀπολέσωσιν; 12:14). These contests continue intermittently throughout Matthew's Gospel (e.g., 12:22–32; 15:1–9; 16:1–4; 19:3–9) until Jesus enters Jerusalem in chapter 21.

The entry into Jerusalem and the temple action in 21:1–17 are hinge episodes depicting prophetic acts on the part of Jesus.[1] From here, the plot moves to the next day (21:18), illuminating the previous day's events with Jesus' further judgement on the temple and its leaders (21:18–22), more disputes with the community leaders (21:23–27; 22:15–46), and polemical parables (21:28—22:14). Some of the pericopes concern further criticisms of the community leaders for their lack of discernment and faithfulness and their stubbornness (21:24–26, 28–32), their violence toward God's representatives in the past and present (21:33–46), and for all of the above reasons (22:1–14). Other pericopes are implicit criticisms, demonstrating the theological acuity of Jesus in response to the ill-willed traps set by the blundering leaders (22:15–46). In short, Matthew tells of leaders who do not do the will of God and who will be judged for it.

The setting for most of these scenes, with the exception of the entrance and fig tree episodes, is the temple. Jesus has already told his disciples that he must go to Jerusalem and suffer many things at the hands of the leaders and be killed and raised (16:21; 17:22–23; 20:17–19). Following 21:1–11, Jesus and his followers find themselves in the very heart of Jerusalem, the center of power. We should remember that the people of Jerusalem were agitated by both advents of Jesus into their midst (2:3; 21:10). Moreover, as we have seen previously, the nature of the clashes that Jesus has with the leaders is an indication of the antagonistic nature of Jesus' relationship to the temple and the broader system it represents. Most pertinently for us, Jesus has gone to the place that kills the prophets and stones those sent to it (23:37a), among whom Jesus is to be numbered. It is in this context that we find Matt 23, a continuation of Jesus' critique of the temple and those who uphold and benefit from it.

---

1. Carter refers to Jesus' entry into Jerusalem as "a prophetic sign action," and on this I think he is correct. Jesus adopts elements of Graeco-Roman processions and subverts them in accordance with prophetic tradition (Zech 9:9). Carter, *Matthew and the Margins*, 414. In regard to Jesus' temple action, most scholars identify it as "prophetic symbolic action"; see Luz, *Matthew 21–28*, 11.

7.2 Does Matt 23 Belong with Matt 24–25?

Related to the literary context of Matt 23 is the question of whether it is part of a larger discourse that continues in chapters 24–25. There is no scholarly consensus on this topic. A minority sees chapters 23–25 as one long discourse,[2] whereas the majority sees Matt 23 as a distinct literary unit.[3] Then there are those, such as Carter and Luz, who offer opposing views within their own respective works.[4] Those who see Matt 23–25 as one discourse are supported by the fact that Matt 23 looks in many ways like Matt 5:3–12 and both may function as introductions to their respective discourses. On the other hand, those who see chapter 23 as being separate from chapters 24–25 are supported by the thematic link between chapters 23 and 21–22. The latter view might also be supported by the fact that the audiences described in 23:1 and 24:1–2 are different, thus implying distinct discourses. However, it should be noted that in Matt 13 there are different audiences being addressed within the one discourse, with a shift at 13:36.[5]

Part of the problem with both perspectives is the assumption that narrative structure is rigid. There is no reason why Matt 23 cannot be linked thematically with chapters 21–22 whilst also being part of a discourse spanning chapters 23–25.[6] I am convinced that there is no good reason to separate Matt 23 from chapters 24–25, since the thematic link of the former with chapters 21–22 in no way precludes chapters 23–25 being one large discourse. In fact, I think it makes sense that successive sections move seamlessly into one another. I am also persuaded that the literary similarities between Matt

2. See for example Bacon, "'Five Books,'" 56–66; Blomberg, *Matthew*, 23–27; Gundry, *Matthew*, 10–11, 453; Hood, "Matthew 23–25," 527–43; Keener, *Gospel of Matthew*, 37, 535; Lohr, "Oral Techniques in the Gospel of Matthew," 403–35, esp. 427.

3. See for example Davies and Allison, *Matthew 1–7*, 61; France, *Gospel of Matthew*, 853; Hagner, *Matthew 14–28*, 653–55; Nolland, *Gospel of Matthew*, 57–59; Osborne, *Matthew*, 699; Riches, *Matthew*, 12; Smith, "Literary Evidences of the Five Fold Structure," 540–41; Turner, *Matthew*; Witherington, *Matthew*, 15–16, 421.

4. As pointed out in Hood, "Matthew 23–25," 528. See Luz, *Matthew 1–7*, 9–12; Luz, *Matthew 21–28*, 92; Luz, *Theology of the Gospel of Matthew*, 121; Carter, *Matthew*, 47, 60, 106, 137, 140–41, 150.

5. Balabanski, *Eschatology in the Making*, 136. Balabanski, citing Luz, goes on to discuss the fact that in Matt 13 there is a narrative movement away from the crowds to the disciples because the crowds do not understand. This, she says, reflects the situation of Matthew's own community in relation to its Jewish neighbors. This theme, says Balabanski, is also present in the comparable division between Matt 23 and 24. Balabanski, *Eschatology*, 136–37.

6. So Syreeni, "Methodology and Compositional Analysis," 94–96, cited in Garland, *Reading Matthew*, 239.

5–7 (with 5:3–12 as an introduction) and chapters 23–25 (with chapter 23 as an introduction) are such that chapters 23–25 warrant being viewed as one discourse.[7] The issue of a change in audience at 24:1–2 is not a problem when viewed in comparison to Matt 13(:36).[8]

By viewing chapters 23–25 as one discourse, we are able to point out some attendant implications. Since Matt 23, with its strong focus on ethics, is included in the eschatological discourse, we can say with Vicki Balabanski that for Matthew there is a necessary link between ethics and eschatology: "The Pharisees are reproached not for their teaching but for their actions, and the results of their actions are viewed against the backdrop of the coming judgement."[9] Moreover, just as Matt 13:36 moves to private discussion with disciples about the content of the teaching in the earlier part of that discourse, so too does 24:1–2 mark a shift to private discussion in chapters 24–25 regarding the teaching in Matt 23. This has significant ramifications for the interpretation of chapters 24–25 since the eschatological discourse found in those chapters is shaped by the proclamation in the previous chapter. But there are also implications for our reading of Matt 23 since Jesus' polemic there cannot be relegated to being an expression of mere frustration or condemnation—there is an eschatological undertone to what he is proclaiming regarding the community leaders and, by extension, those who might follow them (the crowds).

7.3 The Structure of Matt 23

Matthew 23:1 marks off a new pericope with the phrase τότε ὁ Ἰησοῦς ἐλάλησεν τοῖς ὄχλοις καὶ τοῖς μαθηταῖς αὐτοῦ. This establishes the audience of the chapter: the crowds and the disciples. According to Luz, the structure of the chapter is "not controversial," there being three main sections: 23:1–12; 13–33; 34–39.[10] This, however, is not necessarily true. The first section (23:1–12) is indeed uncontroversial.[11] Also widely accepted is the

7. Hood, "Matthew 23–25," 540–42, contains a good discussion of the numerous links between Matt 5–7 and 23–25.

8. As Hood discusses, there is also a geographical shift in both Matt 13 (from the boat [13:1–2] to "the house" [13:36]) and Matt 23–25 (from the temple [21:23] to outside the temple [24:1] and onto the Mount of Olives [24:3]). The shift in the latter cannot be used to separate Matt 23 from 24–25 unless Matt 13 is also split. Hood also notes that the discourse in Matt 18 seems to contain a move to private conversation at 18:21. Hood, "Matthew 23–25," 530–31.

9. Balabanski, *Eschatology*, 137.

10. Luz, *Matthew 21–28*, 92.

11. Apart from Luz, those who take 23:1–12 to be the first section in the chapter

view that the seven woes featured in Matt 23 make up the second section. But where exactly this second section ends, and where the third and final section begins, is disputed. Luz, Davies and Allison, Nolland, and Hagner think the second section ends at 23:33; Carter, France, and Garland[12] think 23:36; Keener and Harrington think 23:32; Garland (in a work preceding his commentary) claims the second section is in fact 23:13–28, with the seventh woe constituting the beginning of the concluding section.[13]

The reasons given by Garland for ending the second section at Matt 23:28 are that the verse "forms an appropriate conclusion to the first six woes, while verse 29 introduces a sudden shift in the charges to the very direct accusation of murder."[14] This, he says, is "the nexus which binds the remaining verses together along with the indication of its punishment."[15] But it is doubtful that the seventh woe and the following verses are any more topically related to, say, 23:37–39 than 23:13–28. Moreover, Garland allows for the possibility that Matthew could destroy literary patterns, such as a series of seven woes, though I hardly find such an explanation, on which the burden of proof lies, very convincing.[16] The similarities in imagery between the sixth and seventh woes—tombs, aesthetic appearance, and dead bodies—as well as the continued claim of hypocrisy, suggest the seventh woe belongs in the second section.

Luz argues that the third section should begin at Matt 23:34 because it begins with "an emphatic 'I.'"[17] He also argues that 23:33 contains an inserted addition inspired by the Baptist's discourse (3:7) that "marks a close and at the same time creates a transition to the pronouncements of judgment that follow."[18] But it is not at all clear why such discourse marks a close within the chapter. Luz also suggests that γέεννα (23:15, 33) is the catchword that

---

include Davies and Allison, *Matthew 19–28*, 264–66; Carter, *Matthew and the Margins*, 451–55; Garland, *Reading Matthew*, 233; Hagner, *Matthew 14–28*, 655–62; Nolland, *Gospel of Matthew*, 920; Keener, *Gospel of Matthew*, 535–46; France, *Gospel of Matthew*, 857–64; Gundry, *Matthew*, 453–59; Harrington, *Gospel of Matthew*, 319–24.

12. In his commentary, at least. Garland, *Reading Matthew*, 233.

13. Garland, *Intention of Matthew 23*, 32–33. In addition, Gundry identifies no third section at all, seeing the second section running from 23:13–24:2. Gundry, *Matthew*, 459–75.

14. Garland, *Intention of Matthew*, 33.

15. Garland, *Intention of Matthew*, 33.

16. Garland, *Intention of Matthew*, 33.

17. Luz, *Matthew 21–28*, 93.

18. Luz, *Matthew 21–28*, 93.

brackets the section,[19] but this is odd given 23:15 is not considered by any scholar (including Luz) to be the beginning of a section.[20]

If there is a literary marker in the latter part of Matt 23, I would suggest it is ἀμὴν λέγω ὑμῖν (23:36). This formula appears numerous times throughout Matthew, and it has multiple uses, in most cases marking a shift in a pericope.[21] It is used as a way of summarizing a pericope (5:26; 10:15, 42; 13:17; 16:28; 17:20; 18:13;[22] 24:2, 34;[23] 25:45; 26:13), concluding a subsection within a pericope (10:23; 25:40), transitioning from one thought to another within a pericope where the next verse/sentence contains a formulaic introductory conjunction (οὖν, 5:18; 25:12; γὰρ, 21:31; δὲ, 6:2, 5, 16; 11:11; 24:47; πάλιν, 18:18; 19:23), and introducing a pericope or introducing Jesus' speech within a pericope (18:3; 19:28; 21:21; 26:21). This suggests that ἀμὴν λέγω ὑμῖν in 23:36 functions either to conclude or to introduce a section within the pericope. In 23:37, there is a shift in tone from judgement to grief, and the object shifts from the Pharisees and scribes to Jerusalem. From this I conclude that ἀμὴν λέγω ὑμῖν in 23:36 is the conclusion to the chapter's second section. This seems like a stronger shift than the "I" in 23:34. Thus, the three sections that make up Matt 23 are 23:1–12, 13–36, and 37–39.

7.4 The Meaning of the "Woes"

In Matt 23 Jesus proclaims seven "woes" (οὐαί) on the scribes and Pharisees (23:13, 15, 16, 23, 25, 27, 29). As with the makarisms in 5:3–12, there is little agreement as to what the woes actually are. Opinions as to the meaning of woes include announcements of God's disapproval and judgement,[24] invectives associated with pronouncements of judgement,[25] public denunciations,[26] prophetic lamentations "for those whose

19. Luz, *Matthew 21–28*, 93n4.

20. Such a marker would also break up the seven woes, which Luz argues against. Luz, *Matthew 21–28*, 92.

21. With either a plural object (ἀμὴν λέγω ὑμῖν) or a singular object (ἀμὴν λέγω σοι).

22. In this case the sentence containing ἀμὴν λέγω ὑμῖν is followed by another before the end of the pericope that summarizes the meaning of the parable.

23. In this case the sentence containing ἀμὴν λέγω ὑμῖν is followed by another that reinforces it before the end of the pericope.

24. Carter, *Matthew and the Margins*, 255, 455.

25. Luz, *Matthew 21–28*, 112.

26. Saldarini, "Delegitimation of Leaders in Matthew 23," 672n37.

situation is miserable (whether they realize it or not),"[27] lamentations as creative prophetic announcements of judgement,[28] expressions of painful displeasure,[29] and descriptions of cursedness.[30]

Many scholars note the intertextual relationship between the woes in Matt 23:13–36 and the Beatitudes in 5:3–12. These texts appear to be contrasting announcements in Matthew, naming opposite realities. This has important ramifications for our view of Matthew's woes in this study, since we have already gone into some detail about the meaning of the Beatitudes, in particular using the cultural analysis of K. C. Hanson. Might Hanson's approach work as well for the woes in Matt 23 as it does for the Beatitudes?

As with the Beatitudes, Hanson locates the woes found in Matt 23 in the foundational Mediterranean values of honor and shame.[31] Honor, we recall, is not self-esteem or pride, but a status-claim that is affirmed by one's community[32] and a commodity over which people compete.

Just as Hanson points out a distinction between blessings and makarisms,[33] so too is this the case for what he calls curses (κατάρα and cognates) and reproaches (woes; Heb: יהֹ; Gk: οὐαί), both in terms of form and content. Whereas curses, like blessings, are words of power whose source is God and whose social setting is ritual/cult,[34] reproaches/woes are the counterparts of makarisms, that is, they are part of the word-field of honor and shame.[35] Hanson points to Eccl 10:16–17 as an example of the juxtaposition of a reproach and makarism, and of the standard content.[36]

> [Shame (הוֹי) on] you, O land,
>   when your king is a servant,
>   and your princes feast in the morning!
> [How honored] (אַשְׁרֵי) are you, O land,
>   when your king is a nobleman,

---

27. Nolland, *Gospel of Matthew*, 467.

28. Keener, *Gospel of Matthew*, 547.

29. Hagner, *Matthew 1–13*, 314.

30. Witherington, *Matthew*, 422.

31. Hanson, "How Honorable! How Shameful!," 81–111.

32. Hanson, "How Honorable! How Shameful!," 83.

33. "אַשְׁרֵי and μακάριος may be related to, but are not synonymous with, the terms for blessing [בָּרַךְ, בֵּרַךְ, בָּרוּךְ, בְּרָכָה; εὐλογία, εὐλογέω, εὐλογήμενες]." Hanson, "How Honorable! How Shameful!," 85.

34. Hanson, "How Honorable! How Shameful!," 86–7.

35. Hanson gives exhaustive example of makarisms as ascriptions of honor in "How Honorable! How Shameful!," 87–89. We will show below that makarisms and reproaches are connected.

36. Hanson, "How Honorable! How Shameful!," 95.

and your princes feast at the proper time—
for strength, and not for drunkenness!

Important to note is that the LXX here uses οὐαί to translate הוֹי. Hanson provides other non-canonical examples confirming the relationship between makarisms and reproaches (1 En. 99:10–16; 103:5–6; 2 En. 52:1–15; Gos. Thom. 102–3; 2 Bar. 10:6–7; b. Ber. 61b; b. Yoma 87a; Thom. Cont. 143.8—144.40; 145.1–7),[37] some of which we explored in our study of the Beatitudes. If, as we have discussed previously, makarisms are not expressions of emotion,[38] nor formal blessings, but ascriptions of honor, then it follows that reproaches are the related-but-opposite ascription, that is, of shame, rather than emotions or formal curses. In this way, just as Matthew's makarisms are best translated as "O how honorable," his reproaches, and those found elsewhere in the Bible, are best rendered "O how shameful."[39] Therefore some of the suggested meanings of "woes" listed above miss the mark, such as woes being expressions of displeasure (emotion) and descriptions of cursedness (related to formal curses). That woes might be public denunciations or announcements of judgement are suggestions that are closer to the mark, so long as they describe attributions of shamefulness and are not understood as instrumental actions of cursing or elucidations of emotion (either that of the subject or object).

Οὐαί is sometimes also used "in the sense of a funeral cry, 'Alas!' (Rev 18:10, 19), in addition to the reproach of 'O how shameful.'"[40] Given the way Matt 23 ends in what is often considered a lament (23:37–39), it is not inconceivable that a funeral cry is intended. So, is οὐαί as used in Matt 23 a reproach or a funeral cry? I am convinced the former is the case. First, the presence of a formal lament in 23:37–39 is debatable (to be explored below) and, even if 23:37–39 were a lament, that is no guarantee that οὐαί is a funeral cry. Second, I agree with Hanson that the usage of οὐαί in Matt 23 is equal and opposite to the makarisms in 5:3–12 as demonstrated by the intertextual relationship between the two passages.[41]

37. Hanson, "How Honorable! How Shameful!," 95–96.

38. At least, expression of emotion is not their primary function.

39. Or perhaps "Shame on those who . . . " or "How disreputable are those who . . . " See Hanson, "How Honorable! How Shameful!," 96–97.

40. Hanson, "How Honorable! How Shameful!," 98. See also Clifford, "Use of *Hôy* in the Prophets," 458–64, for a discussion of הוֹי in the prophetic literature. The author argues that *hôy* "appears in the OT 53 times (counting the two instances of *ho* in Am 5,16)," and has three uses, one being "to describe actual funeral laments (8x; 1 Kgs 13,30; Am 5,16; Jer 22,18; 34,5)" (458).

41. Hanson, "How Honorable! How Shameful!," 102: "the makarisms in Matthew 5 and reproaches in 23 form an inclusio on Jesus' public ministry. The antithetical

7.5 The Form and Content of Reproaches

The form of reproaches in the Bible is fairly consistent—הוֹי/οὐαί followed by a nominal construction.[42] Sometimes there is a reason or threat attached. Hanson lists several variations:

> Singular proper noun: Isa 10:5; 29:1; Jer 48:1. Singular common noun: Isa 1:4; 18:1; 28:1; Jer 23:1; Nah 3:1; Zech 11:17. Plural common noun: Isa 30:1; Ezek 13:3; 34:2. Singular participles: Isa 45:9, 10; Jer 22:13; Hab 2:6, 9, 12, 15, 19; Zeph 3:1. Plural participles: Isa 5:8, 11, 18, 20; 10:1; 29:15; 31:1; Ezek 13:18; Amos 5:18; Mic 2:1; Zeph 2:5. Preposition + singular pronominal suffix: Jer 50:2. Plural adjective: Isa 5:21, 22; Amos 6:1.[43]

Important to note here is that all of the above texts derive from the prophetic corpus, a point to which we will return.[44] It is also important to point out that the typical reproach has two parts:

> (1) the exclamation הוֹי ("woe") followed by a participle denoting the criticized action, or a noun characterizing people in a negative way, and (2) a continuation with as variety of forms, including threats (Isa 5:9,13–14, 24; 28:2–8), accusations (Ezek

---

character of the makarisms and reproaches is not only formal, but semantic as well. . . . The antithetical parallels between the two could hardly be accidental."

42. Hanson, "How Honorable! How Shameful!," 94, 98. A nominal construction might also be called a "noun phrase," in which a phrase including a noun and its modifiers collectively plays the role of a noun.

43. Hanson, "How Honorable! How Shameful!," 94. "For reproaches with οὐαί in the Apocrypha see: Jud 16:17; Sir 2:12–14; 41:8. Reproaches with the Latin equivalent (vae) appear in: 2 Esd 2:8; 15:24, 47; 16:1a, 1b, 63, 67. For other ancient Judean and Christian reproaches, see: 4Q184 1.8; 4Q378 6 1.7; 4Q404 10 1.1; 4Q511 63 3.5; 4QapLam 1.10; 6QHymn 1.7; MasShirShabb 1.2; 1 Enoch 94:6–8; 95:4–7; 96:4–8; 97:7–8; 98:9–99:2; 99:11–16; 100:7–9; 103:5; 2 Enoch 52:4, 6, 8, 10, 12, 14; Sib. Or. 2.339–44; 5.89–91; 7.118–19; 8.95–99; Gos. Thom. 102; Pap. Oxyr. 840; Prot. Jas. 3.1b, 2a, 2b, 2C, 3a, 3b; Inf. Thom. 19.4." Hanson, "How Honorable! How Shameful!," 98.

44. This observation is important. Hanson seems to think that makarisms and reproaches find their origin in the sages, and only secondarily come to be used by the prophets. Hanson notes uses of makarisms (e.g., Pss 40:5; 112; Prov 14:21) and reproaches (e.g., Qoh 10:16–17; Prov 14:31; 23:29–35) in wisdom literature, but it is not at all clear that any of these texts predate the prophetic literature. Ecclesiastes, for example, is often dated to the Persian period or Ptolemaic period. See for example Seow, "Social World of Ecclesiastes," 189–217; Harrison, "Qoheleth among the Sociologists," 162–65; Perdue, *Scribes, Sages, and Seers*, 221–24; Boccaccini, *Roots of Rabbinic Judaism*, 120.

13:3–9; 18:19 [*sic*: 18–19]), or rhetorical questions (Isa 10:3–4; Amos 6:2).[45]

The formula οὐαί + nominal construction is used throughout the NT, including in Matt 23.[46] The reproaches in Matt 23 include reasons given for the ascriptions of shame, as well as negative characterizations of Jesus' opponents (hypocrites, 23:13, 15, 23, 25, 27, 29; blind guides/fools/men, 23:16, 17, 19; serpents/brood of vipers, 23:33). There is generally an accusation following the negative characterization and, in one case, there is also a threat (23:32–36[47]) which seems to relate to both the final reproach and the collection of reproaches as a whole. It seems reasonably clear that the reproaches of Matt 23 conform to a common pattern of reproaches found elsewhere. The formulaic nature of these reproaches suggests that Jesus' announcements follow the traditional pattern and were likely planned (in the narrative world at least). That the sayings were planned is further demonstrated by the identical form of six of the reproaches in Matt 23, as shown by Hanson:[48]

1. Reproach proper

   a. Value judgment: οὐαί ὑμῖν ("Shame on you")

   b. Subject: plural noun/s

2. Reason

   a. Conjunction: ὅτι ("for")

   b. Description of actions

---

45. Hals, *Ezekiel*, 358–59.

46. "The Greek οὐαί formula parallels the Hebrew construction; οὐαί is followed by a nominal construction, and sometimes a reason or a threat. The different variations on the formulaic use are as follows. Singular pronoun: 1 Cor 9:16. Plural pronoun: Luke 11:44, 47; Jude 11. Pronoun + singular proper noun: Matt 11:21a, 21b; Luke 10:13a, 13b. Pronoun + plural common noun: Matt 23:13, 15, 16, 23, 25, 27, 29; Luke 11:42, 43, 46, 52. Singular common noun: Matt 18:7a, 7b; Mark 14:21; Luke 17:1b; 22:22; Rev 12:12. Plural participle: Matt 24:19; Mark 13:17; Luke 6:25a; 21:23; Rev 8:13. Plural adjective: Luke 6:24a, 25b. Adverbial clause: Luke 6:26." Hanson, "How Honorable! How Shameful!," 98.

47. Hanson does not think 23:32–36 belongs to the original oral form of this reproach series, but that the pre-Matthean form ended in 23:31. This is irrelevant to our study, since we are not seeking to study a pre-Matthean form, but the final form of the narrative. He also does not seem to think 23:32–36 constitutes a threat. Hanson, "How Honorable! How Shameful!," 101–2.

48. Hanson, "How Honorable! How Shameful!," 101.

The exception is the woe that begins at 23:16:[49]

1. Reproach proper

    a. Value judgment: οὐαί ὑμῖν ("Shame on you")

    b. Subject: plural nouns

2. Reason

    a. Quotation formula: οἱ λέγοντες ("who say")

    b. Quotation proper

Such uniformity suggests that Jesus' reproaches here are to be thought of as scripted and not improvised, or if improvised, done so according to a well-known form. For the hearers, the distinction between planned and improvised is somewhat moot; what would have mattered is that Jesus' reproaches conformed to a recognizable form that made his speech identifiable as a reproach.

The content of such "woe" formulations is, according to Hanson, "the problems of social ethos commonly addressed in the wisdom literature: oppression of the poor (e.g., Isa 10:1–2//Prov 14:31), illegal acquisition of property (Isa 5:8//Prov 23:10), drunkenness (Isa 5:11–12//Prov 23:29–35), etc."[50] Hanson thinks such concerns may have originated with the sages, but this is questionable.[51] Certainly the bulk of OT reproaches occur in the prophets, and most often in relation to forms of social oppression. The instances are too numerous to list here, but Isa 5:8 is a well-known example:

> Shame on you who join house to house,
>> who add field to field,
> until there is room for no one but you,
>> and you are left to live alone
>> in the midst of the land![52]

Isaiah 10:1–2 is also representative:

> Shame on you who make iniquitous decrees,
>> who write oppressive statutes,
> to turn aside the needy from justice
>> and to rob the poor of my people of their right,

49. Hanson, "How Honorable! How Shameful!," 102.

50. Hanson, "How Honorable! How Shameful!," 95.

51. Hanson, "How Honorable! How Shameful!," 98. See previous footnote about the problems of dating wisdom books prior to prophetic books. It is also questionable whether the sapiential tradition pre-dates the prophetic tradition such that ideas or concerns shared by the traditions can be said to be "of the sages."

52. This is a variation of the NRSV, with "Ah" replaced by "Shame on" to reflect the argument of this chapter.

> that widows may be your spoil,
> and that you may make the orphans your prey![53]

Other examples include Jer 22:13; 23:1; Ezek 34:2; Mic 2:1; Hab 2:6, 9, 12; Zech 11:17. In addition, problems such as idolatry (Isa 31:1; 45:9–10; Jer 50:2; Hab 2:19), debauchery (Isa 5:11; 28:1; Hab 2:15), violence (Nah 3:1), rebellion (Isa 1:4; 5:20; 29:15; 30:1), false prophecy (Ezek 13:3), or compilations of such problems (Zeph 3:1–5) are addressed by the prophets' reproaches. The content of reproaches does not take the form of general prophetic complaints about such social problems. Rather, they are public challenges to the honor of those whose actions embody such problems. As such, they are directed both at the people/group responsible for the problems (polemical), and at the problems themselves, since the polemic is unnecessary if the problems do not exist. By criticizing a particular group for their behavior, and by naming that behavior, reproaches seek also to name implicitly what is right behavior and to pronounce a particular group's honor, namely, those represented by the prophet, including YHWH.

In Matt 23, the polemic exists on at least two levels—it is directed against the scribes and Pharisees in the narrative as well as against those opponents of the Matthean community of whom the community leaders in the story are representative. We will return to discuss Matthew's text in more detail. For now, it suffices to say that the reproaches of Matt 23, as those that conform to the broader pattern of reproaches, fulfill the purpose of challenging the honor of Matthew's opponents, represented by the scribes and Pharisees, for their behavior. They are also an honor-claim by Matthew's community regarding its own behavior.

7.6 Sociological Aspects of Verbal Contests

Jesus' words in Matt 23 are well-known for their vitriolic force, often being considered by commentators to represent violence and thus to stand in strong tension with Jesus' earlier command to love one's enemies.[54] While

---

53. See previous footnote.

54. For example, Luz claims that the critique in Matt 23 is "wholesale and therefore unjust." He goes on to label the critique "prejudice" and says that it is "certainly very remote from the commandment to love one's enemy." He concludes, "Matthew should never have allowed him to speak so unfeelingly as he does in chapter 23." Luz, *Theology,* 121–25. Viviano calls Matt 23 "the unloveliest chapter in the Gospel." Viviano, "Social World and Community Leadership," 3. Saldarini says the chapter "strikes the liberal Westerner or ecumenically minded Christian as malevolent and offensive." Saldarini, "Delegitimation of Leaders," 659. For Carter it is the "bleakest spot" in Matthew. Carter, "Matthew 23:37–39," 66. Johnson notes that, "The power of such language to shape hostile and destructive attitudes and actions toward Jews has often been realized." Johnson, "New Testament's Anti-Jewish Slander," 421.

modern sensitivities regarding Jesus' verbal force are not unimportant,[55] they are not a direct concern for this study. I am, however, interested in how such apparent vitriol should be understood in the context of Matthew's Gospel.[56] Such an understanding ought to shed light on the meaning of Matt 23 and Jesus' prophetic vocation described therein.

To a modern mind, Jesus' public challenges in Matt 23 are indeed problematic. But such challenges were common in the ancient world. Malina and Rohrbaugh describe them as part of the phenomenon they call "challenge-riposte."[57] Played out in public, it consists of a challenge seeking to undermine the honor of the other person, followed by a response that answers in equal or greater proportion, thus challenging in return.[58] Matthew 21–22 pictures the chief priests, elders, Pharisees, and Sadducees all challenging Jesus on a range of topics. In each case, Jesus responds in such a way as to gain the rhetorical upper hand. All of these pericopes contain examples of "challenge-riposte." In Matt 23, Jesus initiates his own challenges toward his opponents. But here, unlike those challenges mounted against Jesus in the previous chapters, they go unanswered. This would have resulted in a serious loss of face for the community leader characters within Matthew's story world.[59]

Luke Timothy Johnson's oft-cited study on the NT's anti-Jewish vilification, what he calls "the rhetoric of slander," is helpful at this point.[60] Johnson begins by outlining the historical circumstances of such slander, explaining that "Christianity" did not yet exist in the NT period, and that followers of Jesus ("messianists") were unnoticed, persecuted, and outnumbered by non-messianist Jews.[61] He goes on to describe the diversity of both the messianic sect and first-century Judaism, noting of the latter that there was fierce debate about what it meant to be a real Jew.[62] These areas have been variously covered in earlier chapters and so we avoid summarizing Johnson's points at length. What is important for us is the next section

---

55. I do not wish, for instance, to ignore or be insensitive regarding the history of Christian anti-Semitism, in-part based on certain readings of Matt 23.

56. In the words of Johnson, "I do not worry about what to do with this language so much as about what the language was doing." Johnson, "New Testament's Anti-Jewish Slander," 419.

57. Malina and Rohrbaugh, *Social-Science Commentary*, 41–42.

58. Malina and Rohrbaugh, *Social-Science Commentary*, 42.

59. Malina and Rohrbaugh, *Social-Science Commentary*, 42.

60. Johnson, "New Testament's Anti-Jewish Slander," 420.

61. Johnson, "New Testament's Anti-Jewish Slander," 423–25.

62. Johnson, "New Testament's Anti-Jewish Slander," 425–28.

of Johnson's article in which he outlines the social context and language conventions of the rhetoric of slander.[63]

Johnson suggests that Judaism from the Hellenistic period onwards ought to be thought of as a philosophy. By this period, philosophy had become "less a matter of metaphysics than of morals."[64] Philosophy was a way of life lead by leaving vice and seeking virtue. While the character and goals of philosophy were, according to Johnson, universally acknowledged, the best way to realize them was disputed. This led to ongoing debate and, eventually, to the development of stereotyped polemic and conventional expression. Johnson describes some of this standardized slander, as found in Hellenistic literature, which passed between philosophical schools and concludes that,

> Certain standard categories of vice were automatically attributed to any opponent. They were all lovers of pleasure, lovers of money, lovers of glory. The main thing that such slander signified, therefore, was that someone *was* an opponent.[65]

Indeed, Johnson goes on to suggest that facts did not affect slander and the purpose of the polemic was not primarily rebuttal, but rather the edification of one's own school.[66] From there, Johnson details such slander in Jewish texts, both Hellenistic and Palestinian. The sheer number of references means it is impractical to provide a detailed summary, but one of the notable examples given by Johnson, one worthy of specific attention, is that of Qumran. Johnson makes note of Qumran's hostility to outsiders and their dualistic paradigm of "sons of light" and "sons of darkness."[67] 1QS describes outsiders in this way:

> But the ways of the spirit of falsehood are these: greed, and slackness in the search for righteousness, wickedness and lies, haughtiness and pride, falseness and deceit, cruelty and abundant evil, ill-temper and much folly and brazen insolence, abominable deeds (committed) in a spirit of lust, and ways of lewdness in the service of uncleanness, a blaspheming tongue, blindness of eye and dullness of ear, stiffness of neck and heaviness of heart, so that man walks in all the ways of darkness and guile. And the visitation of all who walk in this spirit shall be a multitude of plagues by the hand of all the destroying angels,

63. Johnson, "New Testament's Anti-Jewish Slander," 428–41.

64. Johnson, "New Testament's Anti-Jewish Slander," 429.

65. Johnson, "New Testament's Anti-Jewish Slander," 432–33; emphasis original.

66. Johnson, "New Testament's Anti-Jewish Slander," 433.

67. Johnson, "New Testament's Anti-Jewish Slander," 439.

everlasting damnation by the avenging wrath of the fury of God, eternal torment and endless disgrace together with shameful extinction in the fire of the dark regions. The times of all their generations shall be spent in sorrowful mourning and in bitter misery and in calamities of darkness until they are destroyed without remnant or survivor. (1QS 4.9–14)[68]

This passage is aimed at both gentiles and Jews who "do not match the Qumranites' ideas of purity."[69] In other words, the harsh critique is not directed at any particular demographic, nor even necessarily known enemies. On the contrary, those being described are not demonstrably intimately connected to the Qumranites. There is no indication that the rhetoric of 1QS arises in response to tense or painful relationships such as we have assumed is the case between Matthew's community and its Jewish opponents.[70] That such a tender situation is behind 1QS is possible, but we cannot know either way and so we ought not assume that the situation which apparently led Matthew to place such emotional and vitriolic rhetoric on the lips of Jesus in Matt 23 is present in the background of 1QS. This is not to say that the *Yahad* were not living in the midst of clashes with other groups. Indeed, a text such as 4Q171, a commentary on Ps 37, suggests a very hostile relationship between the *Yahad* and the Wicked Priest, who is almost certainly the Hasmonean high priest who persecutes the Teacher of Righteousness.[71] However, despite the existence of such relationships, 1QS does not describe one particular group with whom the *Yahad* are in conflict, but rather all those who are unfaithful according to the standards of Qumran.[72] This suggests the Qumranic vitriol was not motivated by passion, but was an expression of stock categories of vice and fulfilled the purpose of edifying those within the community.

---

68. Translation from Vermes, *Complete Dead Sea Scrolls in English*, 104.

69. Johnson, "New Testament's Anti-Jewish Slander," 440. It is worth noting that "Qumranites" may here be a misnomer. Wise et al. argue that 1QS refers not to a single community living at Qumran, but to groups scattered through Palestine. The text was not attached specifically to the site of Qumran. Wise et al., *Dead Sea Scrolls*, 223. See also Regev, *Hasmoneans*, 123.

70. We ought to keep in mind that the final form of 1QS includes redactions of earlier documents. See Davila, "Damascus Document."

71. "The wicked person spies on the just person and tries to kill him. . . . Its interpretation concerns the Wicked Priest who spies on the just man and wants to kill him." 4Q171 4.7–8. Translation from Martínez and Tigchelaar, *Dead Sea Scrolls Study Edition*, 1:347. See also Regev, *Hasmoneans*, 93–94.

72. Additionally, we ought not assume that Qumran texts date from the same time. On varied dates of 1QS and 4Q171, see Qimron, "Some Works of the Torah," 3:188.

There are some similarities between 1QS and the reproaches in Matt 23, even if there are no reproaches in the former text. In both texts, the enemies are referred to as hypocrites (1QS 4.10; cf. Matt 23:13, 15, 23, 25, 27–29), blind (1QS 4.11; cf. Matt 23:16), greedy (1QS 4.9; cf. Matt 23:25), foolish (1QS 4.9; cf. Matt 23:17), and neglectful of righteous deeds (1QS 4.9; cf. Matt 23:23). If 1QS does indeed utilize stock criticisms of opponents, then it is quite possible that the author is doing the same in Matt 23. Johnson remarks:

> First-century Jews who disputed with each other used language conventional to their world. These conventions provide the appropriate context for properly assessing the polemic of the NT. If by definition sophists are hypocritical, and philosophers of all opposing schools are hypocritical, and philosophers in general are hypocritical, and Alexandrian pagans are hypocritical, and Apion is a hypocrite, are we really surprised to find scribes and Pharisees called hypocrites?[73]

Johnson goes on to make the same point regarding the criticisms of blindness and possession by evil spirits. It is not so much that these criticisms accurately describe one's opponents in the first century CE, it is just that such things should be said about them *because* they are opponents. This is the nature of such stock language. The purpose of such language was not, as we have said, to describe accurately the opponent. Rather, the purpose of such language was to provide a negative example. In this way, a positive alternative is implied, either explicitly or implicitly, and the group would be expected to emulate this positive example. Johnson calls this protreptic discourse.[74] Such language reinforced group values and expectations, thus strengthening the identity of the community. This has a clear connection with one of the purposes of Matthew's Gospel, outlined previously, to create a narrative that helps form and maintain the identity of the Matthean community.[75] We must also keep in mind that, as stated previously, the

---

73. Johnson, "New Testament's Anti-Jewish Slander," 440. Weinfeld makes the point that the charge of hypocrisy was leveled against the Pharisees even in the rabbinic sources. Weinfeld, "Charge of Hypocrisy," 52–58. In another article Weinfeld lists specific cases of Talmudic critique of the hypocrisy of Pharisees owing to their lack of practice: *m. Hag.* 2:1; *m. Yebam* 8:7; *b. Sabb.* 31b. Weinfeld, "Jewish Roots of Matthew's Vitriol," 31.

74. Johnson, "New Testament's Anti-Jewish Slander," 433.

75. David Sim comes to much the same conclusion: "[The presentation of Jesus was] constructed by the evangelist himself in response to the situations of crisis his small Christian community was experiencing." Sim, however, goes on to preference modern presuppositions over a contextual understanding of Matthew's presentation of

conflict being discussed is not between "Christianity" and "Judaism," but rather between two groups that perceive themselves as Jewish and are in conflict over the correct interpretation and practice of Torah. In other words, the conflict is *intra muros*.

There is a tension between the notion of challenge-riposte as honor challenge and the rhetoric of slander as standard polemic. If the rhetoric of slander need not necessarily be accurate, but rather is stock language denoting opposition, can such language function as a meaningful honor challenge? In other words, can inaccurate polemic function as an honor challenge that is taken seriously by the one challenged and those who observe? This is a difficult question because it depends on a number of factors. Perhaps the most important is how the one challenged interprets the challenge itself. This, as Malina notes, includes a judgement about how the community will judge the challenge—"for the victim of an affront or challenge is dishonored only when and where that person is forced by the public to recognize that one has been challenged and did not respond."[76] In this way the challenge is only serious if the community takes it seriously. Matthew's author no doubt shaped chapter 23 so as to direct challenges at those characters within the narrative that represented the opponents of the real-life Matthean community. In this way, the challenges in Matthew 23 are not only polemical patterns common to the time period, but also criticisms shaped by Matthew's current situation. This is perhaps most obvious in the Matthean Jesus' criticism of the title *rabbi*, which is an anachronism deriving from Matthew's time. We can be fairly confident, then, that the Matthean community recognized Jesus' pronouncements as meaningful challenges to the scribes and Pharisees and thus to their own real-life opponents. Looking at the narrative internally, Jesus' challenge in 22:43–44 has already gone unanswered and the implication in 22:46 is that this is not because the leaders deemed the challenge unworthy of response, but rather because they were unable to respond. Matthew does not make explicit whether Jesus' address in chapter 23 is deemed by the crowd to be a meaningful challenge, but given its inclusion in the Gospel and continuation from 22:43–46, this is implied.

It is additionally worth pointing out that, as previously noted, Matthew places the reproaches of Matt 23 alongside the eschatological material in chapters 24–25. This suggests that neither section can be read in isolation from the other. The eschatological discourse is shaped and purposed by Jesus'

Jesus: "Finally and sadly, [Matthew's] Jesus fails to provide the perfect role model for his readers and for Christians today." Sim, "Jesus as Role Model," 20.

76. Malina, *New Testament World*, 41.

criticism of the community leaders in Matt 23. Conversely, Jesus' polemic in Matt 23 only makes sense against the imminent eschatological backdrop of chapters 24–25. The destruction of Jerusalem, described in chapters 24–25, is, for Matthew, the result of the unfaithfulness (e.g., hypocrisy, blindness) of the community leaders and vindicates the critique that Jesus proclaims. In short, the critique is not only a stock reflection of group conflict, but also constitutes an eschatological announcement expressing God's judgement of the injustice present amongst Israel's leadership, an announcement subsequently[77] and ostensibly vindicated by historical events. This may not necessarily allay our modern sensitivities regarding the force of Jesus' language, but combined with the discussion above regarding the stock nature of Jesus' rhetoric, it is legitimate to view Matt 23 as a standard expression of opposition within an urgent period requiring imminent repentance in order to avoid national disaster.

In summary, the challenges offered by Jesus in Matt 23, including the reproaches, are not to be thought of as necessarily emotional and vitriolic statements, but rather as the conventional language of group or school opposition. Such language functions instructively for those internal to the group, and as an honor challenge to the opponent. The challenges also have an underlying eschatological current, implying a marked urgency in light of impending disaster. More broadly, we note that Jesus' prophetic vocation included the task of employing harsh critiques of Israel's leaders, not unlike his OT predecessors. Such critiques took the rhetorical form of the time, and it is difficult to know whether such form was essential to Jesus' vocation or simply a contextual aspect of it. Either way, we can be certain that Matthew viewed harsh criticism of injustice and the unjust as a part of Jesus' prophetic vocation and that, if we assume Matthew was consistent, shaming enemies did not constitute a failing to love them (cf. 5:43–48). After all, Jesus' mourning in 23:37–39 appears to signal his desire that his enemies repent in response to his critique. Finally, in terms of Matthew's rhetorical use of these challenges, Jesus' skill in challenge and riposte demonstrates that he is an honorable and authoritative prophet.[78]

---

77. Subsequent, at least, to the time of Jesus depicted in Matthew's story. Obviously Matthew's audience lives after the vindicating event of Jerusalem's destruction. Whether Matthew is adapting this material *ex eventu* is disputable and not particularly important in this study.

78. Malina and Rohrbaugh, *Social-Science Commentary*, 42.

7.7 Comparison with Jesus Son of Ananias

We have already seen how Jesus' speech in Matthew 23 fits into a pre-existing pattern found in OT and other prophetic literature. What is necessary from here is a comparison of Matthew's Jesus with another figure from the first century CE. By using a contemporary of Jesus of Nazareth as a point of comparison we will find a way to orient our understanding of Jesus' prophetic vocation according to his milieu.

We previously gave attention to Josephus' account of Jesus son of Ananias (*J. W.* 6.300–309), including comparing him to certain OT prophets and prophetic episodes. Josephus' account of Jesus may be of particular value since its wider context is Josephus' description of events that foreshadowed the downfall of Jerusalem and the temple (*J. W.* 6.288–315); such is not dissimilar to the relationship between Jesus of Nazareth's reproaches in Matthew 23 and predictions of Jerusalem's downfall in Matt 24–25.

Jesus of Ananias' reproaches are directed at four objects:

1. Jerusalem (αἰαί Ἱεροσολύμοις, *J. W.* 6.304, 306; αἰαί πάλιν τῇ πόλει, 6.309)

2. The people [of Jerusalem] (αἰαί . . . τῷ λαῷ, *J. W.* 6.309)

3. The temple (αἰαί . . . τῷ ναῷ, *J. W.* 6.309)

4. Himself (αἰαί δὲ κἀμοί, *J. W.* 6.309)

The word αἰαί here is typically translated "woe,"[79] the same as οὐαί in Matthew 23. Liddell and Scott render αἰαί "alas!" in the sense of an exclamation[80] and other renderings are hard to find. The word appears frequently in Greek literature, such as in the following Aristotelian passage citing a drinking song about Athenian exiles who, having fortified a post in Attica, Lipsydrium, were besieged and forced to surrender. The song, describing their failure, says:

> Ah! (αἰαί) Lipsydrium, faithless friend!
> Lo, what heroes to death didst send,
> Nobly born and great in deed!
> Well did they prove themselves at need

---

79. As in the Whiston and Loeb translations.

80. Liddell and Scott, *Lexicon Abridged*, 17. More recently is Nordgren, *Greek Interjections*, 60 who also translates αἰαί as "Alas!" or "O!" in the sense of an expression of grief. Nordgren states that he often prefers to leave αἰαί untranslated since the Greek is more powerful than the English equivalent owing to "the impoverished vocabulary for lamentation in the latter (p. 129n183).

Of noble sires a noble seed.[81]

And Plutarch, quoting the sayings of "intemperate persons," sayings of "incontinence":

> Alas! (αἰαῖ) from God this evil comes to men
> When, knowing what is good, they do it not.[82]

The English translations imply a cry of grief, which is no doubt correct. But it is probably also the case that the grief expressed implies shame. The lexical similarities between αἰαῖ and οὐαί suggest the two words are related,[83] though admittedly even if true this would not prove they share a meaning. However, it would be consistent with what we have said about shame so far that a song about failed exiles begins with an announcement of shame. The same goes for Plutarch's saying, derived from the mouths of uncontrollable people and speaking about the consequences of their own captivity to their passions.

An example from one of the plays of Euripides serves as a further example:

Phaedra

> Oh, oh! (αἰαῖ) How I long to draw a drink of pure water from a dewy spring and to take my rest lying under the poplar trees and in the uncut meadow![84]

Here some context is necessary. Phaedra is discussing with her nurse why she is sick. In the midst of the discussion she admits to her nurse that she is sick because she loves Hippolytus. She claims that she must starve herself unto death in order to retain her honor. The above statement relates to Phaedra's desire to drink, which would ruin her honor. In light of this, αἰαῖ makes sense as an expression of Phaedra's shamefulness that she desires such a thing.

In these examples, we can see how αἰαῖ might function similarly to οὐαί, namely as a reproach for shameful behavior. I would contend that, given the lexical and contextual factors, αἰαῖ ought to be considered part of the honor/shame lexicon as a reproach. If this is correct, and Jesus of Ananias' use of αἰαῖ does indeed represent a reproach, then we can see how

81. Aristotle, *Ath. pol.*, 19.3.

82. Plutarch, *Virt. mor.*, 6.

83. Rossing claims that αἰαῖ, found in classical and modern Greek lament texts, is related to οὐαί. Rossing, "Alas for Earth," 182–83. See also Alexiou, *Ritual Lament in Greek Tradition*, 151.

84. Euripides, *Hipp.*, 208–11.

he is like some of the OT prophets. Perhaps the most pertinent expression of reproach similar to that of Jesus of Ananias is that found in Jer 13:

> I have seen your abominations,
>   your adulteries and neighings, your shameless prostitutions
>   on the hills of the countryside.
> Shame on (οὐαί [LXX]) you, O Jerusalem!
>   How long will it be
>   before you are made clean? (Jer 13:27)[85]

This passage comes at the end of a section in which Jeremiah proclaims impending judgement on Judah in the form of exile. The chapter describes "those who come from the north" (13:20) bringing violence (13:22) and scattering the people like chaff (13:24) because of their iniquity. In the LXX, Jeremiah issues a reproach against Jerusalem, saying their sin has caused them to be in need of cleansing. Jesus of Ananias' reproaches are not attached to a lengthy oracle or an explicit identification of sin as with those of Jeremiah, but the literary and historical contexts of national threat are similar. The same can also be said of Jesus of Nazareth in Matt 23, who also utters reproaches, albeit against community leaders rather than Jerusalem or the people as a whole. In saying this, Jesus of Nazareth does express that Jerusalem as a whole is receiving the consequences of its actions (Matt 23:37–39).

Josephus also records a poetic oracle of Jesus son of Ananias that is not a reproach:

> A voice from the east,
>
> a voice from the west,
>
> a voice from the four winds;
>
> a voice against Jerusalem and the sanctuary,
>
> a voice against the bridegroom and the bride,
>
> a voice against all the people.[86]

This is almost certainly influenced by Jeremiah 7:[87]

---

85. This is a variation of the NRSV, with "Woe to" replaced by "Shame on" to better reflect the argument so far.

86. Josephus, *J.W.* 6.301.

87. Jesus ben Ananias' oracle is by no means a verbatim quote from Jer 7, but as Ferda says, "Even when Josephus' biblical subtext is known there are often few if any verbatim agreements." Ferda notes Josephus' retelling of the Decalogue as an example (*Ant.* 3.91–92 and Exod 20:2–17 have only four words in common). Ferda continues: "Josephus often shows a "paraphrastic freedom" that follows the rhetorical principle of not retelling a story in the same way. Thus, near direct quotations are particularly noteworthy, and [*J.W.* 6.301] is one such case." Ferda, "Jeremiah 7 and Flavius Josephus,"

And I will bring to an end the sound of mirth and gladness, the voice of the bride and bridegroom in the cities of Judah and in the streets of Jerusalem; for the land shall become a waste. (Jer 7:34)

Indeed, Josephus wrote more about Jeremiah than any other biblical prophet, in particular Jeremiah's warnings of judgement prior to the Babylonian exile.[88] It is unsurprising that Josephus would liken Jesus of Ananias to Jeremiah. Both oracles above are found in a similar historical context whereby they are proclaimed in a socio-political situation that appears peaceful and prosperous, prior to the materialization of national calamity. Both correctly prophesy regarding Jerusalem's fate. Both messages are proclaimed in the temple (Jer 7:2; cf. *J.W.* 6.300–301) and both in the context of declaring the destruction of the temple. Ferda also notes the mournful character of Jesus, a Jeremian motif, as well as his opposition to the religious leaders.[89] In terms of a wider Jeremian context, Jesus of Ananias is like the prophet in that both are mistreated and imprisoned.

There are strong echoes of Jeremiah in Josephus' account of Jesus son of Ananias, both in Jesus' reproaches and in his initial "voices" oracle. This suggests, at the very least, that there existed in Palestine in the first century CE the symbolic literacy necessary to understand the meaning of such Jeremian echoes. Jesus of Nazareth explicitly relates his action of clearing the temple with Jeremiah (Matt 21:13; cf. Jer 7:11) and by such identification seems to associate his prophetic actions and speech regarding the temple, the leaders, and Jerusalem as a whole with that of the lamenting prophet. Jesus of Ananias' prophesying also kindled the anger of the "leading citizens" (*J.W.* 6.302), not unlike Jeremiah (Jer 26:7–24). Again, this is similar to Jesus of Nazareth in his ongoing clashes with the community leaders; after Jesus' Jeremiah-like oracles against them, the leaders make their final plans to kill him (Matt 26:3–5). Finally, the son of Ananias used a poetic form for his initial oracle. As we have said above, this oracle was probably based on Jer 7:34, which was likely well-known. This similarity suggests the poetic form used by Jesus son of Ananias was probably composed in advance, or was at least based on stock language known in that time and place. Such premeditation is similar to Jesus of Nazareth who used a well-known form for his reproaches in Matt 23, a form derived from OT prophetic reproaches, as we have seen. This form was a prophetic reproach followed by a pronouncement of judgement, such that a prophetic attribution of shame was connected to its consequences, and hearers/readers knew what they heard/

166–67.

88. Ferda, "Jeremiah 7 and Flavius Josephus," 163.

89. Ferda, "Jeremiah 7 and Flavius Josephus," 168.

read was within the prophetic tradition.[90] Like the son of Ananias, Jesus of Nazareth probably planned his speech.

That there are numerous similarities between the two Jesuses suggests also that their use of prophetic oracles styled from OT prophets (especially Jeremiah), their critique of Jerusalem and its leaders, and their predictions of national calamity were all comprehensible in their social environment. This may imply that prophetic oracles occurred somewhat regularly at that time, but this is far from certain. Moreover, the form of the oracles of these Jesuses is not identical—in fact they only share the use of reproaches and even there they use different words—but the ideas expressed in both, as well as their respective contexts, share many elements of likeness. They shared a critique that must have reflected the minds of some of the people, one that the ruling authorities understood as a critique when they heard it. That both Jesuses make use of such Jeremiah-like critiques, whether in form, content, or context, suggests that there was a feeling amongst some groups at the time that Israel's sin would eventually lead to some catastrophic event. Of course, for Matthew's communities this event had already occurred by the time they read Matthew's story. In terms of the story itself, however, the prophecies of Jesus in Matt 23 are before the fact, and their recipients are expected to take urgent action to avoid calamity.

7.8 Matt 23 and Torah

In addition to resonances with OT prophetic literature and figures from the first century, Jesus' prophetic announcements in Matt 23 also have strong ties with Torah. As we discussed previously, the Beatitudes are, in a sense, an interpretive foundation for Torah put forward in the Sermon on the Mount and throughout Matthew. They are an expression of the underlying reality of Torah. Indeed, Jesus' prophetic vocation is centered on a call to covenantal faithfulness that for Matthew necessitates Torah interpretation and obedience. Given the connection in Matthew between the makarisms in Matt 5 and the reproaches in Matt 23, it is reasonable to assume that the reproaches have a connection with Torah similar to the Beatitudes. In some ways such a connection is expected. We have already established that Jesus' mission as a whole in Matthew's Gospel is intimately tied to Torah. Still, it is important to draw the parallels between the Beatitudes and the reproaches in Matt 23 and their relationship to Torah as prophetic speech.

---

90. Luz, *Matthew 21–28*, 112. Luz does not recognize οὐαί as a reproach, but rather as a "woe." Still, this does not affect his observation about the formula.

We begin by recalling the fivefold structure of Matthew's discourses. Earlier we noted that these five discourses formed a prominent structural component of Matthew's Gospel, punctuating the overarching story with direct teaching for Matthew's communities. We did not, however, discuss the meaning of this fivefold block. The idea that each of Matthew's teaching blocks, plus their preceding narrative material, correspond to the books of the Pentateuch is unconvincing.[91] Yet, we can agree that Matthew is thoughtfully crafted, and that the fivefold structure is not accidental. What is the intention of such a structure? Wright thinks that the Pentateuch is indeed the clue to this question, not in the sense of a sequence of five books, nor a scheme of repetition, but rather Pentateuch as covenant.[92] Wright goes on to posit a connection between Matthew's makarisms and reproaches (Matt 5:3–12; 23:13–38) and the Deuteronomic blessings and curses (Deut 27–30).[93] Wright is correct except for this final point which mistakes Matthew's makarisms and reproaches (μακάριος/οὐαί) as functional equivalents of the Deuteronomic blessings/curses (εὐλογέω/ἐπικατάρατος [LXX]). Though we could draw a comparison between Jesus' prophetic vocation as a whole and Deuteronomism more generally, this does not apply specifically to Matthew's makarisms and reproaches in comparison to Deut 27–30. As we have seen in this chapter and previously, it is not the case that Matthew's "blessings" and "curses" are blessings and curses at all, but rather ascriptions of honor and shame. For this reason, I would contend that Matthew is not drawing a special relationship between Jesus' teaching in Matt 5:3–12; 23:13–38 and Moses' concluding speech in Deut 27–30.[94]

What then is the connection, if any, between Matt 23 and Torah? Previously I noted that the Beatitudes describe a people who find themselves at home in the kingdom of heaven, in part because they are faithful to God according to Torah. If the reproaches of Matt 23 are, as we have said, meant as a contrast to the makarisms of Matt 5—a description of opposing realities—then we might expect them to be describing a people *not* at home in the kingdom of heaven, precisely because they have not been faithful to Torah. If this is correct, the connection between Matt 23 and Torah looks

---

91. Bacon, *Studies in Matthew*, xiv. "A half-century ago it was recognized that its compiler has followed the plan of aggregating his teaching material from all sources into five great discourses corresponding to the oration codes of the Pentateuch, each introduced, like the Mosaic codes, by a narrative section, each closing with a transition formula as the reader passes from discourse to narrative."

92. Wright, *New Testament*, 387.

93. Wright, *New Testament*, 387–88.

94. The word groups used in Matt 5 and 23 differ from those used in Deut 27–30 (LXX).

different from what Wright suggests. Rather than referencing the Deuteronomic blessings and curses, Jesus' speech in Matt 23 alludes to the whole
scope of Torah and the expected faithfulness to that vision of life. Unlike
the Deuteronomic code, Jesus does not name the potential consequences
of hypothetical actions, but rather, like the prophets against Israel's leaders,
announces judgement against the sins of the scribes and Pharisees for the
injustice they have actually done. What, then, does Matt 23 have to do with
Torah?

In Matt 23, the substance of Jesus' disagreement with the scribes and
Pharisees, and thus his critique of their faithfulness to Torah, begins not with
the reproaches themselves, but rather with the introductory remarks in 23:1–
12. Here Jesus, speaking to the crowds and disciples, begins by describing
the scribes and Pharisees as those who sit on Moses' seat. It is not clear what
is meant by "Moses' seat" (*Μωϋσέως καθέδρας*). Cecil Roth has suggested
a piece of synagogue furniture[95] and this has been followed more recently,
at least tentatively, by Carter and Nolland.[96] More common today is to see
the expression as metaphorical or abstract in meaning, for example, Garland
("The seat of Moses . . . refers to their claim to be the rightful interpreters of
the Mosaic tradition") and Viviano ("meaning that the scribes and Pharisees teaching [*sic*] with the authority of Moses").[97] Both interpretations see
the phrase as ultimately referring to the Torah interpretations of the scribes
and Pharisees, which Jesus seems to affirm. As Powell states, however, both
suggestions are only guesses.[98] Powell proposes an alternative interpretation
to the phrase, one that helps make sense of 23:3 in which Jesus advises his
disciples to do what the leaders say, but not what they do:

> When Jesus says that the scribes and Pharisees sit on the seat of
> Moses, he might not be referring to their role as teachers at all,

95. Roth, "Chair of Moses and Its Survivals," 100–111.

96. Carter, *Matthew and the Margins*, 451–52; Nolland, *Gospel of Matthew*, 922–23,
though Nolland only offers it as a possible interpretation. See also Rabbinowitz, "Matthew 23:2–4," 424; Cohen, "Were Pharisees and Rabbis the Leaders," 272. Cohen notes
that few of these objects have ever been found, and that they all date from at least 150
years subsequent to Matthew's Gospel. Rabbinowitz seems to think that these arguments do not cast doubt over the evidence, a point with which I disagree; Rabbinowitz,
"Matthew 23:2–4," 425.

97. Garland, *Reading Matthew*, 233; Mason, "Pharisaic Dominance," 371–72; Viviano,
"Social World," 11. See also Bornkamm, "End Expectation and Church in Matthew," in
Tradition and Interpretation in Matthew, ed. Bornkamm, Barth, and Held, 15–51 (24);
France, *Gospel of Matthew*, 859; Hagner, *Matthew 14–28*, 659; Stanton, *Gospel for a New
People*, 140; Keener, *Gospel of Matthew*, 541. Luz argues that "the archaeological-realistic
and metaphorical meanings of the term belong together." Luz, *Matthew 21–28*, 99.

98. Powell, "Do and Keep," 430–31.

but to their social position as people who control accessibility to Torah. They are the ones who possess copies of the Torah and are able to read them. They are the ones who know and are able to tell others what Moses said. . . . Jesus may be simply acknowledging the powerful social and religious position that they occupy in a world where most people are illiterate and copies of the Torah are not plentiful. Since Jesus' disciples do not themselves have copies of the Torah, they will be dependent on the scribes and the Pharisees to know what Moses said on any given subject. In light of such dependence, Jesus advises his disciples to heed the words that the scribes and Pharisees speak when they sit on the seat of Moses, that is, when they pass on the words of the Torah itself.[99]

Building on Powell, Nolland suggests we might say that the scribes and Pharisees were "walking copies of the Law."[100] This interpretation is convincing for a number of reasons, not least because it results in a consistent approach on the part of Matthew to the authority and Torah-interpretation of the scribes and Pharisees. One of the major problems with understanding the seat of Moses as either a literal seat or as a reference to the teaching authority of the community leaders is that, in separating the teaching and the deeds of these leaders,[101] and assuming that Jesus criticizes only the latter, a contradiction is created between Jesus' words in Matt 23:2–3 and the insistence throughout the First Gospel that the leaders have no authority to teach (e.g., 7:29).[102] Moreover, such a reading of Matt 23:2–3 creates a contradiction in chapter 23 itself, since Jesus calls the leaders "blind guides" (23:16) and attacks their interpretations (23:16–24), not merely their actions. Indeed, for Matthew, the practice of Torah is not characterized only by actions, but also by teaching, as reflected by Jesus' teaching in 5:19.

Ultimately, in Matt 23:2–3 Jesus is telling his disciples to do not what the scribes and Pharisees teach, but what *Moses* teaches, a point that is consistent throughout Matthew. Thus 23:2–3 is not an endorsement of the authority of the scribes and Pharisees. The now-common rendering "they *preach* (λέγω) but do not practice"[103] is misleading since it suggests preaching in the sense of proclaiming interpretation. But λέγω more commonly

99. Powell, "Do and Keep," 431–32.

100. Nolland, *Gospel of Matthew*, 923.

101. An anachronistic approach in any case; So Powell, "Do and Keep," 432.

102. "Either we must admit that here Jesus greatly exaggerates the facts or else he contradicts himself." Douglas, *Overstatement in the New Testament*, 90.

103. English translations using "preach" include ESV, GW, GNT, NIRV, NIV, NLV, Phillips, RSV. For the rendering "teach" see CEV, HCSB, MSG, NET, NLT, NRSV.

means "to say," a broad verb that in no way necessitates the didactic over-tones of "preaching." Inasmuch as the leaders speak the teachings of Moses when they read Torah, what they say should be observed.

All of this is important because it properly frames the argument in Matt 23. Jesus begins by warning the crowd and his disciples that, though the leaders speak the words of Moses in Torah, they do not practice (i.e., interpret and do) accordingly. He then moves to critique some of the practices that arise from their hermeneutic (23:4–7). The reproaches that follow fall into the same pattern for, as I have already said, Torah interpre-tation was not only a matter of doctrinal purity, but additionally entailed a vision and pattern of community life. For Matthew's Jesus, the Torah interpretation of his opponents leads to expressions of community life that are harmful and contrary to the will of God.

This approach also helps to rectify the suggestions of Wright out-lined above in regard to the Deuteronomic blessings and curses. While we maintain that Matthew's makarisms and reproaches are not echoes of Deut 27–30, they do find their basis in God's will expressed in Torah as a whole. Inasmuch as Deut 27–30 confronts Israel with the question of whether they will choose life or death—covenant faithfulness or infidelity[104]—we can say that Matthew's makarisms and reproaches are much the same, confront-ing the faithful community with a vision of life to embody (Matt 5), and a vision of death to avoid (Matt 23). But any correlation only exists because both Matt 5 and 23 and Deut 27–30 are derived from Torah as a whole, not because these passages are directly related. Just as Israel in the time of Moses must choose whether it will live in the covenant of life given as a gift from God, so too must Matthew's communities make the same choice in the time of the new Moses.

If Matthew portrays Jesus as a new Moses figure, he also portrays him as a prophet enforcing the covenant, including right interpretation of Torah. This image finds its reference point in the classical OT prophets who called Israel back to faithfulness to the covenant of the God who brought them up out of the land of Egypt (e.g., Exod 22:21; Jer 7:21–26; 11:1–17; Ezek 20:1–44; Hos 13; Amos 3:1–2; Mic 6; cf. Exod 20:2). This image is reflected in Jesus' criticisms of his opponents, including his seven reproaches. Jesus' critique begins, as I have said, with the insistence that the leaders speak Torah but do not practice it. Their interpretation of Torah burdens others while they evade this burden (Matt 23:4).[105] Their deeds are ultimately done that they may

---

104. Wright, *New Testament*, 388.

105. The phrase "they themselves are not willing to move them with their finger" (αὐτοὶ . . . τῷ δακτύλῳ αὐτῶν οὐ θέλουσιν κινῆσαι αὐτά) is difficult to understand on its own. Luz claims there is "no proverbial saying behind it," and that "move" (κινέω) is

be seen by others (23:5–7). Jesus here criticizes the use of Torah as a means of attaining honor, a self-criticism present in later rabbinic teaching.[106] The discipleship community is to avoid such practices and the hierarchical social arrangements implied by them (23:8–12).

Matthew's seven reproaches continue this Torah-based critique. They are, as Garland suggests, best grouped into three pairs and a concluding reproach:[107]

a. *1* (23:13), *2* (23:15): The effects of the teaching of the scribes and Pharisees on their followers (cf. 23:4)

b. *3* (23:16–22), *4* (23:23–24): Scribal and Pharisaic interpretation of Torah

c. *5* (23:25–26), *6* (23:27–28): The hypocrisy of the leaders (cf. 23:5–7)

d. *7* (23:29–31): Persecution

The fact that there are seven reproaches is significant,[108] representing the fullness of the leaders' shamefulness.[109] The first reproach contrasts the scribes and Pharisees with Peter (cf. 16:19) for they shut the kingdom of heaven in people's faces.[110] This may relate to the criticism of laying heavy burdens (φορτίον) on people in 23:4. That is to say, they teach Torah in such a way as to shut the kingdom in people's faces. This is in contrast to the light burden (φορτίον) of Jesus (11:30), the implications of his teaching of Torah. The narrative itself suggests this connection. Following the declaration in 11:30 that Jesus' burden is light, Matthew moves into two stories dealing with the competing Torah interpretations of Jesus and his opponents, and their effects in the community (12:1–8, 9–14), followed soon after by the teaching

---

a verb with multiple possible meanings. Luz goes on, however, to say the metaphor is clear from the context of bearing burdens. "'Moving burdens' is what a bearer of burdens does, and that obviously is what the Pharisees and scribes themselves do not want to do, even though they demand it of others. Thus the image means: they themselves do not do what they say." Luz, *Matthew 21–28*, 102–3.

106. See *b. Sotah* 22b. In addition, Josephus critiques the Pharisees for their skill in the law which made men think they were favored by God; *Ant.* 17.41.

107. Garland, *Reading Matthew*, 234–36.

108. In asserting that there are seven reproaches, I am taking Matt 23:14 as an interpolation. See Metzger, *Textual Commentary*, 50.

109. Hagner suggests it points to the "fullness of corruption." Hagner, *Matthew 14–28*, 666. This interpretation is right, but neglects the honor/shame element of the reproaches.

110. Peter (and the disciples) are given the keys (κλεῖδας) of the kingdom of heaven (16:19) while the scribes and Pharisees shut (κλείετε) the kingdom of heaven in people's faces (23:13).

regarding a tree and its fruit (12:33–37). This context suggests that the issue of "burdens" does indeed relate to the interpretation of Torah and the resultant social effects. It is here, among other places, that the leaders are charged with being hypocrites (ὑποκριτής; play-actors)[111] since they will not bear that with which they burden others. If the first reproach (23:13) does relate to the imposing of burdens in 23:4, then Jesus ascribes shame on the basis of the unfaithful teaching of the Pharisees that rests heavily on the people, such as their teachings regarding Sabbath in Matt 12.

The following reproach (23:15) deals with scribal and Pharisaic practices of converting gentiles to their version of Judaism.[112] It is not clear what precisely a "child of Gehenna" is,[113] but it is at the very least the negative counterpart of a child of the kingdom (cf. Matt 13:38). That is to say, those who become proselytes to the scribal and Pharisaic interpretation of Torah become twice as much children of Gehenna as those who convert them. Context suggests that the reason for this is the burden placed on them by the scribes and Pharisees, the underlying reason for the reproach.

The third reproach (23:16–22) is longer, dealing with oaths. The precise meaning of Jesus' saying here is not crucial to our argument; what is important is that Jesus' reproach is clearly a criticism of the leaders' Torah interpretation. Jesus has already taught on oaths (5:33–37), and this teaching was an explicit interpretation of Torah (cf. Lev 19:12; Num 30:2; Deut 23:21).[114] The similarity of the subject matter suggests that 23:16–22 should

111. Ὑποκριτής referred to a stageplayer, one who appears to be what they are not.

112. McKnight raises the problem of the lack of evidence for the conclusion that there was a lively Jewish mission among the gentiles. McKnight, *Light Among the Gentiles,* 106–8. Likewise, Luz: "There is no evidence that scribes or Pharisees of that day went on long missionary journeys like the early Christian apostles, and certainly not for the sake of a single proselyte." He deems the statement in Matt 23:15 to be exaggeration—"they 'move heaven and earth' for the sake of a single proselyte." Luz, *Matthew 21–28,* 118. The issues raised here are solved if Nolland is right when he notes that a proselyte (προσήλυτος) refers in the LXX to resident aliens in Israel (*gr*). "Since the resident alien was expected to live in accord with Mosaic Law, the term came to mean 'convert to Judaism.'" Nolland, *Gospel of Matthew,* 933. It may simply be that the proselytes referred to in Matt 23 would have been those resident aliens—God-fearing gentiles—already within the land. It may also be that this verse refers to drawing other Jews into the Pharisaic version of Judaism.

113. Suggestions include that a child of γέεννα refers to one who will incur divine judgement after death (implied by Hagner, *Matthew 14–28,* 668; Carter, *Matthew and the Margins,* 457), one who is the opposite of a child of the kingdom (Luz, *Matthew 21–28,* 118; Nolland, *Gospel of Matthew,* 934), or to one whose destiny is to be thrown onto the literal place called Gehenna, the burning rubbish heap outside of Jerusalem (a possible reference to the conclusion of the events of 70 CE). These readings are not mutually exclusive.

114. Matt 5:33 is not a direct quote from Torah, but seems to be an amalgamation

be read in light of 5:33–37. Jesus seems to be saying that the perplexing and relativizing teaching of the leaders regarding oaths—teaching that defies common sense (23:16–19)—obscures the plain meaning of Torah, that one who makes an oath must keep it. Their interpretation of Torah is such that it undermines the trustworthiness of transactions and relationships in the community, a reason why perhaps Jesus' abolishes oaths altogether for the discipleship community (5:33–37).

Jesus again attacks the scribal and Pharisaic interpretation of Torah in 23:23–24. Here, though, the issue is hermeneutical. While some commentators have seen the issue here as the scribes and Pharisees neglecting "what really matters,"[115] this assumes the existence of an obviousness as to what "really matters" in Torah.[116] To be sure, from a Matthean point of view "what really matters" in Torah is clear because Jesus outlines it in 23:23. However, the nature of Jesus' assertion is obfuscated by commentators' simplification of ancient debates about Torah interpretation. Jewish scholar Phillip Sigal suggests that "Biblical principles and institutions were sometimes 'forever,' but the detailed forms were not. Essence and form are two separate aspects of a whole."[117] In this way, Torah is more correctly understood, according to Sigal, as "instruction" rather than "law."[118] Torah was not absolutist in its requirement, but allowed for "flexibility in application."[119] In other words, there was no singularly obvious way to interpret it. For the Pharisees in Matthew's story, there was no principal command—each halakhah had equal validity, and none could be elevated.[120] The love commands, then, did not take precedence in (Matthew's account of) Pharisaic interpretation

of multiple verses. The first half, "You shall not swear falsely," probably derives from Lev 19:12. The second half, "but shall perform to the Lord what you have sworn," could derive from Num 30:2 or Deut 23:21–23 (or both). Nolland has suggested that Matthew has fashioned this sentence to call to mind the commandment from the Decalogue to not take YHWH's name in vain (Exod 20:7; Deut 5:11). His reasoning for this is that the first two "antitheses" cite two of the Ten Commandments, and so Matthew continues this pattern. This does not explain 5:31, however, which quotes Torah (Deut 24:1), but not the Decalogue. Nolland, *Gospel of Matthew*, 248–49.

115. Garland, *Reading Matthew*, 235. See also Carter, *Matthew and the Margins*, 458 ("missing the big picture of doing God's will"); France, *Gospel of Matthew*, 872 ("meticulous concern for detail which leaves the essential principles of religion untouched"); Hagner, *Matthew 14–28*, 670 ("neglect of things that really mattered"); Luz, *Matthew 21–28*, 122 ("ignoring what is the most important thing in the law").

116. This might be acceptable from the point of view of Christian theological interpretation, but it is questionable from a socio-historical perspective.

117. Sigal, *Halakhah of Jesus*, 15.

118. Sigal, *Halakhah of Jesus*, 17–18.

119. Sigal, *Halakhah of Jesus*, 19.

120. Sigal, *Halakhah of Jesus*, 21.

(what Sigal calls a "constructionist" approach).[121] Jesus, on the other hand, gives priority to the love commands, and allows them to be the lens through which he interprets Torah. This, says Sigal, amounts to "halakhic obedience within the parameters of the prophetic interpretation," the fulfillment of Torah in the spirit of the prophets.[122] If Sigal is correct, Jesus' criticism is not that the scribes and Pharisees do not interpret Torah according to an obvious and singularly correct hermeneutic, but rather that his approach is superior since it focuses on those elements that affect the community the most ("weightier matters").

Another approach is that of William Herzog, following Fernando Belo, who discerns two distinct systems in Torah, a purity code and a debt code.[123] The former was designed to avoid uncleanliness, the latter to ensure the extension of God's blessing (in the form of land and wealth) to all the people.[124] Herzog suggests that the two codes are "not necessarily complementary," and that the "scribal Pharisees made the debt code a function of the purity code."[125] In other words, the Pharisaic approach to Torah interpretation prioritized the purity code. If Herzog is correct, the issue is, again, the contestation of competing interpretative approaches to Torah.

The two approaches to Pharisaic hermeneutics above are not easily harmonized since the former suggests a flat approach to Torah commands, while the latter implies a preference for the purity code. Which approach is correct is not for us the point, however, since we are concerned with showing that debates about how to interpret Torah were present in first-century Palestine and that there was no self-evident hermeneutic that the Pharisees were disregarding. The issue in 23:23–24 is the contested nature of such interpretation. Jesus' attack is against the Pharisaic approach to Torah vis-à-vis his own, not their failure to interpret in a way that was, in first-century Judaism, self-evident. This brings the comparative benefits of competing interpretations into view. The ability to control Torah was significant because, as Herzog says,

> the carrier of the great tradition in first-century Palestine was Torah, and the group that could control the interpretation of Torah could define "world," that social and political construction

---

121. Sigal, *Halakhah of Jesus*, 21.

122. Sigal, *Halakhah of Jesus*, 70.

123. Herzog, *Parables as Subversive Speech*, 182.

124. Herzog, *Parables as Subversive Speech*, 182–83.

125. Herzog, *Parables as Subversive Speech*, 184.

of reality that could specify the meaning of purity, demand tithes, and control behavior.[126]

The Pharisaic insistence on scrupulous tithing (23:23), even beyond the dictates of Torah,[127] was highly regarded by Jewish teachers.[128] It was, however, a source of economic pressure for small farmers.[129] Their interpretation was not simply a matter of doctrine—it had serious effects on the lives of those who trusted them for their leadership and became a source of their power in the community. Thus, the issue is again an interpretive approach to Torah that places heavy burdens on the people while the interpreters are relatively unburdened (23:4). Jesus' alternative hermeneutic includes a prophetic critique that the most important commandments are justice (κρίσις), mercy (ἔλεος), and faithfulness (πίστις).[130] In his hermeneutic, Jesus "represents the Bible's prophetic heritage more than its priestly-cultic heritage."[131] His words contain strong resonances with Amos 4:1–4 and probably Mic 3. Jesus does not condemn tithing (cf. 23:23; "these you should have done, without neglecting the others"), but he does condemn an approach to Torah that treats debatable, and thus minor, matters as more important than the practice of just judgement, mercy, and covenantal faithfulness[132]—in other words, he criticizes an approach that allows for the exploitation of people rather than the enhancing of their well-being. Jesus' alternative Torah hermeneutic, prophetic in nature, is characterized by the supremacy of the OT love commands (cf. 7:12; 22:37–40).

The following two reproaches (23:25–26; 27–28) flow on naturally from the previous one, moving from hermeneutics to hypocrisy regarding application of Torah. While Jacob Neusner has claimed that 23:25–26 relates

---

126. Herzog, *Jesus, Justice, and the Reign of God*, 149.

127. See Keener, *Gospel of Matthew*, 549–51. Keener argues that the insistence on tithing dill (anise), cumin and mint was debatable because it was unclear whether they constituted foodstuffs, and thus whether they were covered under the OT agrarian tithe (Lev 27:30; Num 18:21–32; Deut 14:22–29). "Later rabbis settled on dill (probably m. Ma'aś. Sh. 4:5) and cummin (m. Dem. 2:1) being tithed but later denied mint."

128. Keener, *Gospel of Matthew*, 550.

129. Borg, *Jesus, a New Vision*, 84–85.

130. Luz, *Matthew 21–28*, 124, notes the prophetic language in Matt 23:23. κρίσις, ἔλεος, and πίστις appear together in Hos 2:21–22. Κρίσις and ἔλεος: Mic 6:8; Zech 7:9; Hos 12:7; Jer 9:23. Κρίσις: Isa 1:17; Jer 22:3. Ἔλεος: Hos 6:6.

131. Luz, *Matthew 21–28*, 124.

132. Hence the criticism in 23:24 ("You blind guides! You strain out a gnat but swallow a camel!")—this criticism hyperbolically suggests the leaders are willing to eat a camel even though they will not let small insects enter their mouths.

to purity laws,[133] I am inclined to agree with Hyam Maccoby that "The best explanation is the simplest: that Jesus was talking about clean and dirty cups as a straightforward metaphor for clean and dirty personalities."[134] The context allows for an indirect critique of scribal-Pharisaic compulsiveness regarding washing of utensils—indeed, the washing of vessels was a contemporary discussion[135]—but this is tangential to the core criticism of the leaders appearing clean on the outside but remaining unclean within. Anthony Saldarini puts it well when he says that "The ritual cleanliness of cups and plates remains a valid concern, but it is subordinated to the contrast of the inner and outer human being and the cleansing of the inner self from extortion and intemperance."[136] This is demonstrably true given that there was, according to Maccoby, no ritual custom for washing only the outside of a cup; the only way to wash ritually unclean vessels was "to immerse them totally in the water of the *Miqveh* (ritual immersion pool)."[137] The debate between the first-century Shammaites and Hillelites was not about whether the inside of a cup should be washed, but rather the *outside*.[138] In other words, Jesus' criticism of washing only the outside of a cup does not describe an actual practice of any Pharisaic group, but "appears instead to make fun of the subtle distinction between inside and outside";[139] his saying must be taken metaphorically. The true criticism is about robbery (ἁρπαγή) and self-indulgence (ἀκρασία)—the "cups" are defiled because they are filled with the extortion of the vulnerable by the leaders, a practice linked to their lack of self-control. In its form, Jesus' statement houses an economic judgement within a metaphor about purity and in doing so contrasts the two

---

133. Neusner, "First Cleanse the Inside," 486–95.

134. Maccoby, "Washing of Cups," 12.

135. Keener, *Gospel of Matthew*, 552. "The Mishnah regularly distinguishes between inner and outer parts of vessels with respect to cleanness . . . and some discussions of cleanness go back to the first-century disputes between the schools of Shammai and Hillel (b. Shab. 14b, bar.). The Shammaite school of Pharisees were less concerned whether one cleansed the inner or outer part first. By contrast the Hillelite Pharisees thought that the outside of cups were typically unclean anyway and thus, like Jesus, insisted on cleansing the inner part first."

136. Saldarini, "Delegitimation of Leaders," 676.

137. Maccoby, "Washing of Cups," 5.

138. M. Ber 8:2. This is why Keener's suggestion that Jesus sides with the Hillelites is not correct. Keener, *Gospel of Matthew*, 552. The Hillelite position was that it was acceptable to use a cup whose outside was unclean because the outside was defiled only to the second degree. Jesus' concern in Matt 23 is not whether it is possible to have the contents inside the cup clean even when the outside is unclean; if anything it is the opposite.

139. Luz, *Matthew 21–28*, 127.

concerns, unveiling the skewed priorities of the leaders. Such a judgement is linked to Jesus' critique of the leaders' hermeneutic in 23:23–24; their corrupt practices arise from their flawed interpretive approach to Torah that places scrupulousness above human need.

The saying in 23:27–28 makes a point similar to 23:25–26. Whatever the actual purpose of whitewashing tombs,[140] Jesus acknowledges that such tombs are outwardly beautiful. Inside, however, they are filled with "the bones of the dead and all kinds of filth." The contrasting image is striking, since what is beautiful hides what is corrupt. This image is used to describe the scribes and Pharisees, who outwardly appear righteous, but are full of hypocrisy (ὑπόκρισις) and lawlessness (ἀνομία). The strength of the metaphor should not be overlooked—the leaders are full of *all* uncleanness (πᾶς ἀκαθαρσία), inwardly comparable to corpses, which caused to become impure those who came into contact with them.[141] A connection with Ezek 13:10–12 is possible. Here Ezekiel depicts an image of prophets smearing whitewash on walls that will nonetheless fall. The image illustrates God's coming judgement for the lies uttered by the prophets. Luz suggests this passage may have inspired a "common topos of insult."[142] If so, we have another example of Jesus' adoption and adaptation of prophetic imagery in his discourse. The suggestion may then be that the leaders are liars. The charge that the leaders are full of hypocrisy and lawlessness echoes earlier judgements in Matt 23. Ἀνομία has already been used in Matthew, in 7:23 and 13:41, in both cases to describe those who do not do the will of the Father. In both pericopes these people do not enter the kingdom of heaven. In 7:23, there is the suggestion that these lawless ones are those who say, "Lord, Lord." In chapter 23, Matthew explicitly reveals that these lawless ones are the scribes and Pharisees, the leaders of the people, those who would say "Lord, Lord." For Matthew, lawfulness is related to faithfulness to Torah, specifically Jesus' interpretation of Torah. The leaders, in not abiding by the love-centered interpretation of Jesus, are deemed lawless, those who do not do the will of God and are unfaithful to covenant. From the point of view of Matthew's story, Jesus the prophet announces the truth about those who do not practice the will of God, but who instead merely

140. Keener suggests Jews whitewashed tombs to warn passersby to avoid them because they were unclean. Keener, *Gospel of Matthew*, 553. Luz notes that whitewashing was decorative. Luz, *Matthew 21–28*, 130. Both are probably true.

141. According to Sanders, some even believed that anything which overshadows a corpse, or anything it overshadows, would become impure. Sanders, *Jewish Law from Jesus to the Mishnah*, 34.

142. Luz, *Matthew 21–28*, 130n124. Luz cites CD 8.12; 19.24–25; Acts 23:3 as additional usages of this phrase.

appear to do the Father's will. They, as shameful ones, represent the opposite of those who are honorable (5:3–12).

The imagery of tombs continues into the next and final reproach (23:29–36). It begins with yet another charge of hypocrisy (23:29). This hypocrisy expresses itself in this reproach in the way the leaders apparently honor the prophets who have died, decorating their monuments and denying that they would have shared with their fathers in shedding the blood of the prophets. But for Jesus, the fact that the scribes and Pharisees self-identify as the sons of those who murdered the prophets means that they are of the same kind, even if they try to distance themselves from their fathers. "Sons" here could refer to one being like another, or it could refer to literal lineage.[143] While it is not explicit which is the case, it would seem odd for the leaders to self-identify as metaphorical sons of those whose murders they condemn (unless the self-identification is rhetoric attributed to them but without a historical referent, in which case it holds little power). In any case, their sonship will be reflected in the way they will kill, crucify, flog, and persecute the prophets, wise men, and scribes that Jesus will send (23:34), including Jesus himself. This theme, one that stands in the OT tradition of the murder of the prophets, has already been explored in Matthew's story in 21:33–39 and 22:2–6, and we will explore it further below. Such treatment is a reference to contemporary events in the Matthean community, events that have fulfilled Jesus' words.[144] By persecuting these figures, the leaders demonstrate that they are in fact what they say they are not—murderers of God's faithful ("from the blood of innocent Abel to the blood of Zechariah"; 23:35) and thus hypocrites. They are invited, then, to fill up the measure of their fathers (23:32)—to be what they are—and this will mean their being sentenced to γέεννα.

As in the sixth reproach, the final reproach in 23:29–36 makes an implicit claim about the faithfulness of Jesus' opponents to the covenant obligations found in Torah. In this case, the specific charge of unfaithfulness to Torah is both obvious and serious—the scribes and Pharisees contravene even the Decalogue command not to murder (Exod 20:13; Deut 5:17). In terms of the gravity of the accusation, this reproach is the strongest and concludes the series of seven. It frames the extent of the leaders' covenant

---

143. Keener, *Gospel of Matthew*, 554.

144. Historically this notion is difficult, since it is not at all clear whether the early rabbinic movement, with which Matthew's communities were in conflict, was murdering Christians. Moreover, crucifixion was a Roman punishment, not one that the Jews could carry out. Luz suggests that Matthew's picture here is not real, but merely axiomatic, a result of understandable psychological distress resulting from suffering at the hands of present enemies. Luz, *Matthew 21–28*, 154.

infidelity: they are willing even to murder those sent from God (prophets, wise men, and scribes) to enforce and interpret the covenant obligations that the leaders appear so zealous to uphold.

Jesus' self-identification as a prophet is most clear in this final reproach. The reference to his opponents killing and crucifying prophets, wise men, and scribes is a less than subtle allusion to Jesus' own fate. The shape of his prophetic vocation as reflected in the seven reproaches has been shown to be covenantal in its concern—Jesus' critique of the leaders is that they are unfaithful to God's covenant enshrined in Torah. This critique arrives at a point in Matt 23:32 where Jesus urges the scribes and Pharisees to carry out the evil of their fathers. No longer does Jesus attempt to warn the leaders of the consequences of their actions or call them directly to repent; now he encourages them to carry out the evil of their ancestors, the very thing they should not do. Luz argues this imperative is ironic, citing examples of the same technique from the OT prophets.[145] Keener thinks the:

> Filling of the cup to the brim refers to meriting all the "blood," that is, bloodguilt, saved up among past generations, never punished as was deserved (cf. Is 40:2; Deut 32:43; Ps 79:10; Rev 6:10; Sifre Deut. 332.2.1). (Jesus may allude here to the Jewish eschatological concept that a predetermined quantity of suffering was prerequisite for the end . . .). That generation would receive the fruit of this judgment.[146]

Both Luz and Keener are probably correct and their suggestions are compatible. Both relate Jesus' statement in 23:32 to the prophets, both in tone and content. Keener's suggestion helps make sense of Jesus' statements about all the bloodshed of the earth/land (γῆ) coming upon the leaders (23:35) and all "these things" coming upon this generation (23:36).[147] Jesus' statements

---

145. Luz, *Matthew 21–28*, 133, 133n149. His examples are Isa 8:10; Jer 7:21; Amos 4:4; Nah 3:14, all of which are followed by an announcement of judgement.

146. Keener, *Gospel of Matthew*, 555–56.

147. On the identity of "this generation," Rieske suggests that this phrase refers to "the wicked people of *all* time, those before the Messiah and those after" (emphasis original). Rieske, "What Is the Meaning," 209–26. This is certainly a possibility since γενεά can have a qualitative sense, speaking of a group with shared characteristics, in addition to a chronological sense. A number of factors complicate one's interpretive choice, not least the nature of the judgement declared in Matt 23–25—is it the destruction of Jerusalem, eschatological judgement, or both? Rieske's proposal relies on eschatological judgement being in view, since those in "this generation" who have already died are apparently yet to face the consequences of the judgement. There is also the question, raised by Rieske, as to whether it is befitting divine justice for the bloodguilt of all past generations to fall on Jesus' contemporaries. The assumption here is that judgement implies the action of God, rather than being the inevitable consequence of

here are to be associated with the prophets, whose oracles were rooted in Torah, and are intended to enforce God's covenant with Israel. As was often the case in the prophets, there is in Jesus' words an announcement of impending judgement. This coming judgement is also implied in Jesus' reiteration of John's accusation of the leaders being a "brood of vipers" (23:33; cf. 3:7), which for John was connected to the need for repentance and/or coming judgement ("the wrath to come").

In sum, Jesus' reproaches in Matt 23 represent accusations of shamefulness for the failure of the community leaders, the scribes and Pharisees, to live faithfully in light of God's covenant outlined in Torah. For Matthew, they have failed to live according to God's will, which is expressed by Jesus' own interpretation of Torah centered on justice, mercy, and faithfulness. Because for Matthew covenant faithfulness is defined by God's revelation in Torah, Jesus' prophetic speech here takes the form of accusations of breaches of Torah commands, both specifically (regarding oaths, greed, and murder) but also in a more general sense, encapsulating interpretive and ethical failings that negatively impact on the life of the community. That the leaders have led others astray is an example of the latter kind of accusation and constitutes part of what Jesus means by placing "heavy burdens" on people's shoulders. Just as the prophets of the OT were tasked with announcing God's judgement in light of Israel's covenantal infidelity—particularly that of its leaders—so too does Jesus announce God's judgement, first upon the blind guides themselves and then upon "this generation." This is the consequence of stubborn failure to do God's will, and hypocritically to attempt to counterfeit faithfulness.

7.9 Jesus' Grief (23:37–39)

The stubbornness of the leaders is a cause for grief (23:37–39). Many commentators have categorized this section as a lament.[148] D. Keith Camp-

---

sin. A problem for Rieske's view is that immediately after Jesus' reference to "this generation" in 23:36 he addresses Jerusalem, suggesting the city's destruction in 70 CE is the declared judgement, which falls upon a particular chronological group. The temple is also in view for destruction (cf. 23:38). Since the meaning of this phrase is not crucial for my case in this section, and since Rieske's position is not definitive, I have opted for the majority position, namely, that "this generation" refers to those community leaders contemporary to Jesus whom he is addressing in his speech.

148. See, for example, Carter, *Matthew and the Margins*, 463; Davies and Allison, *Matthew 19–28*, 319; France, *Gospel of Matthew*, 883; Garland, *Reading Matthew*, 236; Gundry, *Matthew*, 472–73; Hagner, *Matthew 14–28*, 678–81; Keener, *Gospel of Matthew*, 557; Meier, *Vision of Matthew*, 166; Nolland, *Gospel of Matthew*, 948; Witherington, *Matthew*, 433–34.

bell, however, suggests this label has taken on a technical meaning in OT studies such that identifying Matt 23:37–39 as lament—a specific literary genre—is incorrect because it does not meet the criteria.[149] Thus, mourning is more appropriate than lament.

In Matt 23:37, Jesus addresses the city with an emphatic double vocative, names its sin (killing those sent to it, especially the prophets), and expresses mourning over Jerusalem's refusal to be embraced.[150] The image of a hen gathering its chicks—based on a well-known OT image[151]—contrasts with that of the scribes and Pharisees placing burdens on people's shoulders (23:4). Whatever the possible meaning of the "house" in 23:38,[152] the most probable options based on OT usage are the city of Jerusalem, Israel as a people, or the Jerusalem temple. That Matthew will soon move to discuss the destruction of the temple in chapter 24 suggests it is in view (cf. 21:13). Even if this is technically true, the temple probably functions metonymically for the whole city;[153] in 70 CE, both were destroyed. It is noteworthy that the temple, previously referred to as "my house" (ὁ οἶκός μου; 21:13; cf. Isa 56:7), is now called "your house" (ὁ οἶκος ὑμῶν)—God is no longer present in it. This is almost certainly an allusion to Ezek 9–11, where the prophet proclaims that YHWH's glory exits the temple (10:18–19). Indeed, in Ezekiel the glory went up from Jerusalem to the Mount of Olives (Ezek 11:23), as does Jesus in Matt 24:1–3; the connection is almost certainly deliberate—Jesus is the locus of divine glory. In any case, Jesus' announcement of judgement on the temple conforms to the traditional prophetic pattern, at least as found in Ezekiel.

---

149. Campbell, "NT Scholars' Use," 213–26. Campbell argues that in OT studies, in contrast to classical English usage, lament refers to a specific literary genre that connotes significant theological implications. While referring to Jesus' speech in 23:37–39 as a lament in a general sense is acceptable, it is not helpful in the field of biblical studies in the period following the form-critical work of Gunkel. Campbell says that Westermann, refining Gunkel's work, "suggests three determinant elements in classifying a lament: 'the one who laments, God, and the others.' He further clarifies these elements by describing what he calls the 'component parts of the lament': (1) the complaint against God (often asks 'Why?' or 'How long?'), (2) the lament over personal suffering (which is dependent on the 'complaint against God'), and (3) the complaint about the enemy" (217).

150. On the image of a hen gathering its chicks, see Blevins, "Under My Wings," 365–74.

151. See Exod 19:4; Deut 32:11; Pss 17:8; 36:7; 63:7; 91:4. See also 1 En. 39:7.

152. It could refer to a royal palace (cf. Jer 22:5). Keener, *Gospel of Matthew*, 559.

153. Observe the close relationship in Isa 64:8–12, for example.

Ezekiel announces destruction and exile (Ezek 11:1–13) but also conditional restoration (11:14–21).[154] Jesus also announces conditional restoration in Matt 23:39, again demonstrating his conformity to Ezekiel's prophetic pattern. Allison notes that some commentators have seen in 23:39 a reference to unqualified judgement.[155] Hagner, Keener, and Luz all express, in their own way, agreement with this reading.[156] Allison notes, however, that the quotation in 23:39 is Ps 118:26a (LXX 117:26a) and that, in the LXX and NT, the words εὐλογεῖν and εὐλογημένος (used in LXX 117:26, the latter also in Matt 23:39) express joy rather than fear and trembling.[157] There is, he says, no precedent for the wicked uttering a blessing when the Lord or the Messiah comes.[158] That Jesus' words here refer to judgement is unlikely. Allison suggests that the text "means not, when the Messiah comes, his people will bless him, but rather, when his people bless him, the Messiah will come."[159] Thus, for Allison the prophecy is conditional—the time of seeing Jesus again is dependent on the leaders blessing him. Seeing Jesus again, he says, is a reference to the final redemption, the consummation of the age, "the end."[160] This need not necessarily be the case since, as we have discussed, the notion of "seeing God," found also in the Beatitudes (5:8), can refer to a special revelation of God within history.[161] In that discussion it was argued that Matthew's notion of seeing God in 5:8 is an alternative way of speaking about inheriting the kingdom of heaven in the present. This may be in view in 23:39. In this reading, rather than Israel's blessing of Jesus the Messiah being the condition for the final

154. Conditional on the basis of whether their heart "goes after detestable things" (Ezek 11:21).

155. For example, John Calvin, "He [Jesus] will not come to them [the Jews] until they cry out in fear—too late—at the sight of His Majesty, 'truly He is Son of God.'" Also T. W. Manson, "The time will come when you will be ready to say to me, 'Blessed is he that cometh in the name of the Lord'; but then it will be too late," and J.C. Fenton, "Jesus will not be seen by Jerusalem again before he comes in judgement, and then they will greet him, but with mourning." See Allison, "Matt. 23:39," 75.

156. Hagner, *Matthew 14–28*, 680–81; Keener, *Gospel of Matthew*, 558–59; Luz, *Matthew 21–28*, 162–64. See also Crawford, "Near Expectation," 234.

157. Allison, "Matt. 23:39," 75.

158. Allison, "Matt. 23:39," 75–76.

159. Allison, "Matt. 23:39," 77.

160. Phrases used throughout Allison's article. Allison, "Matt. 23:39," 75–84.

161. There is a long history of "theophanic" experiences in the OT, meaning simply that God was revealed in a special way to people. In the OT it relates to close relationship with the divine; it does not require a futuristic interpretation (see e.g., Exod 24:9–11; Num 12:8; 14:14; Isa 6:5; Jer 29:12–13; Pss 11:7; 17:15; 24:6; 27:4, 8; John 1:18; Rev 22:4). See Malina, "Patron and Client," 10.

consummation, it is the condition for Israel (corporately or individually) to enter the kingdom of heaven in a present sense.[162] Whichever reading of the meaning of "you will not see me again" is correct, the more important point for us is that the prophecy Jesus utters is conditional in nature and a consolation following the announcement that judgement will come upon Israel for its sin—God does not finally reject Israel, but is faithful to God's covenant in offering salvation through Jesus.[163]

The image of the house being desolate (ἔρημος; 23:38) calls to mind the common OT image of the wilderness, but also the OT prophetic images of Jerusalem lying desolate. Sometimes the word is explicitly connected to the judgement of exile (e.g., Isa 6:11–13). Even so, in the wilderness there is hope for restoration (e.g., Isa 40:3; 43:19; 48:20–21; 52:9). This restoration requires at once the action of God and the obedience of the people (e.g., Isa 52:7–12). Jesus echoes the same tradition that, as Stanton outlines, follows the trajectory of Sin–Exile–Return.[164] Like the OT prophets, Jesus proclaims that the sins of the people will result in desolation, but that there will be hope for return for those who welcome the one who saves. But this will require repentance, and 23:39 is Jesus' only call for repentance in this section; it is his final word. That the leaders appear unlikely to repent before catastrophe comes upon them is a cause for grief.

7.10 Jesus the Martyred Prophet

Finally, and on a more general note, the murder of the prophet is a well-known theme expressed in the texts of the early church. Though there are only a handful of occurrences of or allusions to the murder or attempted murder of specific prophets in the biblical texts (e.g., 1 Kgs 18:4, 13; 19:10; Jer 26:20–23; 38:4; Matt 23:35), the tradition of the murder of the prophets is common, particularly in the NT (e.g., Neh 9:26; Matt 21:34–36; 23:30–31, 35, 37; Acts 7:52; 1 Thess 2:15; Heb 11:32, 36–37; Rev 16:6).[165] This tradition exists in at least one non-biblical text earlier than or contemporary

162. The advantage of this reading is that it does not have the problem of the "rhetorically awkward" (Luz) change of tone from judgement to hope, as noted by Luz, *Matthew 21–28*, 163, and Stanton, *Gospel for a New People*, 249.

163. For further support of the notion that 23:39 is conditional, see Garland, *Reading Matthew*, 236–37.

164. Stanton, *Gospel for a New People*, 247–55.

165. See Turner, *Israel's Last Prophet*, 13–53, for a comprehensive survey of the theme of the rejected prophet in the OT and Jewish literature of the Second Temple period. Turner, *Israel's Last Prophet*, 55–113, provides an equally comprehensive survey of the same theme in NT texts.

to Matthew, namely, *Lives of the Prophets*.[166] This text (or at least an early version of it) may have influenced New Testament martyrdom perspectives, though we cannot be sure.[167] Whether Jesus' eventual death as a prophet conforms to a widespread martyred-prophet trope within Second Temple Judaism is not immediately clear. However, the existence of *Lives of the Prophets*, as well as the *Martyrdom of Isaiah*,[168] along with hints in Josephus (e.g., *Ant.* 3.307; 4.21–22; 9.168–69; 10.37–39) and rabbinic texts (e.g., *b. Yebam.* 49b; *b. Giṭ.* 57b; *y. Sanh.* 10.2; *Pesiq. Rab.* 4.3; 26.1–2), suggest that there was some pre-existing martyred-prophet motif in at least some segments of Judaism.[169]

In the *Lives of the Prophets*, we find traditions about the OT prophets, including stories of the martyrs among them:

- Isaiah is sawn in half by King Manasseh, with no specific reason given;
- Jeremiah is stoned to death by "the people" (Israel[170]) in Egypt, with no specific reason given;
- Ezekiel is slain by the leader of the Israelite exiles because he rebuked him for idolatry;

166. At least an early version of it. See Hare, "Lives of the Prophets," 2:380–81. Interestingly, this martyrdom tradition was strong enough to have endured in much later texts, like the *Book of the Bee* (thirteenth century CE).

167. David Satran cautions that though we can see the martyrdom traditions in the NT as having their basis "in attitudes and beliefs current in first century Jewish circles," care must be taken not to naively project the early Church's focus onto the whole of Judaism in the Second Temple period since this tradition is, according to Satran, given prominence because of the rejection and martyrdom of Jesus. Satran, *Biblical Prophets in Byzantine Palestine*, 59. This is certainly possible, although I am not convinced of the implication that the Jesus sayings about the martyrdom of the prophets are merely projections of the early Church into the Jesus story.

168. The *Martyrdom of Isaiah* is the first section of the composite Christian text *Ascension of Isaiah*. *Martyrdom* is generally regarded as pre-Christian, and Knibb suggests that while it was written no later than the first century CE, the narrative dates back from Antiochus Epiphanes' persecution of the Jews (167–164 BCE): Knibb, "Martyrdom and Ascension of Isaiah," 149. Blenkinsopp agrees that the stories could have been in oral circulation for centuries before being committed to writing: Blenkinsopp, *Opening the Sealed Book*, 49.

169. Donaldson, in his study on Moses typology in Acts, makes an interesting statement, albeit tangential to our concerns: "because a similar tendency to depict Moses as a persecuted figure is to be found already in Josephus, and also because it is highly unlikely that rabbinic tradition was influenced by Christian thought at this point, it can be concluded that the [rabbinic] tendency to link Moses and the 'prophet like Moses' with the theme of the persecution of the prophets was at least latent in first-century Judaism." Donaldson, "Moses Typology," 43.

170. Hare, "Lives of the Prophets," 386n2c.

- Micah is thrown off a cliff by King Ahab's son Joram after rebuking him for the wickedness of his fathers, having previously given much trouble to Ahab;

- Amos was often beaten by Amaziah, priest of Bethel, and was eventually clubbed and killed by Amaziah's son, though no specific reason is given;

- Zechariah son of Jehoiada was slain by King Joash beside the temple altar, with no specific reason given.

The *Martyrdom of Isaiah* adds to the tradition of Isaiah, claiming his death is the result of sustained opposition to King Manasseh. Before the death of Manasseh's father Hezekiah, Isaiah prophesies that the son will be a follower of Beliar (and more: "Beliar shall dwell in Manasseh") and that Manasseh will cause many in Judea to abandon the true faith (1:1–2, 6b–10a). Moreover, Isaiah prophesies that Manasseh will saw him in two (1:7–8a, 9–10a). Manasseh, having become king, does indeed turn away from the God of his father Hezekiah, serving Satan instead and facilitating the spread of lawlessness (2:1–6). Manasseh's ascension and subsequent deeds cause Isaiah and other prophets to withdraw to a desert mountain for two years (2:7–11). Isaiah is eventually accused of being a false prophet for prophesying against Jerusalem and the king (3:6–7), for claiming greater prophetic insight than Moses (3:8–10b), and for denouncing the lawlessness of Jerusalem and its leaders (3:10c). The result is that Isaiah is seized (3:12) and executed to the accompaniment of laughing and mockery (5:1–3).

In every case where a reason is given for the prophet's murder, that reason is tied to the prophet's denunciation of the monarch or some other powerful figure. Such denunciations consist of rebukes for wickedness/lawlessness or idolatry. Even in cases where no specific reason is given, the prophet's demise comes almost invariably by the hand of a powerful person, either a king or priest, with the exception of Jeremiah who is killed by the Israelites in Egypt. Josephus confirms this pattern of prophets being killed by the powerful (*Ant.* 9.168–69 [Jehoash]; 10.37–39 [Manasseh]) but also has clashing examples in which Moses and Aaron are almost stoned by the congregation in the wilderness (*Ant.* 3.307; 4.21–22). What we can say from all of this is that there are no hard and fast rules as to the pattern of the martyrdom or persecution of the prophets, but that in most cases such violence is perpetrated by the powerful against figures who have spoken against their idolatry or wickedness.

This pattern is repeated in the first century CE by Jesus son of Ananias (Josephus, *J. W.* 6.288–315). In Josephus' view, Jesus is one of a number of signs given to the people of Jerusalem to show them "the way to salvation." Jesus appears four years prior to the Jewish–Roman war and for seven years and five months declares doom on Jerusalem and its inhabitants. His prophesying began, like Amos, in a time of apparent peace and prosperity, at least from the perspective of the ruling classes. Like Jesus of Nazareth, he makes use of Jer 7 in his prophecies (Jer 7:34). Though Jesus son of Ananias is not murdered, his oracles do inspire some of the leaders of the city to have him arrested, chastised, and taken to the Romans where he is whipped to the bone. Jesus' only response to this violence is to cry out, "Woe to Jerusalem!" His oracle is clearly threatening to the Jerusalem leadership and they are the ones to detain and punish him. In Jesus of Ananias we see a continuation of the theme of persecuted and martyred prophets and, like most figures in that tradition, he is violated at the hands of Israel's leaders. Two other things about Jesus are also noteworthy: his message and behavior are similar to the OT prophets and his proclamation begins at the temple during a feast.

Such a background provides some cross-references for Matthew's use of the martyred prophet theme. In Matthew's narrative, the first prophet to experience this paradigmatic fate was John.[171] The Baptizer's activities were multidimensional and his preaching about repentance and the One to come, his action of baptizing, and his announcements of judgement stirred up the opposition of the Pharisees, Sadducees, and other groups. Yet, according to Matthew, these did not lead to his demise. Whatever the historical reasons might have been for John's arrest and execution,[172] Matthew simply states that "Herod had arrested John, bound him, and put him in prison on account of Herodias, his brother Philip's wife, because John had been telling him, 'It is not lawful for you to have her'" (Matt 14:3–4). Matthew takes for granted that John, a prophet, will meet a prophet's end, and little explanation is needed—it is enough to know that John called out the lawlessness of a powerful figure and suffered the expected fate.

The connection between the fates of John and Jesus in Matthew is narratively clear in chapter 14. As Webb notes, Matthew has Jesus say of himself that "a prophet is without honor" immediately before the account of John's death (13:53–58), and John's death results in his disciples telling Jesus what has occurred and Jesus withdrawing to a desolate place in response (14:12–13a).[173] The audience should expect that Jesus, who is a prophet like

---

171. See Turner, *Israel's Last Prophet*, 129–50, for a more detailed study of John as rejected prophet.

172. See Webb, *John the Baptizer and Prophet*, 373–77.

173. Webb, *John the Baptizer and Prophet*, 59, 59n38.

John, will meet a prophet's end since he has already hinted at his own status as a rejected prophet and has fled from populated areas, not to mention his predictions of his impending death (17:22–23; 20:17–19).

Though the event of Jesus' death is outside the scope of this chapter, we need not traverse that far in Matthew's story to understand the dynamics that lead to that point. The temple episode is a key event whose narration is a focal point in the exposition of Jesus' prophetic ministry and its response from Israel's leaders. After all, it is the first time Jesus challenges Israel's covenantal infidelity in the context of its center of power. Matthew's Jesus has already twice predicted his death prior to his action in the temple, which he apparently undertakes with full awareness that his prophetic message will be rejected. That the judgement is leveled primarily against Israel's leadership is clear from the setting and, as we have seen, Jesus' critique of the temple system as a center of national power is consistent with other first-century critiques of the temple. In the action's aftermath, the conflict between Jesus and the leaders escalates and it does not take long for the leaders to plan Jesus' arrest (21:45–46; 26:3–5). Jesus' activities do nothing to ease the tension and Matt 23 marks another focal point in the ongoing conflict, with dynamics similar to the temple action in the interplay of a (vainly) call for repentance and announcement of judgement.

Jesus as prophet undertakes bold actions and utters speeches of judgement with the knowledge that they will contribute in no small way to his eventual torture and execution.[174] Although we have seen that the martyred prophet is a well-known theme, it is worth reflecting on the relationship between Jesus' intentionality and his vocation.[175] Thematic patterns are not sufficient to explain the conviction of individuals. If Matthew's Jesus thought that his vocation as a prophet simply required his assimilation to a well-known pattern (martyred prophet), then he could have emulated John's example and remained on the geographical margins whilst calling out the sin of Herod and the community leaders. The fact that he did not, and that at times he fled danger (4:12; 12:15; 14:13), suggests that he understood his vocation—including its prophetic dimension—as being distinct from that of John. The OT is clear at several points that the prophets had been called by God into their

---

174. "Merely prophesying the temple's destruction invited scourging and the threat of death (Jer 26:11; Jos. *War* 6.300–09), and execution was especially the solution if a leader already had a significant gathering of followers." Keener, *Gospel of Matthew*, 495–96.

175. I am of course aware of the pitfalls of the notion of "intentionality." Here I am referring only to Jesus' intentionality within Matthew's story world, determined only by details given by Matthew. I am not attempting to discern the intentionality of the historical Jesus.

vocation (e.g., Exod 3–4; 1 Sam 3; Isa 6; Jer 1; Ezek 2–3; Amos 7:14–15).[176] It is not clear whether every prophet had experienced a equally dramatic call, but each prophet held the conviction that they had heard the word of YHWH and, with the exception of Jonah, felt compelled to communicate it. This call varied from prophet to prophet, as did the specific message. We are not given the details of Jesus' prophetic commissioning in Matthew, save the scant detail of the event at his baptism (3:16–17). However, we are confronted with a story of a traveling prophet who makes intentional decisions throughout his ministry (e.g., where to go, when to flee) which indicates a degree of specific conviction and intentionality. Later in the garden of Gethsemane, Jesus will even agonize over the path on which he is called to walk (26:36–46), a sign that the external call of God was, in whatever way, determining his vocational direction and that it was not arbitrary. Like John the Baptizer, Jesus is presented as embodying a conviction that God had spoken to him in a particular way and that this message needed to be communicated to Israel. Some OT examples suggest that the martyred prophet theme was not universal, that God's calling of a prophet did not necessitate the invocation of the wrath of the community in receipt of the prophet's message. We could think of prophets that *Lives of the Prophets* suggests died in peace, or those whose message resulted in repentance (Jonah[177]). Still, many of the prophets were ignored, rejected, and/or killed, hence the existence of the martyred prophet motif. For these prophets, their vocation came at a great cost, such that it must have required a sufficiently robust conviction that God had called them to deliver a message.

All of this is important to make a crucial point—the prophetic vocation, including that of Matthew's Jesus, did not consist simply of the communication of truths, abstract or otherwise. Nor was it the communication of a stock politico-religious message. Rather, it was the dynamic call of God on the individual to take on the burden of speaking God's message to a chosen group of people, typically (but not limited to) Israel. In other words, in Matthew's presentation, Jesus' particular speech events and actions, such as in Matt 23, are not merely the result of experience, creativity, or intelligence, but are the result of a conviction that YHWH had spoken in a particular way at a particular time, albeit in a fashion consistent with past revelation and eschatological conviction. In this general vocation, Jesus is joined by John and Jesus son of Ananias, though

176. For a valuable discussion on and comparison of the call narratives of Jeremiah and Ezekiel, see Rochester, "Prophetic Ministry," 13–79. See also Hafemann, *Paul, Moses, and the History*, 47–62.

177. It is highly likely that the Jonah story is fictional, but this is irrelevant to its contribution to the prophetic tradition.

the particular vocation of each is distinct. That the Matthean Jesus acts in ways to bring about his execution reflects his faithfulness to God's will, namely that Israel would turn from its sin and embody its corporate vocation reflected in its covenantal obligations.

7.11 Conclusion

Throughout Matt 23, Jesus conforms to patterns set by the OT prophets. This is the case in terms of form, content, and concerns. Jesus' so-called "woes" (23:13–36) are the centerpiece of the chapter. They take the form of reproaches, ascriptions of shame, as opposed to expressions of displeasure or formal curses. Jesus announces such attributions of shame using conventional language in a well-known form as a response to behaviors and actions related to problems of social ethos. The particular problems in view for Jesus are related to the community leaders' specific breaches of Torah, but also more general interpretive failings that negatively affect the life of the community. Jesus also announces the consequences of such actions, predicting the destruction of the temple and, by extension, the whole of Jerusalem. Such proclamations of national threat are not unlike those of Jeremiah from the past. They also share aspects of form, content, and context with those of another first-century figure, Jesus son of Ananias. In particular, they share their mournful character, critique of Jerusalem's leaders, and prediction of national calamity. Matthew's Jesus also conforms to patterns set by other OT prophetic figures, not least Isaiah and Ezekiel. This is true in terms of adopted imagery, but it also extends to an insistence on God's judgement of sin and the hope for restoration through repentance. At an overarching level, Jesus shares the vocation of the OT prophets, including the common element of martyrdom. Like these previous prophetic figures, those who called Israel back to faithfulness to the covenant of the God who brought them up out of the land of Egypt, so too is Jesus' prophetic task centered on God's will expressed in Torah.

Conclusions

THE CHIEF AIM OF this study has been to delineate ways in which Matthew's Gospel depicts the prophetic vocation of Jesus. This is, as I acknowledged in the introduction, a neglected area of investigation—prophecy is typically associated with Luke in Gospel studies—even though Matthew's Gospel makes mention of prophets and prophecy more than the other canonical Gospels. It is true that this study has not been a systematic journey through the entirety of Matthew, though I addressed such limitations in the introduction.

The primary thread running through this study's argument is this: Matthew presents Jesus as a popular prophet who calls Israel, and those beyond it, to faithfulness to Israel's God by way of covenant fidelity. Such a prophetic vocation is presented by Matthew as multi-faceted, reflecting a number of prophetic traditions, including various OT prophets (especially Moses, Isaiah, and Jeremiah) and first-century Jewish popular prophecy.

In chapter 1, we explored some of the foundational questions related to reading Matthew's Gospel. Typical historical-critical elements such as author, location, audience, and date provided crucial glimpses into the social world behind the text, and thus to the historical parameters of interpretation. We noted that Matthew's Gospel was written in a period of tumult and socio-political change, owing in part to the destruction of the temple by the Romans and the growth of the new rabbinic movement. Matthew's communities, in light of competing interpretations of Torah and mythologies about the world, found themselves in a time of significant conflict on the basis of identity, theology, and community—who are we, whose world is this, and how ought we to live together? Literary-critical elements of the Gospel, like structure, genre, and purpose, further helped us understand what Matthew was aiming to do in composing his story. We found that by portraying Jesus as a prophet, Matthew seeks to cut through competing Jewish and Roman claims about identity, theology, and community by pointing to a figure who authoritatively proclaims God's will, critiquing the current dominant consciousness and nurturing a new one in its place. This, for Matthew, provides a pattern for ongoing discipleship.

In chapter 2, we investigated first-century occurrences of popular prophetic activity in Palestine. It is here that we settled on a typology of prophets in this period, one suggested by Robert Webb. We concluded that, notwithstanding the artificial nature of such typologies, Jesus of Nazareth ought to be considered among the popular prophets, though these prophets were diverse. Popular prophets can be further separated into action and oracular prophets, according to the typology of Richard Horsley. Popular prophets were reminiscent of OT prophetic figures such as Moses, Joshua, Elijah, Amos, Jeremiah, or others, and their words and/or deeds often embodied ancient Israelite traditions in the midst of the common people among whom they operated. All Jewish prophets, including the popular prophets, had Moses as their model, since in Moses we find the pattern of all subsequent prophets—messengers who proclaim God's will to Israel and seek to keep them within the covenant. This could be expressed through messages of hope and/or judgement, since both functioned to ensure covenantal faithfulness. Popular prophets also embodied a further vocational dimension, one distinctive to them, namely the hope for divine liberation in the midst of dire circumstances. In this sense, they could be considered apocalyptic. Thus, the prophets often sought to mediate manifestations of divine power that brought either salvation or judgement. We concluded that a Jewish popular prophet was *a divinely inspired person who, operating primarily within the social milieu of the common populace, through intentional action or spoken oracle, influenced by apocalyptic eschatology, and displaying characteristics found in a biblical prophetic tradition, mediates or announces God's covenantal will—including God's deliverance and/or judgement—in order to call the recipients back to covenantal fidelity and/or point to a divine act of judgement and/or liberation.*

Chapter 3 bridged the initial foundational sections of the study (chapters 1 and 2) with the subsequent exegetical section (chapters 4–7). Here we briefly discussed the question of which of Jesus' prophetic words and actions ought to be considered "prophetic." I explained my inclination to include far more of Jesus' actions under the rubric of "prophetic" than are some others. This is because of the definition of prophecy outlined in chapter 2 and because I agree with Morna Hooker that prophetic actions need not be accompanied by prophetic speech in order to be considered "prophetic." Indeed, prophetic actions can be the equivalents of oracular speech in and of themselves. By looking with a broad gaze at Jesus' various prophetic words and actions in Matthew, we concluded that the Evangelist's depiction of Jesus as prophet cannot be reduced to a new Moses or Elijah figure, nor merely to an action prophet or oracular prophet; Jesus is all of the above, which no doubt ties into Matthew's Christology.

In chapter 4, we commenced our exegetical work, beginning with the Beatitudes. Here again we found that Jesus' prophetic vocation was multi-faceted, embodying elements of a number of prophetic traditions, including the OT prophets, apocalyptic, and first-century Jewish popular prophecy. His proclamation in the Beatitudes echoes Isa 61's announcement of good news to the poor. In the Beatitudes, Jesus as prophet announces a new set of values, critiquing the dominant values of his world and offering a new way of (covenantal) life according to his interpretation of Torah. These values subvert socio-cultural norms and call hearers to repentance. They also form the basis of a renewed community that embodies God's will (ex-pressed in the Sermon on the Mount). This prophetic proclamation is both a call *back* to covenantal faithfulness as expressed in Torah as read by Jesus, and also a call to look *forward* eschatologically to enact in the present the New Genesis reality that God will bring to fulfillment in the future. In this sense, Jesus' prophetic vocation functions to critique the current oppres-sive order and point to an alternative way of life. For this, Jesus and those who follow after him will face persecution.

Chapter 5 focused our attention on Jesus eating with sinners in Matt 9:9–13, a potent but oft-ignored episode in Jesus' prophetic ministry. This act redefines the boundaries of Israel in light of the coming kingdom, the kingdom Jesus is inaugurating. Meals functioned to repair relation-ships between two parties and Jesus' action enacts God's desire to repair relationships within Israel, both by redefining boundaries and by inviting people to repentance. For those who do not heed the prophet's invitation, Jesus proclaims judgement since their obstinacy means they are not pres-ent at the table. The debate that gives context to Jesus' action relates to Torah interpretation—Jesus' opponents give precedence to the purity code and thus retain exclusionary practices. In announcing judgement on the leaders, Jesus continues the prophetic tradition of critiquing power in light of God's covenant with Israel. Moreover, his quotation of Hos 6:6 reveals an aspect of his distinctive hermeneutic; following the prophet, Jesus calls on Israel to embody the mercy YHWH had shown to them at the exodus and, by doing this, Jesus defines Torah righteousness as prioritizing mercy. Furthermore, the table fellowship facilitated by Jesus previews the eschato-logical banquet and thus Jesus as prophet brings together the past, present, and future as a sign of future completion. In terms of the form of Jesus' action—the provision of food—it is reminiscent of past prophetic actions by Moses, Elijah, and Elisha. Jesus dramatizes the well-known ritual of table fellowship and infuses it with covenantal and eschatological meaning. Jesus is also similar to first-century popular prophets in that his action embodies judgement and liberation. However, Jesus also goes further than the nationalistic fervor of other popular action prophets of the period in his concern for personal and communal liberation, a sign of a fuller notion of covenantal existence. Jesus was like the OT prophets and other first-century popular prophets, but he was also bringing the prophetic imagination to life in a distinctive way in a new situation.

Chapter 6 saw us turn to a more predictable text for the study of Jesus' prophetic vocation: Jesus' temple action in Matt 21. This complex episode finds Jesus critiquing the temple and its leaders, not unlike prophets of Israel's past like Isaiah and Jeremiah and roughly contemporary figures like Jesus son of Ananias. Like Isaiah and Jeremiah, Jesus, in his temple action, proclaims the centrality of covenantal fidelity and the inclusion of foreigners within God's people whilst critiquing Israel's nationalism, exclusiveness, and the shirking of covenantal obligations, particularly by Israel's leaders. Jesus proclaims judgement on the temple and its leadership but also offers in his healing of the blind and lame a sign of God's healing kingdom in order that Israel might repent. Such healings challenge certain notions of purity and holiness and offer an alternative understanding of God's will and covenantal faithfulness characterized by merciful love. In light of 2 Sam 5:8, Jesus' healing of the blind and the lame in the temple also functions as an implicit revision of Israel's covenantal obligations, a distinctly prophetic practice.

Finally, chapter 7 saw us turn to Jesus' so-called "woes" in Matt 23. These "woes," more accurately seen as ascriptions of shame rather than as curses, conform to patterns set by various OT prophets. Jesus utilizes conventional language in a well-known form in response to certain behaviors and actions related to social maladies. The behaviors addressed by Jesus are specific breaches of Torah by the community leaders, acts that impact the wider life of the community in the form of various injustices. But Jesus is also entering more broadly into conflict over the interpretation of Torah itself, and Matthew portrays him as the authoritative interpreter of God's will. Jesus also announces judgement against the leaders for their actions, predicting the destruction of the temple and the whole of Jerusalem. Such judgement is not unlike that of Jeremiah, and also shares aspects of form, content, and context with the first-century prophet, Jesus son of Ananias. Further, Jesus stands in the line of OT prophets like Isaiah and Ezekiel in his use of imagery and insistence on God's judgement of sin and the hope for restoration through repentance. We saw that Jesus shares the vocation of the

OT prophets, centered on enforcing God's will expressed in Torah, and this extended to the traditional element of martyrdom.

In sum, we find that throughout these Matthean passages we are met with a portrayal of Jesus' prophetic vocation that is consistent both within itself and with wider prophetic traditions from Israel's past and present. This prophetic portrayal of Jesus does not exist in a vacuum but, as we would expect, plays a part in Matthew's wider narrative and socio-historical situation. This brings us full circle back to chapter 1, and the questions raised there regarding identity, theology, and community. There is a rhetorical purpose to Matthew's depiction of Jesus as prophet. Amid communal and ideological conflict with the burgeoning rabbinic movement and with Roman powers, Matthew's Jesus represents a prophetic figure who authoritatively expounds the will of YHWH by way of inspired Torah interpretation and actions embodying divine revelation. In doing so, Jesus offers an alternative ideology to that of Matthew's opponents, one that answers those crucial questions of identity, theology, and community, and provides a form of legitimation for Matthew's distressed communities.

Regarding identity, Matthew's Jesus constantly reminds hearers of the Gospel that they are people of the covenant, of God's gracious connection to God's people in terms set down by God. This covenant is not a "new" covenant, but a renewal of the old in the life, death, and resurrection of Jesus, and a revision of how it is understood according to Jesus' life and teaching. Such revision primarily takes the form of Jesus' authoritative interpretation of the covenant charter, the Torah, and as we have seen such a task is distinctively prophetic in character. Through Jesus' prophetic elucidation of the Torah, Matthew's audience is taught the nature of their relationship to God and thus who it is that they are.

Jesus' prophetic words and actions also teach Matthew's community about theology, that is, about the identity and character of God. God is revealed by the prophet as merciful and as judge, and this has particular importance in responding to the implicit question, "Whose world is this?" Over against Roman myths and competing interpretations of Torah, the God revealed in and by Jesus rules over the world as judge, thus guaranteeing covenant justice as the pattern and trajectory of the world, and as one who is merciful, thus negating exclusivist notions of covenant membership.

This revelation of the identity of God's people and their understanding of the character of God leads to a distinctive picture of community. Jesus' embrace of outsiders—sinners, tax collectors, gentiles—is not simply an example to the Matthean community, although that is true, but is also an embodiment of what the prophet has revealed about Israel's vocation and the character of God. Jesus fully embodies Israel's vocation, thus fulfilling the Torah and the prophets, and teaches others to do the same, such as in the Sermon on the Mount. As we have seen in our study of Matt 23 and elsewhere, Torah interpretation, far from being a purely intellectual exercise, has a marked effect on community life. This is why Matthew's Jesus is so harsh toward those leaders whose interpretations are faulty. Jesus, as prophet, reveals the true nature of God's law, and thus the way God's people ought to live.

By providing a model that embodies answers to these crucial questions in the midst of conflict, Matthew provides his communities with a foundation for their lives together within the context of embattled situations. This model is thoroughly Jewish, only intelligible within the context of Israel's prophetic tradition.

Bibliography

Adams, Samuel L. *Social and Economic Life in Second Temple Judea*. Louisville: Westminster John Knox, 2014.

Ådna, Jostein. *Jesu Stellung zum Tempel: Die Tempelaktion und das Tempelwort als Ausdruck seiner messianischen Sendung*. Wissenschaftliche Untersuchungen zum Neuen Testament 2/119. Tübingen: Mohr Siebeck, 2000.

————. "Jesus' Symbolic Act in the Temple (Mark 11:15–17): The Replacement of the Sacrificial Cult by His Atoning Death." In *Gemeinde ohne Temple/Community without Temple*, edited by Herausgegeben von Beate Ego et al., 461–76. Tübingen: Mohr Siebeck, 1999.

Aernie, Jeffrey W. *Is Paul Also Among the Prophets? An Examination of the Relationship between Paul and the Old Testament Prophetic Tradition in 2 Corinthians*. London: T. & T. Clark, 2012.

Alexander, Philip S. "'The Parting of the Ways' from the Perspective of Rabbinic Judaism." In *Jews and Christians: The Parting of the Ways A.D. 70 to 135*, edited by James D. G. Dunn, 1–25. Grand Rapids: Eerdmans, 1999.

Alexiou, Margaret. *The Ritual Lament in Greek Tradition*. 2nd ed. Revised by Dimitrios Yatromanolakis and Panagiotis Roilos. Lanham, MD: Rowman & Littlefield, 2002.

Allison, Dale C., Jr. *Constructing Jesus: Memory, Imagination, and History*. Grand Rapids: Baker, 2010.

————. *The End of the Ages Has Come: An Early Interpretation of the Passion and Resurrection of Jesus*. Philadelphia: Fortress, 1985.

————. *Jesus of Nazareth: Millenarian Prophet*. Minneapolis: Fortress, 1998.

————. "Matt. 23:39 = Luke 13:35b as a Conditional Prophecy." *Journal for the Study of the New Testament* 18 (1983) 75–84.

————. *The New Moses: A Matthean Typology*. Eugene, OR: Wipf & Stock, 2013.

————. "A Plea for Thoroughgoing Eschatology." *Journal of Biblical Literature* 113 (1994) 651–68.

Andersen, F. I. "2 (Slavonic Apocalypse of) Enoch." In *The Old Testament Pseudepigrapha: Apocalyptic Literature and Testaments*, edited by James H. Charlesworth, 1:91–221. Peabody, MA: Hendrickson, 1983.

Anderson, Bernhard W. "Biblical Theology and Sociological Interpretation." *Theology Today* 42 (1985) 292–303.

Assmann, Hugo. *Theology for a Nomad Church*. Translated by Paul Burns. Maryknoll, NY: Orbis, 1976.

Aune, David E. "The Apocalypse of John and the Problem of Genre." *Semeia* 36 (1986) 65–96.

———. *Apocalypticism, Prophecy and Magic in Early Christianity.* Tübingen: Mohr Siebeck, 2006.

———. "Beatitudes." In *The Westminster Dictionary of New Testament and Early Christian Literature and Rhetoric,* 75–78. Louisville: Westminster John Knox, 2003.

———. *The New Testament in Its Literary Environment.* Philadelphia: Westminster, 1987.

———. *Prophecy in Early Christianity and the Ancient Mediterranean World.* Eugene, OR: Wipf & Stock, 1983.

Bacon, Benjamin W. "The 'Five Books' of Matthew Against the Jews." *Expositor* 15 (1918) 56–66.

———. *Studies in Matthew.* New York: Henry Holt, 1930.

Balabanski, Vicky. *Eschatology in the Making: Mark, Matthew and the Didache.* Cambridge: Cambridge University Press, 1997.

Barnett, Paul W. "The Jewish Sign Prophets—A.D. 40–70: Their Intentions and Origin." *New Testament Studies* 27 (1981) 679–97.

Barton, S. C. "Hospitality." In *Dictionary of the Later New Testament and Its Developments,* edited by Ralph P. Martin and Peter H. Davids, 501–7. Downers Grove, IL: InterVarsity, 1997.

Bauckham, Richard, ed. *The Gospels for All Christians: Rethinking the Gospel Audiences.* Grand Rapids: Eerdmans, 1998.

———. *James.* New York: Routledge, 2002.

———. *Jesus and the Eyewitnesses: The Gospels as Eyewitness Testimony.* Grand Rapids: Eerdmans, 2006.

———. "Jesus' Demonstration in the Temple." In *Law and Religion: Essays on the Place of the Law in Israel and Early Christianity,* edited by Barnabas Lindars, 72–89. Cambridge: James Clarke, 1988.

———. "The Rise of Apocalyptic." In *The Jewish World around the New Testament,* 39–64. Tübingen: Mohr Siebeck, 2008.

———. "Tamar's Ancestry and Rahab's Marriage: Two Problems in the Matthean Genealogy." *Novum Testamentum* 37 (1995) 313–29.

———. *The Theology of the Book of Revelation.* Cambridge: Cambridge University Press, 1993.

Beale, G. K., and Sean M. McDonough. "Revelation." In *Commentary on the New Testament Use of the Old Testament,* edited by G. K. Beale and D. A. Carson, 1081–162. Grand Rapids: Baker, 2007.

Becker, Jürgen. *Jesus of Nazareth.* Berlin: de Gruyter, 1998.

———. *Johannes der Täufer und Jesus von Nazareth.* Neukirchen-Vluyn: Neukirchener, 1972.

Best, Ernest. "Matthew V.3." *New Testament Studies* 7 (1961) 255–58.

Betz, Hans Dieter. *Essays on the Sermon on the Mount.* Translated by L. L. Welborn. Philadelphia: Fortress, 1985.

———. "Jesus and the Purity of the Temple (Mark 11:15–18): A Comparative Approach." *Journal of Biblical Literature* 116 (1997) 455–72.

———. *The Sermon on the Mount.* Edited by Adela Yarbro Collins. Hermeneia. Minneapolis: Fortress, 1995.

Bird, Michael F. "Bauckham's *The Gospel For All Christians* Revisited." *European Journal of Theology* 15 (2006) 5–13.

———. *Jesus and the Origins of the Gentile Mission.* London: T. & T. Clark, 2007.

Black, Matthew. "The Use of Rhetorical Terminology in Papias on Mark and Matthew." *Journal for the Study of the New Testament* 37 (1989) 31–41.

Blenkinsopp, Joseph. "Interpretation and the Tendency to Sectarianism: An Aspect of Second Temple History." In *Aspects of Judaism in the Graeco-Roman Period*, edited by E. P. Sanders, 2:1–26. London: SCM, 1981.

———. *Opening the Sealed Book: Interpretations of the Book of Isaiah in Late Antiquity.* Grand Rapids: Eerdmans, 2006.

Blevins, Carolyn. "Under My Wings: Jesus' Motherly Love: Matthew 23:37–39." *Review and Expositor* 104 (2007) 365–74.

Block, Daniel I. *The Book of Ezekiel, Chapters 1–24.* New International Commentary on the Old Testament. Grand Rapids: Eerdmans, 1997.

———. *The Gods of the Nations: Studies in Ancient Near Eastern National Theology.* 2nd ed. Grand Rapids: Baker, 2000.

Blomberg, Craig. "Jesus, Sinners, and Table Fellowship." *Bulletin for Biblical Research* 19 (2009) 35–62.

———. *Matthew.* New American Commentary 22. Nashville: Broadman, 1992.

Boccaccini, Gabriele. *Roots of Rabbinic Judaism: An Intellectual History, from Ezekiel to Daniel.* Grand Rapids: Eerdmans, 2002.

Booth, Wayne C. *The Rhetoric of Fiction.* Chicago: University of Chicago Press, 1983.

Borg, Marcus J. *Conflict, Holiness, and Politics in the Teachings of Jesus.* Rev. ed. London: Continuum, 1998.

———. *Jesus, a New Vision: Spirit, Culture, and the Life of Discipleship.* San Francisco: Harper & Row, 1987.

———. *Jesus in Contemporary Scholarship.* Harrisburg, PA: Trinity Press International, 1994.

———. Review of *Bandits, Prophets and Messiahs: Popular Movements in the Time of Jesus*, by Richard A. Horsley with John S. Hanson. *Journal of Biblical Literature* 107 (1988) 135–37.

Boring, M. Eugene. "The Apocalypse as Christian Prophecy: A Discussion of the Issues Raised by the Book of Revelation for the Study of Early Christian Prophecy." In *SBL Seminar Papers, 1974*, 2:43–62. Missoula: Scholars, 1974.

———. *The Continuing Voice of Jesus: Christian Prophecy and the Gospel Tradition.* Louisville: Westminster John Knox, 1991.

———. *Sayings of the Risen Jesus: Christian Prophecy in the Synoptic Tradition.* Cambridge: Cambridge University Press, 1982.

Bornkamm, Günther, Gerhard Barth, and Heinz Joachim Held. *Tradition and Interpretation in Matthew.* Translated by P. Scott. New Testament Library. Philadelphia: Westminster, 1963.

Bottrich, Christfried. "The 'Book of the Secrets of Enoch' (2 En): Between Jewish Origin and Christian Transmission. An Overview." In *New Perspectives on 2 Enoch: No Longer Slavonic Only*, edited by Andrei Orlov and Gabriele Boccaccini, 37–67. Leiden: Brill, 2012.

Bowman, John. "Prophets and Prophecy in Talmud and Midrash." *Evangelical Quarterly* 22 (1950) 107–14.

Bowman, Richard G. "Narrative Criticism: Human Purpose in Conflict with Divine Presence." In *Judges and Method: New Approaches in Biblical Studies*, edited by G. Yee, 17–44. Minneapolis: Fortress, 1995.

Bracke, John M. *Jeremiah 1–29*. Louisville: Westminster John Knox, 2000.

Brandon, S. G. F. *Jesus and the Zealots: A Study of the Political Factor in Primitive Christianity*. Manchester: Manchester University Press, 1967.

Brown, Colin. "What Was John the Baptist Doing?" *Bulletin of Biblical Research* 7 (1997) 37–50.

Brown, John Pairman. "Techniques of Imperial Control: The Background of the Gospel Event." In *The Bible and Liberation: Political and Social Hermeneutics*, edited by Norman K. Gottwald, 357–77. Maryknoll, NY: Orbis, 1983.

Brown, Raymond E., and John P. Meier. *Antioch and Rome: New Testament Cradles of Catholic Christianity*. Mahwah: Paulist, 1983.

Brueggemann, Walter. *A Commentary on Jeremiah: Exile and Homecoming*. Grand Rapids: Eerdmans, 1998.

————. *Isaiah 40–66*. Louisville: Westminster John Knox, 1998.

————. *The Prophetic Imagination*. 2nd ed. Minneapolis: Fortress, 2001.

Buchanan, George Wesley. "Symbolic Money-Changers in the Temple." *New Testament Studies* 37 (1991) 280–90.

Bultmann, Rudolf. *History and Eschatology*. Edinburgh: University Press, 1957.

————. *The History of the Synoptic Tradition*. Translated by John Marsh. Oxford: Blackwell, 1963.

————. *Jesus and the Word*. New York: Scribner, 1958.

Burchard, C. "Joseph and Aseneth." In *The Old Testament Pseudepigrapha*, edited by James H. Charlesworth, 2:177–247. Peabody, MA: Hendrickson, 1983.

Burridge, Richard A. *What Are the Gospels? A Comparison with Graeco-Roman Biography*. 2nd ed. Grand Rapids: Eerdmans, 2004.

Caird, George B. "The Language of Eschatology." In *The Language and Imagery of the Bible*, 243–71. Philadelphia: Westminster, 1980.

Campbell, Constantine R. *Verbal Aspect, the Indicative Mood, and Narrative: Soundings in the Greek of the New Testament*. Studies in Biblical Greek 13. New York: Lang, 2007.

Campbell, D. Keith. "NT Scholars' Use of OT Lament Terminology and Its Theological and Interdisciplinary Implications." *Bulletin for Biblical Research* 21 (2011) 213–26.

————. *Of Heroes and Villains: The Influence of the Psalmic Lament on Synoptic Characterization*. Eugene, OR: Wipf & Stock, 2013.

Caneday, A. B. "'Baptized in the Holy Spirit': Epochal Theology in Luke-Acts." Paper presented at the Annual Midwest Regional Meeting of the Society for Biblical Literature. St Paul, Minnesota, April 8–9, 1994.

Carney, Thomas F. *The Shape of the Past: Models and Antiquity*. Kansas: Coronado Press, 1975.

Carr, David. "Narrative and the Real World: An Argument for Continuity." *History and Theory* 25 (1986) 117–31.

Carroll, Robert P. "YHWH's Sour Grapes: Images of Food and Drink in the Prophetic Discourses of the Hebrew Bible." *Semeia* 86 (1999) 113–31.

Carson, D. A., and Douglas J. Moo. *An Introduction to the New Testament*. 2nd ed. Grand Rapids: Zondervan, 2005.

Carter, Warren. "The Crowds in Matthew's Gospel." *Catholic Biblical Quarterly* 55 (1993) 54–67.

————. "Evoking Isaiah: Matthean Soteriology and an Intertextual Reading of Isaiah 7–9 and Matthew 1:23 and 4:15–16." *Journal of Biblical Literature* 119 (2000) 503–20.

————. "Love as Societal Vision and Counter-Imperial Practice in Matthew 22:34–40." In *Biblical Interpretation in Early Christian Gospels, Volume 2: The Gospel of Matthew*, edited by Thomas R. Hatina, 30–44. London: T. & T. Clark, 2008.

————. "Matthew 23:37–39." *Interpretation* 54 (2000) 66–68.

————. *Matthew and Empire: Initial Explorations.* Harrisburg, PA: Trinity Press International, 2001.

————. *Matthew and the Margins: A Socio-Political and Religious Reading.* London: T. & T. Clark, 2000.

————. *Matthew: Storyteller, Interpreter, Evangelist.* Peabody, MA: Hendrickson, 2004.

————. *The Roman Empire and the New Testament: An Essential Guide.* Nashville: Abingdon, 2006.

————. "Some Contemporary Scholarship on the Sermon on the Mount." *Currents in Research: Biblical Studies* 4 (1996) 183–215.

Casey, Maurice. "Culture and Historicity: The Cleansing of the Temple." *Catholic Biblical Quarterly* 59 (1997) 306–32.

Chatman, Seymour. *Story and Discourse: Narrative Structure in Fiction and Film.* Ithaca, NY: Cornell University, 1978.

Chenoweth, Ben. "Apocalyptic Eschatology and the Parables of the Mount of Olives Discourse." *Crucible* 5 (2013). http://www.crucibleonline.net/wp-content/uploads/2016/08/Chenoweth-Apocalyptic-Eschatology-and-the-Parables-of-the-Mount-of-Olives-Discourse-Crucible-5-2-November-2013.pdf.

Chilton, Bruce D. *The Temple of Jesus: His Sacrificial Program Within a Cultural History of Sacrifice.* University Park: Pennsylvania State University Press, 1992.

Chilton, Bruce D., and Jacob Neusner. *Judaism in the New Testament: Practices and Beliefs.* London: Routledge, 1995.

Clark, Kenneth Willis. "The Gentile Bias of Matthew." *Journal of Biblical Literature* 66 (1947) 165–72.

Clarke, Howard. *The Gospel of Matthew and Its Readers: A Historical Introduction to the First Gospel.* Bloomington: Indiana University Press, 2003.

Clements, Ronald E. *God and Temple.* Philadelphia: Fortress, 1965.

Clifford, Richard J. "The Use of Hôy in the Prophets." *Catholic Biblical Quarterly* 28 (1966) 458–64.

Cohen, Shaye J. D. *From the Maccabees to the Mishnah.* Philadelphia: Westminster, 1987.

————. "The Rabbi in Second-Century Jewish Society." In *The Early Roman Period*, edited by William Horbury et al., 922–90. Cambridge: Cambridge University Press, 1999.

————. "The Significance of Yavneh: Pharisees, Rabbis, and the End of Jewish Sectarianism." *Hebrew Union College Annual* 55 (1984) 27–53.

————. "Were Pharisees and Rabbis the Leaders of Communal Prayer and Torah Study in Antiquity? The Evidence of the New Testament, Josephus and the Early Church Fathers." In *The Significance of Yavneh and Other Essays in Jewish Hellenism*, 266–81. Tübingen: Mohr Siebeck, 2010.

Collins, John J. "Introduction: Towards the Morphology of a Genre." *Semeia* 14 (1979) 1–20.

————., ed. *The Oxford Handbook of Apocalyptic Literature.* Oxford: Oxford University Press, 2014.

Combrink, H. J. Bernard. "The Structure of the Gospel of Matthew as Narrative." *Tyndale Bulletin* 34 (1983) 61–90.

Cook, Michael J. "Interpreting 'Pro-Jewish' Passages in Matthew." *Hebrew Union College Annual* 54 (1983) 135–46.

Cook, Stephen L. *The Social Roots of Biblical Yahwism.* Atlanta: Society of Biblical Literature, 2004.

Cope, O. Lamar. *Matthew: A Scribe Trained for the Kingdom of Heaven.* Washington, DC: Catholic Biblical Association, 1976.

Corley, Kathleen E. "The Anointing of Jesus in the Synoptic Tradition: An Argument for Authenticity." *Journal for the Study of the Historical Jesus* 1 (2003) 61–72.

———. *Private Women, Public Meals: Social Conflict in the Synoptic Tradition.* Peabody, MA: Hendrickson, 1993.

Cousland, J. R. C. "The Feeding of the Four Thousand *Gentiles* in Matthew? Matthew 15:29–39 as a Test Case." *Novum Testamentum* 41 (1999) 1–23.

Crawford, Barry S. "Near Expectation in the Sayings of Jesus." *Journal of Biblical Literature* 101 (1982) 225–44.

Croatto, J. Severino. "Jesus, Prophet like Elijah, and Prophet-Teacher like Moses in Luke-Acts." *Journal of Biblical Literature* 124 (2005) 451–65.

Crossan, John Dominic. *The Birth of Christianity.* Edinburgh: T. & T. Clark, 1998.

———. *The Historical Jesus: The Life of a Mediterranean Jewish Peasant.* San Francisco: HarperCollins, 1991.

Crossan, John Dominic, and Jonathan L. Reed. *Excavating Jesus.* New York: HarperCollins, 2001.

Daly-Denton, Margaret M. "David in the Gospels." *Word and World* 23 (2003) 421–29.

Dapaah, Daniel S. *The Relationship Between John the Baptist and Jesus of Nazareth: A Critical Study.* Lanham, MD: University Press of America, 2005.

Davies, G. I. "The Presence of God in the Second Temple and Rabbinic Doctrine." In *Templum Amicitiae: Essays on the Second Temple Presented to Ernst Bammel,* edited by W. Horbury, 32–36. Sheffield, UK: JSOT, 1991.

Davies, W. D. *The Setting of the Sermon on the Mount.* Cambridge: Cambridge University Press, 1977.

Davies, W. D., and Dale C. Allison Jr. *Matthew 1–7.* International Critical Commentary 1. London: T. & T. Clark, 1988.

———. *Matthew 8–18.* International Critical Commentary 2. London: T. & T. Clark, 1991.

———. *Matthew 19–28.* International Critical Commentary 3. London: T. & T. Clark, 1997.

———. *Matthew: A Shorter Commentary.* London: T. & T. Clark, 2004.

Davila, James R. "The Damascus Document and the Community Rule." https://www.st-andrews.ac.uk/divinity/rt/dss/abstracts/ddcr/.

Deines, Roland. "The Pharisees Between 'Judaisms' and 'Common Judaism.'" In *Justification and Variegated Nomism,* edited by D. A. Carson et al., 1:443–504. Tübingen: Mohr Siebeck, 2001.

Dempsey, Carol J. "'Turn Back, O People': Repentance in the Latter Prophets." In *Repentance in Christian Theology,* edited by Mark J. Boda and Gordon T. Smith, 47–66. Collegeville, MN: Liturgical, 2006.

Dever, William. *Who Were the Early Israelites and Where Did They Come From?* Grand Rapids: Eerdmans, 2006.

Dobschütz, Ernst von. "Matthew as Rabbi and Catechist." In *The Interpretation of Matthew*, edited by Graham N. Stanton, 27–38. Translated by Robert Morgan. Edinburgh: T. & T. Clark, 1995.

Dodd, C. H. "Jesus as Teacher and Prophet." In *Mysterium Christi: Christological Studies by British and German Theologians*, edited by G. K. A. Bell and A. Deissmann, 53–66. London: Longmans, Green & Co., 1930.

———. *The Parables of the Kingdom*. Glasgow: Collins, 1978.

Donaldson, T. L. "Moses Typology and the Sectarian Nature of Early Christian Anti-Judaism: A Study in Acts 7." *Journal for the Study of the New Testament* 12 (1981) 27–52.

Douglas, Claude C. *Overstatement in the New Testament*. New York: Henry Holt, 1931.

Douglas, Mary. "Deciphering a Meal." *Dædalus* 101 (1972) 61–81.

Duhm, Bernhard. *Das Buch Jesaia*. Göttingen: Vandenhoeck & Ruprecht, 1892.

Duling, Dennis C. "The Matthean Brotherhood and Marginal Scribal Leadership." In *Modelling Early Christianity*, edited by Philip F. Esler, 159–82. London: Routledge, 1995.

———. "Matthew and Marginality." In *SBL Seminar Papers, 1993*, 642–71. Atlanta: Scholars, 1993.

———. "Matthew as Marginal Scribe in an Advanced Agrarian Society." *HTS Teologiese Studies/Theological Studies* 58 (2002) 520–75.

Dumbrell, William J. *The Faith of Israel: A Theological Survey of the Old Testament*. Grand Rapids: Baker, 2002.

Dunn, James D. G. *Jesus Remembered*. Christianity in the Making 1. Grand Rapids: Eerdmans, 2003.

———. *The Partings of the Ways: Between Christianity and Judaism and Their Significance for the Character of Christianity*. 2nd ed. London: SCM, 2006.

Eck, Ernest van. "A Prophet of Old: Jesus the 'Public Theologian.'" In *Prophetic Witness: An Appropriate Contemporary Mode of Public Discourse?*, edited by Heinrich Bedford-Strohm and Etienne de Villiers, 47–74. Zurich: Lit Verlag, 2011.

Eckhardt, Benedikt. "Meals and Politics in the Yaḥad: A Reconsideration." *Dead Sea Discoveries* 17 (2010) 180–209.

Edin, Mary Hinkle. "Learning What Righteousness Means: Hosea 6:6 and the Ethic of Mercy in Matthew's Gospel." *Word and World* 18 (1998) 355–63.

Elliott, John H. "Jesus Was Not an Egalitarian. A Critique of an Anachronistic and Idealist Theory." *Biblical Theology Bulletin* 32 (2002) 75–91.

Ellis, E. Earle. *Prophecy and Hermeneutic in Early Christianity: New Testament Essays*. Tübingen: Mohr Siebeck, 1978.

Ellis, P. F. *Matthew: His Mind and His Message*. Collegeville, MN: Liturgical, 1974.

Esler, Philip E. "Community and Gospel in Early Christianity: A Response to Richard Bauckham's Gospels for All Christians." *Scottish Journal of Theology* 51 (1998) 235–48.

Eusebius. *Ecclesiastical History*. Volume 1. Translated by Kirsopp Lake. London: William Heinemann, 1926..

Evans, Craig A. *Jesus and His Contemporaries: Comparative Studies*. Leiden: Brill, 1995.

———. "Opposition to the Temple: Jesus and the Dead Sea Scrolls." In *Jesus and the Dead Sea Scrolls*, edited by James H. Charlesworth, 235–53. New York: Doubleday, 1992.

Eve, Eric. *The Jewish Context of Jesus' Miracles*. London: Sheffield, 2002.

Ferda, Tucker S. "Jeremiah 7 and Flavius Josephus on the First Jewish War." *Journal for the Study of Judaism* 44 (2013) 158–73.

Fletcher-Louis, Crispin H. T. "2 Enoch and the New Perspective on Apocalyptic." In *New Perspectives on 2 Enoch: No Longer Slavonic Only*, edited by Andrei Orlov and Gabriele Boccaccini, 127–48. Leiden: Brill, 2012.

Flusser, David. "Blessed Are the Poor in Spirit." *Israel Exploration Journal* 10 (1960) 1–13.

Foley, J. M. *Immanent Art: From Structure to Meaning in Traditional Oral Epic.* Bloomington: Indiana University Press, 1991.

Forbes, Christopher. *Prophecy and Inspired Speech in Early Christianity and its Hellenistic Environment.* WUNT 2/75. Tübingen: Mohr Siebeck, 1995.

France, R. T. *The Gospel of Matthew.* New International Commentary on the New Testament. Grand Rapids: Eerdmans, 2007.

———. *Matthew.* Tyndale New Testament Commentaries 1. Grand Rapids: Eerdmans, 1985.

Fredriksen, Paula. "The Historical Jesus, the Scene in the Temple, and the Gospel of John." In *John, Jesus and History, Vol. 1: Critical Appraisals of Critical Views*, edited by Paul N. Anderson et al., 249–76. Atlanta: Society of Biblical Literature, 2007.

———. "Jesus and the Temple, Mark and the War." In *SBL Seminar Papers, 1990*, 293–310. Atlanta, Scholars, 1990.

Freedman, David Noel, ed. *Anchor Bible Dictionary.* 6 vols. New York: Doubleday, 1992.

Freire, Paulo. *Pedagogy of the Oppressed.* 30th anniv. ed. Translated by Myra Bergman Ramos. New York: Continuum, 2000.

Gabba, Emilio. "The Social, Economic and Political History of Palestine 63 BCE–CE 70." In *The Cambridge History of Judaism: The Early Roman Period*, edited by William Horbury et al., 3:94–167. 8 vols. Cambridge: Cambridge University Press, 1999.

Garland, David E. *The Intention of Matthew 23.* Leiden: Brill, 1979.

———. *Reading Matthew: A Literary and Theological Commentary.* Macon, GA: Smith & Helwys, 2001.

Gillespie, Thomas W. *The First Theologians: A Study in Early Christian Prophecy.* Grand Rapids: Eerdmans, 1994.

Gilmour, Rachelle. *Juxtaposition and the Elisha Cycle.* London: Bloomsbury, 2014.

Glancy, Jennifer A. "Violence as Sign in the Fourth Gospel." *Biblical Interpretation* 17 (2009) 100–117.

Goldenberg, Robert. "The Destruction of the Jerusalem Temple: Its Meaning and Its Consequences." In *The Late Roman-Rabbinic Period*, edited by Stephen T. Katz, 191–205. Cambridge: Cambridge University Press, 2006.

Goldstein, Ronnie. "The Provision of Food to the Aramean Captives in II Reg 6,22–23." *Zeitschrift für die alttestamentliche Wissenschaft* 126 (2014) 101–05.

Good, Deirdre. "The Verb ἀναχωρέω in Matthew's Gospel." *Novum Testamentum* 32 (1990) 1–12.

Goodman, Martin. "The First Jewish Revolt: Social Conflict and the Problem of Debt." *Journal of Jewish Studies* 33 (1982) 417–27.

———. *The Ruling Class of Judaea: The Origins of the Jewish Revolt Against Rome, A.D. 66–70.* Cambridge: Cambridge University Press, 1987.

Grabbe, Lester L. "Prophetic and Apocalyptic: Time for New Definitions—And New Thinking." In *Knowing the End from the Beginning: The Prophetic, the Apocalyptic, and their Relationships*, edited by Lester L. Grabbe and Robert D. Haak, 107–33. London: T. & T. Clark, 2003.

Gray, Rebecca. *Prophetic Figures in Late Second Temple Jewish Palestine.* New York: Oxford University Press, 1993.

Green, H. B. "The Structure of St Matthew's Gospel." In *The New Testament Scriptures,* edited by F. L. Cross, 4:47–59. Berlin: Akademie Verlag, 1968.

Greenspahn, Frederick E. "Why Prophecy Ceased." *Journal of Biblical Literature* 108 (1989) 37–49.

Grimsrud, Ted. *Instead of Atonement: The Bible's Salvation Story and Our Hope for Wholeness.* Eugene, OR: Cascade, 2013.

Grudem, Wayne. *The Gift of Prophecy in the New Testament and Today.* Wheaton: Crossway, 2000.

Guelich, Robert A. "The Matthean Beatitudes: 'Entrance-Requirements' or Eschatological Blessings?" *Journal of Biblical Literature* 95 (1976) 415–34.

———. *Sermon on the Mount: Foundation for Understanding.* Waco, TX: Word, 1982.

Guerin, Wilfred L., et al. *A Handbook of Critical Approaches to Literature.* 5th ed. Oxford: Oxford University Press, 2005.

Gundry, Robert H. *Matthew: A Commentary on his Handbook for a Mixed Church Under Persecution.* Grand Rapids: Eerdmans, 1994.

———. *Matthew: A Commentary on His Literary and Theological Art.* 2nd ed. Grand Rapids: Eerdmans, 1982.

Gutiérrez, Gustavo. *The Power of the Poor in History.* Translated by Robert R. Barr. Maryknoll, NY: Orbis, 1983.

Hafemann, Scott J. *Paul, Moses, and the History of Israel: The Letter/Spirit Contrast and the Argument from Scripture in 2 Corinthians 3.* Paternoster Biblical Monographs. Eugene, OR: Wipf & Stock, 2005.

Hagen, Joost L. "No Longer 'Slavonic' Only: 2 Enoch Attested in Coptic from Nubia." In *New Perspectives on 2 Enoch: No Longer Slavonic Only,* edited by Andrei Orlov and Gabriele Boccaccini, 7–34. Leiden: Brill, 2012.

Hagner, Donald A. *Matthew 1–13.* Word Biblical Commentary 33A. Dallas: Word, 1993.

———. *Matthew 14–28.* Word Biblical Commentary 33B. Dallas: Word, 1995.

———. "The *Sitz im Leben* of the Gospel of Matthew." In *Treasures New and Old: Contributions to Matthean Studies,* edited by David R. Bauer and Mark Allan Powell, 27–68. Atlanta: Scholars, 1996.

Hall, Edward T. *Beyond Culture.* Garden City, NY: Anchor, 1976.

Hals, Ronald M. *Ezekiel.* Forms of the Old Testament Literature 19. Grand Rapids: Eerdmans, 1989.

Hanson, K. C. "How Honorable! How Shameful! A Cultural Analysis of Matthew's Makarisms and Reproaches." *Semeia* 68 (1994) 81–111.

Hanson, Paul D. *The Dawn of Apocalyptic: The Historical and Sociological Roots of Jewish Apocalyptic Eschatology.* Rev. ed. Philadelphia: Fortress, 1979.

Hare, Douglas R. A. "How Jewish Is the Gospel of Matthew?" *Catholic Biblical Quarterly* 62 (2000) 264–77.

———. "The Lives of the Prophets: A New Translation and Introduction." In *The Old Testament Pseudepigrapha,* edited by James H. Charlesworth, 2:379–400. Peabody, MA: Hendrickson, 1983.

———. *The Theme of the Jewish Persecution of Christians in the Gospel According to St. Matthew.* Cambridge: Cambridge University Press, 1967.

Harrington, Daniel J. *The Gospel of Matthew.* Sacra Pagina 1. Collegeville, MN: Liturgical, 1991.

Harrison, Robert C. "Qoheleth among the Sociologists." *Biblical Interpretation* 5 (1997) 160–80.

Hays, Richard B. "The Gospel of Matthew: Reconfigured Torah." *HTS Teologiese Studies/Theological Studies* 61 (2005) 165–90.

Hellholm, David. "The Problem of Apocalyptic Genre and the Apocalypse of John." *Semeia* 36 (1986) 13–64.

Hendrickx, Herman. *The Sermon on the Mount*. London: Geoffrey Chapman, 1984.

Hengel, Martin. *Judaism and Hellenism: Studies in Their Encounter in Palestine During the Hellenistic Period*. 2 vols. Translated by John Bowden. Eugene, OR: Wipf & Stock, 1974.

———. *Was Jesus a Revolutionist?* Translated by William Klassen. Philadelphia: Fortress, 1971.

———. *The Zealots*. Translated by David Smith. Edinburgh: T. & T. Clark, 1989.

Herzog, William R., II. *Jesus, Justice, and the Reign of God: A Ministry of Liberation*. Louisville: Westminster John Knox, 2000.

———. *Parables as Subversive Speech: Jesus as Pedagogue of the Oppressed*. Louisville: Westminster John Knox, 1994.

Hezser, Catherine. *Jewish Literacy in Roman Palestine*. Texts and Studies in Ancient Judaism 81. Tübingen: Mohr Siebeck, 2001.

———. *The Social Structure of the Rabbinic Movement in Roman Palestine*. Tübingen: Mohr Siebeck, 1997.

Hill, David. *New Testament Prophecy*. Atlanta: John Knox, 1979.

Hobsbawm, Eric. *Bandits*. Rev. ed. New York: Pantheon, 1981.

Hollenbach, Paul W. "Jesus, Demoniacs, and Public Authorities: A Socio-Historical Study." *Journal of the American Academy of Religion* 49 (1981) 567–88.

Hollingshead A. B., and F. C. Redlich. *Social Class and Mental Illness: A Community Study*. New York: John Wiley, 1958.

Hood, Jason B. "Matthew 23–25: The Extent of Jesus' Fifth Discourse." *Journal of Biblical Literature* 128 (2009) 527–43.

———. *The Messiah, His Brothers, and the Nations: Matthew 1.1–17*. Library of New Testament Studies. London: T. & T. Clark, 2011.

Hooker, Morna D. *The Signs of a Prophet: The Prophetic Actions of Jesus*. Harrisburg, PA: Trinity Press International, 1997.

———. "Traditions About the Temple in the Sayings of Jesus." *Bulletin of the John Rylands University Library of Manchester* 70 (1988) 7–19.

Horsley, Richard A. "Ancient Jewish Banditry and the Revolt Against Rome, A.D. 66–70." *Catholic Biblical Quarterly* 43 (1981) 409–32.

———. *Galilee: History, Politics, People*. Valley Forge: Trinity Press International, 1995.

———. *Jesus and Empire*. Minneapolis: Augsburg Fortress, 2003.

———. *Jesus and the Spiral of Violence: Popular Jewish Resistance in Roman Palestine*. San Francisco: Harper & Row, 1987.

———. *The Liberation of Christmas: The Infancy Narratives in Social Context*. New York: Continuum, 1993.

———. "'Like One of the Prophets of Old': Two Types of Popular Prophets at the Time of Jesus." *Catholic Biblical Quarterly* 47 (1985) 435–63.

———. "Popular Prophetic Movements at the Time of Jesus: Their Principal Features and Social Origins." *Journal for the Study of the New Testament* 26 (1986) 3–27.

————. *Revolt of the Scribes: Resistance and Apocalyptic Origins.* Minneapolis: Fortress, 2010.

Horsley, Richard A., with John S. Hanson. *Bandits, Prophets and Messiahs: Popular Movements in the Time of Jesus.* Harrisburg, PA: Trinity Press International, 1999.

Howard-Brook, Wes. *"Come Out, My People!": God's Call Out of Empire in the Bible and Beyond.* Maryknoll, NY: Orbis, 2010.

Howell, David B. *Matthew's Inclusive Story: A Study in the Narrative Rhetoric of the First Gospel.* Sheffield: JSOT, 1990.

Humphrey, Edith M. *Joseph and Aseneth.* Sheffield: Sheffield, 2000.

Hutchison, John C. "Was John the Baptist an Essene from Qumran?" *Bibliotheca sacra* 159 (2002) 187–200.

Jeremias, Joachim. *Jerusalem in the Time of Jesus: An Investigation into Economic and Social Conditions during the New Testament Period.* Translated by F. H. Cave and C. H. Cave. Philadelphia: Fortress, 1962.

————. *Jesus' Promise to the Nations.* Translated by S. H. Hooke. Studies in Biblical Theology 24. London: SCM, 1958.

————. *New Testament Theology: The Proclamation of Jesus.* New York: Scribner, 1971.

Johnson, Luke T. "The New Testament's Anti-Jewish Slander and the Conventions of Ancient Polemic." *Journal of Biblical Literature* 108 (1989) 419–41.

Johnson, M. D. "Life of Adam and Eve (First Century A.D.)." In *The Old Testament Pseudepigrapha*, edited by James H. Charlesworth, 2:249–96. Peabody, MA: Hendrickson, 1983.

Jones, A. H. M. *The Herods of Judaea.* London: Oxford University Press, 1938.

Josephus. *Against Apion.* Volume I. Loeb Classical Library. Translated by H. St. J. Thackeray. London: William Heinemann, 1926.

————. *Jewish Antiquities.* Volumes IV–X. Loeb Classical Library. London: William Heinemann, 1961–1981.

————. *The Jewish War.* Volumes II–III. Loeb Classical Library. London: William Heinemann, 1956–1961.

Katz, Steven T. "Issues in the Separation of Judaism and Christianity After 70 C.E.: A Reconsideration." *Journal of Biblical Literature* 103 (1984) 43–76.

Keener, Craig S. "'Brood of Vipers' (Matthew 3.7; 12.34; 23.33)." *Journal for the Study of the New Testament* 28 (2005) 3–11.

————. *The Gospel of Matthew: A Socio-Rhetorical Commentary.* Grand Rapids: Eerdmans, 2009.

Kelhoffer, James A. "Did John the Baptist Eat Like a Former Essene? Locust-Eating in the Ancient Near East and at Qumran." *Dead Sea Discoveries* 11 (2004) 293–314.

————. "Early Christian Studies among the Academic Disciplines: Reflections on John the Baptist's 'Locusts and Wild Honey.'" *Biblical Research* 50 (2005) 5–17.

Kellner, Douglas. "Ideology, Marxism, and Advanced Capitalism." *Socialist Review* 42 (1978) 37–65.

Kermode, Frank. *Poetry, Narrative, History.* Oxford: Oxford University Press, 1990.

Kilpatrick, G. D. *The Origins of the Gospel According to St. Matthew.* Oxford: Clarendon, 1946.

Kingsbury, Jack Dean. *Matthew as Story.* 2nd ed. Philadelphia: Fortress, 1988.

————. "Observations on the 'Miracle Chapters' of Matthew 8–9." *Catholic Biblical Quarterly* 40 (1978) 559–73.

————. "The Title 'Son of David' in Matthew's Gospel." *Journal of Biblical Literature* 95 (1976) 591–602.

————. "The Verb *Akolouthein* ("To Follow") as an Index of Matthew's View of his Community." *Journal of Biblical Literature* 97 (1978) 56–73.

Kittel, Gerhard, and Gerhard Friedrich, eds. *Theological Dictionary of the New Testament.* Translated by G. W. Bromiley. 10 vols. Grand Rapids: Eerdmans, 1964–76.

Knibb, M. A. "Martyrdom and Ascension of Isaiah: A New Translation and Introduction." In *The Old Testament Pseudepigrapha*, edited by James H. Charlesworth, 2:143–76. Peabody, MA: Hendrickson, 1983.

Knowles, Michael. *Jeremiah in Matthew's Gospel: The Rejected Prophet Motif in Matthean Redaction.* London: Bloomsbury, 2015.

Korb, Scott. *Life in Year One: What the World Was Like in First-Century Palestine.* New York: Riverhead, 2010.

Kraybill, J. Nelson. *Imperial Cult and Commerce in John's Apocalypse.* Sheffield, UK: Sheffield, 1996.

Kupp, David D. *Matthew's Emmanuel: Divine Presence and God's People in the First Gospel.* Cambridge: Cambridge University Press, 1996.

Kürzinger, Josef. "Das Papiaszeugnis und die Erstgestalt des Matthäusevangeliums." *Biblische Zeitschrift* 4 (1960) 19–38.

Lang, Bernard. "The Number Ten and the Iniquity of the Fathers: A New Interpretation of the Decalogue." *Zeitschrift für die alttestamentliche Wissenschaft* 118 (2006) 218–38.

Langner, T. S., and S. T. Michael. *Life Stress and Mental Health.* London: Collier-MacMillan, 1963.

Lapin, Hayim. "The Origins and Development of the Rabbinic Movement in the Land of Israel." In *The Late Roman-Rabbinic Period*, edited by Stephen T. Katz, 206–29. Cambridge: Cambridge University Press, 2006.

Laughery, Greg J. "Ricoeur on History, Fiction, and Biblical Hermeneutics." In *"Behind" the Text: History and Biblical Interpretation*, edited by Craig Bartholomew et al., 339–62. Grand Rapids: Zondervan, 2003.

Le Donne, Anthony. *Historical Jesus: What Can We Know and How Can We Know It?* Grand Rapids: Eerdmans, 2011.

LeMarquand, Grant. "The Canaanite Conquest of Jesus (Mt 15:21–28)." *ARC: The Journal of the Faculty of Religious Studies* 33 (2005) 237–47.

Lenski, Gerhard E. *Power and Privilege: A Theory of Social Stratification.* New York: McGraw-Hill, 1966.

Liddell, Henry George, and Robert Scott. *A Lexicon Abridged from Liddell and Scott's Greek-English Lexicon.* Arranged by James M. Whiton. New York: American Book Co., 1906.

Lieber, Andrea. "I Set a Table before You: The Jewish Eschatological Character of Aseneth's Conversion Meal." *Journal for the Study of the Pseudepigrapha* 14 (2004) 63–77.

Lierman, John. *The New Testament Moses.* Tübingen: Mohr Siebeck, 2004.

Liverani, Mario. *Myth and Politics in Ancient Near Eastern Historiography.* Edited by Zainab Bahrani and Marc Van De Mieroop. New York: Cornell University Press, 2004.

Lohr, C. H. "Oral Techniques in the Gospel of Matthew." *Catholic Biblical Quarterly* 23 (1961) 403–35.

Long, Phillip J. "Jesus the Bridegroom (Mark 2:18–22)." *Journal of Grace Theology* 1 (2014) 37–51.

Luther, Martin. *Commentary on the Sermon on the Mount*. Translated by Charles A. Hay. Philadelphia: Lutheran Publication Society, 1892.

Luz, Ulrich. *Matthew 1–7*. Edited by Helmut Koester. Translated by James E. Crouch. Hermeneia. Minneapolis: Fortress, 2007.

———. *Matthew 8–20*. Edited by Helmut Koester. Translated by James E. Crouch. Hermeneia. Minneapolis: Fortress, 2001.

———. *Matthew 21–28*. Edited by Helmut Koester. Translated by James E. Crouch. Hermeneia. Minneapolis: Fortress, 2005.

———. *Studies in Matthew*. Grand Rapids: Eerdmans, 2005.

———. *The Theology of the Gospel of Matthew*. Translated by J. B. Robinson. New Testament Theology. Cambridge: Cambridge University Press, 1995.

Maccoby, Hyam. "The Washing of Cups." *Journal for the Study of the New Testament* 14 (1982) 3–15.

MacDonald, Margaret Y. *The Pauline Churches: A Socio-Historical Study of Institutionalization in The Pauline and Deutero-Pauline Writings*. Cambridge: Cambridge University Press, 1988.

Macintosh, A. A. *A Critical and Exegetical Commentary on Hosea*. International Critical Commentary. Edinburgh: T. & T. Clark, 1997.

Malina, Bruce J. *Christian Origins and Cultural Anthropology: Practical Models for Biblical Interpretation*. Atlanta: John Knox, 1986.

———. *The New Testament World: Insights from Cultural Anthropology*. 3rd ed. Louisville: Westminster John Knox, 2001.

———. "Patron and Client: The Analogy Behind Synoptic Theology." *Forum* 4 (1988) 2–32.

Malina, Bruce J., and Richard L. Rohrbaugh. *Social-Science Commentary on the Synoptic Gospels*. Minneapolis: Fortress, 1992.

Mandel, Paul. "The Tosefta." In *The Late Roman-Rabbinic Period*, edited by Stephen T. Katz, 316–35. Cambridge: Cambridge University Press, 2006.

Marcus, Joel. "*Birkat Ha-Minim* Revisited." *New Testament Studies* 55 (2009) 523–51.

Marshall, Christopher D. *Kingdom Come: The Kingdom of God in the Teaching of Jesus*. Eugene, OR: Wipf & Stock, 2015.

Martínez, Florentino García, and Eibert J. C. Tigchelaar, eds. *The Dead Sea Scrolls Study Edition*. Vol. 1. Leiden: Brill, 1997.

———, eds. *The Dead Sea Scrolls Study Edition*. Vol. 2. Leiden: Brill, 1998.

Mason, Steve. *Josephus and the New Testament*. Peabody, MA: Hendrickson, 1992.

———. "Pharisaic Dominance Before 70 CE and the Gospel's Hypocrisy Charge (Matt 23:2–3)." *Harvard Theological Review* 83 (1990) 363–81.

Matera, Frank J. "The Plot of Matthew's Gospel." *Catholic Biblical Quarterly* 49 (1987) 233–53.

Mathews, Kenneth A. "John, Jesus and the Essenes: Trouble at the Temple." *Criswell Theological Review* 3 (1988) 101–26.

McKane, William. *A Critical and Exegetical Commentary on Jeremiah, Vol. 1*. International Critical Commentary. Edinburgh: T. & T. Clark, 1986.

McKnight, Scot. *Jesus and His Death: Historiography, the Historical Jesus, and Atonement Theory*. Waco, TX: Baylor University Press, 2005.

———. "Jesus and Prophetic Actions." *Bulletin for Biblical Research* 10 (2000) 197–232.

————. *A Light Among the Gentiles: Jewish Missionary Activity in the Second Temple Period.* Minneapolis: Fortress, 1991.

————. *A New Vision for Israel: The Teachings of Jesus in National Context.* Grand Rapids: Eerdmans, 1999.

McRae, Rachel M. "Eating with Honor: The Corinthian Lord's Supper in Light of Voluntary Association Meal Practices." *Journal of Biblical Literature* 130 (2011) 165–81.

Meeks, Wayne A. *The First Urban Christians: The Social World of the Apostle Paul.* New Haven, CT: Yale University Press, 1983.

————. *The Moral World of the First Christians.* Philadelphia: Westminster, 1986.

Meier, John P. *Matthew.* Wilmington: Michael Glazier, 1980.

————. "Matthew 5:3–12." *Interpretation* 44 (1990) 281–85.

————. *Mentor, Message, and Miracle.* Vol. 2 of *Jesus, the Marginal Jew: Rethinking the Historical Jesus.* New York: Doubleday, 1994.

————. *The Vision of Matthew: Christ, Church, and Morality in the First Gospel.* Eugene, OR: Wipf & Stock, 2004.

Menken, Maarten J. J. "Sources of the Old Testament Quotation in Matthew 2:23." *Journal of Biblical Literature* 120 (2001) 451–68.

Metzger, Bruce M. *The Canon of the New Testament: Its Origin, Development, and Significance.* Oxford: Oxford University Press, 1987.

————. *Textual Commentary on the Greek New Testament.* 2nd ed. Stuttgart: German Bible Society, 1994.

Meyer, Ben F. *Christus Faber: The Master Builder and the House of God.* Allison Park: Pickwick, 1992.

Miller, Susan. "The Woman Who Anoints Jesus (Mk 14.3-9): A Prophetic Sign of the New Creation." *Feminist Theology* 14 (2006) 221–36.

Mink, Louis O. "History and Fiction as Modes of Comprehension." *New Literary History* 1 (1970) 541–58.

————. "Narrative Form as a Cognitive Instrument." In *The Writing of History: Literary Form and Historical Understanding,* edited by Robert H. Canary and Henry Kozicki, 129–49. Madison: University of Wisconsin Press, 1978.

Mittelstadt, Martin William. "Eat, Drink, and Be Merry: A Theology of Hospitality in Luke-Acts." *Word and World* 34 (2014) 131–39.

Mørkholm, Otto. "Antiochus IV." In *The Hellenistic Age,* edited by W. D. Davies and Louis Finkelstein, 278–91. Cambridge: Cambridge University Press, 1989.

Moule, C. F. D. *The Origin of Christology.* Cambridge: Cambridge University Press, 1977.

Myers, Ched. *Binding the Strong Man: A Political Reading of Mark's Story of Jesus.* Maryknoll, NY: Orbis, 1988.

————. *Binding the Strong Man: A Political Reading of Mark's Story of Jesus.* 2nd ed. Maryknoll, NY: Orbis, 2008.

Neusner, Jacob. "First Cleanse the Inside: The 'Halakhic' Background of a Controversy-Saying." *New Testament Studies* 22 (1976) 486–95.

————. *The Mishnah: A New Translation.* Rensselaer: Hamilton, 1988.

————. "Money-Changers in the Temple: The Mishnah's Explanation" *New Testament Studies* 35 (1989) 287–90.

————. *The Tosefta.* Volume 5. New York: Ktav, 1979.

Neyrey, Jerome H. *Honor and Shame in the Gospel of Matthew*. Louisville: Westminster John Knox, 1998.

Niskanen, Paul V. *Isaiah 56–66*. Berit Olam. Collegeville, MN: Liturgical, 2014.

Nolland, John. *The Gospel of Matthew*. New International Greek Testament Commentary. Grand Rapids: Eerdmans, 2005.

Nordgren, Lars. *Greek Interjections: Syntax, Semantics and Pragmatics*. Berlin: de Gruyter, 2015.

Norman, Andrew P. "Telling It Like It Was: Historical Narratives on Their Own Terms." *History and Theory* 30 (1991) 119–35.

Orlov, Andrei A. "The Sacerdotal Traditions of 2 Enoch and the Date of the Text." In *New Perspectives on 2 Enoch: No Longer Slavonic Only*, edited by Andrei Orlov and Gabriele Boccaccini, 103–16. Leiden: Brill, 2012.

Orton, David E. *The Understanding Scribe: Matthew and the Apocalyptic Ideal*. Sheffield, UK: JSOT, 1989.

Osborne, Grant R. *Matthew*. Zondervan Exegetical Commentary of the New Testament. Grand Rapids: Zondervan, 2010.

Oswalt, John. *The Book of Isaiah: Chapters 40–66*. New International Commentary on the Old Testament. Grand Rapids: Eerdmans, 1998.

Ottenheijm, Eric. "The Shared Meal—a Therapeutic Device: The Function and Meaning of Hos 6:6 in Matt 9:10–13." *Novum Testamentum* 53 (2011) 1–21.

Overman, J. Andrew. *Church and Community in Crisis*. Valley Forge: Trinity Press International, 1996.

Pennington, Jonathan T. *Heaven and Earth in the Gospel of Matthew*. Novum Testamentum Supplements 126. Leiden: Brill, 2007.

———. *Reading the Gospels Wisely: A Narrative and Theological Introduction*. Grand Rapids: Baker, 2012.

Perdue, Leo G. *Scribes, Sages, and Seers: The Sage in the Eastern Mediterranean World*. Gottingen: Vandenhoeck & Ruprecht, 2008.

Perrin, Nicholas. *Jesus and the Language of the Kingdom: Symbol and Metaphor in New Testament Interpretation*. Philadelphia: Fortress, 1976.

———. *Jesus the Temple*. London: SPCK, 2010.

Picirilli, Robert E. "The Meaning of the Tenses in New Testament Greek: Where Are We?" *Journal of the Evangelical Theological Society* 48 (2005) 533–55.

Pilch, John J. "The Health Care System in Matthew: A Social Science Analysis." *Biblical Theology Bulletin* 16 (1986) 102–6.

Pitre, Brant. "Jesus, the Messianic Banquet, and the Kingdom of God." *Letter and Spirit* 5 (2009) 133–61.

Poirier, John C. "The Endtime Return of Elijah and Moses at Qumran." *Dead Sea Discoveries* 10 (2003) 221–42.

Poland, Lynn M. *Literary Criticism and Biblical Hermeneutics: A Critique of Formalist Approaches*. Chico: Scholars, 1985.

Porter, Stanley E. *Verbal Aspect in the Greek of the New Testament, with Reference to Tense and Mood*. Studies in Biblical Greek 1. New York: Lang, 1989.

Portier-Young, Anathea E. *Apocalypse Against Empire: Theologies of Resistance in Early Judaism*. Grand Rapids: Eerdmans, 2011.

Powell, Mark Allan. "Do and Keep What Moses Says (Matthew 23:2–7)." *Journal of Biblical Literature* 114 (1995) 419–35.

———. "Matthew's Beatitudes: Reversals and Rewards of the Kingdom." *Catholic Biblical Quarterly* 58 (1996) 460–79.

———. *What Is Narrative Criticism?* Minneapolis: Fortress, 1990.

Priest, J. "Testament of Moses (First Century A.D.)." In *The Old Testament Pseudepigrapha: Apocalyptic Literature and Testaments*, edited by James H. Charlesworth, 1:919–34. Peabody, MA: Hendrickson, 1983.

Przybylski, Benno. *Righteousness in Matthew and His World of Thought.* Society for New Testament Studies Monograph Series 41. Cambridge: Cambridge University Press, 1980.

Qimron, Elisha. "Some Works of the Torah: 4Q394–4Q399 (=4QMMTa–f) and 4Q313." In *Damascus Document II, Some Works of Torah, and Related Documents*, edited by James H. Charlesworth, 187–251. Louisville: Westminster John Knox, 2006.

Rabbinowitz, Noel S. "Matthew 23:2–4: Does Jesus Recognize the Authority of the Pharisees and Does He Endorse their *Halakhah?*" *Journal of the Evangelical Theological Society* 46 (2003) 423–47.

Rajkumar, Peniel. *Dalit Theology and Dalit Liberation: Problems, Paradigms and Possibilities.* Surrey: Ashgate, 2010.

Reed, Jonathan L. *Archaeology and the Galilean Jesus: A Re-Examination of the Evidence.* Harrisburg, PA: Trinity Press International, 2000.

Regev, Eyal. *The Hasmoneans: Ideology, Archaeology, Identity.* Göttingen: Vandenhoeck & Ruprecht, 2013.

Richardson, Peter. "Why Turn the Tables? Jesus' Protest in the Temple Precincts." In *SBL Seminar Papers, 1992*, 507–23. Society of Biblical Literature Seminar Papers 31. Atlanta: Scholars, 1992.

Riches, John. *Matthew.* New Testament Guides. Sheffield, UK: Sheffield, 1996.

Rieske, Susan M. "What Is the Meaning of 'This Generation' in Matthew 23:36?" *Bibliotheca sacra* 165 (2008) 209–26.

Roberts, Kathryn L. "God, Prophet, and King: Eating and Drinking on the Mountain in First Kings 18:41." *Catholic Biblical Quarterly* 62 (2000) 632–44.

Robinson, John A. T. *Redating the New Testament.* London: SCM, 1976.

Rocca, Samuel. *Herod's Judaea: A Mediterranean State in the Classical World.* Tübingen: Mohr Siebeck, 2008.

Rochester, Kathleen. "Prophetic Ministry in Jeremiah and Ezekiel." PhD diss., Durham University, 2009.

Rohrbaugh, Richard L. "Methodological Considerations in the Debate over the Social Class Status of Early Christians." *Journal of the American Academy of Religion* 52 (1984) 519–46.

Rossing, Barbara R. "Alas for Earth! Lament and Resistance in Revelation 12." In *The Earth Story in the New Testament*, edited by Norman C. Habel and Vicky Balabanski, 180–92. The Earth Bible 5. London: Sheffield, 2002.

Roth, Cecil. "The Chair of Moses and Its Survivals." *Palestine Exploration Quarterly* 81 (1949) 100–111.

Rouwhorst, Gerard. "Table Community in Early Christianity." In *A Holy People: Jewish and Christian Perspectives on Religious Communal Identity*, edited by Marcel Poorthuis and Joshua Schwartz, 69–84. Leiden: Brill, 2006.

Rowland, Christopher. *The Open Heaven: A Study of Apocalyptic in Judaism and Early Christianity.* London: SPCK, 1982.

Saldarini, Anthony J. "Delegitimation of Leaders in Matthew 23." *Catholic Biblical Quarterly* 54 (1992) 659–80.

———. *Matthew's Jewish-Christian Community.* Chicago: University of Chicago Press, 1994.

———. *Pharisees, Scribes, and Sadducees in Palestinian Society.* Grand Rapids: Eerdmans, 2001.

Sanders, E. P. *The Historical Figure of Jesus.* New York: Penguin, 1993.

———. *Jesus and Judaism.* London: SCM, 1985.

———. *Jewish Law from Jesus to the Mishnah: Five Studies.* London: SCM, 1990.

———. *Paul and Palestinian Judaism.* Philadelphia: Fortress, 1977.

Satran, David. *Biblical Prophets in Byzantine Palestine: Reassessing the Lives of the Prophets.* Leiden: Brill, 1995.

Schmidt, Karl Ludwig. *The Place of the Gospels in the General History of Literature.* Translated by Byron R. McCane. Columbia: University of South Carolina Press, 2002.

Schuler, Philip L. *A Genre for the Gospels: The Biographical Character of Matthew.* Philadelphia: Fortress, 1982.

Schwartz, Daniel R. "One Temple and Many Synagogues: On Religion and State in Herodian Judaea and Augustan Rome." In *Herod and Augustus: Papers Presented at the IJS Conference, 21st–23rd June 2005*, edited by David M. Jacobsen and Nikos Kokkinos, 385–98. Leiden: Brill, 2009.

———. *Studies in the Jewish Background of Christianity.* Tübingen: Mohr Siebeck, 1992.

Schwartz, Seth. "Political, Social and Economic Life in the Land of Israel, 66–c.235." In *The Late Roman-Rabbinic Period*, edited by Stephen T. Katz, 23–52. Cambridge: Cambridge University Press, 2006.

Schweitzer, Albert. *The Quest of the Historical Jesus.* New York: McMillan, 1962.

Schweizer, Eduard. "Matthew's Church." In *The Interpretation of Matthew*, edited by Graham N. Stanton, 149–77. Edinburgh: T. & T. Clark, 1995.

Segal, Alan F. "Matthew's Jewish Voice." In *Social History of the Matthean Community: Cross-Disciplinary Approaches*, edited by D. L. Balch, 3–37. Minneapolis: Augsburg Fortress, 1991.

Seow, Choon-Leong. "The Social World of Ecclesiastes." In *Scribes, Sages, and Seers: The Sage in the Eastern Mediterranean World*, edited by Leo G. Perdue, 189–217. Gottingen: Vandenhoeck & Ruprecht, 2008.

Sigal, Phillip. *The Halakhah of Jesus of Nazareth According to the Gospel of Matthew.* Studies in Biblical Literature 18. Atlanta: Society of Biblical Literature, 2007.

Sim, David C. *The Gospel of Matthew and Christian Judaism: The History and Social Setting of the Matthean Community.* Edinburgh: T. & T. Clark, 1998.

———. "The Gospels for All Christians? A Response to Richard Bauckham." *Journal for the Study of the New Testament* 84 (2001) 3–27.

———. "Jesus as Role Model in the Gospel of Matthew: Does the Matthean Jesus Practise What He Preaches?" *Australian eJournal of Theology* 16 (2010) 1–21.

Sloyan, Gerard S. "The Holy Eucharist as an Eschatological Meal." *Worship* 36 (1962) 444–51.

Smith, Christopher R. "Literary Evidences of the Five Fold Structure in the Gospel of Matthew." *New Testament Studies* 43 (1997) 540–51.

Smith, Dennis E. *From Symposium to Eucharist: The Banquet in the Early Christian World.* Minneapolis: Fortress, 2003.

Smith, Gary V. *Isaiah 40–66*. New American Commentary 15B. Nashville: B&H, 2009.

Smith, Monica L. "Networks, Territories, and the Cartography of Ancient States." *Annals of the Association of American Geographers* 95 (2005) 832–49.

Smith, Morton. "The Troublemakers." In *The Early Roman Period*, edited by William Horbury et al., 501–68. Cambridge: Cambridge University Press, 1999.

———. "Zealots and Sicarii, Their Origins and Relation." *Harvard Theological Review* 64 (1971) 1–19.

Snodgrass, Klyne R. "Matthew's Understanding of the Law." *Interpretation* 46 (1992) 368–78.

———. "The Temple Incident." In *Key Events in the Life of the Historical Jesus: A Collaborative Exploration of Context and Coherence*, 429–80. Grand Rapids: Eerdmans, 2010.

Sobrino, Jon. *Jesus in Latin America*. Maryknoll, NY: Orbis, 1987.

Sommer, Benjamin D. "Did Prophecy Cease? Evaluating a Reevaluation." *Journal of Biblical Literature* 115 (1996) 31–47.

Sprinkle, Preston M. *Paul and Judaism Revisited: A Study of Divine and Human Agency in Salvation*. Downers Grove, IL: InterVarsity, 2013.

Squires, J. T. "'To the Lost Sheep of Israel': Jewish Sectarianism in the Gospel According to Matthew." In *Steps on the Way: Collected Essays on the Partings of the Ways*, 27–45. Sydney: UTC, 1996.

Stacey, David. "The Lord's Supper as Prophetic Drama." *Epworth Review* 21 (1994) 65–74.

———. *Prophetic Drama in the Old Testament*. London: Epworth, 1990.

Stanton, Graham N. *A Gospel for a New People: Studies in Matthew*. Louisville: Westminster John Knox, 1992.

———. *Gospel Truth? New Light on Jesus and the Gospels*. Valley Forge, PA: Trinity Press International, 1995.

———. "The Origin and Purpose of Matthew's Gospel: Matthean Scholarship from 1945–1980." In *Aufstieg und Niedergang der römischen Welt II.25.3, 1889–1951*. Berlin: de Gruyter, 1985.

Stark, Rodney. *The Rise of Christianity: A Sociologist Reconsiders History*. Princeton: Princeton University Press, 1996.

Stassen, Glen H., and David P. Gushee. *Kingdom Ethics: Following Jesus in Contemporary Context*. Downers Grove, IL: InterVarsity, 2003.

Steffen, Daniel S. "The Messianic Banquet and the Eschatology of Matthew's Gospel." *Global Journal of Classical Theology* 5 (2006). http://phc.edu/gj_steffen.php.

Stendahl, Krister. *The School of St. Matthew and Its Use of the Old Testament*. 2nd ed. Philadelphia: Fortress, 1968.

Strecker, Georg. *The Sermon on the Mount: An Exegetical Commentary*. Translated by O. C. Dean Jr. Edinburgh: T. & T. Clark, 1988.

Suter, David W. "Excavating 2 Enoch: The Question of Dating and the Sacerdotal Traditions." In *New Perspectives on 2 Enoch: No Longer Slavonic Only*, edited by Andrei Orlov and Gabriele Boccaccini, 117–24. Leiden: Brill, 2012.

Syreeni, Kari. *The Making of the Sermon on the Mount: A Procedural Analysis of Matthew's Redactoral Activity*. Helsinki: Suomalainen Tiedeakatemia, 1987.

Talbert, Charles H. "Once Again: Gospel Genre." *Semeia* 43 (1988) 53–73.

———. *Reading the Sermon on the Mount: Character Formation and Decision Making in Matthew 5–7*. Columbia: University of South Carolina Press, 2004.

Teeple, Howard M. *The Mosaic Eschatological Prophet*. Journal of Biblical Literature Monograph Series 10. Philadelphia: Society of Biblical Literature, 1957.

Telford, William R. *The Barren Temple and the Withered Tree: A Redaction-Critical Analysis of the Cursing of the Fig-Tree Pericope in Mark's Gospel and Its Relation to the Cleansing of the Temple Tradition.* Journal for the Study of the New Testament: Supplement Series 1. Sheffield: JSOT, 1980.

Theissen, Gerd, and Annette Merz. *The Historical Jesus: A Comprehensive Guide.* Minneapolis: Fortress, 1998.

Thom, Johan C. "Justice in the Sermon on the Mount: An Aristotelian Reading." *Novum Testamentum* 51 (2009) 314–38.

Tilborg, Sjef van. *The Jewish Leaders in Matthew.* Leiden: Brill, 1972.

Turner, David L. *Israel's Last Prophet: Jesus and the Jewish Leaders in Matthew 23.* Minneapolis: Fortress, 2015.

———. *Matthew.* Baker Exegetical Commentary on the New Testament. Grand Rapids: Baker, 2008.

Ulrich, Daniel W. "The Missional Audience of the Gospel of Matthew." *Catholic Biblical Quarterly* 66 (2007) 66–83.

VanderKam, James C. *An Introduction to Early Judaism.* Grand Rapids: Eerdmans, 2001.

VanGemeren, Willem A. *Interpreting the Prophetic Word: An Introduction to the Prophetic Literature of the Old Testament.* Grand Rapids: Zondervan, 1990.

Vanhoozer, Kevin J. *First Theology: God, Scripture and Hermeneutics.* Downers Grove, IL: InterVarsity, 2002.

Vermes, Geza. *The Complete Dead Sea Scrolls in English.* London: Penguin, 1997.

Viljoen, F. P. "Fulfilment in Matthew." *Verbum et Ecclesia* 28 (2007) 301–24.

Viviano, Benedict T. "Social World and Community Leadership: The Case of Matthew 23.1–12, 34." *Journal for the Study of the New Testament* 39 (1990) 3–21.

Vledder, Evert-Jan. *Conflict in the Miracle Stories: A Socio-Exegetical Study of Matthew 8 and 9.* Sheffield, UK: Sheffield, 1997.

Vorster, W. S. "Historical Paradigm—Its Possibilities and Limitations." *Neotestamentica* 18 (1984) 104–23.

Wainwright, Elaine M. "Reading the Gospel of Matthew Ecologically in Oceania: Matthew 4:1–11 as Focal Text." In *Matthew: Texts @ Contexts*, edited by Nicole Wilkinson Duran and James Grimshaw, 255–70. Minneapolis: Fortress, 2013.

Wallace, Anthony F. C. "Revitalization Movements." *American Anthropologist* 58 (1956) 264–81.

Wallace, Daniel B. *Greek Grammar Beyond the Basics: An Exegetical Syntax of the New Testament.* Grand Rapids: Zondervan, 1996.

Waxman, Chaim I. *Stigma of Poverty: A Critique of Poverty Theories and Policies.* 2nd ed. Oxford: Pergamon, 1983.

Webb, Robert L. *John the Baptizer and Prophet: A Socio-Historical Study.* Eugene, OR: Wipf & Stock, 1991.

Weber, Max. *Economy and Society: An Outline of Interpretive Sociology.* Edited by Guenther Roth and Claus Wittich. Berkeley: University of California Press, 1978.

Weinfeld, Moshe. "The Charge of Hypocrisy in Matthew 23 and in Jewish Sources." In *The New Testament and Christian-Jewish Dialogue: Studies in Honor of David Flusser*, edited by Malcolm F. Lowe, 52–58. Jerusalem: Ecumenical Theological Research Fraternity in Israel, 1990.

———. "The Jewish Roots of Matthew's Vitriol." *Biblical Research* 13 (1997) 31.

Weren, Wim J. C. "The Macrostructure of Matthew's Gospel: A New Proposal." *Biblica* 87 (2006) 171–200.

Westermann, D. C. "Salvation and Healing in the Community: The Old Testament Understanding." *International Review of Mission* 61 (1972) 9–19.

White, Hayden. "The Historical Text as a Literary Artifact." In *Narrative Dynamics: Essays on Time, Plot, Closure, and Frames*, edited by Brian Richardson, 191–210. Columbus: Ohio State University Press, 2002.

Whitelam, Keith W. "The Social World of the Bible." In *The Cambridge Companion to Biblical Interpretation*, edited by John Barton, 35–49. Cambridge: Cambridge University Press, 1998.

Willitts, Joel. "Matthew." In *Jesus Is Lord, Caesar Is Not: Evaluating Empire in New Testament Studies*, edited by Scot McKnight and Joseph B. Modica, 82–100. Downers Grove, IL: InterVarsity, 2013.

Wilson, Bryan. *Magic and the Millennium: A Sociological Study of Religious Movements of Protest Among Tribal and Third-World Peoples.* London: Heinemann, 1973.

Wilson, Robert R. *Sociological Approaches to the Old Testament.* Philadelphia: Fortress, 1984.

Windisch, Hans. *The Meaning of the Sermon on the Mount.* Philadelphia: Westminster, 1951.

Wise, Michael, et al. *The Dead Sea Scrolls.* Rydalmere: Hodder & Stoughton, 1996.

Witherington, Ben, III. *The Christology of Jesus.* Minneapolis: Fortress, 1990.

———. *Jesus the Seer: The Progress of Prophecy.* Peabody, MA: Hendrickson, 1999.

———. *Matthew.* Smyth & Helwys Bible Commentary 19. Macon, GA: Smith & Helwys, 2006.

Wright, N. T. "Christian Origins and the Resurrection of Jesus: The Resurrection of Jesus as a Historical Problem." *Sewanee Theological Review* 41 (1998) 107–23.

———. *Jesus and the Victory of God.* Minneapolis: Fortress, 1996.

———. *The New Testament and the People of God.* Minneapolis: Fortress, 1992.

———. *Paul: Fresh Perspectives.* London: SPCK, 2005.

———. *Paul and the Faithfulness of God.* Volume 1. Minneapolis: Fortress, 2013.

Yarbro Collins, Adela, ed. *Early Christian Apocalypticism: Genre and Social Setting.* Atlanta: Scholars, 1986.

Yoder, John Howard. *The Original Revolution: Essays on Christian Pacifism.* Scottdale: Herald, 1971.

———. *The Politics of Jesus.* 2nd ed. Grand Rapids: Eerdmans, 1994.

Yoder Neufeld, Thomas R. *Killing Enmity: Violence and the New Testament.* Grand Rapids: Baker, 2011.

Zamfir, Korinna. "Who Are (the) Blessed? Reflections on the Relecture of the Beatitudes in the New Testament and the Apocrypha." *Sacra Scripta* 5 (2007) 75–100.

Zucker, David J. "Jesus and Jeremiah in the Matthean Tradition." *Journal of Ecumenical Studies* 27 (1990) 288–305.

Zvi, Ehud Ben. "Observations on the Marital Metaphor of YHWH and Israel in Its Ancient Israelite Context: General Considerations and Particular Images in Hosea 1.2." *Journal for the Study of the Old Testament* 28 (2004) 363–84.

Index of Ancient Near Eastern Documents

52:4	272n43
52:6	272n43
52:8	272n43
52:10	272n43
52:12	272n43
52:14	272n43
52:15	177

4 Ezra

4	221

Joseph and Aseneth

8.5–7	191n22
20.6–8	192

Liber antiquitatum biblicarum (Pseudo-Philo)

19.6–7	241

Life of Adam and Eve

29.3	241

Ladder of Jacob

5.8–9	241

Martyrdom of Isaiah

1:1–2	305
1:6b–10a	305
1:7–8a	305
1:9–10a	305
2:1–6	305
2:7–11	305
2:11	141n27
3:6–7	305
3:8–10b	305
3:10c	305
3:12	305
5:1–3	305

Psalms of Solomon

1:8	85n65
8:11–13	85n65
17	135n9

Sibylline Oracles

2.339–44	272n43
3	212n102
4.115–18	241
5.89–91	272n43
7.118–19	272n43
8.95–99	272n43

Testament of Moses

7	241
10	142n28

New Testament

Matthew

1:1—4:16	48–49
1:1—4:11	49–51
1–2	47
1:1	42n174, 177, 260n120
1:1b	134
1:1c	134
1:1d	134
1:2–17	2
1:2	134
1:3	45, 135, 245
1:5	45, 135, 245
1:6	134
1:10–12	136
1:16	134–35
1:18—2:23	59
1:18–25	49
1:18	135
1:21	135–36, 167, 223
1:23	12, 211n97, 222, 246, 252–53
2:1–12	45, 245
2:1	138
2:1a	49